Children's
Literature
Review

Guide to Gale Literary Criticism Series

For criticism on	Consult these Gale series
Authors now living or who died after December 31, 1959	*CONTEMPORARY LITERARY CRITICISM (CLC)*
Authors who died between 1900 and 1959	*TWENTIETH-CENTURY LITERARY CRITICISM (TCLC)*
Authors who died between 1800 and 1899	*NINETEENTH-CENTURY LITERATURE CRITICISM (NCLC)*
Authors who died between 1400 and 1799	*LITERATURE CRITICISM FROM 1400 TO 1800 (LC)* *SHAKESPEAREAN CRITICISM (SC)*
Authors who died before 1400	*CLASSICAL AND MEDIEVAL LITERATURE CRITICISM (CMLC)*
Black writers of the past two hundred years	*BLACK LITERATURE CRITICISM (BLC) AND BLACK LITERATURE CRITICISM SUPPLEMENT (BLCS)*
Authors of books for children and young adults	*CHILDREN'S LITERATURE REVIEW (CLR)*
Dramatists	*DRAMA CRITICISM (DC)*
Hispanic writers of the late nineteenth and twentieth centuries	*HISPANIC LITERATURE CRITICISM (HLC)*
Native North American writers and orators of the eighteenth, nineteenth, and twentieth centuries	*NATIVE NORTH AMERICAN LITERATURE (NNAL)*
Poets	*POETRY CRITICISM (PC)*
Short story writers	*SHORT STORY CRITICISM (SSC)*
Major authors from the Renaissance to the present	*WORLD LITERATURE CRITICISM, 1500 TO THE PRESENT (WLC)*
Major authors and works from the Bible to the present	*WORLD LITERATURE CRITICISM SUPPLEMENT (WLCS)*

ISSN 0362-4145

volume 56

Children's Literature Review

Excerpts from Reviews,
Criticism, and Commentary
on Books for Children
and Young People

Deborah J. Morad
Editor

GALE GROUP

Detroit
San Francisco
London
Boston
Woodbridge, CT

STAFF

Deborah J. Morad, *Editor*

Sara Constantakis, Holly Griffin, Alan Hedblad, Motoko Fujishiro Huthwaite, Maria Job,
Arlene Johnson, Thomas McMahon, *Contributing Editors*

Karen Uchic, *Technical Training Specialist*

Joyce Nakamura, *Managing Editor*

Maria Franklin, *Permissions Manager*
Sarah Chesney, Edna Hedblad, Michele Lonoconus, *Permissions Associates*

Victoria B. Cariappa, *Research Manager*
Corrine A. Stocker, *Project Coordinator*
Gary J. Oudersluys, Cheryl D. Warnock, *Research Specialists*
Patricia Tsune Ballard, Wendy K. Festerling, Tamara C. Nott, Tracie A. Richardson, *Research Associates*
Phyllis J. Blackman, Tim Lehnerer, Patricia A. Love, *Research Assistants*

Mary Beth Trimper, *Production Director*
Cindy Range, *Production Assistant*

Gary Leach, *Graphic Artist*
Randy Bassett, *Image Database Supervisor*
Robert Duncan, Michael Logusz, *Imaging Specialists*
Pamela A. Reed, *Imaging Coordinator*

Library of Congress Catalog Card Number 76-643301
ISBN 0-7876-2905-7
ISSN 0362-4145
Printed in the United States of America

10 9 8 7 6 5 4 3 2 1

Contents

Preface   vii
Acknowledgments   xi

Preface

Literature for children and young adults has evolved into both a respected branch of creative writing and a successful industry. Currently, books for young readers are considered among the most popular segments of publishing. Criticism of juvenile literature is instrumental in recording the literary or artistic development of the creators of children's books as well as the trends and controversies that result from changing values or attitudes about young people and their literature. Designed to provide a permanent, accessible record of this ongoing scholarship, *Children's Literature Review (CLR)* presents parents, teachers, and librarians—those responsible for bringing children and books together—with the opportunity to make informed choices when selecting reading materials for the young. In addition, *CLR* provides researchers of children's literature with easy access to a wide variety of critical information from English-language sources in the field. Users will find balanced overviews of the careers of the authors and illustrators of the books that children and young adults are reading; these entries, which contain excerpts from published criticism in books and periodicals, assist users by sparking ideas for papers and assignments and suggesting supplementary and classroom reading. Ann L. Kalkhoff, president and editor of *Children's Book Review Service Inc.,* writes that "*CLR* has filled a gap in the field of children's books, and it is one series that will never lose its validity or importance."

Scope of the Series

Each volume of *CLR* profiles the careers of a selection of authors and illustrators of books for children and young adults from preschool through high school. Author lists in each volume reflect:

- an international scope.

- representation of authors of all eras.

- the variety of genres covered by children's and/or YA literature: picture books, fiction, nonfiction, poetry, folklore, and drama.

Although the focus of the series is on authors new to *CLR*, entries will be updated as the need arises.

Organization of This Book

An entry consists of the following elements: author heading, author portrait, author introduction, excerpts of criticism (each preceded by a bibliographical citation), and illustrations, when available.

- The **Author Heading** consists of the author's name followed by birth and death dates. The portion of the name outside the parentheses denotes the form under which the author is most frequently published. If the majority of the author's works for children were written under a pseudonym, the pseudonym will be listed in the author heading and the real name given on the first line of the author introduction. Also located at the beginning of the introduction are any other pseudonyms used by the author in writing for children and any name variations, including transliterated forms for authors whose languages use nonroman alphabets. Uncertainty as to a birth or death date is indicated by question marks.

- An **Author Portrait** is included when available.

- The **Author Introduction** contains information designed to introduce an author to *CLR* users by presenting an overview of the author's themes and styles, biographical facts that relate to the author's literary career or critical responses to the author's works, and information about major awards and prizes the author has received. The introduction begins by identifying the nationality of the author and by listing the genres in which s/he has written for children and young adults. Introductions also list a group of representative titles for which the author or illustrator being profiled is best known; this section, which begins with the words "major works include," follows the genre line of the introduction. For seminal figures, a listing of major works about the author follows when appropriate, highlighting important biographies about the author or illustrator that are not excerpted in the entry. The centered heading "Introduction" announces the body of the text.

- **Criticism** is located in three sections: **Author's Commentary** (when available), **General Commentary** (when available), and **Title Commentary** (commentary on specific titles).

  - The **Author's Commentary** presents background material written by the author or by an interviewer. This commentary may cover a specific work or several works. Author's commentary on more than one work appears after the author introduction, while commentary on an individual book follows the title entry heading.

  - The **General Commentary** consists of critical excerpts that consider more than one work by the author or illustrator being profiled. General commentary is preceded by the critic's name in boldface type or, in the case of unsigned criticism, by the title of the journal. *CLR* also features entries that emphasize general criticism on the oeuvre of an author or illustrator. When appropriate, a selection of reviews is included to supplement the general commentary.

  - The **Title Commentary** begins with the title entry headings, which precede the criticism on a title and cite publication information on the work being reviewed. Title headings list the title of the work as it appeared in its first English-language edition. The first English-language publication date of each work (unless otherwise noted) is listed in parentheses following the title. Differing U.S. and British titles follow the publication date within the parentheses. When a work is written by an individual other than the one being profiled, as is the case when illustrators are featured, the parenthetical material following the title cites the author of the work before listing its publication date.

  Entries in each title commentary section consist of critical excerpts on the author's individual works, arranged chronologically by publication date. The entries generally contain two to seven reviews per title, depending on the stature of the book and the amount of criticism it has generated. The editors select titles that reflect the entire scope of the author's literary contribution, covering each genre and subject. An effort is made to reprint criticism that represents the full range of each title's reception, from the year of its initial publication to current assessments. Thus, the reader is provided with a record of the author's critical history. Publication information (such as publisher names and book prices) and parenthetical numerical references (such as footnotes or page and line references to specific editions of works) have been deleted at the discretion of the editors to provide smoother reading of the text.

- Centered headings introduce each section, in which criticism is arranged chronologically; beginning with Volume 35, each excerpt is preceded by a boldface source heading for easier access by readers. Within the text, titles by authors being profiled are also highlighted in boldface type.

- Selected excerpts are preceded by **Explanatory Annotations**, which provide information on the critic or work of criticism to enhance the reader's understanding of the excerpt.

- A complete **Bibliographical Citation** designed to facilitate the location of the original book or article precedes each piece of criticism.

- Numerous **Illustrations** are featured in *CLR*. For entries on illustrators, an effort has been made to include illustrations that reflect the characteristics discussed in the criticism. Entries on authors who do not illustrate their own works may also include photographs and other illustrative material pertinent to their careers.

Special Features: Entries on Illustrators

Entries on authors who are also illustrators will occasionally feature commentary on selected works illustrated but not written by the author being profiled. These works are strongly associated with the illustrator and have received critical acclaim for their art. By including critical comment on works of this type, the editors wish to provide a more complete representation of the artist's career. Criticism on these works has been chosen to stress artistic, rather than literary, contributions. Title entry headings for works illustrated by the author being profiled are arranged chronologically within the entry by date of publication and include notes identifying the author of the illustrated work. In order to provide easier access for users, all titles illustrated by the subject of the entry are boldfaced.

CLR also includes entries on prominent illustrators who have contributed to the field of children's literature. These entries are designed to represent the development of the illustrator as an artist rather than as a literary stylist. The illustrator's section is organized like that of an author, with two exceptions: the introduction presents an overview of the illustrator's styles and techniques rather than outlining his or her literary background, and the commentary written by the illustrator on his or her works is called "illustrator's commentary" rather than "author's commentary." All titles of books containing illustrations by the artist being profiled are highlighted in boldface type.

Other Features: Acknowledgments, Indexes

- The **Acknowledgments** section, which immediately follows the preface, lists the sources from which material has been reprinted in the volume. It does not, however, list every book or periodical consulted for the volume.

- The **Cumulative Index to Authors** lists all of the authors who have appeared in *CLR* with cross-references to the biographical, autobiographical, and literary criticism series published by The Gale Group. A full listing of the series titles appears before the first page of the indexes of this volume.

- The **Cumulative Index to Nationalities** lists authors alphabetically under their respective nationalities. Author names are followed by the volume number(s) in which they appear.

- The **Cumulative Index to Titles** lists titles covered in *CLR* followed by the volume and page number where criticism begins.

A Note to the Reader

CLR is one of several critical references sources in the Literature Criticism Series published by The Gale Group. When writing papers, students who quote directly from any volume in the Literature Criticism Series may use the following general forms to footnote reprinted criticism. The first example pertains to material drawn from periodicals, the second to material reprinted from books.

[1]T. S. Eliot, "John Donne," *The Nation and the Athenaeum*, 33 (9 June 1923), 321-32; excerpted and reprinted in *Literature Criticism from 1400 to 1800*, Vol. 10, ed. James E. Person, Jr. (Detroit: Gale Research, 1989), pp. 28-9.

[1]Henry Brooke, *Leslie Brooke and Johnny Crow* (Frederick Warne, 1982); excerpted and reprinted in *Children's Literature Review*, Vol. 20, ed. Gerard J. Senick (Detroit: Gale Research, 1990), p. 47.

Suggestions Are Welcome

In response to various suggestions, several features have been added to *CLR* since the beginning of the series, including author entries on retellers of traditional literature as well as those who have been the first to record oral tales and other folklore; entries on prominent illustrators featuring commentary on their styles and techniques; entries on authors whose works are considered controversial; occasional entries devoted to criticism on a single work or a series of works; sections in author introductions that list major works by and about the author or illustrator being profiled; explanatory notes that provide information on the critic or work of criticism to enhance the usefulness of the excerpt; more extensive illustrative material, such as holographs of manuscript pages and photographs of people and places pertinent to the careers of the authors and artists; a cumulative nationality index for easy access to authors by nationality; and occasional guest essays written specifically for *CLR* by prominent critics on subjects of their choice.

Readers who wish to suggest authors to appear in future volumes, or who have other suggestions, are cordially invited to contact the editor. By mail: Editor, *Children's Literature Review*, The Gale Group, 27500 Drake Road, Farmington Hills, MI 48331-3535; by telephone: (800) 347-GALE; by fax: (248) 699-8065.

Acknowledgments

The editors wish to thank the copyright holders of the excerpted criticism included in this volume and the permissions managers of many book and magazine publishing companies for assisting us in securing reproduction rights. We are also grateful to the staffs of the Detroit Public Library, the Library of Congress, the University of Detroit Mercy Library, Wayne State University Purdy/Kresge Library Complex, and the University of Michigan Libraries for making their resources available to us. Following is a list of the copyright holders who have granted us permission to reproduce material in this volume of *CLR*. Every effort has been made to trace copyright, but if omissions have been made, please let us know.

COPYRIGHTED EXCERPTS IN *CLR*, VOLUME 56, WERE REPRODUCED FROM THE FOLLOWING PERIODICALS:

Arts Magazine, v. 61, May, 1997 for "English Book Designers and the Role of the Modern Book L'Art Nouveau; Part One: Modern Merriment and Morality in the Art of Walter Crane" by Colleen Denney. © 1997 by The Arts Digest Inc. Reproduced by permission of the author.—*Best Sellers,* v. 23, December 15, 1963. Copyright 1963, by the University of Scranton. Reproduced by permission.—*Bookbird,* v. 24, December 15, 1986. Reproduced by permission.—*Booklist,* v. 69, November 15, 1972; v. 70, March 1, 1974; v. 75, September 1, 1975; v. 72, December 15, 1975; v. 73, May 15, 1977; v. 74, December 15, 1977; v. 74, June 1, 1978; v. 75, November 15, 1978; v. 76, November 15, 1979; v. 77, October 1, 1980; v. 77, October 15, 1980; v. 78, January 15, 1982; v. 79, January 15, 1983; v. 79, April 1, 1983; v. 79, July, 1983; v. 80, September 15, 1983; v. 82, November 1, 1985; v. 86, September 1, 1989; v. 87, December 15, 1990;; v. 88, November 1, 1991; v. 88, March 1, 1992; v. 88, May 1, 1992; v. 89, September 1, 1992; v. 89, September 15, 1992; v. 89, October 15, 1992; v. 89, November 1, 1992; v. 90, September 15, 1993; v. 90, October 1, 1993; v. 90, February 15, 1994; v. 90, March 1, 1994; v. 90, March 15, 1994; v. 90, May 1, 1994; v. 91, October 1, 1994; v. 91, August, 1995; v. 92, September 15, 1995; v. 92, February 15, 1996; v. 92, March 15, 1996; v. 93, September 1, 1996; v. 93, October 1, 1996; v. 93, March 1, 1997; v. 94, September 1, 1997; v. 94, September 15, 1997; v. 94, November 1, 1997; v. 94, December 15, 1997. Copyright © 1972, 1974, 1975, 1977, 1978, 1979, 1980, 1982, 1983, 1985, 1989, 1990, 1991, 1992, 1993, 1994, 1995 1996, 1997 by the American Library Association. All reproduced by permission.—*Books for Keeps,* November, 1987. © School Bookshop Association 1987. Reproduced by permission.—*Books for Your Children,* v. 16, Autumn-Winter, 1981. © Books for Your Children 1981. Reproduced by permission.—*Bulletin of the Center for Children's Books,* v. 20, February, 1967; v. 23, October, 1969; v. 25, October, 1971; v. 25, June, 1972; v. 36, January, 1983; v. 38, October, 1984; v. 39, October, 1985; v. 41, December, 1987; v. 45, March, 1992; v. 46, November, 1992; v. 46, December, 1992; v. 47, September, 1993; v. 47, November, 1993; v. 47, March, 1994; v. 47, April, 1994; v. 48, October, 1994; v. 48, November, 1994; v. 48, March, 1995; v. 49, September, 1995; v. 49, March, 1996; v. 49, May, 1996; v. 50, February, 1997; v. 50, April, 1997; v. 50, May, 1997; v. 50, June, 1997; v. 51, December, 1997; v. 51, January, 1998; v. 51, June, 1998. Copyright © 1967, 1969, 1971, 1972, 1983, 1984, 1985, 1987, 1992, 1993, 1994, 1995, 1996, 1997, 1998 by The University of Chicago. All reproduced by permission.—*Catholic Library World,* v. 68, March, 1998. Reproduced by permission.—*Children's Literature: Annual of The Modern Language Association Group on Children's Literature and The Children's Literature Association,* v. 8, 1980. Reproduced by permission.—*The Christian Science Monitor,* November 6, 1974. © 1974 The Christian Science Publishing Society. All rights reserved. Reproduced by permission from The Christian Science Monitor.—*Five Owls for Parents,* v. I, January-February, 1991. Reproduced by permission.—*Five Owls,* v. VI, March-April, 1992; v. VIII, January-February, 1994; v. X, September-October, 1995; v. X, May-June, 1996. All reproduced by permission.—*Growing Point,* v. 15, December, 1976 for a review of "The Hobbit" by Margery Fisher/ v. 18, March, 1980 for a review of "Under the Mountain" by Margery Fisher/ v. 24, January, 1986 for areview of "Rose Blanche" by Margery Fisher/ v. 24, January, 1986 for a review of "The Priests of Ferris" by Margery Fisher. All reproduced by permission of the Literary Estate of Margery Fisher.—*The Horn Book Magazine,* v. XLV, June, 1969; v. L, October, 1974; v. LIII, August, 1977; v. LIV, April, 1978; v. LIV, August, 1978; v. LV, October, 1978; v. LV, February, 1979; v. LVI, February, 1980; v. LVI, October, 1980; v. LVIII, April, 1982; v. LIX, June, 1983; v. LIX, October, 1983; v. LXIII, May-June, 1987; v. LXV, March-April, 1989; v. LXVII, March-April, 1991; v. LXVIII, November-December, 1992; v. LXIX, March-April, 1993; v. LXX, January-February, 1994; v. LXX, May-June, 1994; v. LXX, July, 1994; v. LXX, November, 1994; v. LXXIII, November-December, 1997; v. LXXIV, January-February, 1998. Copyright, 1969, 1974, 1977, 1978, 1979, 1980, 1982, 1983, 1987, 1992, 1994, 1997, 1998 by The Horn Book, Inc., 11 Beacon St., Suite 1000, Boston, MA 02108. All rights reserved. All reproduced by permission./ v. XI, November-December, 1935; v. XVI, November-December, 1940; v. XIX, January-February, 1943; v. XIX, November-December, 1943; v. XXI, January-February, 1945; v. XXI, March-April, 1945; v. XXII, January-February, 1946; v. XXII, November-December, 1946; v. XXIV,

Children's
Literature
Review

Eve Bunting

1928-

(Full name Anne Evelyn Bunting; born Anne Evelyn Bolton; has also written as Evelyn Bolton and A. E. Bunting) Irish-born American author of fiction, nonfiction, and picture books.

Major works include *Ghost of Summer* (1977), *The Wall* (1990), *Jumping the Nail* (1991), *Smoky Night* (1994), *Your Move* (1998).

For more information on Bunting's career prior to 1991, see *CLR*, Vol. 28.

INTRODUCTION

A diverse and prolific writer noted for honesty and sensitivity, Bunting is the author of thought-provoking, entertaining, and commercially successful works for preschoolers, primary graders, middle graders, and young adults. She is perhaps best known for her realistic fiction, mysteries, and picture books about holidays as well as for introducing science fiction to readers in the early grades. In *Something about the Author* (*SATA*), Bunting likens herself to a Shanachie, the traditional Irish storyteller "who went from house to house telling his tales of ghosts and fairies, of old Irish heroes and battles still to be won." Widely acclaimed for her lyrical language and storytelling ability, Bunting has approached topics ranging from folklore and ghost stories to inner-city violence and the lives of such sea creatures as sharks, whales, and squids. Many of her works, which are often published as a series, are recognized as being among the most substantial in their respective genres and are often noted as the first books on their subjects.

Throughout the great range of work she produces, Bunting is consistently commended for her impressive empathy for her young readers. Praised for her compassion and humor, she creates characters that are vibrant and realistic and of a variety of ages and backgrounds: her main characters are from such nationalities as Japanese, Chinese-American, Inuit, Puerto Rican, Hawaiian-Irish, and Northern Irish, as well as black and white American. She also includes characters who are abused, homeless, and disabled. Her protagonists respond to difficult decisions and complicated situations in true-to-life ways, particularly because Bunting takes contemporary problems as her inspiration. Always aware of the pressures affecting children's lives, Bunting noted in *SATA*, "because ninety percent of my ideas come from reports of current news and the other ten percent from what I see happening around me, I guess what I write has to be contemporary." In her books Bunting has dealt with abortion, teenage prostitution, gang membership, racial conflicts, terrorism, the deaths of parents and siblings,

suicide, and the Los Angeles riots. Sometimes criticized for exposing children to disturbing material, Bunting told Michael Cart, "as long as you give kids the truth, you needn't be ashamed of anything you write. Children are living in this real world, and we adults can't protect them from its realities. My father used to say to me when I had troubles, 'I can't stand between you and the wind. 'I often think of that now when I'm writing for children."

Although she does not believe in hiding the truth from her readers, Bunting often incorporates moral messages in her books, with a greater or lesser degree of success. Critics have accused her at times both of being heavy-handed in her moralizing and of being disturbingly non-judgmental, perhaps indicating the difficulties inherent in dealing with complex contemporary issues. Yet, through their experiences, Bunting's characters often become more self-confident and learn to accept life as it is. Bunting told Allen Raymond of her personal goal in writing for children: "Each of us has a choice of what we do with our lives. I hope the children make the right choice, whatever it is, and in my books I try to help them make it."

Biographical Information

Born in 1928 in Maghera, Northern Ireland, Bunting was the daughter of a postmaster and shopkeeper. As an author, she draws from her childhood experiences in the Irish countryside, such as in *Market Day* (1996), the story of an Irish town on its vibrant monthly market day and the friendship between two children, Tess and Wee Boy. Bunting has also written about the folktales of Ireland, and has explored its political and religious conflicts in books for young adults. When she was nine years old, she went to boarding school in Belfast, where she developed her love of books and reading. "Perhaps it was there, in the telling of tall tales after 'lights out,'" she explained in *SATA,* "that I got my first taste of storytelling." In 1945, Bunting graduated from Methodist College in Belfast and attended Queens University before coming to the United States with her husband and three children in 1960, settling first in San Francisco and later, in Pasadena. Since then she has lived in California. While her children were growing up, Bunting enrolled in a Writing for Publication class at Pasadena City College. Her first book, *The Two Giants,* was published in 1972 when she was forty-three. Bunting has since published well over 130 books for children and young adults, and has taught writing classes at universities and writers' conferences.

Major Works

While sometimes criticized for approaching topics thought to be too difficult for young readers, Bunting has remained committed to dealing with contemporary issues. When asked by Stefanie Weiss whether children should be protected from troubling subjects, Bunting replied, "I think the protection we can give them is the truth. I think we have to try somehow to extend their understanding of the difficult problems we have. Children can deal with the truth if they have a caring person to help them try to understand it." Bunting attempts to bring truth to her young readers in works such as *Ghost of Summer,* a book about her native Northern Ireland. Bunting takes as her subject the violent conflicts between Protestants and Catholics, and connects those prejudices with the problem of racism in the United States. She explained in *SATA,* "I tried to write a story that children would find exciting but that would also show them the insidious horror of prejudice and the tragedy of a people torn apart by old hatreds." In *A Sudden Silence* and *Jumping the Nail,* both novels for young adults, Bunting is equally candid in her treatment of the problems faced by teenagers. *A Sudden Silence* (1988) is told by Jesse, whose younger brother Bry has been killed in a hit-and-run accident. While Jesse struggles with his feelings of guilt over his brother's death and the confusion of his growing attraction to his brother's girlfriend, Bunting sends a warning message about the extreme effects of alcohol abuse. Bunting portrays the romance of danger and peer acceptance in *Jumping the Nail.* The novel features a group of young people caught in the frenzy of a dangerous coming-of-age rit-

ual: jumping over the Nail, a local cliff above the ocean where earlier daredevils died in similar stunts. Dru, the novel's heroine, must make serious decisions about standing up to peer pressure and the influence of her boyfriend, who wants her to remain in their town instead of leaving for college. Dru also struggles with what to do about her friend Elisa, a fragile girl dangerously dependent upon her boyfriend; Elisa ultimately breaks down in the face of difficult adult decisions. *Jumping the Nail* manages to represent the complexities of teen relationships and sends a positive message about standing up to peer pressure. Susan Knorr noted that Bunting "does . . . well in recalling the uncertain stirrings and emotions inherent in new relationships. Dru's perceptions and observations are right on target, and Bunting shows clearly that the pressure to conform or concede can be as blatant as a demand to jump off a cliff or as subtle as a request couched in gentle words."

Even in her works for younger children Bunting does not shy away from difficult subjects. In the picture book *Smoky Night,* Daniel and his mother witness the Los Angeles riots from their inner-city apartment building. When their building catches fire, Daniel's cat Jasmine and his neighbor Mrs. Kim's cat—sworn enemies—disappear, and their owners are thrown together in a shelter worrying about them. Although she deals honestly with the violence and confusion of the riots, Bunting ends her story with a note of hope: the two cats return and drink out of the same bowl, hinting at future reconciliation and even friendship. Betsy Hearne recognized that, with *Smoky Night,* the "author . . . managed to portray a politically charged event without pretension or preaching." In a similar vein, Bunting's popular picture book, *The Wall,* presents the difficulties of dealing with grief and loss and understanding the tragedies of war. The story focuses on the journey of a young boy who goes to the Vietnam War Memorial with his father to find the name of his grandfather on the wall. Another picture book, *Your Move,* tells the story of James, a ten-year-old who wants to be a member of the cool K-Bones gang. James passes the gang's dangerous initiation, but when a rival gang threatens James and his little brother Isaac with a gun, James declines membership. Praised for her moral approach, Bunting has also been criticized for the too-simple ending; Elizabeth Bush acknowledged that Bunting captured "the allure, even the romance, of James's gutsy escapade," but also called her ending "facile."

Awards

Bunting received a PEN Special Achievement Award in 1984 for her contributions to children's literature. *One More Flight* was awarded the Golden Kite Award from the Society of Children's Book Writers and Illustrators in 1976, *The Wednesday Surprise* received the Jane Addams Honor award in 1990, *A Sudden Silence* won the 1990-91 Sequoyah Young Adult Book Award, and *Coffin on a Case* received the 1993 Edgar Allen Poe Award. *Is Anybody There?* received the Golden Sower

Award in 1992. *Our Sixth Grade Sugar Babies* was honored with a Young Reader's Choice Awards nomination in the youth division in 1993, while *SOS Titanic* was nominated in the senior division in 1999. *Smoky Night* was recognized by the American Library Association as a notable children's book, and *Night of the Gargoyles* was cited by the Young Adult Library Services Association of the American Library Association as a recommended book for reluctant young adult readers, both in 1995. *Spying on Miss Müller* was nominated for the 1996 Edgar Allen Poe Award, while *Nasty Stinky Sneakers* was nominated for the Young Reader's Choice Awards in 1997. Bunting received the 1999 Kerlan Award from the University of Minnesota for singular achievement in the creation of children's literature. In addition, she has also received many children's choice and regional awards in her home state of California.

AUTHOR'S COMMENTARY

Stefanie Weiss

SOURCE: An interview with Eve Bunting, in *NEA Today,* Vol. 13, No. 8, April, 1995, p. 7.

[*Bunting's 1995 book,* **Smoky Night,** *created enormous controversy because of its subject—a boy who loses his cat during an inner-city riot. This interview addresses the concerns raised by reviewers about the appropriateness of the setting and topic for young children.*]

Why write about a riot?

I live in Pasadena, 10 miles from downtown L.A. The night the Rodney King verdict came in, I was speaking in the public library.

When I got home and turned on the TV, almost instantly my thoughts went to the children who were there. What would it be like to be one of those children? How does a parent explain this to a child? How does a teacher explain why schools were damaged or closed?

Is the book appropriate for young children?

It's not meant for kids below seven or eight, but there's no upward level on it. I meant it for any kid and every kid. I think we can all use it.

How do you respond to those who say this book will only scare kids?

I knew this book might be criticized as not suitable for children. People say, "Do children need to know this? Can't children be children?" Well, I write my share of books that are full of little bears—and I think bedtime stories are terribly important. But this is not a bedtime story, and there was a time when it could not have been published.

Is there no protecting our children anymore?

I think the protection we can give them is the truth. I think we have to try somehow to extend their understanding of the difficult problems we have. Children can deal with the truth if they have a caring person to help them try to understand it. I don't want to write down to children at any age.

Your book about the Vietnam War Memorial, **The Wall,** *is a real tear-jerker. Do kids need sad books?*

Yes. Sadness is going to touch every child's life. I think in **The Wall,** I was trying to say that sometimes a war can be necessary, but people are dead just the same, so let's not glorify war any more than we have to.

I get more letters on **The Wall** than any of my other books. So many children have had grandfathers who died in the war. It's very touching to me to know that my book can make them feel that someone understands.

How do you come up with your ideas?

I'm inspired by things I read or hear or see on television that touch me in some way. I won't write a book unless I feel it emotionally and, having grown up in Northern Ireland, prejudice and violence bother me a lot.

Do you try to send a message?

I don't ever start off to give a message in my books, although often it must seem as though I do. I like to write about loving and caring and how both can ease everyone's way through life. Maybe that sounds Pollyana-ish, maybe it's optimism carried to the nth degree, but that's what I want to do.

How should your books be taught?

I'd like teachers to use my books to open up topics that aren't easy to talk about. I'd like teachers to read my books out loud, then ask the kids what they think. A teacher could say, "This is fiction, but does this kind of thing really happen? Is there something we can do to make this wrong a little better?"

Do your books change kids or inspire kids to change the world?

Maybe my books change their thinking or promote thinking. I got a letter from a little girl who'd read *Fly Away Home,* which is about a boy and his father who live in an airport because they can't afford an apartment.

"There's a girl in my class who lives in an abandoned building," the little girl wrote. "She always looks dirty, and we make fun of her. We're not going to make fun of her anymore." There it is! That's why I wrote the book.

Do you visit schools to talk to children?

Not anymore. I speak to teachers and librarians—they're the messengers. And my message to them is simple: Help your students take pleasure in reading—it's something they'll have all their lives.

Paul E. Pojman

SOURCE: "Conversations with Eve Bunting," in *Catholic Library World,* Vol. 68, No. 3, March, 1998, pp. 19-25.

[*After her acceptance speech for the Regina Medal on April 3, 1997, in Minneapolis, MN, Bunting participated in a "chat" session attended by about fifty librarians and teachers. The following questions and answers were edited for* Catholic Library World *from the original audio-taped session.*]

Question: Would you tell us a little bit about how writing is a part of your day?

Bunting: I'm a very unscheduled person. I only write when I want to write. The thing is that I want to write all the time! So this works fine for producing books. I write with a pencil in a notebook—you know the lined ones with pretty covers. I buy a pile of them: little ones for picture books; middle-sized for middle-grade books; and big, fat ones for my novels. This is what I tell kids when I talk to them. I write only on one side of the page. The other side is for my "second thoughts" or my corrections, so that I don't have to scribble all over my work. Sometimes there's more writing on the "other" side! Preferably I write in the morning. I don't just sit down right away and write but try to take care of my correspondence first.

After writing in the notebook is done, I type the book out on my old IBM Selectric, which I love dearly. I fear they will stop making ribbons for it. (I bought a computer and word processor, a lovely one, last year and tried it for about three days before giving it to my son.) Then I have a typist who can make up for my very bad typing, with the strike-outs and so on. Basically I do two drafts—one hand written and one typed. Then, when the typist sends it back to me, very often while reading it I find something else I need to change; it will go to my typist a second time. That's another thing I tell kids; you seldom get it right the first time. Also, I'm very aware of how a story sounds; so I'm a great believer in reading aloud, especially picture books because I like the rhythm of the words. I like words that sound beautiful, as beautiful as I can make them. Then I send the manuscript off to a publisher. . . .

Question: How long does it take you to write a book?

Bunting: It depends on the book, really. I can't even say that a picture book takes me a short time or a long time, because sometimes it doesn't work that way. *The Wall,* for instance, took me three years, even though it's such a short book. I'd been thinking about it for three years, but it took probably two hours to actually write. I just finished a young-adult novel called *The Black Water.* It was hard to write because of all the "psychological" kind of action. I'd write a couple of chapters and get stuck. Then I'd leave it and go and write something else that was burning in my head (because there's *always* something burning to write). I told one of my editors about this book I had started to write two and a half years or so before, about two kids in a river. Every time she saw me, she'd say, "Well, where is this book? Are those kids still in the river?" I finally got them out! So it just depends. Some books go very fast and easy and some don't.

Question: Do you work on two or three pieces at one time?

Bunting: I usually work on one piece at a time, except in those cases where I get stuck. I would hate to get stuck and not write at all. I usually have something that I'm just dying to do; so if I am stuck on one thing, I start another. Normally, however, I write one thing until I'm finished. I get really into it and really absorbed, and I can't think about anything else. . . .

Question: How many publishers have you used for your books?

Bunting: Oh my, well there was a time when I had thirteen different publishers, which is not a good idea. But I was a beginning writer and was eager and anxious. . . . It used to be that people would write only for one publisher, but I don't think it works anymore like that. Of those thirteen I had, I weaned them down through the years to four major ones. These are the ones I like the best for one reason or another. And sometimes I have a paperback sub-right which gives me another publisher, but that's not for me.

Question: How many illustrators have you used and how do you choose them?

Bunting: I don't know how many I've had. I've had an awful lot. Of all the illustrators who have done work for my books (163 of them)—only for three books did I not like the illustrator. It used to be that I didn't see anything of the picture book until it was finished. Then I'd walk to the mail and see the brown package and there was my book. Yes, I hope when they buy the book or see the book, people will read the text and the story will "grab" them; but the first thing they see is the cover and the art. I know my book won't sell well if the art is not good. So I open that envelope—saying a small prayer as I do so—and pull the book out. I've really been exceedingly fortunate. When I love the illustrations, I immediately sit down and write this "gushy" letter, telling the illustrator he's a genius. If I don't like them, I don't write anything because there's no point. I just let it be.

I don't choose the illustrators, unfortunately. They're chosen for me. Yet I really shouldn't say "unfortunately" because the publisher probably does a better job of choosing than I would. However, what I can do now (that I couldn't do at the beginning) is *suggest*. For *I Am the Mummy Heb-Nefert*, I said to the editor I would really like David Christiana to illustrate it since I'd seen other work he'd done that I really liked. Of course, asking for or suggesting someone doesn't necessarily mean I'll get that person. The illustrator can choose to say no; or the illustrator can be booked up. For one of my current illustrators I have to wait three years before he can even start.

Mostly, when I'm doing a picture book—not even mostly, *always* actually—the publisher keeps the illustrator and the author well apart. People think that we're together, discussing the work, but no. What they do for me now (and I'm happy to have it this way) is send me samples of the art; so I get a little preview, which is lovely. . . . But, even if there's something I don't like, there's not much I can do about it. The paintings are done. They're quite careful not to send you anything until there's nothing you can do about it, you know.

Question: Could you talk a little about the editor and the writing process?

Bunting: I've had wonderful editors. That's the first thing I would say. . . . I feel that the editor and the author are working together to produce a good book. I think you and your editor need to have a rapport, which I have with all of mine—maybe more with some than with others. There's one house I work with where the editor and I are good friends. Although I don't really like the publisher, I like the *editor* so much that I want to stay with that house.

A good editor doesn't really "change" your work. If an editor has problems with a book, she'll contact me to explain and maybe make suggestions; and, if we can't agree, we won't do the book. That's the kind of relationship I have, really, with all my editors. One of my publishers, for example, took the text of a new story and cut it up to make a "dummy" book, to see if text and pictures would balance on the pages. (It's amazing how much thought goes into these books.) My editor sent me the dummy, and she said, "Now I feel we need to put more text on this page and take some text out of this page. I've gone ahead and done it and tell me if you agree." I started to read and suddenly this awful sentence jumped out at me. I learned from this experience. Editors are very good at being editors, but they are not writers. I have to be aware of that and I just have to tread carefully. Both author and editor are working toward the same end—to make a better book—and perhaps don't always see things the same way. Personally I don't like to have somebody cut too many sentences because

the story loses the meaning or feeling I'm trying to get across. But I've been lucky.

Question: Are you or any of your family members in any of your books?

Bunting: Are you kidding? We are in all of them practically. Let's see, there's a book I did called *A Day's Work*—I don't know if you've seen that one. It's about a grandfather who is Mexican-American and who comes to stand around on a farm with a lot of other men waiting to get work. They're all waiting for a day's work. You know. I see them all the time. One of my sons is a landscape designer. There was this new development where he was employed to do all the landscaping. One day he was driving his truck along and looking for somebody to do weeding for him in an embankment that bordered new homes. He stopped and asked a group of people if anybody was a gardener. This man said, *si, si,* that he was a gardener. The man spoke no English and my son didn't speak Spanish. He took the man in his truck to the housing place and explained how he wanted him to weed and clean around the new plants. Well, you probably know the rest of the story. My son went off to inspect the other houses. When he came back, all the new plants were out and all the weeds still in! My son said he could do nothing but laugh. He felt it was his own fault for leaving the man by himself. I put all of this in the book. My little granddaughters were reading the book when it had just come out—they were probably six-years old at the time—and said to me, "Oh, Grandma, this same thing happened to my daddy!" I said, *"Really?"*

I use them shamelessly. *No Nap,* another picture book, features one of my granddaughters. Every time I took her hand, even if we were in the middle of the mall, she'd say, "No nap, Grandma, no nap." She was always thinking I was taking her for a nap. So they all give me ideas all the time. They don't really give them to me, I just take them. It's wonderful to have them.

Question: Have you written about Ireland?

Bunting: I write about it quite a lot. *Spying on Miss Müller* is a young-adult novel I did a couple of years ago. It's a story about World War II and myself in boarding school. In fact, I'm one of the four girls on the cover [of the hard bound editions]. I had sent a photograph to the artist, who drew a picture of me. (It's hard to believe I ever looked like that!) The story takes place in Belfast, which was bombed quite a lot during the War. Then I've done *Market Day,* a picture book about Maghera on "market day." It's supposed to be my father on the inside, but he never looked like that. And I have *St. Patrick's Day in the Morning, Clancy's Coat, Barney the Beard, The Haunting of Kildoran Abbey* and *The Ghost of Summer.*

Question: I have always loved *The Wednesday Surprise* from the moment I held it in my hands. Could you give the background for it?

Bunting: Yes, I'd love to because it's one of my favorites too. I was having dinner with a friend, Penny, a teacher in Sacramento. Penny was talking about her mother who had come from Greece when Penny was a baby. "You know," she said, "my mother could speak a little English but couldn't read it when she first came to this country. I taught her to read using my picture books." Then Penny went on talking while I was poised with the fork halfway to my mouth. (You run the risk of people thinking you're a little slow!) Then, after she's finished about ten more sentences, I said, "You taught your mother to read using picture books? Oh, I'd love to write a story about that. Would it be OK if I wrote a story about that?" She said, "Oh sure." Then I said, "You know, it's really your mother's story. Maybe you could ask your mother if she would mind if I wrote her story." Penny called sometime later to tell me what her mother said: "You tell that writer lady that if she wants any more stories I've got millions of them!" So I wrote *The Wednesday Surprise*. It was really funny, I never did meet her mother. I kept getting messages through Penny: "My mother wants to know how you're getting along with *her* book?" And so on. When I write a book, I never know if a publisher will buy it or not. I began to think, please God let me sell this book because otherwise this woman is going to be so disappointed. So when I finished the book and sold it, she was so excited. Of course, the book was dedicated to her. She turned out to be a very well-known person in Sacramento. She had arranged that, when the book was published, we'd have a big publication party. She, of course, would be the "queen bee." The mayor was coming. Everybody was coming and it was going to be this wonderful party. Then, maybe a month before the book was to come out [in 1989], she died very unexpectedly. Penny called me and she could hardly speak. We cried a little bit on the phone. I felt I'd come to know her mother just through the "back and forth." Penny said, "You know, this party's all scheduled. We're going to have it because my mother would have wanted that." She wasn't Irish, but it was as if she had an Irish wit. We had the party and practically all of Sacramento came since they all knew her. We had the band from a local high school. It was very wonderful.

I remember, at that time, a bridge over a river there. The bridge had been dark and you could buy a light in memory of someone to light the bridge. Penny had bought a light for her mother. I came home after that party and was telling my granddaughter (about five-years old at the time) how sad it was that Penny's mother had died and about the light. And my little, wise granddaughter—you know that they are sometimes wiser than we are—said, "It's all right, Grandma, everybody has to die." Then she said, "I know you're going to be dying soon. Just wait a while and I'll come too." *The Wednesday Surprise* is a simple, little story, but people really seem to like it. Barbara Bush wrote me and said she really liked the book. I have the letter framed and hanging in my hallway. If anyone walks past without noticing it, I immediately point it out.

Question: What was that story you told us about a house you once lived in you suspected could be haunted and you tied it in with a novel?

Bunting: The novel was called *Ghost Behind Me*. The house was our first one in the United States, in Sausalito. We didn't know [when we moved in] it was supposed to have been haunted. We never saw a thing. I was so lonely that I would have been quite happy to see a ghost! We wondered why we got it for quite an inexpensive rate.

Question: Could you talk a little bit about *The Wall?*

Bunting: Oh, *The Wall* I wrote after I heard some teachers talking about a class trip to Washington, D.C., and how the children had been more impressed with the Vietnam Memorial than any of the other monuments. Some of the children had laid their hands on it and been very quiet. Their remarks to each other were not flippant but were really sensible. As the teachers told me about it, I thought I would really like to write a book about this. (I always think first "picture book" because that's my love.) I began to mull over in my mind how I could do this. It was really hard. How do you write about "war" and the Vietnam War? How do you write about dead soldiers? So that book took me a long, long time to write. I couldn't seem to get a handle on it. Then one night I went to bed and woke up in the morning with the first two lines. So often when I get those first lines, the rest of the story follows. "This is the wall, my grandfather's wall. On it are the names of those killed in a war long ago." When I heard those lines, I suddenly saw the little boy walking hand in hand with his father to find his grandfather's name on the Wall. Then I had the story.

After that, I think the book took me probably not more than four days to write. At the time, I had not yet been to see the Wall. I had just heard teachers talking about it. Then I'd started to think about it and taken "everything" out of the library. (I have a nextdoor neighbor who's a librarian and she was really wonderful; she put in a search at the library and got me articles and articles out of periodicals. I was actually swamped.) I went through all the material. It was so sad. When I wrote the book and sent it in, I wasn't sure if my editor would buy it since the subject was "iffy"; but he loved it right away. When I first saw the "F&Gs"—which are the "folded and gathered" sheets that are more like a loose-leaf book than the real published book—I went to Washington and went to the Wall. I left this first copy of *The Wall* leaning against the Wall and had a good cry. I guess now it's in the museum they have there.

I get so many letters on that book. I've had signings for the book. Sometimes a woman will just hand the book to me and stand there and sob. Then I just cry with her. A gift shop at the Wall has the book for sale. I was there one time when a woman was buying one and saying to the clerk, "I'm taking this book home to explain the Wall to my children and to have their teacher read it." I stood there and thought, "Shall I, shall I, shall I?" Finally I said, "I wrote it!" The woman was very happy. But I should have kept quiet because then the clerk said, "Oh, you did? We have these cases of them for you to autograph." Which I was happy to do.

Question: Would you describe your personal reading habits?

Bunting: I don't read an awful lot of other children's authors unless something comes highly recommended. I read mostly for pleasure, for relaxation. I like to have a good mystery, or sometimes I'll find a new author whom I think is really wonderful. Or I'll just take a walk through the library shelves of adult reading. I don't exactly read "trash"—but close to it! I mean, I don't read Danielle Steel or things like that, but for instance I just found a very good new author. I think her books are wonderful. I like a nice, good novel with good characterization and a good story that I can read in bed at night.

Question: How about when you were very young?

Bunting: When I was very small, I loved the *Anne of Green Gables* books. In fact I pretended I was Anne but couldn't quite convince my parents! I renamed everything around my house. I would say to my mother, "I'm going out to the 'Lake of Shining Waters' now." I loved those books. I loved all the wonderful children's books in my day, such as *Little Women* and all of those books. I wanted to be "Jo" in *Little Women*—I think we all did.

Question: So you've been reading from early on?

Bunting: Oh yes, oh yes. And my father was a big, rough, burly, country man who kept sheep and pigs and used to go to pubs (which were many in Maghera) to be with his friends who were as big and rough as he was, to share his secret passion which was for poetry. He absolutely loved poetry. If you ever asked him, he could tell you honestly what was a good poem and what wasn't. He would take me on his lap by the fire and read me poetry all the time. Then he would stop at the end of the page to make sure I wasn't asleep or something and say, "All right, darlin' what does that mean? What was the man sayin' there?" Through it I got the sense of it all. Then he'd say, "Now listen to this absolutely beautiful line." So I think that, from my father, I really got that love of, not only of reading, but of the sound of words, the sounds that words make on the page.

Question: How about some words of encouragement for an adult who is an aspiring children's book writer and who has researched and found that the topic for a story has never been written about in a children's book before?

Bunting: That's a great start—a topic that's never been written about before. Well, I think first of all he would need to show some of his work, not just say he has this topic. He would need to do two or three chapters. [*Comment: It's a picture book.*] Oh a picture book. Well then, has he tried to sell it? [*Comment: Yes, but no luck. He was trying to get an agent.*] No, he doesn't need an agent at this point. I would just say, as words of encouragement, have him be persistent, keep trying, have faith in what he's done. The difference is what editors say to you. When an editor sends back a judgment slip and says something, it's really true even if you don't want to believe it. You don't, you know. If that editor says, "This is too long" or "You have too much description" or "It doesn't ring true" or "It's too slight" or "It's not saying anything worthwhile" your first instinct is "Well, what does he mean? Of course it's saying something worthwhile." But *look* at it and see if it really is. Be willing to change it, but don't be willing to change it for everybody. You know, just look at it for the truth of what the book is saying. Then keep sending it out. That's really about all you can do. And maybe put in a little note saying, "I have really researched this book." If he has any special qualifications, maybe his job relates to what he's doing—I mean suppose the book is about a dancer and he can say he danced for three years with the New York Ballet or whatever—anything that is pertinent should be put in the letter.

Question: What has been your most memorable award? What advice would you give to encourage children to write?

Bunting: Let's not count the Regina Medal in this conversation. Even if this is sort of a sloppy thing to say, I think my most memorable awards are those that I get from children. Certainly it was wonderful when *Smoky Night* won the Caldecott Award. That was terrific. The State awards that you get are wonderful. The Mystery Writers Guild and others all mean a great deal to a person. But I think the awards that come when children actually vote for you in their classroom are just supernice. I love it when kids like my books. A book I did a few years ago, *Nasty, Stinky Sneakers,* you can tell is cleaning up with the kids. It's winning a lot of State awards. I think they like that title. Although one kid wrote to me (they're so funny and so honest) and said, "I took your book *Nasty, Stinky Sneakers* out of the library. To tell you the truth, I thought it was going to be better than it was." Maybe nasty, stinky sneakers aren't so funny after all! But I love the awards I get.

Then to encourage kids to write, the obvious thing is just to encourage them to read. Get them to read the good books they like and encourage them to write, to write their own stories, not to worry so much about their spelling or punctuation or whatever. Just encourage them to be creative. If they like to keep a journal—but if they are anything like I was when I was their age, my journals always stopped at January 4th, I don't know if that really works too well—you can always try to do that. I think just be appreciative and encouraging and never negative with them. When I was at university, before I dropped out to get married, my professor of literature told me I should never consider English or writing in any form as a career because I was no good.

Of course, I wasn't exactly a kid; I mean, I was eighteen or whatever, but I don't think anyone should ever do that with the children. All my grandchildren write and show me their stories. I just think that's great. I always tell them: "Be careful. I might steal that."

Question: When we go back to our classrooms after this convention and talk to our students about meeting with you, what message may we convey, as words to them from you?

Bunting: Well, tell them that I love them. I really do. I can't see children without smiling. I find their letters charming and amusing, often interesting and helpful, and sometimes taking me to task. For example, "I didn't like the ending of that book." I find the letters very interesting, but I find it very difficult to answer them all. We do. Ed helps me. He does all the envelopes. We answer every letter that we get, but I want you to know that it's hard. Also I want you to know that I do a lot of soul searching periodically. One thing I could say is, please send a stamped envelope. I get about eighty letters a week and it is so hard to answer them. We take a weekend a month and try to answer them. I'm telling you that it's wonderful when we get the letter box empty. Then comes the next day with twelve or fourteen more. HarperCollins gets letters for me and saves them; then they send me a big envelope. I open it and all these letters pour out and it's so distressing. I open and read them as I get them. And I enjoy them. Yet I just wish that teachers could say—and it's so heartwarming when they do—"You don't have to answer this letter, but I just want you to know that I really liked your book." That is like a little blessing. Then there are so many that say "I have to write a letter to you" or "I have to do an essay" or "We all have to write a letter to an author and I chose you. I haven't read any of your books, but I hear you're a good author."

Last night I had dinner with Marion Bauer and we were talking about this. She said, "Sometimes I feel like I'm on the edge of having a nervous breakdown because these letters that keep on coming." You never really finish. Katherine Paterson once said that she does not answer any more letters. She said she's really sorry about that, because kids who really write from the heart are being left out. Yet there are so many that aren't that she just cannot do it, cannot keep up with it.

So we're kind of struggling with that at the moment. Ed thinks I should answer them all selectively. What he means by "selectively" is that we do one letter for a class, even if we get thirty letters from a class and the teacher says, "Our students would be very disappointed if they don't each get a letter." Ed says, "no." But it's a constant struggle. When we get all the letters done, I think that it was really worthwhile and I'm glad we did it. I picture all those children getting all these letters and how happy they'll be. But then when the box is full, believe me that I am a much crueler person!

Question: Do you write your responses in longhand?

Bunting: No. Actually what we usually do is use forms I have from the publishing company and I attach a little hand written note. I don't do a big long letter, but if I'm asked a question I'll answer it. I try to make it pertinent to the letter-writer.

Question: Have you considered writing an autobiography?

Bunting: I've done one. It's called **Once Upon a Time**—part of a series published by R. C. Owen. It's one of these very simple books.

Question: What about one for older readers?

Bunting: Please no. Well, *Something about the Author* has quite a long piece. A lot of these journals cover a lot. I think that's enough. Maybe someday. I like to write biographical fiction you know. I would be tempted to make my life more interesting!

GENERAL COMMENTARY

Michael Cart

SOURCE: "Barriers against the Wind," in *Booklist,* Vol. 92, No. 2, September 15, 1995, p. 150.

Eve Bunting, author of the 1995 Caldecott Medal-winning **Smoky Night**, laughed ruefully when I asked her the now-inevitable question about the *c* word. "Honestly," she answered, "I think when Harcourt reprints the book, they should officially change its title to *The Controversial Smoky Night.*

She was referring, of course, to the heated debate that has been raging over the suitability of her subject—an urban riot—to a picture book published for the very young. The brouhaha has even bubbled over from the professional literature into the mass media, thanks to essayist Charles Krauthammer's outraged observation in the March 27 issue of *Time:* "Teaching the most wrenching social history to the very young assaults their innocence by deliberately disturbing their cozy, rosy view of the world. For what purpose? They live only once, and for a very short time, in a tooth-fairy world. Why shorten that time further?"

Well . . . maybe, but I would answer his question with a sad one of my own: "What innocence?" For it seems to me that the cozy, rosy worldview being compromised here is Krauthammer's, not that of beleaguered kids who must live in a real world where the tooth fairy has just been mugged at the corner and robbed of its pocketful of quarters. Rioting is only one public strain of the epidemic of violence that infects the world of today's kids. According to a recent issue of the *Journal of the American Medical Association,* 1 in 4 kids from 10 to 16 report having being assaulted or abused within the previous year. The streets are bad enough, but the home is no longer a sanctuary, either. The U.S. Advisory Board on Child Abuse and Neglect reports that 2,000 kids die every year from domestic violence, while 140,000 more are seriously injured. And the heartbreaking fact is that a vast majority of these abused and neglected children are under 4 years of age. Are we, I wonder, doing these kids any favors by continuing to pretend that theirs is a "tooth fairy world"?

Bunting thinks not. "There's no way I feel I shouldn't have written **Smoky Night,**" she told me, "because I know it is a true book and as long as you give kids the truth, you needn't be ashamed of anything you write. Children are living in this real world, and we adults can't protect them from its realities. My father used to say to me when I had troubles, 'I can't stand between you and the wind.' I often think of that now when I'm writing for children."

Books can be barriers against the wind, though, and **Smoky Night** . . . [is a] perfect example of [a] picture book that, in [its] treatment of tough topics, invite[s] reading and healing discussion, not only by kids of the traditional target age—6 through 9—but also by older kids, even those in high school. The problem is getting the books into the hands of these older kids. Because the production, marketing, and distribution of books all hinge on the perceived need to categorize, any title that can't be easily labeled with an "age appropriate" designation runs the risk of being lost. . . .

The Five Owls for Parents

SOURCE: "Making Good Choices," in *The Five Owls for Parents,* Vol. 1, No. 1, January-February, 1999.

For the last quarter-century, an increasing number of books for young people have dealt with challenging subject matter drawn from the mean streets and world that too many children are forced to endure. No subject is taboo—divorce, terminal illness, death, gang activity, child abuse, substance abuse. All of these books deal with the difficult choices that life brings. Most of these books are directed, understandably, to teens. Relatively few are suitable for younger readers.

But books by Eve Bunting are the exceptional exceptions. She has written many books for preteen readers that are set in the reality of the world. "Ninety percent of my ideas come from reports of current news, and the other ten percent from what I see happening around me," said Bunting. "What I write has to be contemporary."

Eve Bunting's take on reality is honest, thoughtful, and positive. "It would be dishonest to write a novel about characters free from any problems of a serious nature. But the problems should be an integral part of the book, not the entire substance of the book."

"I'd never have a kid messing with drugs or messing with sex. In my books my kids are always tempted, because I think that's life. But whatever the tempting situation, kids will find a message, well-hidden I hope, that says, 'better not.' Each of us has a choice of what we do with our lives. I hope the children make the right choice, whatever it is, and in my books I try to help them make it."

TITLE COMMENTARY

JUMPING THE NAIL (1991)

Kirkus Reviews

SOURCE: A review of *Jumping the Nail,* in *Kirkus Reviews,* Vol. LIX, No. 20, October 15, 1991, p. 1340.

Impelled by a heady blend of peer pressure and vainglory, a group of recently graduated California teens revive the local stunt of leaping from a 90-foot cliff into the sea where some of their predecessors died.

Skillfully, Bunting hones in on the dynamics of daredevil behavior, omitting such trappings of teen rebellion as alcohol, drugs, or problem parents. Conscientious Dru, her narrator, is about to be a scholarship student at Northwestern; Dru's new boyfriend, Mike, is rich but very nice. Dru's anxiety especially concerns her close friend Elisa, whose mental health she knows is fragile. Elisa's charismatic but boorishly insensitive boyfriend, Scooter, cajoles Elisa into joining him in the first jump. Afraid to lose him, Elisa complies; though neither is physically hurt, the effect on Elisa is traumatic. Next, driven by the growing exhilaration plus competition over Mike's sexy former girlfriend, twin boys jump, surviving with minor injuries but adding to the tension—to which Elisa tragically succumbs before Mike and Dru are able to carry out their difficult resolution to inform the police.

Satisfying suspense that unobtrusively incorporates wholesome values while drawing a credible picture of ordinary teens enthralled by their own escalating frenzy.

Stephanie Zvirin

SOURCE: A review of *Jumping the Nail,* in *Booklist,* Vol. 88, No. 5, November 1, 1991, p. 505.

Dependency and *danger* are the operative words in Bunting's latest novel about a teenage couple who take a perilous risk that eventually leads to tragedy. Dru is terrified when she discovers that her friend Elisa is going to accompany Scooter, the boy Elisa's been dating, in a treacherous leap off the Nail, a nearby cliff that looms large in local legend as a place to "prove" oneself.

Knowing Elisa is emotionally unstable, Dru fears for more than her friend's physical safety. Her concerns prove well grounded. Though the pair survive the plunge, the shock of it unhinges fragile Elisa. Boastful Scooter, in the meantime, becomes a hero to his peers and has his pick of pretty, fawning girls. Powerless to help her friend, Dru wonders at Scooter's selfishness and Elisa's loyalty and obedience. At the same time, Dru faces her own personal crisis—should she stay in La Paloma with her boyfriend, Mike, or make her own leap of faith by leaving for college in the fall and possibly losing Mike when she does? Characters and plot are simply but effectively sketched. It's Bunting's acknowledgment of the allure of danger and the power that comes from facing it, as well as her on-target depiction of how easy it is to lose perspective when you fall in love, that makes her novel more than just a good, fast read.

Susan Knorr

SOURCE: A review of *Jumping the Nail,* in *School Library Journal,* Vol. 37, No. 12, December, 1991, p. 135.

Rising 90 feet above the water, the cliff known as the Nail looms large in the legends of the teens in the coastal community of Paloma, California. A jump off the cliff into the ocean below rates an entry on the roster of names carved into the cliff's "danger" sign, and now, despite the risk, Dru's best friend, Elisa, is jumping in order to please her boyfriend. This jump causes her chronic depression to resurface, and raises for Dru all sorts of issues regarding peer pressure, insecurity, and parental demands. Bunting's message is obvious—distraught Elisa will do anything to keep her chauvinistic boyfriend and commits suicide when he is unfaithful; another boy jumps in order to impress flirtatious Diane; and Dru feels pressure from her boyfriend, who requests that she change her plans and go to a local college, and from her mother, who urges her not to let this boy (the rich son of mom's first sweetheart) slip away. While the characters tend to be narrowly drawn, Bunting excels in her descriptions of the cliff, the anticipation of the jump, and Elisa's wild imaginings of what she experienced in the watery depths. The author does equally well in recalling the uncertain stirrings and emotions inherent in new relationships. Dru's perceptions and observations are right on target, and Bunting shows clearly that the pressure to conform or concede can be as blatant as a demand to jump off a cliff or as subtle as a request couched in gentle words.

SUMMER WHEELS (1992)

Susan Patron

SOURCE: A review of *Summer Wheels,* in *The Five Owls,* Vol. VI, No. 4, March-April, 1992, p. 79.

Here is a story about trust and rules and fairness—a

story in which a kind older man makes a difference in the lives of some "underprivileged" kids. It works as a story, without becoming sentimental or didactic, because it's told from the perspective of a kid who loves the Bicycle Man without even knowing it.

The Bicycle Man keeps a garage full of old bikes that he lets neighborhood children borrow. He works it on an honor system: you choose any bike you want (first come, first served), you sign it out, you get it back by 4:00 that day. If the bike you borrowed needs repair, you fix it or you help the Man fix it. Those are the only rules.

But so much trust is risky business. When a new boy who signs himself "Abrehem Lincoln" borrows the narrator's favorite bike and fails to return it, Lawrence is furious. That boy violated the honor system! The Man shouldn't have trusted him so easily! "You should have suspected!" Lawrence says. "I'm not here to suspect," the man answers.

He *is* there, it seems, to nurture those neighborhood kids. Some of them hang around the garage, helping him fix bikes. Some of them, like "Abrehem Lincoln," test just exactly to what degree that amazing offer of trust will hold up. What if they keep the borrowed bike *overnight,* without even asking? What if that bike has been badly damaged?

The Man has high expectations of kids; he wants them to observe the rules because they elect to do so, not because they're forced or coerced. He empowers them through love and trust.

This handsomely formatted book has wide margins, a large, clear typeface, and an illustration for every page or double-page spread. It will be inviting to a reader who needs a bridge from controlled-vocabulary books to easy fiction. Thomas B. Allen's full-color pastel/crayon drawings reinforce and support the text. (The stately if shabby old houses of these neighborhoods—probably south-central Los Angeles—provide a backdrop to the real center of activity: the streets and sidewalks.) The pictures exactly capture that hot and dusty and free quality of school-less summer days, when you and your best friend have great wheels for doing cherry pickers and Vander rolls.

The interracial friendship between the narrator and his best friend, while not a focus of the story, underscores the themes of trust and support. The final illustration, of the two t-shirted boys on a palm tree-lined street, their arms draped across each other's backs, is like an anthem to boyhood. Bravo Bunting and Allen for capturing this universal and intimate moment of it.

Elizabeth S. Watson

SOURCE: A review of *Summer Wheels,* in *The Horn Book Magazine,* Vol. LXVIII, No. 4, July-August, 1992, pp. 447-48.

Thanks to the Bicycle Man, any neighborhood child can borrow a fixed-up bicycle for the day as long as he or she has it back by four p.m. and agrees to fix the bike if it breaks. When a bully tries to buck the system, Lawrence and Brady are intent upon bringing the culprit to justice. What they learn about giving the other guy a second chance, human nature, and human kindness causes them to take another look at the gray areas of life and will provide the reader with the same opportunity. The story is brief; the moral, straightforward but subtle. With its illustrated format, the book can help in that transition from picture book to novel and is an incentive for less skilled readers. Depicting the neighborhood from varying angles and perspectives, the subdued charcoal and pastel drawings underlie the mood. The book works both as a discussion-starter for values clarification and as an enjoyable story to read.

Susan Giffard

SOURCE: A review of *Summer Wheels,* in *School Library Journal,* Vol. 38, No. 8, August, 1992, p. 134.

The Bicycle Man lends bicycles to the neighborhood kids with two rules: they must be returned by four o'clock, and if they break, the kids must fix them. Lawrence, the African-American narrator, and his friend Brady spend their summer days riding. When a new kid doesn't return a bike, the two friends find him and make him take it back. In the process, they discover that his toughness is just a mask for his need for adult attention, and that the Man cares more about kids than bicycles. This gentle, warm story, divided into chapters, has an understated message. The immediacy of the present-tense narration and the colloquial dialogue help to create the sense of freedom and space that is peculiar to summer. Allen's pastel drawings shimmer with the heat as they capture the energy and movement of the boys on their bikes. The numerous illustrations, generous amount of white space, and good-sized print make this a perfect choice for beginning chapter-book readers.

📖 *THE DAY BEFORE CHRISTMAS* (1992)

Publishers Weekly

SOURCE: A review of *The Day before Christmas,* in *Publishers Weekly,* Vol. 239, No. 40, September 7, 1992, p. 68.

Bunting's tale alludes to ghosts from Christmas past—in this case, the seven-year-old heroine's long-dead mother. Allie doesn't remember her, but Grandpa does, and Allie worries that their attendance at a performance of *The Nutcracker* will trigger sad memories in him (Grandpa had made a ritual of taking Allie's mother in *her* childhood). Bunting handles this tricky subject with her customary delicacy and candor and, while [Beth] Peck's oil paintings are perhaps too gray to appeal to children, her illustrations of the ballet convey . . . motion . . .

School Library Journal

SOURCE: A review of *The Day before Christmas,* in *School Library Journal,* Vol. 38, No. 10, October, 1992, p. 38.

Just before Christmas, a girl and her grandfather take the train into the city to see *The Nutcracker.* But it's not just the season that makes this day and this trip special. They are going to the ballet together—just as the man had taken the child's mother, now dead, when she was seven. The story is told with a loving tone, filled with childlike wonder. But it's an odd combination: a fun trip to a holiday ballet is tinged with sadness. The paintings are oils done on canvas and have a formal, somewhat heavy look. Although each one is beautiful, as illustrations they are uneven and confusing. The historical period seems to change with almost every page; some pictures show characters who could have lived perhaps 30 or 40 years ago, while others depict vehicles that seem more modern. The lack of consistency in both time frame and social milieu detracts from the whole. Mixed messages, both in art and text, give what should have been a lovely book an uneven quality.

Carolyn Phelan

SOURCE: A review of *The Day before Christmas,* in *Booklist,* Vol. 89, No. 5, November 1, 1992, pp. 518-19.

On the day before Christmas, Allie's grandfather takes her to see *The Nutcracker,* just as he had taken her mother to see it when she was seven. They take the train into the city, enjoy the performance, then ride the train back home. Told by the child, who confides that her mother died when she was three and that she hardly remembers her, the story has a patina of sadness despite Allie's excitement and Grandpa's statement that "a loving memory is happy, not sad." Perhaps the emotional shading arises from the gray undertones of Peck's palette, which seem to belie the story's upbeat sentiments, despite the occasional warmth of colors. Still, her painterly, impressionistic illustrations often show promising finesse in composition, gesture, and narration. This picture book brings up the issue of parental death, which many parents prefer not to discuss with preschoolers except in the most reassuring terms. While the book is not what most parents are looking for as a pre-*Nutcracker* or holiday read-aloud, it may strike a chord in children who are themselves dealing with the story's emotional issues. Recommended for larger collections.

📖 *OUR TEACHER'S HAVING A BABY* (1992)

Kathryn Broderick

SOURCE: A review of *Our Teacher's Having a Baby,* in *Booklist,* Vol. 89, No. 2, September 15, 1992, p. 153.

Mrs. Neal informs her students that she's going to have a baby. They take the news well but have lots of questions, all of which are legitimate. And Mrs. Neal proves to be a responsible teacher, answering their questions and involving the children in her situation. Through the fall and winter, this multicultural class works on projects relating to the approaching birth—deciding what to name the baby, writing letters of welcome, pinning up pictures of baby's things on the bulletin board. Bunting's story is realistic and accurate, while [Diane] de Groat's beautiful watercolor spreads show much of the emotion that seven-year-olds can feel, from the excitement at hearing the news to the fear of not seeing their teacher again. Overall, this book provides great feelings of reassurance, which children need during times of change.

Jeanne Marie Clancy

SOURCE: A review of *Our Teacher's Having a Baby,* in *School Library Journal,* Vol. 39, No. 3, March, 1993, p. 171.

Considering the tremendous number of books available on new babies and pregnancy, it is truly amazing that almost all of them deal with mothers and aunts. *Our Teacher's Having a Baby* will certainly fit the bill on that special occasion. Mrs. Neal's first grade class is thrilled, after some initial skepticism, to learn that she is expecting. The woman works life and birth into her curriculum, and really involves her class in her pregnancy. Finally, the baby arrives. Classroom life continues with a substitute teacher, and Mrs. Neal brings Isabel (in a Moses basket decorated with their stickers) for a visit, reassuring the children that she will be back. While Mrs. Neal's assurances about her future in teaching are positive, it seems highly unlikely that someone who delivered in February would return from maternity leave to the same class. Otherwise, Bunting's wise and wonderful tale deserves its place on every school and public library shelf. De Groat's warm watercolor illustrations portray a nurturing and joy-filled classroom. She successfully reflects all the emotions of the action from excited anticipation to complete joy to worried concern. An excellent collaboration.

COFFIN ON A CASE (1992)

Deborah Stevenson

SOURCE: A review of *Coffin on a Case,* in *Bulletin of the Center for Children's Books,* Vol. 46, No. 3, November, 1992, p. 69.

Henry Coffin's father is a private detective who models himself after Sam Spade, while Henry hopes to model himself after his father. The summer after sixth grade, Henry falls into a doozy of a case: Lily, a sexy older woman (sixteen), has lost her mother, and with Henry's father out of town, Henry takes on the case. He and Lily eventually track down her mom to a basement where

thieves have hidden her after she witnessed their crime, and Henry saves the mom, the loot, and the day. This is a cheerful homage to hard-boiled detecting, with its own twists and charm: when arranging a signal with Lily, for instance, Henry says "I can't whistle. I'll cluck like this," and a brief argument ensues as to whether the cluck belongs to a hen or a woodchuck. Lily is no dumb blonde but still seems a likely enough fantasy for boys Henry's age, as does the rest of this blithely improbable boy-wonder tale. A good mystery for young romantics, this will set them on the Bogart trail.

Kirkus Reviews

SOURCE: A review of *Coffin on a Case,* in *Kirkus Reviews,* Vol. LX, No. 21, November 1, 1992, p. 1373.

Here, Bunting brings a glib, easy style to the tale of Henry Coffin, son of a partner in the detective agency "Coffin and Pale." When his father is unable to take on a case, sixth-grader Henry hooks up with "gorgeous babe" Lily—several years his senior—whose mother has disappeared. Figuring in the plot are the theft of a jade figurine, the appearance of two shady newcomers in a still-under-construction development, and the discovery of a missing wooden stork. It's a point-blank mystery that gets its atmosphere from Henry's funny narration and the frequent invocation of the name and talents of "Sam Spade"; and though Bunting's more sophisticated fans may not find much to get their claws into, those who like uncomplicated suspense will be (albeit briefly) entertained.

Kim Carter

SOURCE: A review of *Coffin on a Case,* in *Voice of Youth Advocates,* Vol. 16, No. 1, April, 1993, p. 24.

Twelve-year-old Henry Coffin is determined to follow in his detective father's footsteps, especially when doing so enables him to play Sam Spade for lovely Lily Larson, who thinks she has lost her mother (for the fourth time). Riding around L.A. in Lily's big red car is fun until the case gets serious, putting both Henry and Lily in positions that could cost them their lives!

Similar in style to Jay Bennett's mysteries, the somewhat lighter *Coffin on a Case* will appeal to middle school readers with a taste for easily read, fast paced plots. Recommended, especially for developing middle school/junior high hilo collections.

SOMEDAY A TREE (1993)

Kirkus Reviews

SOURCE: A review of *Someday a Tree,* in *Kirkus Reviews,* Vol. LXI, No. 4, February 15, 1993, p. 223.

The team who collaborated on *The Wall* (1990) and *Fly Away Home* (1991, both ALA Notables) takes on another contemporary issue in a story about a beloved tree, an ancient oak, succumbing to pollutants. Alice describes the tree's importance to her family—not just a favorite picnic spot but the site of events like her christening. When Alice notices a "funny" smell, withering grass, and leaves falling (it's spring), a tree doctor is summoned; she reports that the tree has been poisoned, perhaps by illegal dumping. Neighbors pitch in for a rescue effort involving spraying, sunscreens, laborious soil replacement, and more whimsical gestures like get-well cards and chicken soup, but to no avail; even Mom weeps. Still, with youthful hope, Alice plants some acorns she gathered while the tree was still healthy. Deliberately poignant but more plausible and skillfully written than most of the recent spate of consciousness-raising books about trees; [Ronald] Himler's sensitive, evocative watercolors make a fine complement to the lyrical, perceptive text.

Publishers Weekly

SOURCE: A review of *Someday a Tree*, in *Publishers Weekly*, Vol. 240, No. 11, March 15, 1993, pp. 86-7.

Nostalgia and timeliness merge seamlessly in this uncommonly evocative picture book. A sprawling oak tree grows in the field next to Alice's house, and it holds many memories for her family. Her mother reminisces about the first picnic she and Alice's father shared underneath it, and about Alice's christening on the very-same spot. When the grass around the tree begins to turn yellow, and the branches begin to drop leaves in springtime, a tree doctor surmises that someone has dumped chemicals by its roots. Alice and her parents, as well as their neighbors, try desperately but vainly to save the poisoned tree. Finally, when its branches are bare, Alice plants acorns she had once gathered from the then-healthy tree, telling her dog that if even one of them grows, another tree will sprout up "someday." While filling her cogent tale with poignant details (neighbors bring food and get-well cards; one knits a scarf to tie around the trunk of the ailing oak), Bunting never allows it to become sentimental or didactic. The story's emotional impact—and environmental message—are movingly reinforced by Himler's delicate paintings, which deftly portray the robust oak's pathetic deterioration into a rickety skeleton of a tree.

Jacqueline Elsner

SOURCE: A review of *Someday a Tree*, in *School Library Journal*, Vol. 39, No. 5, May, 1993, p. 81.

A sensitive book with an environmental theme. A family relaxes and engages in picnics, naps, storytelling, and plain fun under a gigantic old oak tree on their country property. One day, young Alice notices that the grass under the tree smells funny and is turning yellow. The

oak's leaves start to fall, even though it is spring. A tree doctor discovers that the soil has been poisoned, probably by illegally dumped chemicals. Neighbors pitch in: the poisoned dirt is carted off, the fire department sprays water, sacking is wrapped around top branches, and the telephone company loans poles from which to hang sunscreens. The tree dies despite the efforts to save it. Finally, Alice remembers her collection of acorns, which she rushes out and plants in healthy ground near the tree. Himler's soft, realistic watercolors spread over double pages and complement the sensitive, poetic mood of the story. In increasing numbers, teachers are asking for picture books on ecological issues. This title joins [Chris] Van Allsburg's *Just a Dream* and Ruth Brown's *The World That Jack Built* in serving that demand.

RED FOX RUNNING (1993)

Publishers Weekly

SOURCE: A review of *Red Fox Running*, in *Publishers Weekly*, Vol. 240, No. 36, September 6, 1993, pp. 95-6.

Bunting's rhymes freeze-frame moments of a red fox's winter day. The urgent tempo of the narrative echoes the animal's growing hunger: "Red fox running, / Running through the snow, / White sky above / And white earth below. / . . . / Hunger runs beside you / On this cold and frozen day." Elegant metaphors (the silence of an eagle's shadow, the loneliness of being left behind by migrating cranes) convey the emptiness within the starving fox. But "red fox, weary" turns to "red fox, joyous" when he sniffs out prey and returns to feed his family. The book hints at the cost of the hunt—"Your paws are raw and bleeding, / Your body's sore and spent"—but identifies the unlucky victim only in the illustrations, as a vague furriness. Facing each page of verse is a full-page painting; alternating with these are textless full-spread depictions of the fox's outdoor world. [Wendell] Minor's grainy paintings combine down-to-earth representations with an ethereal use of lighting.

Sara Stein

SOURCE: "The Little Foxes," in *The New York Times*, November 14, 1993, p. 24.

I wish that Eve Bunting, a veteran children's book author, had . . . done her homework for **Red Fox Running**. The story, told in verses that alternate with full-spread paintings by Wendell Minor, hinges on a fox's quest to bring food to his mate and cubs in early spring, when "winter should be over, but it didn't go away." That time of year is breeding and birthing season for red foxes (the previous year's cubs have long since dispersed), and though the male may bring food for his mate, he does not enter the maternal den. Yet the final illustration shows this out-of-synch fox family "all curled together in a warm, furry heap." Between Ms. Bunting's sing-song verse and Mr. Minor's beautiful but lifeless art, the story is as limp as the prey the fox finally finds, which is unidentified in the text, unidentifiable in the illustrations, but apparently already dead. In fact, it looks rather like a fox's tail.

Valerie Lennox

SOURCE: A review of *Red Fox Running,* in *School Library Journal,* Vol. 39, No. 12, December, 1993, p. 80, 85.

Bunting draws readers into the winter world of a red fox. In a simple, rhyming text—eight short lines per page—its quest for food unfolds. Suspense builds as it runs through the snow encountering other woodland creatures (will one become its prey?). As night falls, the animal wearies and becomes vulnerable itself. Finally, a meal is captured—details of the kill are discreetly omitted from both text and illustrations—and the creature staggers home with its "prize" to a cozy den and hungry cubs. The serious topic brings to mind a documentary, but the verse and fine watercolor paintings heighten its drama. Sweeping landscapes dominated by snowy ground, bleak skies, and rich evergreens appear regularly on double-page spreads that alternate comfortably with the sedately framed white pages of measured text. Compelling closeups of the wildlife are appropriately naturalistic and marvelously textured. Overall, Bunting provides an unromanticized glimpse of survival in the wild. Her lyrical language and Minor's large-format art render this an ideal choice to read aloud or independently.

SMOKY NIGHT (1994)

Publishers Weekly

SOURCE: A review of *Smoky Night,* in *Publishers Weekly,* Vol. 241, No. 5, January 31, 1994, p. 89.

Bunting addresses urban violence in this thought-provoking and visually exciting picture book inspired by the Los Angeles riots. Although they're neighbors, Daniel's cat and Mrs. Kim's cat don't get along. Nor do Daniel and his mother shop at Mrs. Kim's market. "It's better if we buy from our own people," Daniel's mother says. But when Daniel's apartment building goes up in flames, all of the neighbors (including the cats) learn the value of bridging differences. Bunting does not explicitly connect her message about racism with the riots in her story's background, but her work is thoroughly believable and taut, steering clear of the maudlin or didactic. [David] Diaz's dazzling mixed-media collages superimpose bold acrylic illustrations on photographs of carefully arranged backgrounds that feature a wide array of symbolic materials—from scraps of paper and shards of broken glass to spilled rice and plastic dry-cleaner bags. Interestingly, Diaz doesn't strongly differentiate the presumably Asian American Mrs. Kim from the

African American characters—even the artwork here cautions the reader against assumptions about race.

Betsy Hearne

SOURCE: A review of *Smoky Night,* in *Bulletin of the Center for Children's Books,* Vol. 47, No. 7, March, 1994, p. 217.

Eve Bunting has a good track record for vitalizing what would be docudrama in the hands of a lesser storyteller. Here the scenario is an inner-city riot that young Daniel and his mother and his yellow cat Jasmine watch from their apartment window. "It can happen when people get angry," explains Mama. "They want to smash and destroy. They don't care anymore what's right and what's wrong." Among the stores looted is Mrs. Kim's market, and when Daniel's building catches fire in the middle of the night, both he and Mrs. Kim end up in the local church shelter, worrying about whether their cats—archenemies in the past—have escaped the blaze. It's the authentic child's perspective that makes the tale so touching. What impresses Daniel in the midst of an adult-size crisis are the kind of details that adults wouldn't notice ("I've never seen a bigger jar of mayo," he observes in the shelter) or wouldn't be honest about ("Mrs. Kim takes her big, fat, mean old orange cat and holds him close"). It's these very observations that lead Daniel to a truth about what caused the riot to begin with. Diaz has not been afraid to take risks in illustrating the story with thickly textured paintings against a background of torn-paper and found-object collage; the heavy outlines are a bit reminiscent of John Steptoe's early work. Without becoming cluttered or gimmicky, these pictures manage to capture a calamitous atmosphere that finally calms. His choice of a stylized medium to express a frighteningly realistic situation will allow young listeners to get the emotional impact without becoming overpowered by it—just as the first-person narrative succeeds in doing a lot by not trying to do too much. In fact, both author and artist have managed to portray a politically charged event without pretension or preaching.

Ellen Fader

SOURCE: A review of *Smoky Night,* in *The Horn Book Magazine,* Vol. LXX, No. 3, May-June, 1994, p. 308.

Daniel's mother explains that the rioting in the street outside their apartment "'can happen when people get angry.'" The aberrant behavior of the people who are smashing windows, cars, and street lights and the looters who look angry and happy at the same time fascinate Daniel. When the smell of smoke wakens the two of them during the night, they flee to a shelter with other residents of their building. Daniel is frantic because he cannot locate his cat, Jasmine. Mrs. Kim's mean orange cat, who always fights with Jasmine, is missing, too. Daniel and his mother don't have too much to do with

Mrs. Kim and do not shop at Kim's Market because "Mama says it's better if we buy from our own people." Eventually, a fire fighter appears at the shelter with one cat under each arm, claiming to have discovered the cats "'holding paws'" under the stairs of the burning building. When the cats drink from the same dish, Daniel observes that the animals might not have previously liked each other because they didn't know each other. Silence follows Daniel's innocent comment, until his mother introduces herself to Mrs. Kim: "'My name is Gena. Perhaps when things settle down you and your cat will come over and share a dish of milk with us.'" Clearly, the African-American woman's attempt to reach out to the Korean-American woman is a result of surviving the riots together and understanding the commonality of their lives. Although the CIP page mentions that these events took place during the recent Los Angeles riots, young readers may need some additional explanation, since the setting is not mentioned anywhere in the book. Diaz's bold artwork is a perfect match for the intensity of the story. Thick black lines border vibrant acrylic paintings that are reminiscent of Picasso's early work, especially in the composition of the characters' faces. Diaz's work also evokes images of the French impressionist Georges Rouault and of the early books of John Steptoe, both of whom used black to outline individual elements in their paintings. Diaz places these dynamic paintings on collages of real objects that, for the most part, reinforce the narrative action. For example, a painting of Daniel observing someone looting a dry cleaners is superimposed on a collage composed of wire hangers and clothes wrapped in clear plastic. Because each double-page spread is so carefully designed, because the pictorial elements work together harmoniously, the overall effect is that of urban energy, rather than cacophony. Both author and illustrator insist on a headlong confrontation with the issue of rapport between different races, and the result is a memorable, thought-provoking book.

Selma G. Lanes

SOURCE: "Violence from a Distance," in *The New York Times,* May 21, 1995, p. 25.

Children and adults, we live in volatile and perilous times. From the bombing of the Oklahoma City Federal Building to the nerve-gas attack in the Tokyo subway, the world has come to accept deliberately orchestrated as well as mindlessly random acts of violence as familiar, everyday components of our lives. With almost daily exposure to horrors we can do nothing about—they have, after all, already taken place by the time we see and hear about them on ubiquitous television newscasts—we are rendered impotent. By slow degrees, we become impervious to normal human reactions of revulsion and outrage. Overexposure induces numbness. As the film director Marcel Ophuls has chillingly observed, "No violence, real or fictional, is taken seriously any longer. It's all just imagery—video clips."

It is in this context that *Smoky Night,* a troubling and

curiously affectless picture book, becomes comprehensible. Eve Bunting, who has written more than 100 children's books, both fiction and nonfiction, for various age levels, here bravely attempts to give us a child's-eye view of the rioting in Los Angeles three years ago. The text chronicles one evening's sorry spectacle of crime and violence from a relatively safe, dispassionate distance. ("Mama and I stand well back from our window, looking down," the boy hero begins. "We don't have our lights on though it's almost dark. People are rioting in the street below.")

Though Ms. Bunting writes about wanton vandalism, looting and arson, her prose remains disconcertingly detached and nonjudgmental. Perhaps as apologia for this disquieting neutrality, there is another early quote from the young narrator: "Mama explains about rioting. 'It can happen when people get angry. They want to smash and destroy. They don't care anymore what's right and what's wrong.'" And, somehow, neither do the book's readers. As innocent on-lookers, all we want is to keep out of the path of the maelstrom. We partake of the powerlessness of victims and, for a thoughtful child, this may be little short of nightmarish. . . .

Smoky Night falls into a category of knock-'em-dead artwork for an au courant if less-than-riveting story. Young children are unlikely to be satisfied.

They are, in the end, impassioned and highly impressionable, eager to make sense of the world around them and pleased when what they perceive as being good and right prevails. In *Smoky Night* evil goes unpunished, undefined and almost unacknowledged. True, the author would have us believe that because two feuding pet cats—one belonging to the story's black narrator, the other to a Korean storekeeper—have become friends as a result of a horrific trial by fire, then so too will their owners. This is likely to seem a dubious triumph to young listeners, who will be worrying that the book's victims have been left temporarily homeless, their neighborhood in ruins.

📖 *FLOWER GARDEN* (1994)

Elizabeth Bush

SOURCE: A review of *Flower Garden,* in *Booklist,* Vol. 90, No. 12, February 15, 1994, p. 1076.

From grocery cart to checkout stand, from bus to third-floor walk-up, an excited little girl totes home a heavy armload of flowering plants. Sitting on the newspaper-strewn floor, she and her father transplant them, creating a "Garden in a window box / High above the street / Where butterflies can stop and rest / And ladybugs can meet." The garden is much admired by passing pedestrians, but the true object of this labor of love will discover the surprise upon her return home. "Candles on a birthday cake / chocolate ice cream, too. / Happy, happy birthday, Mom! A garden box—for you." The simple rhymed verse, which skips along in pace with the child's anticipation, is smoothly integrated with the vibrant, lifelike paintings. The garden's progress from pots to planter is seen from several startling perspectives—from the little girl's lap, from the base of a staircase, from directly overhead, from street level. Pre-readers can trace the floral motif, repeated in the child's tights, the bus passenger's dress, the birthday cake, and the plate, or they can discover such hidden treats as the girl's reflection in the bus mirror. Almost as a bonus, one splendid close-up of the blooms is accompanied by verse identifying five common flowers. This title succeeds both as an introduction to the pleasures of gardening, and as a picture of a family, African American in this case, in which gifts are fashioned by loving hands.

Kirkus Reviews

SOURCE: A review of *Flower Garden,* in *Kirkus Reviews,* Vol. LXII, No. 7, April 1, 1994, p. 478.

A young girl carries a carton of potted flowers from the supermarket home and up the stairs; she and her father replant them in a window box and light candles on a birthday cake to surprise Mom when she comes wearily home from work. In [Kathryn] Hewitt's expansive oil paintings, the girl's honey-brown face shines as brightly as the daisies and daffodils; Bunting's brief rhymed text ("Garden in a cardboard box/Walking to the bus/Garden sitting on our laps/People smile at us!") celebrates the child's contagious happiness, the warm response of everyone who sees her, and the pleasure of having "a color jamboree" of flowers in the window of an inner-city apartment, high above the street. A simple, pleasing episode with a contemporary subtext.

Maeve Visser Knoth

SOURCE: A review of *Flower Garden,* in *The Horn Book Magazine,* Vol. LXX, No. 3, May-June, 1994, p. 307-08.

Kathryn Hewitt's realistic oil paintings and Eve Bunting's rhyming text pull the reader into a story of surprise and fun. The young narrator has, with the help of her father, assembled a "garden in a shopping cart" and invites the reader to come home with her and see what they are planning to do with their boxes of tulips and geraniums. She leads the reader on a bus, along the sidewalk, and up the stairs to her apartment past many friendly smiles, as neighbors and strangers admire the colorful picture this lovely African-American child and her plants make. The objects and figures are very large on the page so the reader is very close to the action, and each double-page spread uses a different perspective, adding to the surprise of the simple text. When the child arrives home, she and her father plant the flowers in a windowbox high above the city and light candles on a cake just in time for her mother's arrival home and a birthday cel-

ebration. This story of the gift of love and beauty is suitably illustrated with warm colors—rich reds, yellows, and golds. The child wears flowered tights, mirroring the flowers she carries home. Their urban world is a benevolent one—"people smile at us"—so the last painting of the loving family looking out past the windowbox to the city and night sky beyond expresses their joy in life and their secure home.

SUNSHINE HOME (1994)

Kirkus Reviews

SOURCE: A review of *Sunshine Home,* in *Kirkus Reviews,* Vol. LXII, No. 4, February 15, 1994, p. 223.

Timmie and his parents make their first visit to Gram at a nursing home; she's had to move there since "the doctors said she needed full-time nursing care." Until now, Gram has lived with Timmie's family, and it's so hard for Mom to see her here that she talks in an unnaturally bright voice, only to weep once she's outside. Rushing back to deliver a picture he forgot to leave and discovering Gram in tears too, Timmie pulls Mom back inside, where the honesty of shared grief provides at least some comfort. Bunting catches the nursing home ambience with empathy and precision—the sharp smell "like mouthwash, or the green bar that Mom hangs in the toilet bowl"; the elderly dozing in wheelchairs, intruding on one another's visitors, or joshing; their families filling time with small talk. In perceptive, realistic watercolors, [Diane] de Groat characterizes Timmie's family with loving care and depicts the residents of the home in enough realistic variety to give young readers a good idea of what to expect on such a visit. A poignant slice of life in the 90s; Timmie's successful intervention sends the message that even a child can offer real consolation.

Ellen Mandel

SOURCE: A review of *Sunshine Home,* in *Booklist,* Vol. 90, No. 14, March 15, 1994, p. 1371.

About to visit his grandmother at the Sunshine Home for the first time, seven-year-old Timmie is scared but won't say so. Yet he describes the building as "barf green," his stomach hurts when he enters, and he notices his mom speaks in a "bright and sparkly" voice he's never heard before. Once inside, the visit goes well. Best of all, Gram seems the same. But as soon as Timmie and his parents leave, Timmie's mom dissolves into tears. When Timmie runs back inside to give Gram the school picture he'd forgotten, he finds her also sobbing. Gram apologizes and explains she doesn't want anyone to know she's unhappy because it's easier on everyone that way. But Timmie, remembering how his fears were allayed when he confessed them to his dad, insists, "It's better when you tell. Honest. You don't feel so scared." With that, Timmie hurriedly retrieves his parents, and the four share their feelings about missing each other. In her realistic watercolors, de Groat defines the images of Bunting's tender, true-to-life story: Timmie's face stares out at readers with apprehension before he enters the home, then registers discomfort at seeing a bib tied to Gram when she eats, and finally relaxes when he talks with Gram. Scenes in the home are painted in institutional greens, yellows, and corals culled from the floral motifs in the wallpaper and curtains. Youngsters whose families are wrestling with similar concerns over an elderly or unwell grandparent will especially relate to the dilemma conveyed here with honesty and some sadness but with a prevailing hopefulness.

Betsy Hearne

SOURCE: A review of *Sunshine Home,* in *Bulletin of the Center for Children's Books,* Vol. 47, No. 8, April, 1994, pp. 253-54.

A story that could have stayed at the level of bibliotherapy instead cuts to the heart as the narrator suffers through his family's forced-cheerful visit to Gram's nursing home, discovers his mother and grandmother separately in tears afterwards, and confronts them with the fact that everything is not all right. The ending makes no promises beyond honesty, "because maybe Gram will never be well enough to ride in a red convertible" (for which she has threatened to trade her wheelchair). Yet it's clear that an admission of sorrow will at least allow mutual comforting. It's also clear that isolation is the real curse of old age, something a child not far removed from the throes of separation anxiety can understand with special intensity. De Groat's watercolors are well composed and colored, if heavily literal; in fact, they have a photo-realistic quality that weights the total impact without becoming somber.

NASTY, STINKY SNEAKERS (1994)

Stephanie Zvirin

SOURCE: A review of *Nasty, Stinky Sneakers,* in *Booklist,* Vol. 90, No. 17, May 1, 1994, p. 1601.

Bunting's latest story banks on the idea that middle-graders will love the thought of disgustingly grungy sneakers—and they probably will. Colin thinks he has a good chance to win a prize for his smelly shoes, which are so foul that his mom won't even let them in the house. Even Bruno, the bulldog belonging to Mr. Sabaton upstairs, is awed. When the sneakers inexplicably vanish, Colin, convinced it's rival Jack Dunn's doing, decides to retaliate by stealing Jack's reeking shoes. Imagine Colin's surprise when he discovers he's wrong, and that Jack's shoes have now disappeared. Nice kid Colin's sense of right and wrong eventually takes over, something Bunting accomplishes without heavy moralizing, and rightly, neither boy (Jack cheats) wins. This is good fun that begs a sequel, especially one that gives

bulldog Bruno (deliciously pictured on the jacket) more of a part.

Dot Minzer

SOURCE: A review of *Nasty, Stinky Sneakers,* in *School Library Journal,* Vol. 40, No. 6, June, 1994, p. 124.

The Slam Dunker company is sponsoring a contest—the kid who produces the stinkiest sneakers will win three pairs of prized Slam Dunkers. The footwear must be made smelly by natural means, and Colin, coached by his friend Webster, knows them all—no socks, jogging, sleeping with the sneakers on, no washing of feet, etc. Colin has his mind on other things, too, like Poppy Roginski, the prettiest girl in his class. Missing sneakers, false accusations, and good intentions gone awry all play a part in the story; in the end, it is Poppy who wins the contest, along with Colin's heart. As its title suggests, this book is nasty and stinky—and because of that—children will love it. Bunting's dialogue is on target, and although the story is light, it has some twists that will keep readers hooked.

Kirkus Reviews

SOURCE: A review of *Nasty, Stinky Sneakers,* in *Kirkus Reviews,* Vol. LXII, No. 12, June 15, 1994, p. 841.

When 10-year-old Colin's dirty sneakers disappear from outside his apartment door, he's sure the culprit is Jack, his chief rival in a contest for the most offensive footwear (the prize: two new pairs of Slam Dunkers). Colin retaliates by hiding Jack's sneakers—only to discover that a well-meaning neighbor had actually rescued, washed, and returned his own, thus ruining his chance of winning. Hoping to undo the mischief, Colin, his little sister Amy, and best pal Webster plunge into the depths of a garbage truck, retrieve Jack's sneakers, and return them just in time. However, since obnoxious Jack and his bully brother Shrike have broken the sneaker-messing rules, none of the boys wins; the prize goes to Colin's secret sweetheart. Curiously, the icky appeal, kid-tickling story line, and lesson about integrity and fairness here all closely parallel those in Julie Ann Peters's half-as-long *The Stinky Sneaker Contest* (1992).

A DAY'S WORK (1994)

Publishers Weekly

SOURCE: A review of *A Day's Work,* in *Publishers Weekly,* Vol. 241, No. 32, August 8, 1994, p. 434, 436.

Francisco, trying to find work for his grandfather, or *abuelo,* who has just arrived from Mexico, acts as a liaison between Abuelo, who doesn't speak English, and

Ben, who wants to hire a gardener for a day's work. Eager to earn the badly needed pay, Francisco assures Ben that his grandfather is a skilled gardener (Abuelo is in fact a carpenter). Returning at the end of the day, Ben is shocked to discover that Francisco and Abuelo stripped his field of the plants and left the weeds. Abuelo is also angered, learning only now that Francisco had lied to Ben, and refuses payment until they have done the job correctly. Recognizing the older man's integrity, Ben rewards Abuelo and Francisco with the promise of "more than just one day's work." Says Ben of the plants: "The roots are still there. If they've replanted early, they'll be alright." Similarly, Francisco is given a chance to start over. He changes from a naïvely parental figure to a child who "had begun to learn the important things." The shift in the boy's role quietly suggests not only the importance of a work ethic but also Francisco's need to be a child, guided by a caring adult. With expressive, gestural watercolors, [Ronald] Himler, who illustrated Bunting's *Fly Away Home* and *Someday a Tree*, conveys the boy's complex relationship with his grandfather and strongly invokes both the harsh and the tender landscapes of Francisco's world.

Elizabeth Bush

SOURCE: A review of *A Day's Work,* in *Bulletin of the Center for Children's Books,* Vol. 48, No. 2, October, 1994, pp. 38-9.

Street-smart, aggressive Francisco fast-talks the owner of a gardening service into hiring his *abuelo,* a recent immigrant, for day labor: "And my grandfather is a fine gardener, thought he doesn't know English." Although grandfather protests in Spanish to his grandson that he's a carpenter with no knowledge of gardening, Francisco assures him it will be okay. Returning to inspect the job site that afternoon, the employer is furious to find the weeds in place and the flowers uprooted, and Abuelo realizes Francisco has lied their way into the job. He insists on returning the next day to rectify the damage and is rewarded for his honesty with a promise of future work, as his employer remarks, "The important things your grandfather already knows. And I can teach him gardening." The vagaries of day labor are concisely sketched—the scramble for a seat on an employer's truck, difficulties of communication between Spanish-speaking workers and American employers, long, hot hours of toil across the fence from inviting backyard swimming pools. The focus of Bunting's work, however, is the price of Francisco's lie—another day's hard labor for a single day's pay—but adults seeking a palatable dose of lying-doesn't-pay moralizing to pour into young listeners must look elsewhere, for implicit in this tale is the strong probability that, but for Francisco's lie, Abuelo would never have had even the opportunity to display those qualities of fortitude and honor that so impressed his employer. Himler's watercolors in tans, yellows, and grays nicely catch the parched rises and heat-soaked pavements that circumscribe Francisco and Abuelo's world.

Jessie Meudell

SOURCE: A review of *A Day's Work,* in *School Library Journal,* Vol. 41, No. 1, January, 1995, p. 82.

A charming story about an elderly man who has just come from Mexico to live with his daughter and grandson Francisco in California. The boy convinces a man to hire him and his Abuelo by saying that " . . . my grandfather is a fine gardener, though he doesn't know English yet," in spite of the fact that he has always lived in the city and worked as a carpenter. After their new employer drives off in his van, the two set to work—but they pull up all of the plants and leave the weeds. "We do not lie for work," Abuelo tells Francisco when he learns what they have done, and they return the next day to rectify their mistake for no extra pay. Bunting perfectly captures the intergenerational love and respect shared by these two characters and the man's strong sense of honesty and integrity. Himler's softly colored illustrations reflect the feelings of the characters and the setting.

NIGHT OF THE GARGOYLES (1994)

Kirkus Reviews

SOURCE: A review of *Night of the Gargoyles,* in *Kirkus Reviews,* Vol. LXII, No. 16, August 15, 1994, p. 1122.

At night a motley assortment of gargoyles come alive to "creep on stubs of feet," to fly "if they have gargoyle wings, straight up to lick the stars with long stone tongues," or to land in "sleeping trees." But eventually they all gather at a fountain to "gargoyle-hunch around the rim and gargoyle-grunt with friends from other corners who have come for company" and complain all night long about the sun, the rain (which "pours in torrents through their gaping lips and chokes their throats with autumn leaves") and—of course—the "humans who have made them so and set them high on ledges where dark pigeons go." These monsters, defined at the beginning of the book as waterspouts representing grotesque human or animal figures, come in a variety of forms—all surprisingly unsinister, despite Wiesner's gray palette. Somehow, these gargoyles appear stone-like and cuddly at the same time.

Caldecott medal-winner [David] Wiesner's charcoal drawings are as breathtaking as Bunting's prose in this wildly successful attempt to prove what we've always suspected: The gargoyle lives.

Hazel Rochman

SOURCE: A review of *Night of the Gargoyles,* in *Booklist,* Vol. 91, No. 3, October 1, 1994, p. 331.

In a macabre and funny picture book, those stone gargoyles that squat all day on public buildings get free at night and come down from their shadowy corners. Bunting's words are creepy and poetic, scary because they are so physically precise. The stone creatures are "pockmarked," their tongues "green-pickled at the edges." They have unblinking, bulging eyes and their mouths gape like empty suits of armor in museum halls. Wiesner's duotone charcoal illustrations capture the huge heaviness of the stone figures and their gloomy malevolence as they bump and fly and tumble free in the dark. They are so ugly. They're like fiends that come from the graves at night. They're also very human. Wiesner's funniest scene is a double-page spread of a group of gargoyle creatures hunching and grunting together at a spitting water fountain. They could be the gossips and grousers at your local neighborhood hangout. This book is more a situation than a story, but it makes you face what you've always feared but hadn't quite seen. Even the word *gargoyle* makes you choke.

Elizabeth Bush

SOURCE: A review of *Night of the Gargoyles,* in *Bulletin of the Center for Children's Books,* Vol. 48, No. 3, November, 1994, p. 82.

Bunting sets the scene for an exposé on the midnight rites of the grotesque title beasts. Free verse that tolls as steadily and solemnly as a church bell is rich with moody imagery: " . . . rain/ that pours in torrents through/ their gaping lips/ and chokes their throats/ with autumn's leaves") and the promise of some child-pleasing menace. But when it comes to the big question—What do gargoyles *do* in the dead of night?—the answer is disappointing. They lurk and they creep and they peer and they swoop, and then they gather and complain about the weather, make rude faces at the museum guard, and go home. Wiesner, with his sharp insight into the nocturnal antics of frogs, seems the ideal artist to illuminate Bunting's theme. Indeed, his grainy, deeply shadowed charcoal images, which are bound to be compared with Van Allsburg's Conté pencil work, expertly blend frolic and fright; vertical panels cleverly incorporated into the book's design offer an appropriately Gothic look. But absence of plot provides Wiesner little to work with, and so his stone figures mostly pose and mug. A provocative title and enticingly creepy cover art are certain to attract and even please browsers, but youngsters looking for a good scare will only find a mild shudder.

SPYING ON MISS MÜLLER (1995)

Roger Sutton

SOURCE: A review of *Spying on Miss Müller,* in *Bulletin of the Center for Children's Books,* Vol. 48, No. 7, March, 1995, p. 229.

"She's not a teacher anymore," says a classmate of narrator Jessie, "She's a German." Like the other stu-

dents, Jessie had admired Miss Müller, the German-language teacher and dorm supervisor at Jessie's Belfast boarding school, but the war has changed their feelings, especially since Miss Müller has been spotted leaving her room at night and going up onto the roof. When the Germans bomb Belfast, Jessie and her friends become more convinced than ever that Miss Müller is a spy, but their attempt to catch her out becomes complicated when taciturn Greta, a Jewish refugee, insists on joining the plot. "Will you kill her?" asks Greta eagerly, and seeks to see her wish come true. Suspenseful and romantic, this is a strong combination of boarding-school story and spy-hunting theme, with the details of 1940s British girls' life worked smoothly into the plot—one of the funnier moments comes during an air-raid when the boy- and girl-boarders at the school chaotically meet in the cellar. "I will not have this!" screams the headmistress. "This is a serious, life-changing experience." Recollects Jessie, "It surely was. Us and the boys," and ponders her first kiss. While Miss Müller does have a secret, it has nothing to do with spying for her fatherland; nevertheless, the girl's conspiracy to find her out has sad repercussions that leave them wiser. The subject is serious and the treatment is cozy but honest, with Miss Müller a figure of Jessie's ambivalent empathy: "Those awful maids spreading the story that Miss Müller's father was a Nazi. As if everyone wasn't against her enough, me included."

Martha Davis Beck

SOURCE: A review of *Spying on Miss Müller,* in *The Five Owls,* Vol. X, No. 1, September-October, 1995, pp. 15-17.

Eve Bunting has tackled difficult subjects in many of her books for children; in fact, she has made it something of a trademark. But her stories come alive as a result of her refusal to preach and her unerring ability to put herself inside the mind of a child caught in the midst of an often confusing world.

What's different with **Spying on Miss Müller** is that here Bunting has mined her own past for her story. The novel is based on her girlhood experiences at a boarding school in Belfast during World War II. The focus of the narrative is the prejudice that spreads among a group of schoolgirls against one of their teachers, who happens to be half German. Bunting has referred to it as "the book I always knew I would write," but it didn't come early or easily.

Jessie, the novel's protagonist, is thirteen, a girl both sensitive and sensible, not initially inclined to judge others harshly or hatch meanspirited schemes. She has a good heart, but (like all of us) is capable of misguided actions. She is even capable of acting as a ringleader. We see the all-too-human face of prejudice in this likable character.

Miss Müller, the target of the girls' ostracism, is a

vulnerable figure—more vulnerable than they realize. Though she is not, as they suspect, a German spy, she does have a secret, and their eventual unmasking of it has profound consequences. The novel deals in part with the universal experience teenagers have of going along with a group, ultimately realizing that they are in over their heads and that their actions have a real effect.

Spying on Miss Müller is a book whose seriousness sneaks up on you. Bunting captures the easy banter and whispered secrets of teenage girls just perfectly, and the narrative skips along in a casual vein, gathering its power discreetly.

The unavoidable world of adult problems and the equally powerful reality of young desires collide in this story, as they do in the lives of all teenagers, but at this particular moment in history the collision is especially powerful. Jessie's first kiss is overshadowed by an air raid. She and her friends witness the visible suffering of the school's one Jewish student, a Polish refugee who will probably never see her parents again. Jessie's cousin, a boy she loves like a brother, is taken prisoner by the Germans. And then there's Miss Müller, whose father was a Nazi, which seems evidence enough of her disloyalty in the eyes of her students, despite the fact that she has been a friend to many of them.

Perhaps the most painful collision of all is Jessie's gradual facing of her own father's alcoholism. (Her shame of her father provides an interesting parallel to Miss Müller's situation.) When Jessie is finally able to talk about this problem with her closest friend, she feels unexpectedly free, as if she's "in an open meadow, filled with sunshine." The truth is tough, Bunting seems to say, and often elusive, but it is worth confronting. Collisions have their rewards.

Ada Demlow

SOURCE: A review of *Spying on Miss Müller,* in *Voice of Youth Advocates,* Vol. 18, No. 4, October, 1995, p. 216.

Bunting has drawn from her experiences living in a boarding school in Belfast, Ireland, in this story of mystery, friendship and coming-of-age during World War II. Thirteen-year-old Jessie Drumm has a lot on her mind. Her three best friends all believe that their teacher, Miss Müller, is a Nazi agent, and after seeing her out on the roof the night before their first air raid and over-hearing the maids talking about the picture they saw of Miss Müller's father bearing a swastika, Jessie is starting to believe them. She is also worried about her own father's drinking problem, and her cousin Bryan who is in the British Army. Then there is Ian McManus, the boy whose picture she keeps in her emergency suitcase. During an air raid when the students are led to the basement for shelter, they share their first kiss! Somehow that seems more important than what is going on in the world!

Spying on Miss Müller takes a dark turn when Greta, a student who lost her father to Nazi forces, wants to join the girls to "take care" of her. When Jessie's cousin becomes a prisoner of war, she too turns against Miss Müller. One final night the girls follow Miss Müller out to the roof and discover her secret—a romantic tryst. Greta reports the incident and Miss Müller is sent away, but not before Jessie learns an important lesson about accepting her father.

Even while dealing with some dark themes, the book has a warmth to it—especially in the believable depictions of the girls as they share their lives and secrets. Mystery readers will be satisfied by the intrigue, fans of Lois Lowry's *Number the Stars* (1989) and Carol Matas's *Lisa's War* (1987) will appreciate the perspectives on this time period, and with encouragement—readers who enjoy fresh stories about people "just like them" will give the book a try—with satisfying results.

CHEYENNE AGAIN (1995)

Hazel Rochman

SOURCE: A review of *Cheyenne Again,* in *Booklist,* Vol. 91, No. 22, August, 1995, p. 1946.

A young Cheyenne boy tells how he's taken from his parents on the reservation in the late 1880s and sent to a boarding school, where he's forced to learn white ways. . . . This is a picture book for older readers, a grim story of painful separation and forced assimilation. Although Young Bull's mother urges him to hide, his father says the boy must learn the "White Man's" ways if he is to survive. We feel the boy's loneliness ("At night I hear the train . . . and cry for home") as the school authorities cut off his braids and teach him Christianity and the white view of history ("You will be like us"). The short, spare lines of free verse are illustrated by double-page-spread oil and acrylic paintings [by Irving Toddy] that contrast the open landscape with the stiffness of figures forced into uniform and regimentation. The artist went through a similar experience as a child.

Roger Sutton

SOURCE: A review of *Cheyenne Again,* in *Bulletin of the Center for Children's Books,* Vol. 49, No. 1, September, 1995, p. 8.

Young Bull, aged ten, is taken from his Cheyenne tribe to live in an Indian boarding school, where his people are absent from the pages of history books, where he learns to worship the White Man's God instead of the Great Spirit, and where wall plaques remind students to "SPEAK ENGLISH." This is a piece of American history most students won't know about, but the picture-book format seems young for the material. Perhaps inevitably, it is a solemn, even dour, book, with a prose poem text that is stilted and monotonous: "The bugle calls us in to dinner/ and to work./ There's carpentry,/ so we who lived in teepees/ can repair/ the wooden buildings where we sleep/ and shed our tears." The pictures, reminiscent of Ronald Himler's work, are composed in appropriately moody tones but are as stiff and glum as the text—no one cracks an expression, much less a smile. Do picture books have to be fun? Of course not. But surely we can expect more of them than this kind of ponderous preaching.

Sally Margolis

SOURCE: A review of *Cheyenne Again,* in *School Library Journal,* Vol. 41, No. 12, December, 1995, pp. 72-3.

A poignant look at the pain inflicted upon one child by a dominant culture's heavy-handed attempt to "help." Near the turn of the century, a Cheyenne boy, Young Bull, is forced to attend the off-reservation Indian school so that he can learn to become a part of the white world. He is housed in soulless barracks and shown repeatedly and quite blatantly that the Indian ways are no good. When he rebels and tries to run home in a snowstorm, he is caught, returned, and shackled for a day. The story, told from Young Bull's point of view, is not so much judgmental as empathetic—none of the authority figures is an ogre. The agents for change here are not white bureaucrats, but Indians who have adopted white ways, and Young Bull clearly feels betrayed by them. Toddy's acrylic and oil paintings add to the emotions expressed in the narrative. The openness, light, color, and individuality of the boy's home surroundings are in sharp contrast to the formality, emptiness, and uniformity of the school. Young Bull's struggle to hold onto his heritage will touch children's sense of justice and lead to some interesting discussions and perhaps further research.

DANDELIONS (1995)

Elizabeth Bush

SOURCE: A review of *Dandelions,* in *Bulletin of the Center for Children's Books,* Vol. 49, No. 1, September, 1995, p. 8.

For Papa, the fulfilled promise of a fresh start on his own homestead is close to a religious experience, which narrator Zoe and her younger sister are eager to share, but Mama's quiet grief at leaving her parents' Illinois home for the solitude of the prairie casts a pall on the family's optimistic spirit. To help reconcile her to their new life, Papa and the girls plant two withering, maverick dandelions on the roof of their sod house—flowers which, Mama remarks, may "just die of loneliness." While there is no shortage of picture books about the settlement of the Great Plains, this title addresses the isolation of the settlers, an issue usually left to older

readers' fiction. Expect understated but persistent heartstring tugging from the start ("See how the grass closes behind us?" Mama asked. "It's as if we'd never been") to finish ("I hoped maybe one, just one, dandelion might lift its head for us. But not even one did"). [Greg] Shed's large gouache paintings are luminous with the parched golds and wheats of the sun-seared landscape, and characters are meticulously posed in the tradition of pioneer heroism. The closing spread supplies a reassuring visual epilogue—wagon ruts lead to modest fields, a windmill, and the soddie roof blooming with dandelions.

Kay Weisman

SOURCE: A review of *Dandelions,* in *Booklist,* Vol. 92, No. 2, September 15, 1995, p. 162.

Zoe and her family have traveled by covered wagon from Illinois to the Nebraska Territory. As they build a sod house and meet new neighbors. Papa can barely contain his enthusiasm. Mama, on the other hand, remains quiet, thinking of the family and memories left behind. On a trip to town with her father for supplies, Zoe spots a mass of dandelions and realizes that the flowers are much like her family—they may be out of their element on the prairie, but they will survive and bloom in their new land. The gouache paintings capture the lonely panorama of the landscape, and the classically painted, sometimes faceless figures give the book a sense of universality. A solid choice for read-alouds, this may also be used with older, reluctant readers or students learning about the westward movement.

Joanne Schott

SOURCE: "Pigs and Prairies," in *Quill and Quire,* Vol. 61, No.11, November, 1995, p. 47.

At Zoe's bleak homestead in Nebraska Territory, the neighbours are three hours away, the nearest town a day's ride. Papa is full of hope for what will soon develop. Mama, though she says little, feels lost on the prairie, remembering the home she left.

Returning with Papa from a trip to town, Zoe spies a bright patch of dandelions. She persuades Papa to dig it up as her birthday present for Mama, and that night she and her sister plant it on the roof of their sod house. The story is narrated by Zoe, whose strong bond with her mother gives her insight into the feelings of pioneering women of any time or place.

The dandelions are a well-developed symbol of the transplanting process that is the essence of pioneering. Sensitive dialogue brings this one family to life with the hopes, concerns, and regrets common to everyone who puts down new roots. Beautiful paintings focus on the blue sky and golden expanse of the prairie and are filled with the strong light of hot summer. They illustrate the family's solidarity, hope, and isolation with the same sensitivity as the text. Look for this to be one of the highly honoured books of the season.

📖 MARKET DAY (1996)

Publishers Weekly

SOURCE: A review of *Market Day,* in *Publishers Weekly,* Vol. 243, No. 6, February 5, 1996, p. 89.

It's almost impossible to read this winsome tale without lapsing into an Irish brogue. Seven-year-old Tess meets her friend, Wee Boy, at the market held monthly in their Irish village. A lively affair, with a cornucopia of colorful goods for sale, market day also serves as a setting for unusual performances by extravagant characters, such as Baba-Ali, the sword swallower, and Jehosophat, who walks on hot coals. Of course, the streets are filled with plenty of noisy livestock, too. Bunting succeeds in finding just the right sensory ingredients to captivate a child. On bite-size honeycombs: "The honey tastes of the flowers the bees drank from, and the wax is as thick in your mouth as chewing gum." Tess's friendship with Wee Boy, whose growth has been stunted, adds a tender underpinning to the story; Tess spends her last ha'penny on a reassuring fortuneteller, who predicts that Wee Boy will be "big and brave as [he'll] ever need to be." [Holly] Berry illustrates with stylized simplicity, tempering her brio with attention to patterns. Bright natural colors convey the gaiety of the market against a backdrop of fieldstone houses and cobbled streets. A Celtic charmer.

Ilene Cooper

SOURCE: A review of *Market Day,* in *Booklist,* Vol. 92, No. 12, February 15, 1996, p. 1016.

Thursdays are Market Day in this small Irish village, and the excitement begins when Father gives the young narrator her Market Day penny. She'll meet her friend Wee Boy ("he's seven same as me, but he's never grown past four"); and together they will go to the sweetie stall with its gob stoppers and cherry lips and clove rocks, watch the goat steal Mrs. MacAffe's petticoat off the line and gobble up the lace, and admire the sword swallower as he pulls the blade from his throat. Bunting draws from her own childhood in Ireland, and the writing she offers is pure and totally evocative: "My father's in the street in a wallow of pigs. They're all scrubbed up for Market Day." There couldn't be a better match for Bunting's words than Berry's enthusiastic, jam-packed pictures. There's so much to see, so much life swirling around, that kids will hardly know where to look first. Bunting balances all the activity with a lovely pensive moment as Wee Boy and a fortune-teller contemplate his future. A delightful read-aloud, brimming with life.

Betsy Hearne

SOURCE: A review of *Market Day,* in *Bulletin of the Center for Children's Books,* Vol. 49, No. 9, May, 1996, p. 294.

Cast as the present-tense narration of a young girl named Tess, Bunting's memory of a monthly event traditional in Irish towns has the idiosyncratic ring of truth: "There's a bit of a commotion over by the churchyard. One of the goats got away and stole Mrs. McAfee's petticoat off her clothesline and dragged it back to the square. He had the double frill eaten half off before he was caught." What keeps the sights and sounds from becoming a descriptive catalogue is the friendship between Tess and Wee Boy ("He's seven, same as me, but he never grew past four"). They alternate picking out and paying for candy from "Harry Hooey's sweetie stall"—this week Wee Boy treats with a "penny poke of gob stoppers." By the end of the day Tess has given away her penny, half to a musician on the street and half to get Wee Boy's fortune told by Madame Savanna, who predicts from her seat beside the gypsy caravans that Wee Boy will be as big and brave as he ever needs to be. This is more portrait than story, but the place and persons portrayed are authentic and lively. The artist has done her homework, from the opening landscape of sheep grazing along steep seaside mountains, to the town square bustling with people and livestock, to details of clothing and even Wee Boy's typical haircut. The shapes are rounded nostalgically and the contrasting hues softened by shadows and textured blending. A viewer could wish for less-cartooned faces, since Berry's drafting is otherwise subtle, and perhaps for a less obtrusive typeface than the bold and blocky letters jumping out from stark-white half- and full-page sections of text. However, visual motifs related to the compositions help unify each spread, and the overall design is jaunty.

📖 SOS TITANIC (1996)

Kirkus Reviews

SOURCE: A review of *SOS Titanic,* in *Kirkus Reviews,* Vol. LXIV, No. 4, February 15, 1996, p. 292.

From a familiar event, Bunting creates a gripping story that will have readers struggling right along with its hero on the doomed *Titanic.*

Barry O'Neill, 15, leaves Ireland, where he's been living with his grandparents, to join his parents in New York. He sails in first class on the largest oceangoing vessel in the world, the *Titanic.* Also on board, in steerage, are Barry's worst enemies, the fighting Flynn boys, who have threatened to throw him overboard; with them is their gentle sister Pegeen. From the outset, Barry fares badly with the Flynns; in the meantime, his steward—born with a caul—predicts disaster for the ship and its occupants. The one positive force is Barry's crush on Pegeen and her reciprocal interest. When the ship begins to sink, Barry witnesses the other passengers' disbelief and jocularity, and then their panic or (more rarely) stoicism. He makes a desperate attempt to find Pegeen, who is trapped with hundreds of others in steerage until all the lifeboats are launched. Suspense, adventure, romance, and a protagonist who comes of age under terrible circumstances combine in a novel that survives the tragedy at its center without diminishing it, and somehow remains upbeat.

Debbie Carton

SOURCE: A review of *SOS Titanic,* in *Booklist,* Vol. 92, No. 14, March 15, 1996, p. 1252.

Fifteen-year-old Barry O'Neill is traveling from Ireland to New York on the *Titanic.* He is heartsick about leaving the beloved grandparents who raised him for the last 10 years and apprehensive about rejoining his parents, who have been in China. He's also worried about the Flynn brothers, archenemies traveling in steerage who have threatened to throw him overboard. Foreshadowing of impending disaster winds through the early narrative: a psychic steward tells Barry of visions, and a superstitious passenger counts and re-counts the lifeboats. What sets this tale apart from other recent novels about the disaster is Barry's growing awareness of the injustice of the class system that ultimately doomed most of the steerage passengers. With so many characters, most are reduced to a few identifying quirks, but Bunting accurately and dramatically describes the ship's sinking and, at the same time, immerses readers in the many human tragedies. Perfect for middle school, this fast-paced story will satisfy readers looking for the human element in the *Titanic*'s history.

Joel Shoemaker

SOURCE: A review of *SOS Titanic,* in *School Library Journal,* Vol. 42, No. 4, April, 1996, p. 154.

Readers fascinated by the lore surrounding the sinking of the *Titanic* will likely enjoy this exciting, suspenseful, and romantic version of the tragedy. Fifteen-year-old Barry, a privileged, upper-class Irishman raised by his grandparents while his parents were off in China, is bound for America to join them at last. Class conflict comes aboard, too, in the form of Frank and Jonnie Flynn, who blame Barry's grandfather for their forced departure from Ireland via steerage. Frank's threats of revenge add a layer of fear to Barry's on-again, off-again relationship with their sister, Pegeen, as the plot steams steadily toward its inevitably icy climax. The final hundred pages of the book describe post-collision confusion that escalates toward chaos, including Barry's gallant attempt (in vain) to save Frank's life. He does succeed in saving Pegeen, and the two of them end up on the overturned inflatable life raft and are among those few rescued the next morning by the *Carpathia.* Lots of foreshadowing and hints of the supernatu-

ral (Watley, Barry's first-class steward, was born in a caul, which is said to have given him second sight) add interest, as does an interesting range of supporting characters.

📖 *TRAIN TO SOMEWHERE* (1996)

Elizabeth Bush

SOURCE: A review of *Train to Somewhere,* in *Bulletin of the Center for Children's Books,* Vol. 49, No. 7, March, 1996, pp. 220-21.

Marianne's mother left her at St. Christopher's Orphanage in New York with the promise, "I'm going West to make a new life for us. . . . Then I'll come for you." Now, several years later, the plain-faced child is westbound on an orphan train in 1877, anxious that she find her mother before someone else claims her and yet secretly hurt that no one is interested. At the last station, in Somewhere, Iowa, an elderly couple shyly presents her with a toy locomotive, an indication that they had hoped to adopt a boy; recognizing their kindness and resigning herself to her mother's disappearance, Marianne offers them her most prized possession, the feather she plucked from her mother's hair. Bunting lays on the sentiment with a liberal hand, but it's an affecting story, and details of the journey do much to mitigate the slightly dolorous tone. Stretched blankets provide privacy aboard the train, each town greets the train with its own community rite, and if some of the adoptive parents seem less than amiable, Bunting playfully hints that not all the children will prove to be as charming as they feign to be. [Ronald] Himler's warm, hazy watercolor and gouache paintings focus on the poignancy of initial meetings, with orphans courting or avoiding the attention of prospective parents, and adults regarding the children as hired hands or lovable sons and daughters. A brief introduction about the orphan trains is included.

Shirley Wilton

SOURCE: A review of *Train to Somewhere,* in *School Library Journal,* Vol. 42, No. 3, March, 1996, pp. 166-67.

From the mid-19th century until after World War I, thousands of homeless "orphans" were sent West by charitable agencies to find homes with families seeking workers, children to adopt, or mother's helpers. In telling the story of one child, Bunting encapsulates the fears and sometimes happy endings of those fateful trips. Marianne is among the oldest and least attractive of the 14 children sent on a train to the Midwest, and she starts the journey with hopes that her mother will be waiting at one of the stops. At each station, papers are signed and children are placed, until only Marianne remains when the last town of Somewhere is reached. Only an elderly couple, hoping for a boy, is waiting there. They look kindly at Marianne, and the grandmotherly wife sums up the story's theme when she remarks that "Sometimes what you get turns out to be better than what you wanted in the first place." By making this slice of American history into an appealing tale, Bunting offers an opportunity to compare present-day social policies with those of times past. The book is timely yet universal in showing the desire of every child for a loving family. Himler's full-page, bordered paintings portray the people and towns in warm colors and softly blended brush strokes. Beyond this gentle story lie the social issues of our own day.

Wendy E. Betts

SOURCE: A review of *Train to Somewhere,* in *The Five Owls,* Vol. X, No. 5, May-June, 1996, p. 110.

The problem of homeless and unwanted children is just beginning to be touched on in picture books, but it has a long history in American society. One of the more ingenious efforts to solve the problem was the Orphan Train, an exodus of approximately 100,000 homeless children from New York City to adoption in the Midwest, during the mid-1850s to the late 1920s. For this fictional look at one journey on the Orphan Train, Bunting chose to tell a bittersweet but essentially positive story, while still revealing many of the negative aspects of this intriguing episode in our history.

Narrated in the present-tense by Marianne—a sad little girl illustrated with a face full of woe—*Train to Somewhere* tells of her long journey out West. At each stop she sees her friends sent off with whoever asks for them; the children have no choice, even when they are obviously being picked as cheap labor. Marianne doesn't want to be placed, even with a kind family. She is sure her mother, who went west years before, will be waiting for her somewhere along the way. But as the journey goes on, and Marianne is still not chosen, she begins to wonder what will happen if her mother doesn't come. Maybe her mother doesn't really want her; maybe no one will want her.

Himler's rather formally arranged paintings match the poignancy of Bunting's words, emphasizing the contrast between the joyful wanted children and the plain, lonely, unwanted ones. For the quietly happy ending, which unites Marianne with an understanding old couple, we finally get to see her smile and bloom—no longer really plain—as she reaches out to her new family.

Still, even with the promise of happiness for Marianne, there is a frightening undercurrent to this story. The casualness of the adoption process seems staggering today, and the children's helplessness is painful to witness. It is evident that though this program was ostensibly for the children's benefit, it was the adults who got to pick and choose what they wanted. As in her Caldecott winning book *Smoky Night,* Bunting reports without judging, ending her central story on a bright note, but

leaving readers to think about the implications for others who weren't as lucky.

SECRET PLACE (1996)

Kirkus Reviews

SOURCE: A review of *Secret Place,* in *Kirkus Reviews,* Vol. LXIV, No. 12, June 15, 1996, p. 895.

Bunting writes about a small boy who discovers a secret place—a small patch of wildlife—at night in the river that runs through a cacophonous, polluted urban center—"Close by is a freeway where cars and trucks boom, and a railroad track with freight trains that shunt and grunt." He shares this discovery with his father who runs a forklift at night and "is good with secrets," a young married couple, and others who teach him the names of the birds. The snowy egret feeds, green-winged teals and buffleheads skim the water, a mallard duck raises ducklings, and a coyote and possum with babies come to drink. The boy wants to tell even more people about the secret place, but decides to be careful in the name of protecting it. The brief poetic text captures the surprising beauty of nature in the city, where "The phone wires rocked the moon/in their cradle of lines./The stars rested bright on the telephone poles." Luminous watercolors [by Ted Rand] juxtapose the concrete and smoke of warehouses and wharves in an evocative and deeply satisfying work.

Carol Ann Wilson

SOURCE: A review of *Secret Place,* in *School Library Journal,* Vol. 42, No. 9, September, 1996, p. 171.

The cover illustration reveals to readers what the young narrator has discovered—a duck and her ducklings hidden amid the concrete and grime of the city. He shares his precious find with just a few appreciative adults and, in the process, introduces readers to a variety of wildlife. As his enthusiasm for this special spot grows, he wants to tell everyone about it but wise counseling from an adult cautions him to "be careful" because "some people might want to take the secret place and change it." Instead, readers are left with a bit of a hint as to its location—just enough to send them off to explore their own cities and towns. Double-page watercolor illustrations offer varying perspectives, and nature and the urban environment alternate as the dominant element. A dark palette contributes a sense of mystery and solemnity. Nighttime scenes acquire a magical quality when characters are outlined in a golden glow. The spare but lyrical text is boxed in the blues and greens of water and sky with the city's soot often, but not always, intruding. The illustrations are large enough to share with a group, and the text has a natural pacing well suited to reading aloud. Children will be delighted by the opportunity to be included in this secret, and will also share a profound respect for nature and a sense of joy in the triumph of a small piece of wilderness over urban decay and pollution. Like the secret place, this is a story that is gentle yet powerful.

Susan Dove Lempke

SOURCE: A review of *Secret Place,* in *Booklist,* Vol. 93, No. 1, September 1, 1996, p. 140.

A little boy learns that the city, with all its grime and smoke and noise, can also be home for wildlife, when he discovers a "secret place" in a river flowing between concrete walls. When he observes the oasis, he sees such exotic birds as egrets and cinnamon teals as well as mallard families nesting. Returning at night with grown-up friends, he even sees coyotes and possums. But the adults caution him not to reveal the secret place to others, for fear they might change it. Bunting's prose is evocative, if a tad sophisticated for her young narrator, and Rand's paintings vividly convey both the grayness of the city and the colors of the graceful wild creatures.

📖 *GOING HOME* (1996)

Barbara Kiefer

SOURCE: A review of *Going Home,* in *School Library Journal,* Vol. 42, No. 9, September, 1996, p. 171.

Mama and Papa are ecstatic to be going home to Mexico for the Christmas holidays, but Carlos and his sisters, who have beenraised in a labor camp on a farm in the U.S., have difficulty understanding their parents' longing for this unfamiliar place. After the old station wagon crosses the border, however, excitement builds, and when they finally reach La Perla, a noisy and joyous family reunion takes place. After all the guests have left, Mama and Papa steal outside and dance barefoot in the street. Their amazed children then begin to understand the sacrifices their parents have made for them. Bunting conveys her message softly, leaving the major role to [David] Diaz. His distinctive style is well suited to the setting and the mood of the book. End papers feature closeup photographs of brilliant "artesanias Mexicanas," decorative objects, figures, and other popular arts found in the market places. This "arté popular" then forms the background on which the paintings and type are placed. Diaz uses color, shape, and line to evoke the anticipation of the trip and the joy of arrival. Even the layout effectively mirrors the emotional energy and tension of the story. A lovely journey home for Mama and Papa and their children, and for readers, a journey to understanding.

Kirkus Reviews

SOURCE: A review of *Going Home,* in *Kirkus Reviews,* Vol. LXIV, No. 17, September 1, 1996, p. 1320.

From the Caldecott Medal-winning team behind *Smoky Night* (1994), the story of a migrant family returning to Mexico for the Christmas holidays.

Carlos and his sisters are not at all sure that "home" is Mexico, although they were born there. It is difficult for them to understand their parents' enthusiasm for the long journey and for the tiny town of La Perla at the end of it. A tender revelation, when Carlos realizes that his parents left the place they deeply loved to provide their children with "opportunities," ties the tale of the journey to the season, the moment, and the future. Diaz creates an explosion of color in his familiar format of a visual environment that is whole and entire: He designed the eccentric, legible typeface; set the framed illustrations and text blocks on digitally enhanced photographs of flowers, pottery, baskets, and folk art; and filled the pictures with his signature saturated colors in bold, broad planes. These do not bind readers to the tale any more than the words do, hinting at the depth of parental love and sacrifice while distancing children from genuine understanding. An affectionate, but not exceptional offering.

Susan Dove Lempke

SOURCE: A review of *Going Home,* in *Booklist,* Vol. 93, No. 3, October 1, 1996, p. 357.

In a family that has moved to California from Mexico to work, the parents may call one place home, the children, another. When Carlos and his family go to his parents' village for Christmas, Carlos realizes the sacrifices his parents have made in leaving behind a beloved home to do brutally hard work so that their children may have better lives. Although Bunting has a message, her story is also a pleasure; her evocative writing makes each tiny moment in Mexico come alive. Diaz uses photographs as borders (this time mainly of folk art objects) for his paintings, just as he did so effectively in his 1995 Caldecott winner, *Smoky Night,* also written by Bunting. However, the theme here is not the chaos of a riot, and the overall effect is cluttered and frustrating, as his fine paintings are overshadowed.

📖 *THE BLUE AND THE GRAY* (1996)

Kirkus Reviews

SOURCE: A review of *The Blue and the Gray,* in *Kirkus Reviews,* Vol. LXIV, No. 22, November 15, 1996, p. 1666.

Bunting adds to her series of picture books with serious themes with this account of an unnamed Civil War battle framed within a present-day story of two young boys, one black, one white, whose new homes are being constructed within view of an unmarked battlefield. As the two boys, fast friends, explore their new homesites, they learn about the tragic loss of life that happened there in that war of "us against us . . . the saddest kind of war there is." Bunting's text is mostly stated in the manner of a child's brief sentences, but sprinkled with rhyming words and typographically arranged like a poem in short lines that slow the reading to a somber pace. [Ned] Bittinger's oils capture both the bucolic peace of the present-day countryside and the smoke and turmoil of battle, in one case as seen from exactly the same point of view in two consecutive spreads. Particularly effective is the ghostly presence of soldiers, cannon, horses, and wagons as faint silhouettes in some scenes of the two young friends.

Offering only hints of the issues over which the war was fought, this is not a book to read without preparation, but it is a worthy complement to books such as Patricia Polacco's *Pink and Say* (1994) and Karen Ackerman's *The Tin Heart* (1990).

Lauralyn Persson

SOURCE: A review of *The Blue and the Gray,* in *School Library Journal,* Vol. 42, No. 12, December, 1996, p. 85.

The families of two friends, one black and one white, are building new houses on a spot overlooking a field where a Civil War battle took place. The white boy's father describes the battle to the two children, and these imagined scenes are shown, juxtaposed with the everyday calm of the present. Surprised that there is no historical marker, the boys vow that they'll remember, and the father says: *"We'll* be a monument of sorts . . . a part of what they fought for long ago." Bunting uses a first-person narrative, writing in verse that is often evocative and lyrical. When the narrator finds an old bullet, he throws it " . . . high/across the field of bones./How silently it falls/into the tufts of grass/and flowers." The author does not always maintain an authentic child's voice, however. Bittinger's striking oil paintings are technically accomplished and suit the dramatic nature of the text. He's especially good with the contrast between the serene present, with its clear, transparent light, and the dark chaos of the fighting long ago. This well-intentioned story is not quite up to Bunting's best, but there is much potential for classroom use, and the book will make an interesting match with Patricia Polacco's *Pink and Say,* right down to a painting of black hands and white hands reaching toward one another.

Elizabeth Bush

SOURCE: A review of *The Blue and the Gray,* in *Bulletin of the Center for Children's Books,* Vol. 50, No. 6, February, 1997, pp. 200-01.

As the young narrator hangs around the framework of his family's new house, his father tells him and his best friend J.J. tales of a Civil War battle that was fought in the field just beyond their subdivision. The two friends—

one white and one black—are troubled to learn that many of the soldiers who fought on opposite sides of the battle had once been friends too. Since this particular battlefield remains unmarked, the boys resolve to make their own homes and memories a sort of living monument to the fallen soldiers and, when the narrator finds a bullet amid the construction rubble, he throws it into the sky rather than keep it as a souvenir. This slender tale fairly groans under the weight of its good intentions, but neither the sensibility nor the solemn, Veteran's-Day-style text rings true to a child's experience. Two boys living in close proximity to battle sites could scarcely be so ignorant of the Civil War, and the narrator's imaginings, as portrayed in Bittinger's hazy oil paintings, sentimentalize and sanitize the bloody affair. Didactic verse, punctuated by the occasional rogue rhyme, swings from adult ("The three of us look out across a field / all hillocky and hummocky / with tufted grass and stubby flowers") to banal ("My dad says that's the saddest kind of war there is,/ though every war is sad / and most are bad").

ON CALL BACK MOUNTAIN (1997)

Publishers Weekly

SOURCE: A review of *On Call Back Mountain,* in *Publishers Weekly,* Vol. 244, No. 2, January 13, 1997, pp. 74-5.

Bunting and Moser demonstrate their craftsmanship with this carefully calibrated tale. The narrator and his younger brother live at the foot of Call Back Mountain, "on the very edge of the wilderness." Their only neighbor is Bosco Burak, the summer lookout in the fire tower 15 miles away. His annual arrival is the highlight of the boys' year; they look forward to the single night he spends with them as he travels to the tower, his goods piled atop his mules Aida and Traviata (he calls them "the ladies"). Every night, all summer long, the boys flash their lanterns to say good night to Bosco. But one night he fails to signal back, and the boys' parents climb the mountain to discover that he has died. The grieving boys spy an unusually long-legged wolf; as they marvel at the return of the wolf after fire drove the wild animals away a few years earlier, they are at the same time reminded of the unusually long-legged Bosco. They wonderingly recall Bosco's belief that "any creature that loves the wilderness will always come back." This is a quiet, understated story that raises questions without fretting over answers. [Barry] Moser's paintings mirror the tale's subtlety, doing justice to the wilderness setting, and flourishing within the confined palette of night scenes.

Kirkus Reviews

SOURCE: A review of *On Call Back Mountain,* in *Kirkus Reviews,* Vol. LXV, No. 2, January 15, 1997, p. 138.

Joe and Ben anxiously await the annual summer return of their friend Bosco Burak, the elderly lookout in the fire tower that stands on the peak above their family's cabin. Although the forest was devastated by a fire that drove the animals away a few summers ago, Bosco tells the boys that there is new growth and that the animals will return to Call Back Mountain, just as Bosco always does. Every night that Bosco is on the tower, the boys signal goodnight with their lanterns, and Bosco's light answers. Then one night there is no answer—Bosco has had a fatal heart attack, and Ben and Joe must come to terms with his death. The night after Bosco's death, the boys spot a lone wolf with great shining eyes and long, spindly legs, just like Bosco's, on a ledge—the animals have returned. Simply written and gloriously illustrated, this tale of love, loss, and renewal lingers long after the last page is turned. Bunting presents complex issues in a way that even very young readers will grasp.

Judith Gloyer

SOURCE: A review of *On Call Back Mountain,* in *School Library Journal,* Vol. 43, No. 3, March, 1997, p. 149.

A gifted writer creates a world and relationships that will touch her readers. Two young brothers live in an isolated wilderness area. Each June, an elderly man who works as a fire spotter high on the mountain comes to visit before climbing up to the tower for the summer. The fun and affection they share is joyous. The boys read aloud to Bosco to show their new skills; he shares his knowledge of nature and his love of opera with them. Once Bosco assumes his post, they signal him with lanterns each night, and his light always answers theirs. Linked to the story is the disappearance of wolves from the area after a fire caused by arson. One night, he does not return their signal; in the morning the boys' parents climb up the mountain and discover that he has died of a heart attack. The youngest continues to try to signal the old man in disbelief at his death. The older boy takes comfort in the return of the wolves, in the sense of hope and renewal he sees around him in the natural world, and in his memories of his friend. Bunting's words and phrases are lyrical. Moser's watercolors evocatively convey the starkness and majesty of the wilderness setting during the day and at night and the closeness the friends share.

📖 *TROUBLE ON THE T-BALL TEAM* (1997)

Susan S. Verner

SOURCE: A review of *Trouble on the T-Ball Team,* in *Bulletin of the Center for Children's Books,* Vol. 50, No. 8, April, 1997, p. 277.

The Dodgers is a hot T-ball team on a winning streak, except they keep losing something, and it's not games.

Linda is the last one on the team to lose hers and finally she, too, joins the others in losing—her first tooth. Bunting's somewhat coy story features budding baseball players, all consumed by their common (and age-prescribed) losses. Despite numerous hints, the author nevertheless manages to keep the mystery unsolved until the very end. [Irene] Trivas is a fully compliant accessory to the fact—her sly pastel watercolor illustrations hide the gap-toothed evidence while insightfully showing the youngsters' sublime inattention to the game. The greatest mystery of all, however, is the seeming ambidexterity of the players, first wearing their gloves on one hand, then the other. Could Generation Y be loaded with switch hitters? Introduce this one to the fans on opening day—they'll sink their teeth into it.

Christy Norris

SOURCE: A review of *Trouble on the T-Ball Team,* in *School Library Journal,* Vol. 43, No. 5, May, 1997, p. 93.

This picture book centers around a T-ball team on which everyone has "lost one" except for the narrator. Therein lies the dilemma—the elusive "one" that has been lost. It turns out to be a tooth. To no surprise, a home run (and subsequent fall over a wayward dog) ensures that the narrator becomes one of the gang. This story struggles to be a mystery and fails at being a consolation book for children with their baby teeth intact. The average-quality watercolors do little to further the narrative; at one point, the illustrations even contradict the text with the narrator suddenly switching from playing offense to defense while scoring the winning home run. For a seven-year-old, losing a tooth is a rite of passage. Not losing a tooth can therefore be somewhat traumatic and create a sense of isolation in a child. . . . Bunting's title lacks the superior quality usually associated with her books.

📖 *I AM THE MUMMY HEB-NEFERT* (1997)

Kirkus Reviews

SOURCE: A review of *I Am the Mummy Heb-Nefert,* in *Kirkus Reviews,* Vol. LXV, No. 7, April 1, 1997, p. 550.

From Bunting, a remarkably succinct and knowing "autobiography" of a mummy that provides the essence of life in the Egypt of the pharaohs, and which is strikingly illustrated by Christiana.

The favored, beautiful daughter of a monarch dances one evening for the pharaoh's brother, Ti. Soon she is a cherished wife, interrupting her idyllic existence only to revisit the home in which she once lived. Her parents are gone, but a house snake, set to catch grain-thieving mice, remains. "The same snake or another. Who could tell?" Heb-Nefert's ponderings arise from her current museum-display vantage point, a 3,000-year period of mummification in "the silent twilight of the afterlife," taken up "when day changed to eternity" and during which she has seen that all things change. Now she hovers in spirit above the display case at which museumgoers express astonishment that her mummy and the one near it—the mummy of her beloved husband—were once living people. Heb-Nefert thinks them foolish for not foreseeing that soon enough they will be dust and bones while she will remain as she is now, "black as night, stretched as tight as leather on a drum," although, in a stunning final line, there is a proud, immutable, and very human fact: "Once I was beautiful." [David] Christiana provides haunting portraits, hints of a spirit world, and misty glimpses as well as bold scenes of the past. A startling shot of a contemporary child underscores Heb-Nefert's dulcet lament in this compelling work.

Janice M. Del Negro

SOURCE: A review of *I Am the Mummy Heb-Nefert,* in *Bulletin of the Center for Children's Books,* Vol. 50, No. 9, May, 1997, p. 315.

An imaginary voice from the past speaks: "I am the mummy Heb-Nefert,/ black as night,/ stretched as tight/ as leather on a drum./ My arms are folded/ on my hollow chest/ where once my live heart beat." In this evocation of life in ancient Egypt, the mummy Heb-Nefert speaks of what it was like to be the beloved wife of the pharaoh's brother, how they sailed in barges on the Nile, and feasted in gardens while harpists played. And then death: "My golden cat, Nebut, I loved./ She loved me, too,/ and came with me/ into the silent twilight of the afterlife/ when day changed to eternity." Heb-Nefert describes the mummification process, her internment, and her final destination: a glass coffin "under lights in quiet rooms," as people pass by and say "This was a person?" She muses, "How foolish that they do not see/ how all things change and so will they." Bunting's text is deliberately restrained, with a formality that suits the speaker as she comments with longing and wisdom on her life, her own passing, and the passage of time. While the impressionistic tone of Christiana's watercolors is sometimes a little vague, and the compositions vary in effectiveness, for the most part the paintings are as evocative and understated as the text as they reflect the golden days of love on a royal barge, the darkness of the tomb, and the starkness of the mummy wrapped in ancient linens under museum lights. A clearer sense of chronology would be useful, but this will intrigue those kids fascinated by Ancient Egypt and even those who aren't.

Cathryn A. Camper

SOURCE: A review of *I Am the Mummy Heb-Nefert,* in *School Library Journal,* Vol. 43, No. 8, August, 1997, p. 154.

In this quiet, evocative voyage through time, an Egyptian mummy looks back on her life. In her own time, Heb-Nefert was the wife of the pharaoh's brother, with servants who dressed her and a loving husband with whom she explored the royal gardens and hunted birds on the Nile. She recalls visiting her humble childhood home where women baked bread outdoors and a snake was coiled in a basket to catch rats and mice. When she died, her body was anointed with oils and spices, and bandaged to begin the process of mummification. Her loyal cat was mummified, too, so it could follow her into the afterlife. Finally, she looks down on her shriveled body where it lies in a museum and observes the daily stream of visitors that pass by, rarely thinking that a similar fate awaits them. Bunting uses a poetic, lyrical voice to transport readers beyond the withered mummified remains they see and into Heb-Nefert's ancient world. The atmospheric watercolors pick up both the sunlight on Egyptian sands and the dark shadows of sealed tombs.

MY BACKPACK (1997)

Carolyn Phelan

SOURCE: A review of *My Backpack,* in *Booklist,* Vol. 93, No. 17, May 1, 1997, pp. 1500-01.

As a preschool boy tells about his new backpack, he goes around the house happily putting things into it: his brother's baseball mitt, his father's glasses, his mother's shoes, a supply of cookies, and the family cat. After the child strolls out to the backyard, his family start looking for their missing things. Instead of being the hero for collecting scattered belongings and keeping them safe, the boy finds that he's being blamed. A backpack ride from his understanding Dad makes everything all right again. The rhythmic, rhyming text succeeds in sounding childlike but not precious, simple yet not simplistic. Young children will not only enjoy the notion of putting things into a backpack, but they will also empathize with the boy when his actions are misunderstood and his feelings are hurt. Bright and expressive, the colorful artwork [by Maryann Cocca-Leffler] centers on the child, his emotions and his delight in familiar, everyday things. Preschoolers who wear glasses will enjoy seeing that this boy has glasses, too, a rare sight in picture books.

Publishers Weekly

SOURCE: A review of *My Backpack,* in *Publishers Weekly,* Vol. 244, No. 19, May 12, 1997, p. 76.

Call this an accumulative tale: a bespectacled boy gets a backpack from Grandma and proceeds to fill it up with just about everything in the house. When his frantic family finally discovers what he's done, the chastened child is comforted by getting to ride in the backpack himself. Bunting's rhyming text manages to have both a bouncy beat and an authentically colloquial voice. She also shows a keen understanding of how every-day objects—especially those that belong to other people—fascinate very young children. "I like this television thing," says the boy, eyeing the remote control, "You push it and it makes a ping./ Cartoons come on and sometimes news./ I think I'll take my mother's shoes." Cocca-Leffler (previously paired with Bunting for *I Don't Want to Go to Camp*) extends the buoyant mood of the story with cheery illustrations. Jazzy borders, a frisky sense of composition, clean lines and bright colors, along with skillfully deployed white space, give her pictures a strong graphic quality. Like Bunting, Cocca-Leffler is adroit at capturing the comic realities of family life—children should get a particular kick out of seeing Dad peering under an armchair for his missing reading glasses, his derriere in the air.

Anne Knickerbocker

SOURCE: A review of *My Backpack,* in *School Library Journal,* Vol. 44, No. 4, April, 1998, p. 91.

When Grandma sends her grandson a large backpack as a gift, she tells him to fill it with "important stuff." The boy does so joyfully, but he goes a bit overboard. Dad's glasses, Mom's keys, big brother's catcher's mitt—all get packed in the large blue pouch. Family members are dismayed about their missing items until the culprit is found. Saddened by his parents' lack of enthusiasm, the child seeks comfort with his father, who ends up putting his son inside the backpack for a ride. Youngsters will enjoy noting all the things that fit into the backpack and will delight in predicting that the boy may be getting himself into trouble. The rhyming text begs to be read aloud. Each double-page spread includes a framed illustration on the right, with the text and whimsical images of the objects on the left. The colorful artwork, done in gouache, colored pencils, and collage, complements the story, giving the book a playful tone. Pack this in your preschool-storytime bag.

THE PUMPKIN FAIR (1997)

Publishers Weekly

SOURCE: A review of *The Pumpkin Fair,* in *Publishers Weekly,* Vol. 244, No. 21, May 26, 1997, p. 84.

"There's even gooey party stew/ (I'll try them all, except the stew./ It's icky-looking, gross, pew-yew!)"— Bunting's rhymes typically project an authentic voice, and this time the voice belongs to a gangly girl who visits her village's annual Pumpkin Fair. Accompanied by her parents and a sibling dressed in a bunny suit, the girl admires the Pumpkin Princess, enters a pumpkin-seed spitting contest ("Pucker up and let 'em fly!/ Spit 'em far and spit 'em high!") and tastes pumpkin cooked every which way, including the aforementioned stew.

[Eileen] Christelow partners Bunting's text with flavorsome cartoons. Exuding a mild sense of humor and much affection, they capture both the excitement and goofiness of the small-town event. But Bunting has something more important in mind than just a fun outing. Everywhere her heroine goes, she cuddles a pumpkin that she has grown from a seed. It's small and bumpy, she admits, but, "I tell her that it's still OK./ She's very special in her way." Her steadfast affection is rewarded at the end, when she wins the prize for "best-loved pumpkin at the fair/ The best-loved pumpkin anywhere!" This lightly proffered moral, along with Bunting's effortlessly idiomatic verse, makes for a sweet seasonal tale.

Marcia Hupp

SOURCE: A review of *The Pumpkin Fair,* in *School Library Journal,* Vol. 43, No. 9, September, 1997, p. 173.

This story in rhyme celebrates a small town's "Pumpkin Fair," complete with a Pumpkin Princess and Peter Pumpkin Band. Everyone comes to carve pumpkins; bowl pumpkins; spit pumpkin seeds; juggle pumpkins; make pumpkin creatures; and eat pumpkin stew, cake, pie, ice cream, and cookies. The young narrator brings her very own pet pumpkin to the festivities and winds up with two ribbons for the "best-loved pumpkin at the fair. The best-loved pumpkin anywhere!" Christelow's jubilant illustrations in watercolor and pen and ink add to the general atmosphere of gaiety—everywhere readers look, families are interacting happily and having fun. According to a sign, it is October 28th, and many of the children in the pictures are wearing costumes, but Halloween is never mentioned, so the book could be used to celebrate the harvest season in general. Of course, it will also serve as a good non-scary Halloween story.

Ilene Cooper

SOURCE: A review of *The Pumpkin Fair,* in *Booklist,* Vol. 94, No. 5, November 1, 1997, pp. 478, 480.

A bouncy rhyme and delightful artwork bring this pumpkin fair to life. The young narrator is ecstatic to be at the local pumpkin fair, where pumpkins of every size are on display—and that's not all! There's pumpkin bowling, a pumpkin pull, and every sort of food you can imagine made from the orange stuff, from ice cream to stew. But the little girl is most interested in the pumpkin contest. She doesn't think she'll win anything. Her pumpkin isn't the biggest, or even the smallest. It's medium sized and kind of warty. But her name is called for a special prize. "The best-loved pumpkin at the fair / The best loved pumpkin anywhere!" Christelow's good-natured watercolor-and-ink illustrations are filled with things to look at and laugh about, including a marching band in pumpkin suits. Keep this book around to read for autumn story hours—but you might want a piece of pumpkin pie when you're done.

MOONSTICK: THE SEASONS OF THE SIOUX (1997)

Kirkus Reviews

SOURCE: A review of *Moonstick: The Seasons of the Sioux,* in *Kirkus Reviews,* Vol. LXV, No. 14, July 15, 1997, p. 1108.

Bunting turns a sensitive eye to Sioux culture, depicting it truthfully and realistically while incorporating into the book a heartening message to any child whose ancestral ways have passed (even temporarily) into obscurity. The father of the first-person narrator notches a moon-counting stick at the beginning of each of the 13 moons of the Sioux year, a way to mark the passing of the year. [John] Sandford's appealing, unsentimental illustrations link the notches to the passing seasons, from the Moon of the Birth of Calves, through the Cherry-Ripening Moon when the men take part in the Sun Dance, and the Sore-Eyes Moon when snow so dazzles the narrator that his father reassures him that "changes come and will come again. It is so arranged." Soon it is time for a new moonstick, but, in a brief page, readers understand that many moonsticks have come and gone: The child is grown, his culture passed away, and the narrator's livelihood comes from the sale of his wife's beadwork and his own headdresses—"We do not hunt." That's the poignant clincher, so it's a relief that the narrator takes his small grandson to cut a stick, to pass on his father's wisdom, to note that changes will come again. Expertly and beautifully told.

GraceAnne A. DeCandido

SOURCE: A review of *Moonstick: The Seasons of the Sioux,* in *Booklist,* Vol. 94, No. 1, September 1, 1997, p. 132.

The Sioux year, which is marked by 13 moons, begins in spring with the Moon of the Birth of Calves. In this story, the father of a small boy makes a moonstick, a stick with notches for each moon, to note the passage of time. The boy tells of the Strawberry Moon when his mother and sisters and aunts make clothing; the Moon of Frost on the Tipi when his father hunts on snowshoes, and so on for each. The moonstick appears in each text block with the appropriate notches, becoming more elaborately decorated as the moons pass. The language is simple and straight-forward but curiously unengaging: "Changes come and will come again. I was told once that it is so arranged." The full-bleed, double-spread paintings are beautiful, with supple brushwork that is light enough for the canvas texture to show through, but the whole has little child appeal. The story closes with the boy, now a man with a grandson, carving a moonstick for the child. They are in a rural setting that seems too modern since earlier pages depict the boy's father hunting with a bow and arrow.

TWINNIES (1997)

Publishers Weekly

SOURCE: A review of *Twinnies,* in *Publishers Weekly,* Vol. 244, No. 29, July 21, 1997, pp. 201-02.

Both Bunting and [Nancy] Carpenter are in top form in this wise and funny story of a girl who sheds sibling rivalry in favor of affection for her twin baby sisters. Life isn't easy for the unnamed heroine who seems to be four or five and who plays second fiddle to the scene-stealing "twinnies." Bunting captures her angst well: when they are dressed as Raggedy Ann and Andy for Halloween, "everybody, *everybody* said how darling they were"; when their frazzled parents must chase down the toddlers headed toward ocean waves, their big sister forlornly wonders, "Who was left to run in the water after me if I ran into the water, that's what I want to know." But eventually, she wants to keep them, just the way they are: "They are so soft, on either side of me. I think if there was only one, I'd feel lopsided." Carpenter's oil paintings of butter yellow and sky blue have a timeless quality, as with the twinnies at the beach, bursting out of the double-page spread in opposite directions. She also manages to give each twin her own personality (one joyfully flails ahead with mouth open wide, while the other, eyes down, makes a studied dart). Together, author and artist have created a heroine with such a likable mix of mischief and warmth that young ones will likely see themselves in her, whether or not they have their own twin siblings.

Ilene Cooper

SOURCE: A review of *Twinnies,* in *Booklist,* Vol. 94, No. 2, September 15, 1997, p. 240.

"Last June I got twin baby sisters. The worst thing is that there were two of them." So begins this right-on story about a big sister who is having a little trouble redefining her place in the family. All the attention is going to Boo and Gwendolyn, and their sister is not pleased. Bunting does a terrific job of building the story. She moves the narrator from being a child who slyly changes the twinnies' socks so they can't be told apart to a sister who barks at a neighbor displeased by the babies' crying. And when that crying causes the babies to be brought into their parents' bed, their sister comes along too—and to a new realization: "They are so soft, on either side of me. I think if there was only one, I'd feel lop-sided." The story is illustrated in thick oils that can be lively but don't always capture the appeal of the babies and their older sibling. The pleasure here is mostly in the words, and big brothers and sisters, even if not the siblings of twins, will understand exactly where this book is coming from.

📖 *DUCKY* (1997)

Marcia Hupp

SOURCE: A review of *Ducky,* in *School Library Journal,* Vol. 43, No. 9, September, 1997, p. 173.

In 1992, a large crate of bathtub toys traveling from Hong Kong to Tacoma, Washington, was lost at sea. Since then, hundreds of the toys have washed ashore, with scientists recording their positions, plotting their courses, and using the information to further their study of currents, winds, and tides. *Ducky* is the first-person account of one yellow plastic duck that survived the journey to fulfill his destiny in a little boy's tub. In the throes of the adventure, Ducky wishes he could do more than just float, that he could swim, or fly. But, by journey's end, safe and with a child of his own, the contented toy concludes, "How wondrous it is to be able to float!" Bunting's narrative opens with the choppy rhythms and abbreviated sentences of an easy reader, but grows more lyrical as events progress. It is a bit cloying, though. [David] Wisniewski's intricate paper cuts seem a bit grandiose for this modest, somewhat precious text. They will engage readers, however, and they are striking in their use of color and texture, in their composition, and in their interpretation of events. A bit out of sync, then, but likely to find an audience among the bathtub set—and budding scientists as well.

Roger Sutton

SOURCE: A review of *Ducky,* in *The Horn Book Magazine,* Vol. LXIII, No. 6, November-December, 1997, p. 668.

David Wisniewski's Caldecott-winning paper-cutting talents get a comedic workout here, illustrating Bunting's slightly sly text about a plastic duck who, along with thousands of fellow bathtub toys, is washed overboard when a storm hits the freighter ferrying them across the ocean (Bunting supplies a note about the factual event that inspired the story). The duck tells the story ("Our ship has disappeared. The sea is big, big, big. Oh, I am scared!"), including an unfortunate encounter with a shark ("It shakes its head and spits us out. I expect we are not too tasty, though we are guaranteed non-toxic") and the basic existential dilemma of a bathtub toy out of its element: "I wish we could swim and get away. But all we can do is float." The ocean's currents eventually bring the duck to shore alongside many of his compatriots, and he finally achieves his destiny, floating in the security of a bubblebath. This is an out-of-the way excursion for both author and illustrator. . . .

Pat Mathews

SOURCE: A review of *Ducky,* in *Bulletin of the Center for Children's Books,* Vol. 51, No. 5, January, 1998, pp. 155-56.

Based on an actual incident which occurred in 1992, the story chronicles the adventures of Ducky, one of 29,000 plastic bathtub toys shipwrecked during a storm. Sea snakes, sharks, bad weather, and loneliness plague Ducky until he is found by a boy on the coast of Washington state and happily ends up in the boy's bathtub. As anyone who has ever been a kid knows, toys are real and they have feelings, so there can be no doubt that young listeners will relate to the pathetic plight of this yellow plastic duck ("Our ship has disappeared. The sea is big, big, big. Oh, I am scared!"). Bunting's text ably captures the poignant feelings of the lost and found protagonist, even if it is only yellow plastic. Wisniewski's obvious expertise with paper is somewhat overshadowed by a disunity in the color scheme where primary colors unfairly compete with a more subtle palette. The composition is often erratic: the icy blues and whites of one wintry spread showcase the illustrator's craft, while other spreads seem either overdone or lackluster. Children will nevertheless be delighted to learn that the story is factual (a concluding author's note gives details, which may be necessary to understand parts of the story), and everyone should have a, uh, ducky time.

📖 *DECEMBER* (1997)

Ilene Cooper

SOURCE: A review of *December,* in *Booklist,* Vol. 94, No. 1, September 1, 1997, p. 138.

In a picture book for older children, the award-winning combination of Bunting and [David] Diaz presents another story of life on the streets. Here, the narrator and his mother live in a homemade cardboard house; a calendar angel is their decoration. On Christmas Eve, they have only two cookies to look forward to the next day. When an old woman appears at their door, the mother lets her spend the night; the boy gives her a cookie. Early Christmas Day, he sees the calendar angel come to life—wearing a faded rose as did the old woman. After that, the family's luck changes, and the following Christmas finds them in their own apartment. Using elements of traditional folk tales, Bunting provides a simply told story that is infused with the miraculous. The narrator is an Everyboy that readers will respond to, no matter their socioeconomic position, and children will find the ending heartening. The artwork, featuring dramatic backgrounds (actually constructed by another artist and photo-graphed by Diaz), is top-notch. Intricate collages created from scraps of newspaper and images from the story make an arresting backdrop for the bold acrylic-and-watercolor pictures in Diaz's signature style.

School Library Journal

SOURCE: A review of *December,* in *School Library Journal,* Vol. 43, No. 10, October, 1997, p. 40.

A story singular in its originality, its artwork, and its

contemporary, multilayered theme that is ultimately filled with joy and peace despite its stark setting. On Christmas Eve, a homeless boy and his mother share their small cardboard-box home with an elderly stranger. The next morning, she is gone. And outside, the child thinks— but cannot believe—he sees an angel like the one on his December calendar page. The story ends a year later, when his situation has changed. His mother has a job and they have moved to a small apartment. It is then he observes that his calendar angel wears a rose just like the one the stranger had put on his Christmas tree. The message of charity as a risk worth taking in a dangerous world is a sobering, thoughtful holiday message. So deft in her writing, Bunting creates a mood or expresses an emotion with a simple sentence or phrase. Diaz's now-familiar angular, almost stained-glass figures dominate illustrations that are set against backgrounds so striking in their creativity and complexity that they would over-whelm a lesser story. The artist uses a mix of media and repetitive patterns to create unusual designs that give each backdrop a multidimensional look. One of a very few holiday books that has both art and writing so strong that they effectively mesh to create a truly unique title.

Janice M. Del Negro

SOURCE: A review of *December,* in *Bulletin of the Center for Children's Books,* Vol. 51, No. 4, December, 1997, pp. 119-20.

In a cardboard-box room, a homeless boy and his mother celebrate Christmas with a scrawny tree, some found ornaments, the December page of a calendar with a golden angel on it, and two Christmas cookies earned by collecting pop cans. An old woman with a fake rose pinned to her hat knocks on their cardboard door on Christmas Eve. The boy's mother lets the old woman in, and the boy gives her one of their only two Christmas cookies. "It's warm in here," the old woman says. "Warm with love." The three of them sleep, but the boy awakens in the middle of the night to find the old woman gone and, standing in the doorway, the glowing figure of the December angel. After that Christmas, the boy and his mother's luck improves, and the tale closes with the boy celebrating the next Christmas in an apartment, with the same calendar angel on the wall, now with a faded rose in her hair. This tale's effectiveness lies in its controlled brevity and the incorporation of strong folkloric elements, epitomized by the motif of the unfortunate poor giving to the stranger who turns out to be a divinity in disguise. Diaz's illustrations have his trademark strengths: vigorous lines, tight compositions, and beautiful, expressive faces. The text itself is contained in boxes set against what appears to be crumpled brown paper. The painted, textured collage backgrounds (created by Daniel Renner) are a distinct contrast to Diaz's paintings with their smooth, glossy surfaces, adding greatly to the richness of the overall design. This story has all the elements of generosity and magic found in traditional tales; that it reflects a reality of our society is both its strength and its tragedy.

THE DAY THE WHALE CAME (1998)

Publishers Weekly

SOURCE: A review of *The Day the Whale Came,* in *Publishers Weekly,* Vol. 245, No. 8, February 23, 1998, pp. 76-7.

The rotting carcass of a humpback whale is the unlikely focal point of this moralistic story set in the early 1900s. The likable narrator explains that an entrepreneur has rolled into his small Illinois town on a train, selling admission to a "once-in-a-lifetime" viewing ("for educational purposes") of his freakish cargo: a smelly dead whale. Tommy, who has read "a lot about humpbacks," is horrified when his bossy best friend reveals a pen-knife with which he intends to obtain a "souvenir" of the mammal, and foils the plan. When the train breaks down, Tommy helps the townsfolk bury the whale; later, he finds a new best friend (Tommy's mom says, "Sticking up for something you believe in and sticking up for yourself are the same thing"). At spring's arrival the town receives an unexpected reward: a carpet of wildflowers in the shape of a whale blooms at the grave-site. The intriguing look at small-town America long ago gets flattened under Bunting's heavy-handed message. Debut illustrator [Scott] Menchin's unconventional pictures, which are dominated by earth tones, subtly incorporate photographs with stylized drawings that take inventive liberties with perspective and scale. They show a sense of humor missing from the text, but they don't dispel the overwhelmingly somber mood.

Kirkus Reviews

SOURCE: A review of *The Day the Whale Came,* in *Kirkus Reviews,* Vol. LXVI, No. 5, March 1, 1998, p. 335.

When a train pulls into town carting a dead whale, the citizens of Johnstown, Illinois—one in a Model A— eagerly hand over their buffalo-head nickels and dimes to Captain Pinkney for a chance to view the dead behemoth. Tommy, who has read about whales, is nauseated by the spectacle, particularly when it turns out the whale is rotting and smelly. His friend, Ben, wants to cut off a hunk of the whale as a souvenir, intentions that spell the end of his and Tommy's friendship. As the train is about to depart, the engine breaks down, and Captain Pinkney asks for the townspeople's help in burying the smelly carcass. Tommy feels somewhat better about putting the whale to rest, but it isn't until the following spring, when wild flowers flourish over the whale's grave, that Tommy believes that its death is appeased. The language Bunting uses is clear as ever, and the analogy of the story, that standing up for what you believe in is the same as sticking up for yourself, rings true. It's just such an odd story, set in turn-of-the-century America, and made more peculiar by Menchin's collage artwork (which, significantly, gives the dead whale a human eye). That a child would be sensitive to the whale's plight may prove a timeless notion, but it feels more 1998 than 1920, the date on a nickel viewed close up.

Susan Scheps

SOURCE: A review of *The Day the Whale Came,* in *School Library Journal,* Vol. 44, No. 6, June, 1998, p. 97.

This curious story about a traveling whale exhibit seems an odd vehicle for a young boy's discovery of self-esteem. Tommy's first-person account of going to the train station in his small mid-western hometown to see a dead humpback whale is also a story of two opportunists. One is Captain Pinkney, who is touring the country by train and charging people for a look at the dead animal. The other is Tommy's friend Ben, who, to Tommy's disgust, yearns to cut off a piece of the creature's flipper as a souvenir. When the train breaks down just outside the town and the captain threatens to dump the smelly whale, the men and boys bury it and Tommy stands up to Ben. Menchin's collage illustrations are thickly outlined and detailed in pen and ink. Clothing is made of material and buttons; cutouts of ears and hair are added to skintone paper heads with features drawn in. The style is a mix of bold abstract and garish cartoon—the characters are a primitive echo of David Diaz's illustrations. The use of present tense to recount an event that happened in the past is awkward ("That winter I walk out to the place where we buried him"). Bunting's fine quality of writing is lacking here, as is a story that will be of interest to young people.

YOUR MOVE (1998)

Publishers Weekly

SOURCE: A review of *Your Move,* in *Publishers Weekly,* Vol. 245, No. 8, February 23, 1998, p. 77.

Bunting, in a markedly different approach from her ***The Day the Whale Came,*** collaborates with [James] Ransome on a gripping picture book told through the first-person narrative of a boy who nearly joins a gang. One evening, while their mother works at her waitressing job, 10-year-old James takes his six-year-old brother, Isaac, along to meet up with the K-Bones, a gang to which James yearns to belong. As his initiation rite, James must spray-paint the K-Bones name over that of a rival gang, the Snakes, on a freeway sign ("'Cool,' I say, but I'm more nervous than ever"). James does the deed, but learns that the gang also steals for fun, and begins to have doubts about joining. Then, on their way back, they run into the Snakes, who fire a gun. No one gets hurt, but the next night, when James and Isaac are offered membership to the K-Bones, they refuse. Though the ending is a bit facile, Bunting skillfully contrasts James's cool veneer with his inner turmoil, creating a story that will likely resonate with children who have felt pulled against their own conscience. Ransome's full-bleed oil paintings convey the tension and looming danger of the boys' misadventure. His illustrations effectively put readers in James's shoes: in the most dramatic, the K-Bones gang stares out from the page against a swirling gold background as the leader extends the can of spray paint to readers themselves.

Anne Connor

SOURCE: A review of *Your Move,* in *School Library Journal,* Vol. 44, No. 5, May, 1998, p. 107.

A somewhat idealized, but powerful picture book about how a good kid avoids gang involvement. James, 10, and his 6-year-old brother Isaac are alone at night while their single mother works. A neighbor keeps an ear out for James's hourly thumps on her wall assuring her that they are okay. One night James leaves their apartment with Isaac to meet up with the K-Bones crew. To prove himself, he must spray paint a freeway sign with the club's name, thus covering a rival gang's tag. He is frightened but climbs the pole to the sign, high over traffic. Successful, the boys leave the scene, but their elation quickly evaporates when the rival gang challenges them—with a gun. Running away, Isaac falls and is hurt. When they get home their mother is there, called by the worried neighbor. The next night the K-Bones leader comes by to tell James he's in, and Isaac is, too. They both decline the invitation. Bunting's vignette is lent power by Ransome's strong, realistic oil paintings. The text, simple and direct, lets the message come through without preachiness. However, is it realistic for the gang leader to give up on his recruits and for the kids to be able to resist the temptations offered by gang membership? Perhaps the problem isn't this easily solved in real life, but it is good to see a positive view of boys who take control of their lives when danger appears.

Elizabeth Bush

SOURCE: A review of *Your Move,* in *Bulletin of the Center for Children's Books,* Vol. 51, No. 10, June, 1998, p. 354.

"I'm not that dumb. Maybe I did know. But I wanted to be in with them." Ten-year-old James recalls the near-tragic misadventure of the evening he brought his adoring younger brother Isaac along on his initiation into the K-Bones, a young crew of gangsta wannabes. James's mission is to climb up to a sign overhanging the expressway and spraypaint the crew's name over a rival crew's tag. The Snakes, however, are older and armed, and although the K-Bones escape with only terrified Isaac's ripped pants and lacerated knees as the night's damages, this close shave is enough to convince James that he does not want to join the crew. Bunting's text acknowledges the allure, even the romance, of James's gutsy escapade, and his pride in his accomplishment: "When I reach the S, I look. I can read it! Yeah!" Ransome's densely brushed oils poignantly contrast the relative youth and naïveté of the K-Bones with the menace of the more mature Snakes.

The aftermath of James's tale is all too facile, however. Bullets fly and miss their marks; James can simply walk away from the K-Bones with no repercussions; Mom will quit her night job to stay home with her sons; the issue of "belonging" is left at bay. Readers and listeners who have caught a glimpse of the evening news can figure out there's more romance than realism here.

📖 *SO FAR FROM THE SEA* (1998)

Publishers Weekly

SOURCE: A review of *So Far from the Sea*, in *Publishers Weekly*, Vol. 245, No. 16, April 20, 1998, pp. 66-7.

Bunting's eloquent yet spare narrative introduces nine-year-old Laura, who recounts her family's 1972 visit to the site of the former Manzanar War Relocation Camp in eastern California. Thirty years earlier, her father and his parents were interned there, along with 10,000 other Japanese Americans. Soon to move to Boston, Laura, her younger brother and parents pay a final visit to the grave of the children's grandfather, a tuna fisherman robbed of his boat, home and dignity when the U.S. government sent his family to this remote camp, far from the sea he loved. Thoughtful and sympathetic, Laura has brought a chillingly ironic offering for the ancestor she never knew. It is the neckerchief from her father's Cub Scout uniform, which her grandfather had insisted his son wear on the day soldiers arrived at their home to transport them to the camp: "That way they will know you are a true American and they will not take you." [Chris] Soentpiet's portrait of the uniformed boy respectfully saluting the soldiers as his mournful parents embrace is only one of numerous wrenching images that will haunt readers long after the last page is turned. Rendered with striking clarity, the artist's watercolors recreate two vastly different settings, evoking the tense 1940s scenarios in black and white and the serene yet wistful 1970s setting in bright color. An exceptionally effective collaboration.

Jennifer M. Brabander

SOURCE: A review of *So Far from the Sea*, in *The Horn Book Magazine*, Vol. LXXIV, No. 3, May-June, 1998, pp. 329-30.

In 1972, the Iwasaki family visits Grandfather's grave at the site of the Manzanar War Relocation Camp. Seven-year-old Laura is angry at the injustice her father and grandparents experienced at the camp thirty years ago. Her feelings are thought-provokingly juxtaposed with her mother's reticence about her internment in a different camp and her father's simply stated desire to move on past "a thing that happened long years ago. A thing that cannot be changed." Laura has retrieved her father's Cub Scout neckerchief and brought it to place on the grave. (In a poignant, hopeless attempt, her grandparents had their son wear his Cub Scout uniform so the

soldiers might reconsider taking away and interning "a true American.") Laura's grandfather was a fisherman who died "so far from the sea"—and the scarf on his grave fluttering in the wind makes her think of sails and "a boat, moving on." With that, the neckerchief intersects both Laura's anger and her father's desire to forget the past, and father and daughter meet on common ground in their mutual sadness and in their agreement that Grandfather was "a true American." An afterword provides brief information but, like the text, tells only a piece of the story, making no mention, for instance, of the long struggle for reparations that gained momentum in the 1970s. Portraying both the starkness of the landscape and the camp and the beauty of the snow-covered mountains in the background, the watercolors have a photographic quality that suits the story's realism. Frequent scenes from the camp in 1942, presented in black and white, will guide young readers through the flashbacks in the text. The point of view expressed by Laura's father—one shared by many internees because of the shame they felt—is not often seen in books on this topic, and could provide plenty of room for discussion of changing historiographical and cultural expectations.

Shelley Harwayne

SOURCE: A review of *So Far from the Sea*, in *The New Advocate*, Vol. 11, No. 4, Fall, 1998, p. 365.

It is 1972, and we watch the Iwasaki family make their last visit to a grandfather's grave site before moving from California to New England. Laura's grandfather died in the Manzanar War Relocation Camp, an internment center for ten thousand Japanese-Americans during World War II. The author reveals a great deal of information about this historic period through the questioning of Laura's younger brother, her father's stories and memories and Laura's emotional response to the visit. The artist's realistic and finely detailed watercolor illustrations alternate from the dramatic colors of the present to the somber black-and-white of the 1940s wartime. As the writer suggests, "The way it was almost seems like a picture that got wiped out by a giant eraser." Our students were very moved by this compelling story. They appreciated the silk flowers left on the grave. They felt the young brother's socks slipping down into his boots as he walked. They understood why the grandfather named his fishing boat "Arigato," which means "thank you" in Japanese. They, too, agreed with Laura that the internment was not fair and with her father's comment that attacking a country is not fair either. They were touched when Laura places her brother's outgrown Cub Scout neckerchief on their grandfather's gravesite.

📖 *SOME FROG!* (1998)

Publishers Weekly

SOURCE: A review of *Some Frog!*, in *Publishers Weekly*, Vol. 245, No. 46, June 29, 1998, p. 58.

Huckleberry Finn has nothing on Billy when it comes to frog-jumping contests. Enticed by the grand prize of two tickets to a Cubs game at Wrigley Field, Billy plans to catch a whopper of a frog and enter it in the school contest. Best of all, Dad, who no longer lives with Billy and his mom, has promised to come over and help. Billy fights off tears when his unreliable dad just never shows up. But Mom, Grandma and Grandpa make sure Billy has a frog adventure to remember. Bunting's easy-flowing dialogue and realistic situations give this picture book/chapter book both depth and heart. She leads readers to experience disappointment, excitement and joy right along with Billy as he moves through a particularly emotional day. The story, broken into nine brief chapters, is generously illustrated with [Scott] Medlock's slightly impressionistic oil paintings, which feature familiar scenes of home and classroom as well as an arresting sequence showing Billy and Mom's nocturnal trip to the frog pond. The combination of ample art and plentiful dollops of text is just right for early and beginning readers, especially those who may enjoy an alternative to the many paperback series aimed at them.

Judith Constantinides

SOURCE: A review of *Some Frog!,* in *School Library Journal,* Vol. 44, No. 10, October, 1998, p. 87.

In a sensitive and honest story, Bunting captures the heartache of a child whose parent doesn't follow through on a promised excursion. Billy lives with his mother and grandparents, but his father has arranged to take him to catch a frog for his class' frog-jumping competition. When his father fails to show up and the expedition is threatened, his understanding mom and grandparents step in and help the boy learn that his life is really "very good the way it is," although his dad's presence would have enhanced the occasion. The author does an excellent job of presenting a realistic situation and its resolution in straight-forward yet eloquent prose. Medlock's bright oil illustrations appear on almost every page, adroitly mirroring the child's emotions and the contest events. This is an early chapter book, but its subject matter will appeal to slightly older readers as well.

Russ Merrin

SOURCE: A review of *Some Frog!,* in *Magpies,* Vol. 13, No. 5, November, 1998, p. 35.

There is to be a frog-jumping competition at his school, and to enter, Billy desperately needs to catch a frog. Dad has promised to help, but he never arrives. The contest is the big occasion on which Billy has been pinning all of his hopes.

Finally, when it becomes obvious once again that Dad isn't going to come, Mom, Grandma and Grandpa step in. Mom bakes frog cookies, Grandma makes a frog suit and Grandpa paints a frog mask. More importantly, Mom takes Billy to Miller's Pond where she catches the biggest, meanest gigantic frog in the lake. Can this new pet, Amphibian, match Billy's hopes and expectations? With the support of Mom and his grandparents, Billy enters his frog in the contest. Eve Bunting has written a warm, happy, satisfying tale about a small boy's developing awareness of the importance of family, and the painful need to come to terms with occasional adult indifference. Scott Medlock's oil painting illustrations evocatively capture this story's highlights and human details, and celebrate Billy's victory over his sadness and hurt. This moving story reflects the pain of growing up and the rewards of love and kindness in unexpected places. Billy finally does get his moment of glory at the school frog-jumping competition, but more importantly, he comes to value the family that he does have, and who in turn affirm that he is indeed, well-loved.

Additional coverage of Bunting's life and career is contained in the following sources published by The Gale Group: *Authors and Artists for Young Adults,* **Vol. 5;** *Contemporary Authors New Revision Series,* **Vol. 59;** *Junior DISCovering Authors; Major Authors and Illustrators for Children and Young Adults;* **and** *Something about the Author,* **Vols. 18, 64.**

Walter Crane

1845-1915

(Also illustrated as Ennis Graham) English illustrator of picture books, fiction, poetry, and nonfiction; author/illustrator of poetry and nonfiction; editor.

Major works include the "Toy Book" series (1867-76), *Walter Crane's Picture Book* (1872), *The Baby's Opera: A Book of Old Rhymes with New Dresses* (with Lucy Crane, 1877), *The First of May: A Fairy Masque* (written by J. R. de Capel Wise, 1881), *Household Stories from the Collection of the Brothers Grimm* (written by Jakob Grimm and Wilhelm Grimm; translated by Lucy Crane, 1882), *The Faerie Queen* (written by Edmund Spenser, 1894).

Major works about the illustrator include *An Artist's Reminiscences* (by Walter Crane, 1907); *Walter Crane as a Book Illustrator* (by Rodney K. Engen, 1975); *Walter Crane* by (Isobel Spencer, 1975); *Walter Crane, 1845-1915: Artist, Designer, and Socialist,* (edited by Sarah Hyde and Greg Smith, 1989).

INTRODUCTION

Often called the father of the illustrated picture book, Crane is considered one of the most talented and influential illustrators of the nineteenth century. He is also lauded for his contributions to European fine art and the decorative arts as both an artist and an educator. A member, with his contemporaries Randolph Caldecott and Kate Greenaway, of the triumvirate of artists dubbed "the Academicians of the Nursery," Crane is recognized as a pioneer in the development of picture books and illustrated works for children. His titles for this audience, which include nursery rhymes and songs, fairy tales, fables, poems, and concept books, are acclaimed as beautiful works that reflect the artist's skills as a designer, as well as his desire to entertain and educate the young. Crane is credited with transforming the genre of the children's book by using his artistry and technical ability to produce illustrated books that were aesthetically pleasing, appealing to children, and economical to produce. He is perhaps best known as the creator of the "Toy Book" series, approximately forty picture books that were issued in the large, slim format that gave the series its name. These works introduced small children to popular folk and fairy tales and nursery rhymes, as well as to concepts such as multiplication and the alphabet. Before Crane, books of this type were generally unimaginatively designed and cheaply produced; Crane, however, revolutionized the format by investing his works with bright colors, creative page designs, and sudden shifts in points of view, time, and perspective.

Noted for his range and versatility as an illustrator for

children, Crane provided the pictures for European fairy tales such as those of French fabulist Charles Perrault, German retellings by the Brothers Grimm, traditional English folk tales, *The Arabian Nights,* and contemporary stories such as *Goody Two Shoes.* He also created the popular "Baby's Own" series, books on which he collaborated with his sister Lucy, a teacher, and his mentor W. J. Linton. In these works, which were longer and more sophisticated than his toy books, Crane illustrated familiar rhymes and songs, as well as Aesop's fables. He also provided the pictures for fifteen well-received stories for children by Mary Louisa Molesworth, who wrote as Mrs. Molesworth, as well as for retellings of the legends of King Arthur and Robin Hood. In addition to works directed to young people, Crane was a prolific artist for adults. His pictures graced the works of such authors as Homer, Shakespeare, Edmund Spenser, Miguel de Cervantes, Dinah Maria Mulock, Nathaniel Hawthorne, Oscar Wilde, and Robert Louis Stevenson; he also collaborated on a collection of valentines with illustrator Kate Greenaway, who is thought to have created her classic picture book, *Under the Window*, as a companion to Crane's *The Baby's Opera.* In addition, Crane wrote poetry and his autobiography, as well as informational and theoretical books on art and design.

Crane approached each of his works as both an illustrator and a designer. Seeking to make his pictures an integral part of the design of each book, he is regarded as one of the first artists to propose that text and page design be planned in tandem. Blending ordered spacing and graphics with balanced areas of light and dark, Crane used line and color to unify his designs and give them style. Much of his early work shows the artist's use of bold, flat lines in both his black and white and color illustrations. His later pictures reflect a simpler, more open line and delicate use of color. Crane's mature work also demonstrates his interest in architecture and interior design. His illustrations are filled with elaborate furniture and objects such as vases and glassware, and were often used by professional designers to influence prospective clients. In his toy books, Crane's detailed illustrations amplify his texts, which are written into the artwork in script or placed in a box. He typically outlined figures in strong, bright colors such as black, green, and blue; depicted people in elaborate costumes, often reflecting the Elizabethan period; gave his animals a lively demeanor; framed his illustrations with dark lines; and included lavish double-page spreads in the center of each book. In all of his works, Crane included fanciful borders, title pages, and endpapers—many of which depict allegorical or symbolic themes—and places his signature, a long-legged crane set within his monogram, somewhere within each book. As an artist, Crane was influenced by a variety of sources, such as classical Greek art, the drawings and paintings of English poet and engraver William Blake, and the Pre-Raphaelites, a brotherhood of artists and poets organized in the 1840s to bring the beauty of early Italian painting to contemporary art. His most pronounced influences included Japanese prints—works that inspired Crane with their brilliant, yet delicate use of color—and the work of William Morris, an English artist, author, and craftsman who revived the Pre-Raphaelite Brotherhood and founded the Arts and Crafts Movement, an attempt by artists to provide an alternative to the effects of the Industrial Revolution by bringing exquisite design and craftsmanship to furniture and decorative objects.

Biographical Information

Born in Liverpool, England, Crane was the son of Thomas Crane, a well-known portrait painter, and his wife Marie. When he was three months old, Crane and his family moved to Torquay, a coastal city in South Devon, for his father's health. The Cranes then moved to Upton, a picturesque Devonshire village; in his autobiography, *An Artist's Reminiscences,* Crane wrote that here "a very happy child-life was passed, not oppressively shadowed by much governessing or schooling." Influenced by his father's studio work and sketching club, Crane began drawing at an early age. He wrote, "I was always drawing, and any reading or looking at prints or pictures, led to drawing again." After briefly

attending a private school for boys—where he distributed his drawings to his schoolmates on his last day—Crane moved to London with his family for his father's professional advancement. At thirteen, Crane drew a set of colored page designs for *The Lady of Shalott,* a poem by English poet laureate Alfred, Lord Tennyson. These drawings were shown to noted art critic John Ruskin, who praised the young artist's use of color, and to W. J. Linton, a writer, poet, and social reformer who was also considered the leading wood-engraver of his day. Recognizing Crane's potential as an illustrator and designer, Linton accepted the boy—then thirteen years old—as an apprentice. After three years, Crane became a professional freelance artist; he also took night classes at Heatherley's, a prominent London art school, while drawing pictures for books and magazines.

In 1865, Crane met the engraver Edmund Evans, a pioneer in the development of color printing. Evans involved Crane in his campaign to persuade publishers that the public would buy high quality picture books rather than the crude works that flooded the market. Although Crane initially illustrated books for Evans that ranged from cheap novelettes to works of a more refined nature, he soon focused on producing books for children that were influenced by his interest in Japanese color prints. In 1867, Crane and Evans arranged with the English publisher George Routledge to issue the first of their toy books, eight-page volumes that sold for a sixpence and were published approximately four times a year. In 1871, Crane married Mary Frances Andrews; the couple went to Italy for a long honeymoon, a trip that greatly influenced the artist, and later had three children—Beatrice, Lionel, and Lancelot. In 1872, Crane's publisher issued *Walter Crane's Picture Book,* an omnibus volume that was released without the artist's knowledge. The title brought Crane increased attention but no more money, since Routledge did not pay royalties. When his contract expired, Crane began working independently with Evans. In 1877, the pair produced *The Baby's Opera: A Book of Old Rhymes with New Dresses,* a work that combined old songs with forty nursery rhymes and fairy stories told in verse by Lucy Crane. The book became a best-seller and was followed the next year by *The Baby's Bouquet: A Fresh Bunch of Old Rhymes and Tunes.* Although not quite as successful as its predecessor, this work was still well-received. Before her death in 1884, Crane collaborated with his sister on *Household Stories from the Collection of the Brothers Grimm,* a volume of stories that is considered among the artist's best work. In 1886, Crane's teacher W. J. Linton provided the text for *The Baby's Own Aesop; Being the Fables Condensed in Rhyme.*

Crane wrote in *Imprint* magazine that children "like definite statements in design. They prefer well-defined forms and bright, frank colour." He also believed that children can learn "definite ideas from good pictures"; consequently, he created primers and alphabet books and sought to introduce moral and ethical values through his works. However, Crane was also concerned that the child's imagination was consistently stimulated with bright colors, sensitive lines, and symbolic imagery. He wrote, "The best of designing for children is that the imagination and fancy may be let loose and roam freely, and there is always room for humour and even pathos, sure of being followed by that ever-living sense of wonder and romance in the child heart. . . ." Crane also believed that the artist should be a reformer. A devout Socialist, he was considered the movement's most active artist. Crane lectured, published political cartoons in socialist magazines, and illustrated a book for young socialists. In addition, he was a leader in the Arts and Crafts Movement, becoming the first president of the Art Workers Guild in 1884 and the president of the Arts and Crafts Exhibition Society in 1888; except for a three-year period when William Morris took over, Crane remained in this position until 1912. Crane was also a prominent educator: he was director of design at the Manchester School of Art for three years, a period in which he revamped the school's curriculum, and also served as the art director of Reading College. In 1898, he became principal of the Royal College of Art in London. Crane influenced generations of artists by creating the drawing syllabuses for the school. These documents were used by art educators until the middle of the twentieth century. In addition to his work as an illustrator, teacher, and social advocate, Crane designed wallpaper, textiles, friezes, ceramics, carpets, tiles, and stained glass and also painted in oil and watercolor. A traveling exhibition of his work made a great impression on American designers of the era, and his frieze and mosaic decorations can be seen in several buildings in Britain. An internationally known figure, Crane was friends with many notable personalities of his day, including George Bernard Shaw, Howard Pyle, Oscar Wilde, and Edward Burne-Jones.

Critical Reception

Crane is generally considered a brilliant artist, as well as an effective educator, interior designer, and social reformer. As an illustrator, he is praised for his exceptional sense of composition and design and for his inventive use of color. Acclaimed for his knowledge of the engraving process and his skill as a draftsman, he is also celebrated for creating pictures that are imaginative, graceful, and charming and for providing fresh, colorful works that appeal to both children and adult audiences. He is further acknowledged for influencing other illustrators—Caldecott, Greenaway, and Aubrey Beardsley among others—who would continue to take the illustrated book to new heights. Although some critics regard his pictures as too detailed and elaborate, and have noted that the artist sometimes forgot his child audience in his quest to elevate taste, most observers recognize Crane as one of the greatest illustrators of all time, as well as a pivotal figure in the development of the children's book. Writing in *A Treasury of Children's Book Illustrators,* Susan E. Meyer stated, "In only ten years, . . . Crane transformed the children's book as it was known then by applying his considerable design skills to a more advanced method of production, raising the quality of

inexpensive picture books as no one before him had done. . . . Determined to lead his flock out of the darkness into a new era, this reformer promoted English theory and design to a wide audience, inspiring new generations of artists and designers. Yet his most ardent followers were oblivious to his polemics. Innocently turning the pages of his slender picture books, children throughout the world would remember Walter Crane not only for his theories, but for his simple gift of joy, for giving them these cherished moments in an imaginary universe where reason has no place."

Awards

Crane was honored internationally throughout his career. He received two French prizes, the Silver Medal (Paris) for *The Diver* in 1889 and the Gold Medal (Paris) in 1900 for mural tile design. He won the Gold Medal (Munich) for *Chariot of the Hours* in 1895. In 1903, Crane received his first Italian honor, the Commendatore of the Order of the Royal Crown of Italy. In 1906, he won the Gold Medal and Grand Prize at the Milan International Exhibition. In 1911, he was dubbed Caviliere, Order of S. S. Maurizio e Lazzaro in Italy. Crane also received an English award, the Albert Gold Medal, from the Society of Arts in 1904.

ILLUSTRATOR'S COMMENTARY

Walter Crane

SOURCE: *Of the Decorative Illustration of Books Old and New,* George Bell and Sons, reissued 1972, 237 p.

[*The following excerpt from* **Of the Decorative Illustration of Books Old and New** *was originally published in 1896.*]

As, until recently, I suppose I was scarcely known out of the nursery, it is meet that I should offer some remarks upon children's books. Here, undoubtedly, there has been a remarkable development and great activity of late years. We all remember the little cuts that adorned the books of our childhood. The ineffaceable quality of these early pictorial and literary impressions afford the strongest plea for good art in the nursery and the schoolroom. Every child, one might say every human being, takes in more through his eyes than his ears, and I think much more advantage might be taken of this fact.

If I may be personal, let me say that my first efforts in children's books were made in association with Mr. Edmund Evans. Here, again, I was fortunate to be in association with the craft of colour-printing, and I got to understand its possibilities. The books for babies, current at that time—about 1865 to 1870—of the cheaper sort called toy books were not very inspiriting. These were generally careless and unimaginative wood-cuts, very casually coloured by hand, dabs of pink and emerald green being laid on across faces and frocks with a somewhat reckless aim. There was practically no choice between such as these and cheap German highly-coloured lithographs. . . .

It was, however, the influence of some Japanese printed pictures given to me by a lieutenant in the navy, who had brought them home from there as curiosities, which I believe, though I drew inspiration from many sources, gave the real impulse to that treatment in strong outlines, and flat tints and solid blacks, which I adopted with variations in books of this kind from that time (about 1870) onwards. Since then I have had many rivals for the favour of the nursery constituency, notably my late friend Randolph Caldecott, and Miss Kate Greenaway, though in both cases their aim lies more in the direction of character study, and their work is more of a pictorial character than strictly decorative. The little preface heading from his *Bracebridge Hall* gives a good idea of Caldecott's style when his aim was chiefly decorative. Miss Greenaway is the most distinctly so perhaps in the treatment of some of her calendars.

Children's books and so-called children's books hold a peculiar position. They are attractive to designers of an imaginative tendency, for in a sober and matter-of-fact age they afford perhaps the only outlet for unrestricted flights of fancy open to the modern illustrator, who likes to revolt against "the despotism of facts." . . .

I think that book illustration should be something more than a collection of accidental sketches. Since one cannot ignore the constructive organic element in the formation—the idea of the book itself—it is so far inartistic to leave it out of account in designing work intended to form an essential or integral part of that book.

I do not, however, venture to assert that decorative illustration can only be done in *one* way—if so, there would be an end in that direction to originality or individual feeling. There is nothing absolute in art, and one cannot dogmatize, but it seems to me that in all designs certain conditions must be acknowledged, and not only acknowledged but accepted freely, just as one would accept the rules of a game before attempting to play it. . . .

It may not be amiss to add a few words as a kind of summary of general principles to which we seem to be naturally led by the line of thought I have been pursuing on this subject of book decoration.

As I have said, there is nothing final or absolute in Design. It is a matter of continual re-arrangement, re-adjustment, and modification or even transformation of certain elements. A kind of imaginative chemistry of forms, masses, lines, and quantities, continually evolving new combinations. But each artistic problem must be solved on its merits, and as each one varies and presents fresh questions, it follows that no absolute rules or principles can be laid down to fit particular cases, although as the result of, and evolved out of, practice, certain general guiding principles are valuable, as charts and compasses by which the designer can to a certain extent direct his course.

To begin with, the enormous variety in style, aim, and size of books, makes the application of definite principles difficult. One must narrow the problem down to a particular book, of a given character and size.

Apart from the necessarily entirely personal and individual questions of selection of subject, motive, feeling or sentiment, consider the conditions of the book-page. Take an octavo page. . . .

Although we may take the open book with the double-columns as the page proper, in treating a book for illustration, we shall be called upon sometimes to treat them as single pages. But whether single or double, each has its limits in the mass of type forming the full page or column which gives the dimensions of the designer's panel. The whole or any part of this panel may be occupied by design, and one principle of procedure in the ornamental treatment of a book is to consider any of the territory not occupied by the type as a fair field for accompanying or terminating design—as, for instance, at the ends of chapters, where more or less of the type page is left blank.

Unless we are designing our own type, or drawing our lettering as a part of the design, the character and form of the type will give us a sort of gauge of degree, or key, to start with, as to the force of the black and white effect of our accompanying designs and ornaments. For instance, one would generally avoid using heavy blacks and thick lines with a light open kind of type, or light open work with very heavy type. (Even here one must qualify, however, since light open penwork has a fine and rich effect with black letters sometimes.)

My own feeling—and designing must always finally be a question of individual feeling—is rather to acknowledge the rectangular character of the type page in the shape of the design; even in a vignette, by making certain lines extend to the limits, so as to convey a feeling of rectangular control and compactness, as in the tailpiece . . . from *The Faerie Queene.*

But first, if one may, paradoxically, begin with "end paper" as it is curiously called, there is the lining of the book. Here the problem is to cover two leaves entirely in a suggestive and agreeable, but not obtrusive way. One way is to design a repeating pattern much on the principle of a small printed textile, or miniature wallpaper, in one or more colours. Something delicately suggestive of the character and contents of the book is in place here, but nothing that competes with the illustrations proper. It may be considered as a kind of quadrangle, forecourt, or even a garden or grass plot before the door.

We are not intended to linger long here, but ought to get some hint or encouragement to go on into the book. . . .

If we are to be playful and lavish, if the book is for Christmastide or for children, we may catch a sort of fleeting butterfly idea on the fly-leaves before we are brought with becoming, though dignified curiosity, to a short pause at the half-title. Having read this, we are supposed to pass on with somewhat bated breath until we come to the double doors, and the front and full title are disclosed in all their splendour.

Even here, though, the whole secret of the book should not be let out, but rather played with or suggested in a symbolic way, especially in any ornament on the title-page, in which the lettering should be the chief ornamental feature. A frontispiece may be more pictorial in treatment if desired, and it is reasonable to occupy the whole of the type page both for the lettering of title and the picture in the front; then, if richness of effect is desired, the margin may be covered also almost to the edge of the paper by inclosing borders, the width of these borders varying according to the varying width of the paper margin, and in the same proportions, *recto* and *verso* as the case may be, the broad side turning outwards to the edge of the book each way. . . .

If I may refer again to my own work, in the designs to *The Faerie Queene* the full-page designs are all treated as panels of figure design, or pictures, and are enclosed in fanciful borders, in which subsidiary incidents of characters of the poem are introduced or suggested, somewhat on the plan of mediæval tapestries. . . .

A full-page design may, thus inclosed and separated from the type pages, bear carrying considerably further, and be more realized and stronger in effect than the ornaments of the type page, just as in the illuminated MSS. highly wrought miniatures were worked into inclosing borders on the centres of large initial letters, which formed a broad framework, branching into light floral scroll or leaves upon the margin and uniting with the lettering.

Much depends upon the decorative scheme. With appropriate type, a charming, simple, and broad effect can be obtained by using outline alone, both for the figure designs or pictures, and the ornament proper. . . .

The opening chapter of a book affords an opportunity to the designer of producing a decorative effect by uniting ornament with type. He can place figure design in a frieze-shaped panel (say of about a fourth of the page) for the heading, and weight it by a bold initial letter designed in a square, from which may spring the stem and leaves of an arabesque throwing the letter into relief, and perhaps climbing up and down the margin, and connecting the heading with the initial. The initialed page from *The Faerie Queene* is given as an example of such treatment. The title, or any chapter inscription, if embodied in the design of the heading, has a good effect.

Harmony between type and illustration and ornament can never, of course, be quite so complete as when the lettering is designed and drawn as a part of the whole, unless the type is designed by the artist. It entails an amount of careful and patient labour (unless the inscriptions are very brief) few would be prepared to face, and would mean, practically, a return to the principle of the block book.

Even in these days, however, books have been entirely produced by hand, and, for that matter, if beauty were the sole object, we could not do better than follow the methods of the scribe, illuminator, and miniaturist of the Middle Ages. But the world clamours for many copies (at least in some cases), and the artist must make terms with the printing press if he desires to live. It would be a delightful thing if every book were different—a millennium for collectors! Perhaps, too, it might be a wholesome regulation at this stage if authors were to qualify as scribes (in the old sense) and write out their own works in beautiful letters! How it would purify literary style! . . .

It might be possible to construct an actual theory of the geometric relation of figure design, ornamental forms, and the forms of lettering, text, or type upon them, but we are more concerned with the free artistic invention for the absence of which no geometric rules can compensate. The invention, the design, comes first in order, the rules and principles are discovered afterwards, to confirm and establish their truth—would that they did not also sometimes crystallize their vitality!

I have spoken of the treatment of headings and initials at the opening of a chapter. In deciding upon such an arrangement the designer is more or less committed to carrying it out throughout the book, and would do well to make his ornamental spaces, and the character, treatment, and size of his initials agree in the corresponding places. This would still leave plenty of room for variety of invention in the details.

The next variety of shape in which he might indulge would be the half-page, generally an attractive proportion for a figure design, and if repeated on the opposite page or column, the effect of a continuous frieze can be given, which is very useful where a procession of figures is concerned, and the slight break made by the centre margin is not objectionable.

The same plan may be adopted when it is desired to carry a full-page design across, or meet it by a corresponding design opposite.

Then we come to the space at the end of the chapter. For my part, I can never resist the opportunity for a tailpiece if it is to be a fully illustrated work, though some would let it severely alone, or be glad of the blank space to rest a bit. I think this lets one down at the end of the chapter too suddenly. The blank, the silence, seems too dead; one would be glad of some lingering echo, some recurring thought suggested by the text; and here is the designer's opportunity. It is a tight place, like the person who is expected to say the exactly fit thing at the right moment. Neither too much, or too little. A quick wit and a light hand will serve the artist in good stead here.

Page-terminations or tailpieces may of course be very various in plan, and their style correspond with or be a variant of the style of the rest of the decorations of the book. Certain types are apt to recur, but while the bases may be similar, the superstructure of fancy may vary as much as we like. There is what I should call the mouse-tail termination, formed on a gradually diminishing line, starting the width of the type, and ending in a point. Printers have done it with dwindling lines of type, finishing with a single word or an aldine leaf.

Then there is the plan of boldly shutting the gate, so to speak, by carrying a panel of design right across, or filling the whole of the remaining page. This is more in the nature of additional illustration to carry on the story, and might either be a narrow frieze-like strip, or a half, or three-quarter page design as the space would suggest.

There is the inverted triangular plan, and the shield or hatchment form. The garland or the spray, sprig, leaf, or spot, or the pen flourish glorified into an arabesque.

The medallion form, or seal shape, too, often lends itself appropriately to end a chapter with, where an inclosed figure or symbol is wanted. One principle in designing isolated ornaments is useful: to arrange the subject so that its edges shall touch a graceful boundary, or inclosing shape, whether the boundary is actually defined by inclosing lines or frame-work or not. Floral, leaf, and escutcheon shapes are generally the best, but free, not rigidly geometrical. The value of a certain economy of line can hardly be too much appreciated, and the perception of the necessity of recurrence of line, and a re-echoing in the details of leading motives in line and mass. It is largely upon such small threads that decorative success and harmonious effect depend, and they are particularly closely connected with the harmonious disposition of type and ornamental illustration which we have been considering.

It would be easy to fill volumes with elaborate analysis of existing designs from this point of view, but designs, to those who feel them, ought to speak in their own tongue for themselves more forcibly than any written explanation or commentary; and, though of making of many books there is no end, every book must have its end, even though that end to the writer, at least, may seem to leave one but at the beginning.

Walter Crane

SOURCE: "Early Work, 1862-70" and "Life in the Bush, 1873-79," in *An Artist's Reminiscences,* Methuen & Co., 1907, pp. 66-109.

During the year 1863 I had an introduction to Mr. Edmund Evans, and thus commenced a connection which has lasted to the present time, though Mr. Wilfred Evans now manages his late father's business.

Mr. Evans was one of the pioneers in the development of colour-printing, and not only did a quantity of ordinary trade work in this way, but also choice books. One of the directions in which his craft was extensively used was that of covers of cheap railway novels, which we sometimes called, from their generally yellow hue and sensational character, "mustard plaisters." Designs of this kind were my principal work for Mr. Evans at first, but later (about 1865) I began to design for him the children's picture-books published by the house of George Routledge & Sons which afterwards attained such popularity.

The first, however, were done for Messrs. Warne. They were a *History of Cock Robin and Jenny Wren, Dame Trot and Her Comical Cat,* and *The House That Jack Built.* They were designed with solid black or blue backgrounds, the figures being relieved against them in bright colours. The series for Messrs. Routledge commenced with a *Farmyard Alphabet* and a *Railway Alphabet,* printed in two colours only, in addition to the key block. These were followed by designs of figures without backgrounds printed in red, blue, and black, of which *The Song of Sixpence* is a type; but gradually more colours were used as the designs became more elaborate, until a few yearslater they had developed, under various influences, among which that of Japanese colour prints must be counted as an important factor. *The Fairy Ship* and *This Little Pig* are examples of this period.

Mr. Evans was not only a man of business but a clever artist in water colour himself, and aided my efforts in the direction of more tasteful colouring in children's books; but it was not without protest from the publishers, who thought the raw coarse colours and vulgar designs usually current appealed to a larger public, and therefore paid better, and it was some time before the taste for the newer treatment made itself felt. . . .

I . . . continued to do more work for Edmund Evans, and the demand for new picture-books went on at the rate of two a year. About 1869-70 they began to show something like a distinct decorative treatment and style, as I endeavoured to adapt them more both to the conceptions of children and to the conditions of colour-printing. In this I found no little helpful and suggestive stimulus in the study of certain Japanese colour prints, which a lieutenant in the Navy I met at Rode Hall, who had recently visited Japan in his ship, presented me with. He did not seem to be aware of their artistic qualities himself, but regarded them rather as mere curiosities. Their treatment in definite black outline and flat brilliant as well as delicate colours, vivid dramatic and decorative feeling struck me at once, and I endeavoured to apply these methods to the modern fanciful and humorous subjects of children's toy-books and to the methods of wood-engraving and machine-printing. *The Fairy Ship,*

This Little Pig Went to Market, designed in 1869, and *King Luckieboy's Party* (the verses and idea of which were supplied by me), in 1870 made this new departure, and led on to their successors, which shortly became numerous enough to be put in a separate category and labelled with my name by Messrs. Routledge. . . .

In 1874 was commenced the well-known series of children's story-books by Mrs. Molesworth, issued by the house of Macmillan. The first was *Tell Me a Story.* I remember being introduced to Mrs. Molesworth in the late Mr. G. L. Craik's office. Mr. Craik then acted as reader to the firm, and he arranged with me to supply the illustrations to these very pretty stories, which I continued to do for many years. . . .

The series of children's picture-books issued by Messrs. Routledge & Co., which had been added to year by year, had now come to an end with *The Sleeping Beauty in the Wood.* I had offered to continue them if granted a small royalty, but as the firm took the line rather of the provincial trader who said, "We lose on every article we sell, it is only the quantity that makes it pay," there was nothing further to be hoped for in that direction, so I struck. Taking counsel with my friend the printer, Mr. Edmund Evans, we planned a book of another order, and *The Baby's Opera* was the result. . . .

The Baby's Opera turned out a great success, although at first "the Trade" shook its head, as the sight of a five-shilling book not decently bound in cloth and with-

Walter Crane at the age of 21.

out any gold on it was an unheard-of thing, and weighing it in their hands and finding it wanting in mere avoirdupois weight, some said, "This will never do!"— but it *did.* The first edition of 10,000 copies was soon exhausted, and another was called for, and another, and another. It has long passed its fortieth thousand, and, like "Charley's Aunt," is still running.

No doubt the combination of favourite nursery rhymes with pictures, as well as the music of the old airs, made it attractive, and commended it to mothers as well as children.

I was indebted to my sister for the arrangement of the tunes, which she collected with considerable care and research; but she was a pianist of much taste and skill, and possessed a considerable knowledge of music, both ancient and modern, and the task was a congenial one, I feel sure.

I received many gratifying letters about the book, and perhaps I may quote one from Professor von Herkomer, which I thought as coming from an artist of his distinction a particularly spontaneous and generous tribute.

DYREHAM, BUSHEY, HERTS

December 8, 1876

DEAR SIR,—I have not the pleasure of knowing you personally, but I hope you will allow me to express my great admiration for your last book, *Baby's Opera.* The sweet humour, the dainty design, and the good drawing of the pictures make it a delight for every person of taste, no matter what age he or she may be.

Wishing you may enrich the world with many such books yet, I am, dear Sir, yours very truly,

HUBERT HERKOMER

W. CRANE, Esq.

The success of *Baby's Opera* made the publishers "ask for more," and I had a visit from Mr. Edmund Routledge (whose daughters I had painted, by the way, in the spring of that year (1877), a water-colour picture of the two young girls full length sitting upon a settee) to ascertain whether I would do another at once, as he said people were already asking "what was to be Walter Crane's next book."

Having my hands full of other work, and not wishing to produce a less spontaneous book simply to meet commercial demands, I was not prepared to accede to his wishes. He had suggested a Birthday Book, too, an idea which I did not care for, so that I did not follow up this success immediately.

This unbusiness-like laxity on my part at least gave others their opportunity, and if I had opened the door with a new class of books, others soon pressed in.

Among Messrs. Routledge's Christmas announcements (in the *Athenæum*) for that year I was rather startled to observe "Companion Volume to *The Baby's Opera*"(!), Miss Kate Greenaway's first children's book, *Under the Window,* being thus introduced to the world by the publishers. This I thought quite misleading, and wrote to protest, and the announcement was withdrawn. Miss Greenaway, in collaboration with Mr. Edmund Evans as the colour-printer, had produced a pretty book of nursery rhymes, with illustrations, treated, as far as the outline and flat tint method went, in a similar way to mine, but less formal, without the decorative borders, without the music, and of quite a different size. Her success from the appearance of this book was assured. She followed it up quickly, too, so I imagine she made more hay while the sun shone than I did, which, for the time at least, shone brightly enough for her, even if it did not shine so long.

I did not meet Miss Greenaway till some time afterwards, and only once. . . .

The success of *Baby's Opera* even attracted the attention of the Editor of *Punch,* then Mr. (now Sir) F. C. Burnand, who despatched a brief note to me, of which the following is a copy:—

GARRICK CLUB, W.C.

DEAR SIR,—Would you be open to a Christmas book with me?—Yours truly,

F. C. BURNAND

I have the notion.

I did not, however, feel at liberty then to take it up, having my hands full, and so there was another might-have-been to be recorded.

Still another might-have-been must be mentioned. "Lewis Carroll" (Mr. C. L. Dodgson of Christ Church, Oxford) wrote to me early in 1878, saying he had been looking out for a new illustrator for a forthcoming work of his, as after *Alice in Wonderland* and *Alice through the Looking-Glass,* Tenniel would do "no more." This Mr. Dodgson evidently greatly deplored, and naturally felt that it would be most difficult to find a substitute. His letters gave one the impression of a most particular person, and it is quite possible that he may have led Tenniel anything but a quiet life during the time he was engaged upon his inimitable illustrations to the immortal *Alice.* . . .

I believe I agreed to meet his views if possible, but my hands were so full of all sorts of other work that I fear the year went by without my being able to take the matter up. The story, too, of which he sent me a por-

tion, was of a very different character to *Alice*—a story with a religious and moral purpose, with only an occasional touch of the ingenuity and humour of *Alice,* so that it was not nearly so inspiring or amusing.

GENERAL COMMENTARY

Jacqueline Overton

SOURCE: "Illustrators of the Nineteenth Century in England," in *Illustrators of Children's Books 1744-1945,* compiled by Bertha E. Mahony, Louise Payson Latimer and Beulah Folmsbee, The Horn Book Inc., 1947, pp. 25-86.

About 1859, while John Leech and Tenniel were doing their finest for *Punch,* Walter Crane, the son of an artist, was working hard as an apprentice to W. J. Linton, the wood engraver, and learning to draw on the block. . . .

After practical work with Linton he joined evening classes at Heatherley's, a well-known art school in London, in order to study from the life and costume models. His first independent work began with designs for the paper covers of cheap railway novels (mustard plasters, they were called, because of their yellow hue and sensational character). These were executed by Edmund Evans.

At that time, about 1865, Mr. Evans was taking a definite stand against the crude, colored illustrations on the market for children. He had the courage to believe that paper picture books might be made beautiful in color and design and still be sold for a sixpence "if printed in sufficient quantity." Young Crane was interested in the idea and was easily persuaded to try the experiment with him, but the publishers were not so keen. The public, they maintained, must like the "raw colors and vulgar designs" that Evans complained of since they bought them—so why risk losing on something new?

Frederick Warne was the pioneer publisher to fall in with the movement for better color, and Crane's first nursery picture books, *The House That Jack Built, Dame Trot and Her Comical Cat* and the *History of Cock Robin and Jenny Wren,* were published by his firm. These were designed with solid black or blue backgrounds, the figures being relieved against them in bright colors. About 1865, the publisher, Routledge, followed suit, and the series of sixpenny picture books Crane made for Routledge numbered about thirty-five titles.

The use of flat, almost primitive colors, bold, black outline drawn with a sure stroke, an ever-present sense of design, were all characteristics of Crane's work from beginning to end, and this second group of books shows the influence of his growing interest in Japanese prints.

A navy friend brought Crane some prints, more as a novelty than anything else, but he was charmed with them. "Their treatment," he says, "in definite black outline and flat, brilliant as well as delicate colors, their vivid, dramatic and decorative feeling struck me at once and I endeavored to apply these methods to the modern fanciful and humorous subjects of children's toy books and the methods of wood engraving and machine printing."

One, Two, Buckle My Shoe, and This Little Pig are perhaps the simplest of these nursery books in treatment. The Absurd ABC, Valentine and Orson and Puss in Boots show a stunning use of black. Puss begging a pair of boots from the miller's son is one of Crane's most delightful early pictures.

In the Baby's Alphabet we find a gay lot of little individual drawings charmingly placed on a page without a sense of overcrowding, but Blue Beard and The Sleeping Beauty both suffer from too much detail. Design cramps and outweighs the drama of the story of Blue Beard and the classic setting of The Sleeping Beauty seems forced and lacking in charm and humor. The same may be said of the rather disconcerting introduction of contemporary costume into Cinderella.

The Fairy Ship and King Luckieboy's Party, however, are two entirely satisfying and festive picture books. Father Christmas arriving at Luckieboy's party in a snow storm is enough to put anyone in holiday humor.

Several of these early picture books were done while Walter Crane and his bride were enjoying a leisurely honeymoon in Italy. "Mother Hubbard's dog," he says, "I took the liberty of depicting as a poodle—that type flourishing at the time in Rome." The drawings, he tells us, "were made on cards in black and white and sent by post to Edmund Evans in London, who had them photographed on the wood and engraved, returning me the proofs to color. This method of work was beginning to supersede the old practice of drawing direct on the block for the engraver. It certainly had its advantages, not the least among which was that of being able to retain the original drawing."

While abroad, something else occurred which is startling evidence of the lack of protection and appreciation accorded an illustrator in those days. "While I was in Italy," writes Crane in his autobiography, "the publishers who at first were by no means converts to the effort we were making to get more artistic color treatment in their books, perceiving a growing demand for them, issued a set of my sixpenny books bound together and called it Walter Crane's Picture Book, but without my knowledge. This volume, though far from being what I should have approved in its general format, certainly served as a poster for me; and was, I believe, a commercial success; but as I had no rights in it, it was of no benefit to me in that respect. My drawings for these books were done for a very modest sum and sold outright to the publishers. The engraving and printing was

costly, and a very large edition had to be sold in order to make them pay; as many as fifty thousand of a single book, I was told, being necessary. However, if they did not bring in much money, I had the fun out of them." The fun consisted in working out a number of theories in color, design, etc., for Crane's work was in the experimental stage and he was strongly under the influence of William Morris and his school of craftsmen.

Hence Crane took toy books more seriously than any of his predecessors had done, and drew every picture with a two-fold aim—as a piece of illustration and likewise as a piece of design. He was one of the first to feel that text and page should be planned in harmony, and he often carried this theory to the extent of executing parts of the text himself in bold, distinctive, red and black letters. The end papers and title pages of his picture books are delightfully entertaining, and even his signature (a long-legged bird set within his monogram) has a style of its own.

Beginning about 1873, he designed a second series of toy books for Routledge which Edmund Evans again printed. These sold for a shilling each, and a greater and more pleasing variety of colors was used and the plan of the page was more spacious. Occasionally, as in the first series, they lack humor and are too elaborate. One feels at times Crane's interest in design and setting led him to forget the children for whom these books were intended. "I was," he confessed, "in the habit of putting in all sorts of subsidiary detail that interested me and often made them the vehicle for my ideas in furniture and decoration." Nevertheless these books all have real distinction—The Yellow Dwarf, The Frog Prince, The Alphabet of Old Friends, and the Hind in the Wood are delightfully fantastic. Aladdin and Beauty and the Beast both riot in color, and Goody Two-Shoes is the most lovable of them all. . . .

About this time Mrs. Molesworth began a series of children's stories that were destined to become popular on both sides of the ocean. Beginning with Carrots, Walter Crane made the illustrations for about sixteen of them. The majority were done in black and white, with his usual heavy pen strokes; a few were tinted. It is a pity that in the apparently necessary reduction in size the clearness of many of these pictures is lost.

Before telling of Crane's drawings for The First of May, we must go back to the year he was seventeen and still at Linton's. At that time Mr. J. R. Wise was about to publish a book on the history and scenery of the New Forest, and his publishers, Smith and Elder, suggested that young Walter Crane draw the illustrations for the book. . . .

Mr. Wise was in Sherwood Forest in the spring of 1878, working under its spell on a fairy masque to be called The First of May. He sent for Crane to come down and hear the masque read and to plan some illustrations for it. It was to be published as an illustrated gift book and Walter Crane writes, "Together we made out the scheme of arrangement and list of illustrations for the whole book. . . . The work of my friend was steeped in the knowledge and love of the country and was the product . . . of an ardent lover of nature."

The following spring they were again there, working on the book, and the Forest about Edwinstowe and Ollerton was so beautiful that Crane returned in the summer with his wife and family "to enjoy it better and see it in its full panoply of leaves and bracken," while he continued to work on *The First of May.* When the drawings were completed they were so in harmony with the text, so at one with the Forest "as Shakespeare must have imagined it for *Midsummer Night's Dream,*" that it seems impossible the book is not the conception of a single mind. It is by far the most imaginative, whimsical, and beautiful thing Crane ever did and it is executed with rare delicacy and skill. Fairies, elves and imps, children, lovers, shepherds and shepherdesses, and the Queen of the May herself roam the borders of the pages, while birds and insects and beasts of many sorts, real and imaginary, play a part in the revel and dance about their own Maypole.

> Hedgehog, hare, mole, fieldmouse play;
> Squirrel leap with all your might,
> 'Till birds envy you your flight;
> Glitter, insects, scale on scale!
> Dance thou knight in armour, snail!
> Come all creatures here today,
> Welcome to our Queen of May!

The drawings were all made in pencil and were afterwards reproduced by photogravure by Messrs. Goupil and Co., the plates being done in Paris. "The reproductions were slightly reduced in scale, were very well done, and gave the silvery, delicate effect of the pencil drawings most successfully." No font of type was delicate enough to harmonize with the designs, so Crane lettered every word of the text by hand, a tremendous task, but the beauty of the finished page must have rewarded him. The book was dedicated to Charles Darwin, from the author and the artist.

As may be imagined, the cost of the reproduction of *The First of May* was great, and it could only be published in a limited edition; hence this book, which shows Walter Crane at his best, is comparatively little known. . . .

After completing the toy books, Crane and Edmund Evans planned a book of another order, a book of old rhymes with the music set on one side of the page and the illustration on the other. "*The Baby's Opera* turned out a great success, although at first the trade shook its head, as the sight of a five-shilling book not decently bound in cloth and without any gold on it was an unheard-of thing; and weighing it in their hands and finding it wanting in mere avoirdupois weight, some said, 'This will never do'—but it did. The first edition of ten thousand copies was soon exhausted, and another was called for and another," and we might add that *The Baby's Opera* and its two successors, *The Baby's Bou-*

quet and *The Baby's Own Æsop,* which were published as companion volumes during the next two Christmas seasons, still remain favorite picture books. There is a distinct charm about the size of these little square books. The tunes for both *The Baby's Opera* and *The Baby's Bouquet* were arranged by Walter Crane's sister, Lucy, who was a skillful pianist. The text of *The Baby's Own Æsop* was done by Crane's old master, Linton, who sent it to him from America, where he was living in 1886.

Later, in 1892, "when the babies who were present when *The Baby's Opera* had its first season were all grown up," the three little books were published together in a large de luxe edition for collectors—very fine; but *Triplets,* as the special edition was called, lacks the charm of the individual books.

Lucy Crane likewise did the translation of the text of Grimm's *Household Stories,* for which her brother made the illustrations. Some of Crane's most distinctive pen and ink work appears in this book which was engraved by Swain and printed by Clark. The lines are clear-cut and reproduce exceedingly well; the head- and tail-pieces and the initial letters are delightful, and after many years it still holds its place as one of the most pleasing and all-round satisfying editions of the old folk tales, and is perhaps the best known of any of Crane's work.

Martin Hardie

SOURCE: "Neglected Centenaries," in *The Studio,* Vol. 136, No. 666, September, 1948, pp. 75-8.

Walter Crane began publishing his first 'toy-books' fifteen years before Kate Greenaway and [Randolph] Caldecott entered the field. His series of sixpenny books, published between 1864 and 1869, included *The Railroad Alphabet, The Farmyard ABC* and, best of all in decorative aim and quaint humour, *A Song of Sixpence.* At an early stage in producing these books he was amused by a request from the publishers that some children designed for his next book 'should not be unnecessarily covered with hair', this being considered a dangerous innovation of Pre-Raphaelite tendency. In these sixpenny books he was limited to the use of red, blue and black. The range of colour was enlarged for *The Fairy Ship* in 1869, with 'raisins in the cabin; almonds in the hold', all under the command of the captain who said 'Quack!' and anticipated Donald Duck as a marine adventurer. In the famous *Baby's Opera* of 1877 the colours were still more extended. The price was five shillings, and Routledge, who was publishing the volume for Evans, scoffed at the notion of ten thousand copies being printed, especially with no gold on the cover. The public thought differently, and further editions were soon in demand.

In all of Crane's books, ending with the *Floral Fantasy* in 1899, the important element is decoration. His creed, expressed in his *Decorative Illustration of Books,* was that each picture must be an organic element, forming an integral and constructive part of the book as a unified whole. Even end-papers must be 'delicately suggestive of the character and contents of the book . . . a kind of quadrangle, forecourt, or even grass plot before the door'. . . .

Isobel Spencer

SOURCE: In *Walter Crane,* Macmillan Publishing Co., Inc., 1975, pp. 39-100.

Walter Crane's reputation as a children's book illustrator is founded on colour work for sixpenny and shilling picture books printed by Edmund Evans and published by Routledge between 1865 and 1875. . . .

> The books for babies current . . . —about 1865 to 1870—of the cheaper sort called toy books were not very inspiring. These were generally careless and unimaginative woodcuts, very casually coloured by hand, dabs of pink and emerald green being laid across faces and frocks with a somewhat reckless aim. There was practically no choice between such as these and cheap German highly coloured lithographs.

This is how Crane later assessed the range of inexpensive nursery books available when he began to design them. He minimizes the efforts of good printers, other than Evans, such as Vizetelly and Vincent Brooks, who were working variations on Baxter's patent, and the reference to cheap coloured lithographs probably alludes to the firm of Kronheim which, by that date, was run by Oskar Frauenknecht whose standards were not as high as those of the firm's founder. Crane's comments on bright colour are critical of a generally held belief among publishers that the brighter the book the better suited to the taste of children. However, his earliest toy books are as brash as many of their companions in different series, and it was only gradually with Evans's help that this was modified, although Crane rarely made use of the very gentle colour harmonies printed by Evans for Kate Greenaway.

Walter Crane's earliest toy books reveal his skill as an animal draughtsman. The characters in the first, *The History of Jenny Wren,* are drawn with a naturalist's attention to detail and yet are treated in a sympathetic and comical way guaranteed to make an immediate appeal to children. This was one of three titles illustrated by Crane for a New Shilling Series issued by Ward Lock and Tyler at Christmas 1865. All were printed by Evans. *Jenny Wren* was prepared with a black key and backgrounds, a practice quite common in picture book printing at the time, and three colours, red, brown and green. The gold overprinting of the backgrounds in the surviving examples may have been added to relieve what originally must have been a very sombre colour scheme. Crane's designs are well balanced but the amount of stippling and hatching on the key block shows how unfamiliar he was with the effects of colour printing. The other two books were printed in five colours and a

black key, *The House That Jack Built* having bright blue backgrounds with pictures printed in ochre, red, green and brown. The result is quite crude and, as with *Jenny Wren,* confused by too much texture drawing on the key block. Crane remedied this fault by the time he came to design the *Comical Cat* with its clear outline and minimal furry texturing. This picture toy has cheerful red backgrounds. A design such as that of the 'Fox and Cock' in *The House That Jack Built* shows the young artist following a fairly traditional line of animal drawing and in this respect he is every bit as accomplished as well established animal draughtsmen like J. B. Zwecker and T. W. Wood. Other pages are more remarkable for a new wit and vitality and Crane may well have been influenced by Grandville's amusing interpretations published in *Scènes de la vie privée et publique des animaux* of 1842. *The Comical Cat* has a surprising gay abandon and her large scale and anthropomorphic role are oddly disconcerting. She is, nevertheless, a more sympathetic companion for children than the sinister inhabitants of Katzland illustrated by Baxter's former pupil, Harrison Weir, for *The Cat's Tea Party,* one of Routledge's New Shilling Series of Toy Books printed by Vincent Brooks, which also came out at Christmas 1865. . . .

The stylistic development of Crane's colour work for Routledge reveals increasing fluency and confidence as he learned how to make the most of printed colour and to exploit his own talents as an imaginative and decorative draughtsman. He handled the animal subjects of the first Sixpenny Toy, *The Farmyard ABC,* with his accustomed dexterity, but the ABC aspect involved a design problem which resulted in both this and its successor, *The Railroad ABC,* appearing relatively restrained in comparison with the bright bold designs for Ward Lock. The Routledge format was narrower and Evans's colour printing more limited. Both have key designs in black on a white ground, *The Farmyard ABC* with red, yellow and green, and the *Railroad ABC* with red and blue. The large alphabet letters are not particularly impressive and contribute less than they might have done to a strong page design. He carefully researched railway details for the second book but, despite this, something of the stiffness affecting Crane's drawing of everyday life scenes is still evident.

The next two books, *Sing a Song of Sixpence* and *The Waddling Frog,* were unhindered by ABCs and Crane found himself dealing with themes open to more lively and imaginative interpretation. The pages are unframed and emphasis is concentrated on the appropriate figures, animals and accessories. Lines from the rhymes appear at the top of each page in thin Gothic lettering headed by a large initial. He considered *Sing a Song of Sixpence* his first successful attempt at more careful design. In *The House That Jack Built* there had already been an opportunity to introduce medieval decorative features and these also add to the quality and characterisation of his deft drawing for *A Song of Sixpence.* This Pre-Raphaelite legacy was one that the young illustrator was to find useful, for many of the picture books, including *The Old Courtier,* the next to be published, are full of details of gothic architecture, mounted knights, falconry and feasting.

The titles issued in 1867 and 1868 show Crane and Evans experimenting with more subtle colour, but the results in *The Old Courtier* are unsatisfactory. Evans printed here using tint blocks of purple, blue and yellow and the effect does not help to unify or give emphasis to Crane's busy designs, which are further confused by the need to accommodate large portions of text. *Multiplication Table* and *Chattering Jack* are less complicated. The 'Ten Steamboats' and 'Twenty-Two Ships' pages of the former are fine designs, probably deriving from studies made on a visit to Plymouth the previous summer. A similar combination of semi-geometrical principles and shallow illusory space appears in parts of *Chattering Jack* like the 'slice' of modern life in the page with a staircase and abruptly truncated foreground figures. Of the Crane Sixpenny Toys issued in the next year, *How Jessie Was Lost* appeals least, being a feeble story, badly told by Lucy Crane and not visually interesting. On the other hand, the everyday life themes in *Grammar in Rhyme* are quite entertaining and its design is more confident. Pale shades contrast with stronger accents achieved by overprinting the hatched key colour with blue or red. Both these numbers were printed in a dark brown key and three primaries.

It is in the next two toy books, *Buckle My Shoe* and *Annie and Jack in London,* that Crane achieves a fully integrated decorative style. The same colours are used with the addition of a flesh tone, which does away with the striped effect created in earlier books by printing fine red lines to suggest pink, and there are fewer tint effects and more flat colours. Dark accents cover larger areas and are positive factors in creating bold design. A clue to a new factor affecting this change is to be found in a page of *Buckle My Shoe* which has a screen decorated with a design from a Japanese print. The confident outline, diagonal compositions and use of bold page patterns show the important influence of Japanese prints. For the first time Crane is explicit about choosing artistic furniture for his interiors. Blue and white crockery, ebonised clocks and chairs make their own comment on Japanese influences affecting English taste. It is more difficult to see these characteristics in the active pages of *Annie and Jack*—a story by Lucy Crane about children visiting the sights of London—except that they too take on a new assurance with strong outline and confident arrangements of figures against coloured or plain backgrounds. Crane had been given some Toyokuni prints by a naval lieutenant recently returned from Japan. This occurred at an opportune moment because he had not yet resolved the style and presentation of his own picture books. The 'definite black outline and flat brilliant as well as delicate colours, vivid dramatic and decorative feeling' of the woodcuts provided him with the very example needed, and he began to apply these characteristics to the treatment of the historical and humorous subjects of toy books and to the techniques of wood engraving for machine printing.

The four books published in 1870, *The Fairy Ship, The Adventures of Puffy, This Little Pig Went to Market* and *King Luckieboy's Party* owe an obvious debt to Japan in their new compositional freedom and large areas of bright (but not garish) flat colour. Though still using three primaries, a key and a flesh tint, Evans now set off bright colours against softened blues and greens achieved through subtle texturing of the block and overprinting. Every page of *The Fairy Ship* is delightful, with pompous Captain Duck and his bustling and conscientious crew of white mice attending to the satin sails, and cargo of raisins and almonds. *Puffy,* whose story was written by Lucy Crane, presented greater problems with its longer text. To include this the pages were divided into compartments, a device which possibly also owes something to Japanese methods. The five *Little Pigs* are less elaborate, but distinguished by a truly impressive fleshy grandeur, made all the more ridiculous by their pinafores, ruffs and breeches, and their demure domestic setting. *King Luckieboy's Party* illustrates a rhyme written by Crane himself and based on the idea of the months and the zodiac signs presenting their compliments to Luckieboy. Such a theme, lending itself as it did to fantastic personifications, was to prove a favourite with him. Some of the designs are strikingly impressive with their quaint figures set against backgrounds of flat colour. The effect is bolder than is usual in Japanese prints and in this respect he may also have been influenced by recent English book illustrations like

From The Arabian Nights, *illustrated by Walter Crane.*

the decorative chromolithographedgift books *Paradise and the Peri* (1860), and *Scenes from the Winter's Tale* (1866), designed by Owen Jones with figures by Albert Warren. Crane's style of around 1869 is even closer to the work of Henry Stacy Marks which he specifically admired for the 'bold outlines and flat tints' of two toy books published as part of Routledge's Shilling Series in 1865, *Nursery Rhymes* and *Nursery Songs,* each including six full colour pages printed by Vincent Brooks. Crane's earliest books have little in common with these designs and it is only in the simplified style of those of a few years later that the connection becomes more obvious. He was brought directly into contact with this work around 1869 when Routledge had him design a cover for a composite volume to contain reprints of the *Rhymes* and *Songs,* called *Ridiculous Rhymes,* which was published for Christmas 1869. In Crane's view the medieval character of these illustrations almost certainly added to their charm. His debt to them can be seen in a page like the 'Old King Cole' design for Cassell's *The Merrie Heart* (1871), a book containing six colour plates printed by Evans with black-and-white work by other artists. This shows, too, how Crane's own tendency to load his pages with decoration and detail has prevailed, in spite of the lessons in economy which he might have learned from Stacy Marks or from Japanese prints.

The excellent sales of Walter Crane's toy books encouraged Routledge in 1870 to begin to issue composite volumes of several titles, and the rapid consumption of these were proof of the artist's well established popularity as a children's illustrator. In 1873 Routledge began the New Series of Walter Crane's Toy Books at sixpence, following it in the next year with the Shilling Series. A new cover was designed for each: one with a Crane in a blossoming tree and an audience of birds with little children's heads printed in green, black and red on buff; the other with an orange tree printed in two shades of blue and orange on white. The pictures inside were produced somewhat differently from the earlier numbers of the original series and instead of a flat flesh tone, Evans used a hatched flesh colour with denser spots for cheeks, while he continued with the same number of colour blocks—a brownish red, a greyish blue, and yellow, with black or brown key. *Noah's Ark ABC* the very last of the original Sixpenny Toys is a puzzling book stylistically, having weaker outline and less assured design than its immediate predecessors. It seems also to represent a transitional stage in Evans's change of flesh tone printing. Here a hatched brown is used to describe the dark-skinned natives and also for the texture of animals' coats. . . .

Ideas already adopted or invented by Crane are further developed in the picture books of 1873 and 1874: interiors with painted tiles, potted plants and ebonised furniture; elaborate historical costumes and architectural settings; a style involving black as an important decorative element in the rich pattern of the page and the pages themselves framed in a black line with a separate compartment for the text. Animals like the peevish bears who so terrify poor Silverlocks as ever play an impor-

tant part. Some of the richest effects are achieved through quite unorthodox juxtapositions of styles. Owen Jones's works on ornament, Japanese prints, English MSS, early printed books, Renaissance painting—all may have sown the seeds which blossom in profusion in the picture books; but no child nor even an art-historically anxious adult would wish to alter Ali Baba's orient, or inhibit Valentine and Orson's time-travelling in Dark Age France and the Egypt of the Pharaohs. A fine feature of these toy books is the centre spread for which, in the case of **Cinderella, Valentine and Orson** and **Puss in Boots,** Crane drew splendid sequences. Italian influence, discernible in the glimpses of orange trees, cypresses and heraldic devices in **Valentine and Orson,** is very marked in the Renaissance settings of **Bluebeard** and the Titianesque gowns of his wife and her maidservants. In the last of all the Series, he transfers an essentially Gothic French tale to the Mediterranean. The Sleeping Beauty rests in a Roman palace guarded by a maiden, a harper and soldiers. An owl in a spandrel and poppy in a pot symbolize sleep, while the prince struggles through the thicket, his pose like that of a Michelangelesque slave, clad in leather armour and wearing a sun-decorated mazzocho.

Less dense black is used in the books of 1875, the key is often brown, and a more nervous mellifluous line replaces the confident, sometimes quite angular emphasis of earlier books like **The Three Bears.** A technique, to be seen as early as the *Merrie Heart* pages, where leaves and grass texture are indicated by little dots or strokes, is used more often. Obvious geometry is softened by the text now being framed in a parchment scroll instead of a box. Burne-Jones and Botticelli, whose *Spring* and *Venus* Crane sought out on his visit to the Uffizi in 1871, are sources for this style and the flower-strewn grassy carpets and fruit-laden trees derive from these or other Quattrocento examples, although the exaggerated ideal profiles, rather boneless limbs and fleshy tapering hands suggest the mannerism of the Cinquecento. Even spatial arrangements depending on perspective rather than a frieze system become quixotically extreme in such settings as the centre spread of **The Yellow Dwarf** with its gigantic turkey-cocks, or its final page with the goose-drawn chariot and the tiny figure of Toutebelle by the steel castle.

The Shilling Series is the same as that to which Harrison Weir and Stacy Marks had contributed and in it Crane had greater scope than with the Sixpenny Toys. The format was larger and text was printed on separate pages. The colour range was extended too: in addition to a dark brown key, Evans printed in six colours—usually flesh tone, buff, yellow, red and two shades of blue.

In 1874, **The Frog Prince, Goody Two Shoes, Beauty and the Beast** and **The Alphabet of Old Friends** were issued. Crane designed six pictorial alphabets for Routledge: **The Railroad, Farmyard** and **Noah's Ark ABCs** of 1865 and 1872 which may be said to subscribe to a fairly traditional pattern, and **The Absurd Alphabet** (1874), **The Baby's Own Alphabet** and **Alphabet of Old**

Friends (1875) in which he explores different ideas of layout using more flexible subject matter taken from nursery rhymes and stories. The animal characters of the *Absurd ABC* are set in vertical compartments printed in red and yellow, with gold letters, against a black ground. The rollicking mood of these pages is close to contemporary designs by Crane for the coloured covers of Beeton's Humorous Books, also printed by Evans. The ABCs of 1875 are less hilarious but still funny and more artistic in colouring than their absurd forerunner. The sixpenny version, *The Baby's Own ABC,* presents a wealth of witty material in scenes organized in comic strip form, their captions below, and letters on a ladder down one side. The sumptuous shilling *Alphabet of Old Friends* introduces many nursery favourites in a variety of page layouts punctuated with gold roundels carrying the capitals. However, it is for the beast fairy-tales in the Shilling Series that Crane produces some of his finest designs: *Beauty and the Beast* and *The Frog Prince* are rich in decorative detail and convey also, in contrast to their obvious glamour, a real sense of horrific fantasy. Beauty's discomfiture, so well expressed by her despairing countenance and lash-frilled eyes, and the control of design in the perspective interior of the page where Froggy visits his beloved, are just two examples of this masterly handling. Crane's uninhibited enjoyment in such pictorial fantasy is equally obvious from the exotic creations of 1875: *Aladdin, Princess Belle Etoile, The Hind in the Wood* and *The Yellow Dwarf.* . . .

Picture books were appreciated not only in the nursery but by adults in the parlour and library and even by artists and architects who used them to give clients an idea of the way in which their own homes could be decorated. They were a readily available source of ideas for those following the latest modes of the Aesthetic Movement. Routledge had at first been anxious lest Crane's designs would reflect avant-garde sympathies, and had asked him not to make his heroines look like Pre-Raphaelite girls with masses of long hair. Soon the pages of the picture books were characterized by his own unique blend of detail and decoration in which lively narrative was held captive in brilliant kaleidoscopic designs. Despite the obvious enjoyment derived from this work, it was not a self indulgent artistic exercise. Crane wanted to please the children. He had none of his own when he began to design picture books, but he was not long in forming ideas about what was suitable and these show a sensitive understanding of the child's point of view in keeping with the changing Victorian attitude:

> Children, like the ancient Egyptians, appear to see most things in profile, and like definite statement in design. They prefer well defined forms and bright frank colour. They don't want to bother about three dimension. They can accept symbolic representations. They themselves employ drawing . . . as a kind of picture-writing, and eagerly follow a pictured story. When they can count they can check your quantities, so that the artist must be careful to deliver, in dealing with, for instance . . . 'The Song of Sixpence', his tale of twenty-four blackbirds.

Educationally, the picture books served a key function because children could learn 'definite ideas from good pictures' long before they could read or write. Crane is most characteristically a man of his age in the importance he attached to the imagination in a child's early development. Later, when artists like Arthur Rackham peopled their pages of books for the young with Gothic ghouls and bogeys he was anxious that they should not have too disturbing an effect on the young, but he put no curb on the artist appealing to a child's imagination 'in a healthy way'. The imagination freed both the childlike and the artistic spirit:

> The best of designing for children is that the imagination and fancy may be let loose and roam freely, and there is always room for humour and even pathos, sure of being followed by that ever-living sense of wonder and romance in the child heart—a heart which in some cases, happily, never grows up or grows old.

[*The Baby's Opera: A Book of Old Rhymes with New Dresses*] had been issued at Christmas 1876. The nursery songs in this little book were arranged for the piano by Lucy Crane and it was a more ambitious production than previous efforts shared by Crane and Evans. The small quarto format derived from a series of six-inch tiles which Crane had just designed for Maw and Company. Other essentials were worked out during a stay at Evans's home at Witley in Surrey and the printer made up a dummy book for Crane to plan the layout. The experimental nature and success of this venture are clear from the artist's own account:

> . . . at first 'The Trade' shook its head, as the sight of a five-shilling book not decently bound in cloth and without any gold on it was an unheard-of thing, and weighing it in their hands and finding it wanting in mere avoirdupois weight, some said 'This will never do!'—but it *did*. The first edition of 10,000 copies was soon exhausted and another was called for, and another, and another. It has long passed its fortieth thousand and, like 'Charley's Aunt', is still running.

This compact little volume is one of Crane's most successful early decorated books. Its pictorial cover deftly introduces motifs from the lively contents. Hubert Herkomer's response to 'the sweet humour, the dainty design, and the good drawing' and his claim that it would be 'a delight for every person of taste no matter what age he or she may be' indicates the approval with which *Baby's Opera* was welcomed in discerning circles. . . .

[In 1875] Crane made black and white designs for *Tell Me a Story,* the first of eighteen books by Mrs. Molesworth which he was to illustrate for Macmillan. The series followed an octavo format with a red cloth cover printed in black and gold, six full-page illustrations, a frontispiece and a small picture for the title page. Within this scheme there was only limited scope to experiment with cover design. His black and white style for Mrs. Craik's books is rather mannered with very formally posed figures. This is also the case with the frontispiece to *Tell Me a Story.* In the better pictures for Mrs. Molesworth's books he succeeds with a relatively simple and sympathetic interpretation of the various domestic dilemmas and imaginative adventures of her little heroes and heroines. Crane's handling of children is more appealing than his treatment of adults and it must be concluded that despite the enormous popularity of these books their illustrations often fall below the mark. *The Adventures of Herr Baby* (1881) (an exception for the series because it was produced in quarto and had an attractive pink cloth with a design printed in brown) has illustrations which suffer badly from their expansion to a larger format. Best among the earlier books are *The Cuckoo Clock* and *The Tapestry Room* and the happiest results are to be found in the later books like *Christmas Tree Land* (1884) whose illustrations are treated in a more linear technique and are full of lively assurance. . . .

Crane responded more imaginatively when he was using material of his own choice as in the *Baby* books. With Evans he had learned what it was like to have complete control over all design aspects of a book's production and, in the future, he wanted to plan his own format, binding, endpapers and page layout. Up to this time, apart from the single colour outlines of *Mrs Mundi,* his black and white work was chiefly limited to the frontispiece or a few full page pictures set opposite pages of type. His chance to take fuller advantage of his developing ideas on design in monochrome occurred with the commission of a book for his old friend John Wise. *The First of May: A Fairy Masque,* which was dedicated to Charles Darwin, was published by Southeran and Company in 1881 in a lavish oblong folio edition of two hundred copies and one of three hundred in a smaller format. Most of the illustrations were done in 1878 and 1879 during a series of visits to Sherwood Forest, the setting chosen for Wise's fairy-tale adventure in a Mayday variation on *A Midsummer Night's Dream.* Fifty-two pencil designs were finished the following spring. These were reproduced by Goupil and Company using photogravure, a process Crane found highly satisfactory.

It is delightful as an inventory of imaginative design: little studies of animals and birds, grotesques, frogs, flowers and elves woven into a delicate interlace or set against grassy carpets, numerous fairies in déshabillé and dressed for amateur theatricals, even troupes of smocked and bonneted babes and miniature rustics—more decorous, pretty and Kate Greenaway-like than ever before. Burne-Jones greatly admired this gift book. Indeed, the pencil medium may have been suggested by his *Aeneid* drawings. Many other details reflect the influence of the older artist's work such as the flowing bands of drapery of the Rainbow Guardian in the 'Procession of Spring', Crane's androgynous nudes and various perpendicular compositions which echo the gentle spiral of 'The Golden Stairs', one of Burne-Jones's major works of the decade. Although Crane was freed from the geometry which had been imposed by musical notation in the case of *Baby's Opera* and *Baby's Bouquet,* he chose to keep a compartmented page layout here

"Cock Robin and Jenny Wren," from An Artist's Reminiscences, *written and illustrated by Walter Crane.*

also. A similar page layout was also to be used in the songbook *Pan Pipes.* In *The First of May* he introduced little motifs around the text, which was harmoniously incorporated into the design by being hand-written and not, as in the case of the earlier books and *Pan Pipes,* in type. His style at this stage combines fluency with considerable restraint. As the decade advanced it was to become more abandoned and gain the organic linearism generally associated with his maturity.

An energetic line characterizes many examples of his earlier work (in *Mrs Mundi* for instance) but it was only during the 1880s that Crane in the company of other English designers evolved stylistic characteristics which are usually associated with Art Nouveau. This development may be studied in an analysis of the illustration of two books issued by Macmillan in 1880 and 1882 and of three illuminated poems reproduced in the *English Illustrated* Magazine during 1884 and 1885. The first of the Macmillan books was *The Necklace of Princess Fiorimonde* by Mary de Morgan. Her brother, the ceramic designer William de Morgan, had illustrated her previous book, *On a Pincushion,* published by the same firm in 1877. Crane followed this example by including headings and tailpieces as well as full page illustrations. However, where de Morgan chose a deliberately primitive style for the small text embellishments, Crane's were derived from early printed books. His full page illustrations are confidently planned around stable horizontal and vertical axes. They are more relaxed in effect than the earlier frontispiece for R. L. Stevenson's *Inland Voyage,* with more fluent treatment of forms and drapery. *Princess Fiorimonde* has a fine grey cloth cover with devices stamped in black and gold. Crane's skill in handling headings and tailpieces is more vigorously demonstrated in the next Macmillan book, the *Household Stories of the Brothers Grimm* which Lucy Crane translated at the suggestion of Mr. Craik. Crane was delighted with the subject. He tackled the vivid and grotesque fantasies of the text decorations with the enthusiasm of a gothic illuminator let loose on his marginalia. The influence of Renaissance printed books, particularly the work of Dürer and Holbein which had already played its part in the development of Crane's drawing style, is very obvious in the full page designs which are given elaborate geometrical and semi-architectural frames. The flowing rhythms apparent in *Princess Fiorimonde* develop a new urgency in the Germanic pages of the Hausmärchen. The angularity of the seated figure of 'The Goose Girl' is broken down by the hatching lines of the grass, the folds of her dress, her fluttering hair and fleeing Conrad. This new spontaneity is proclaimed with a flourish in many tailpieces. The red and green cover incorporates the design of a fantastic house and there are endpapers with motifs from the stories. . . .

As his young family grew up Crane would invent and illustrate stories for them in little picture books. These were strictly for home consumption. Only *Legends for Lionel* and *Lancelot's Levities* were published in Crane's lifetime. The family knew these as the 'black books' from the shiny covers of the notebooks bought for the purpose. Their author described these sketches as 'the offspring of the odd half hours of winter evenings' and a glance at almost any one of the twenty-nine books at Yale and Harvard reveals a delightful succession of fact and fancy. The early ones are the most inventive. From 1879 to the *Notebooks for Beatrice* of 1882 Crane used pencil and water-colour wash, from *Beatrice's Bearings* of 1883 the medium was ink and water colour. It is fascinating to see how he adapted ideas to suit the characters and taste of his children: fairies and flowers for Beatrice, adventurous and artistic incentives for Lionel, and mostly pure fun for Lancelot, whose chubby form equipped him for a variety of roles.

The earliest surviving 'black book' is one completed for Beatrice's sixth birthday on 20 February 1879, *Beatrice in Fairyland.* Accompanied by her good fairy the little girl explores the heavenly bodies and the mountains of the moon, and is encouraged up the ladder of learning—as inevitably were all the little Cranes. She falls into the clutches of mis-spelling, is rescued by friendly letters of the alphabet and sails on a sea of ink to the kingdom of sums. That same year Lionel has lessons in ABC and drawing, in his *Primer and Copy Book.* He ascends the steps of knowledge to find himself in a painter's paradise where he is taught the primary colours by Major General Red Coat, Miss Daffodil and Bluebell, and then meets Rainbow who introduces him to her band of colours represented by Scarlet Poppy, Orange, Leaf Green

and Violet girls. Designs from *Beatrice Her Book of Beauties* were worked up for publication in two large pages with images arranged like those of comic strips. Some idea of the later books may be had from *Legends for Lionel* and the charming *Mouse's Tale,* which was published by Yale University in 1956.

These private picture books were the testing ground for ideas developed in three publications of the mid-1880s, *Slateandpencilvania* (1885), *Little Queen Anne* (1886) and *Pothooks and Perseverance* (1886). They were issued by Marcus Ward and Company separately and in a composite volume under the title *The Romance of the Three R's* (1886). By this time Thomas Crane was Art Editor of the firm. The designs were drawn on zinc lithographic plates using a very fine brush but Walter Crane was not so pleased with the colour of this printing as he had been with the results Evans achieved. *Slateandpencilvania's* theme was first explored in *Lionel's New Picture Book* of November 1880. *Little Queen Anne* appeared initially only shortly after this in the opening page of *The Adventures of Beatrice* of 1881, where she receives an invitation to meet the occupants of a great house—the Library of Learning. Sir Percyvere's hobby horse tilting at pothooks has its earliest precedent in Lionel's charge at a canvas in a notebook of 1880.

Stylistically this last of the Marcus Ward series is notable for its development of flowing rhythms and flourishes and in this respect may be compared with the last of the triplets, *Baby's Own Aesop,* which was published by Routledge in 1887, a decade later than *Baby's Opera* and *Baby's Bouquet.* These delicately coloured and compact volumes set the precedent for a series of highly successful 'aesthetic little quartos' published by Warne and Marcus Ward in the early 1880s and designed by J. C. Sowerby, Thomas Crane and a cousin of the Cranes, Ellen Houghton. Thus, *Baby's Own Aesop* had to face more serious competition than *Baby's Opera.* Crane used a text devised by his old master W. J. Linton but this was not very suitable for young children. From a commercial point of view the *Aesop* was the least successful of the *Triplets,* as these three Crane-Evans productions were called when they were published together in 1899.

In the spring of 1886 Crane was asked to design a book to commemorate a theatrical event based on new translations of Homer and Aeschylus by Professor Warr of Kings College, London. The first part of this entertainment, 'The Tale of Troy' was performed in 1883 and was repeated, together with 'The Story of Orestes' at a performance at the Prince's Hall in 1886. Crane's *Echoes of Hellas* was published by Marcus Ward in the following year. Many designs were based on stage settings devised by well-known artists; that of 'Aphrodite's Pledge Redeemed' for example from a tableau by Sir Frederic Leighton. This project allowed Crane to indulge his love of the antique. . . .

Some of the finest pages are very simple and reveal an

economy rare in Crane's work. The classical theme encouraged the portrayal of statuesque figures moving with noble calm and heroic gesture but, as in the page of 'The Furies', he occasionally relaxed into a more abandoned linear style. Fluent draughtsmanship, originally developed in **The Sirens Three,** appears in several books of 1887 apart from certain sections of **Echoes of Hellas** and **Baby's Own Aesop.** Most noteworthy perhaps is **Four Winds Farm** by Mrs. Molesworth. This highly personal graphic expression culminated the following year in Crane's designs for **Flora's Feast,** one of the most remarkable contributions to herald the decade of Art Nouveau. **Flora's Feast, A Masque of Flowers,** was published by Cassell and Company in 1889. It contains forty unframed colour-lithographed pages illustrating Flora calling the flowers from their winter sleep, each one appearing according to its place in the yearly cycle. The idea of using flower-clad figures had been worked out earlier in a tentative way in Lionel's unpublished *Primer and Copy Book.* Crane must have also been familiar with Grandville's designs in *Les Fleurs Animées* (1847) but his floral figures have none of the formality which lingers on even in these lively creations. Such apparently effortless invention is misleading however, because Crane's effects could not possibly have been achieved without considerable understanding of plant form.

Natural form was the most usual source for decoration in mid-Victorian design as well as during the Art Nouveau period of the 1890s. Blake's importance is closely linked with the way in which he combined human forms with flowers, flowing water, flames and leaves in a manner highly suited to the linear expression of this organic style. The page of 'Lilies, turned to Tigers' shows Crane responding in a similar fashion as well as introducing a famous piece of Blake imagery. Crane's **Tennyson** set of 1859 and his studies for **The New Forest** reveal an early interest in flora but he soon found that his zoo studies were of more use for picture books. When he turned his attention to commercial design around 1875 he began to rely increasingly on floral motifs and by the later 1880s made free use of such patterns although he still tended to incorporate more animal and figure subjects than did Morris and other wallpaper designers. Plant studies from nature are not as common in Crane's sketchbooks as might be supposed from his surprisingly accurate and apparently spontaneous interpretations of such forms. Instead he made use of early printed herbals and, like Morris, recommended these as sources, not only of information but as models of fine woodcut design. Of the three famous herbals, by John Gerard, Pier Andrea Matthiolus and Leonhard Fuchs, it was the latter's *De Historia Stirpium* which Crane particularly admired and he used illustrations from Morris's copy for one of the Cantor lectures in 1889. Crane praised Fuchs' designs for being drawn 'in fine free style'. This source is quite obvious in the decorative borders of **The Book of Wedding Days** published by Longmans Green and Company the same year. But it is **Flora's Feast** which best represents Crane's achievements at the close of the decade. Here motifs, which by 1889 might have been expected to have quite withered

and died from aesthetic overexposure, are pictured with all the freshness and charm of a new discovery.

Colleen Denney

SOURCE: "English Book Designers and the Role of the Modern Book at L'Art Nouveau; Part One: Modern Merriment and Morality in the Art of Walter Crane," in *Arts Magazine,* Vol. 61, No. 9, May, 1987, pp. 76-83.

In June of 1896 Siegfried Bing held an international exhibition of modern books at his Parisian gallery entitled the "Exposition Internationale de Livre Moderne à L'Art Nouveau," which included the productions of every major international innovator in the resurgence of book design. . . .

This international exhibition was a phenomenal accomplishment which included both books and illustrated magazines. Bing showed contemporary developments, up to April of 1896 in some cases, alongside books which were strategic examples of the historical development of the modern book. Major figures from England included William Morris Kelmscott Press productions, often illustrated by Burne-Jones, toy books and personal texts by Walter Crane, toy books by Randolph Caldecott, examples of the collaborations of Charles Ricketts and Charles Shannon, and the works of Aubrey Beardsley, and Laurence Housman; these English examples numbered some 245 in all. . . .

Bing's interest in English innovations in design was not an isolated example since the English book designers were being emulated, exhibited, and discussed elsewhere in Europe and America prior to Bing's experiments with the book exhibition at *L'Art Nouveau.* . . .

Crane and English book designers in general were being emulated and admired on the Continent and in America prior to Bing's exhibition in France. As a book illustrator, Crane was extremely influential in his theories as well as in his designs. In 1891 he published his series of Cantor lectures on the Decoration and Illustration of Books, which were first delivered to the Society for Encouragement of Art Manufacture and Commerce in 1889. In 1892 **The Claims of Decorative Art** was published which proved extremely influential on the Continent. In 1892 *Arts and Crafts Essays* appeared by members of the Arts and Crafts Exhibition Society that included an introduction by Crane as well as his essay on **"Of Decorative Painting and Design".** The year of Bing's modern book exhibition Crane's study on **Of the Decorative Illustration of Books Old and New** appeared. Crane, therefore, was quite visible and influential in promoting the decorative arts; President of the Art Worker's Guild in 1884, he was also later President of the Arts and Crafts Society as well as Director of Design at The Manchester School of Art.

The implementation of Crane's theories into practice in his series of toy books and personal texts helps to establish the beginning of design reform in the British book which can be characterized by its construction, clarity, simplicity, and spareness, as opposed to the cluttered aspect of previous Victorian design taste. These qualities of British design appealed to Bing as he called for form to follow function in his own workshop.

Crane began working with the printer Edmund Evans in 1865 on his toy book designs which were transferred to color woodblocks and published by various firms. *The Fairy Ship* was part of a group later known as the Sixpenny Toy Series which was exhibited at the 1896 book exhibition. The endpapers of the book represent part of the overall book building aesthetic of which Crane says in *Of the Decorative Illustration of Books Old and New:*

> The problem is to cover two leaves entirely in a suggestive and agreeable, but not obtrusive way. One way is to design a repeating pattern much in the principle of a small printed textile, or miniature wall-paper, in one or more colours. Something delicately suggestive of the character and contents of the book is in place here, but nothing that competes with the illustration proper. It may be considered as a kind of quadrangle, forecourt or even a garden or grass plot before the door.

The idea of a "miniature wall-paper" suggests that the end papers are the walls of a house, of an interior world which we are about to enter. As Crane states, "We are not intended to linger long here, but ought to get some hint or encouragement to go on into the book." We are given a clue of what is inside and the endpapers invite our curiosity. The actual illustrations from the book text repeat the images of the ship and the duck Captain, examples of the continuity of a motif.

Even in these earliest designs, such as *Jack and the Beanstalk,* Crane is thinking in terms of a unified design that works within the confines of the book page. He frames the text and sets it off in a different color so that it will not interfere with the illustration but rather complement it. Crane expresses that:

> A respect for form and style in lettering is . . . one of the most unmistakable indications of a good decorative sense. A true ornamental instinct can produce a fine ornamental effect by means of a mass of good type or MS. lettering alone: and considered as accompaniments or accessories to design they are invaluable, as presenting opportunities of contrast or recurrence in mass or line to other elements in the composition. To the decorative illustrator of books they are the unit or primal element from which he starts.

During this same period of book illustration in the 1870s and 1880s, Crane also produced independent publications with Edmund Evans, of which *Baby's Bouquet* was one. Crane's methods as translated in these designs and the idea of the book's construction exemplify his theory on unification. It was in the planning of *Baby's*

Opera that Evans gave Crane "a dummy book" so that he could "design the volume complete, with the pages in relation to each other and in strict accordance with the exigencies of the press and the cost of production." Crane had full control over the building of this book within certain bounds enforced by the required size and the finances available for the project, as well as the restrictions of the press. What set Crane apart was his sense of decorative unity and "build-up" of suspense in the organization of a book and its ornament. He expresses his consciousness of the functional object of the book thus:

> I think that book illustration should be something more than a collection of accidental sketches. Since one cannot ignore the constructive element in the formation—the idea of the book itself—it is so far inartistic to leave it out of account in designing work intended to form an essential or integral part of that book.

Each individual design becomes part of a whole, just as in designing an interior of a home, each object is taken into account in terms of its function. This concept of unison continues in Crane's book illustrations for the *Household Stories from the Collection of the Brothers Grimm* which are striking examples of Crane's ability to manipulate the structure of various images in different tales within one volume so a sense of continuity is immediately recognized. The elementary compositional features of the frames with their inscriptions and tondos echo, as always, the rectangular structure of the page, and unify the individual designs in a series of fairy tales, just as in the next book, *Pan Pipes,* Crane adapted the shape of the book and its illustrations to suit its special purpose: to sit conveniently on a piano by virtue of its oblong form. Crane incorporates the music as a text which is surrounded by its illustration in *The Three Ravens.*

In relation to Crane's own description of what the experience of opening one of his books should be like, he states:

> A book may be the home of both thought and vision. Speaking figuratively, in regard to book decoration, some are content with a rough shanty in the woods, and care only to get as close to nature, in her more superficial aspects, as they can. Others would surround their house with a garden indeed, but they demand something like an architectural plan. They would look at the Frontispiece like a facade; they would take hospitable encouragement from the title page as from a friendly inscription over the porch; they would hang a votive wreath of dedications, and so pass on into the hall of welcome, take the author by the hand, and be led by him and his artist from room to room, as page after page is turned, fairly decked and adorned with picture, ornament, and device; and perhaps finding it a dwelling after his desire, the guest is content to rest in the single nook in the firelight of the spirit of the author or the play of fancy of the artist, and, weaving dreams in the changing lights and shadows to forget life's rough way and the tempestuous world outside.

"Here We Go Round the Muberry Bush," from Favorite Poems of Childhood, *comprised of selections from* The Baby's Opera *and* The Baby's Bouquet, *illustrated by Walter Crane.*

Again we see Crane using the idea of a house, suggesting that this inspired interior world should truly be a three-dimensional experience for the reader. These book designs emphasize the importance of the function of the object and are examples of utilitarian forms which have been subjected to design reform.

In the image from *King Luckieboy's Party,* which was included in Bing's book exhibition, and also in *Eleven, Twelve, Ring the Bell,* from *One, Two, Buckle My Shoe,* Crane utilizes elements of design and decoration that align him with the Aesthetic Movement, art-for-art's-sake, and ideally, tasteful art for the people's sake. As one critic described it, "One effect of the movement was to revolutionize nursery books with their frequent motifs of sunflowers, pomegranates, cranes, and melancholy girls in languid gowns," a perfect description of the women portrayed in these images. They reflected even further the ideas of the Aesthetic Movement in the inclusion of ebonized furniture, and blue and white tiles, and the illustration from *Buckle My Shoe* even includes a Japanese screen, all of which were items associated with the selected elitism of this tendency. In fact, interior designers would keep toy book illustrations on hand to show clients how to arrange their homes in the Aesthetic mode. This is a further example of architectural thinking on Crane's part since, in these samples and others like them, he not only perceived the book as a house but each illustration as an interior.

The Aesthetes were especially attracted to Japanese objects since each object was seen as equal, no matter what its medium; the fine and the applied arts held the same importance. *The Fairy Ship* was part of a series,

with *This Little Pig Went to Market,* and *King Luckieboy's Party* (all of which were exhibited in the book exhibition), that Crane described as utilizing the influence of Japanese prints that he had received from a naval officer. In these illustrations Crane uses flat planes of simple, sharply delineated color and daring asymmetrical arrangements and the bird's-eye view so common to Japanese wood blocks. He incorporates elements essential to the Aesthetic Movement and later to Art Nouveau—asymmetry and animal imagery—into a unified design. These ideas are extended to his treatment of the human form as the illustration from *King Luckieboy's Party* shows.

Crane's synthesis of Greek and Japanese motifs in a decorative design characteristic of Aestheticism occurs in *Baby's Own Aesop.* The design of *The Fox and the Crane* aligns Crane with the Aesthetic Movement in painting as practiced by Albert Moore and Whistler in which these sources of inspiration are also combined. . . .

Of Crane's later designs in the 1890s, four books were included in the show, one of which was *The Story of the Glittering Plain,* on which Crane collaborated with Morris. Crane did the illustrations while Morris did the ornate borders. The design of the illustrations are characteristic of the Arts and Craft movement in the airless medieval earthiness which is so often associated with Morris' Kelmscott Press. That Bing included Crane's collaboration with Morris in his book exhibition is further documentation of his recognition of Crane's involvement with the Arts and Crafts movement in England.

Crane was also producing works that can now be understood as direct precursors of the Art Nouveau books of the 1890s in their linearity, dependence upon nature for inspiration, and in their two-dimensional flourish. An illustration from *The Sirens Three,* which was written and illustrated by Crane, shows forms that have become organic and flowing. Its linear, swirling movement anticipates the developments of the 1890s. The naiveté of Crane's children's books have been modified in his images from *Flora's Feast* in order to have greater appeal to adults. These flower transformations were a source of admiration for later Symbolists including the French poet Comte Robert de Montesquieu who compared Crane's dreamlike equations of flower and human forms with the flower maidens in Wagner's *Parsifal.* Crane's versatility with these metamorphoses has reached a culmination in this book. The type and the design both take part in this transformation which has that simplicity and spareness coupled with the feeling for architectonics that is a triumph of Crane's ability. This illustration from *Flora's Feast* is a good example of the ideas espoused in Crane's later theory book on *Line and Form* in which he states that objects drawn derived from individual elements in nature. Crane used this idea to place figures and objects within the confines of a rectangular book page. This is another example of linear treatment that is restricted to the form and function of the object it adorns. In his development of forms from nature, Crane can be aligned with Proto-Art Nouveau tendencies which express themselves through the growing cult of plant and line that would eventually explode in Continental Art Nouveau. Thus, the variety and quality of Crane's work in book design was well represented at *L'Art Nouveau*. The sheer volume of Crane's creations and his writings are testimony to the necessity of his inclusion in such a major exhibition which addressed modern developments in book design.

Susan E. Meyer

SOURCE: "Walter Crane," in *A Treasury of the Great Children's Book Illustrators,* Harry N. Abrams, Inc., Publishers, 1987, pp. 79-94.

Nothing irritated Walter Crane more than hearing reviewers describe him as the "Academician of the Nursery." For one, his designs for children represented only a part of his total output as an artist and designer. For another, he felt he had dedicated his entire career to innovation and experimentation, achievements that represented to him the very antithesis of the term, academician. . . .

Although his colorful and delightful books have entertained children for over 100 years, his achievements are more remarkable than these little books might suggest. In only ten years—between 1865 and 1875—Crane transformed the children's book as it was known until then by applying his considerable design skills to a more advanced method of production, raising the quality of inexpensive picture books as no one before him had done. While he was, it is true, a charming illustrator, he also represented a new breed of designer whose work and ideas influenced many generations of artists that followed him.

Born on August 15, 1845, the son of a locally respected portrait painter, Walter Crane was encouraged to paint and draw from the very outset. . . . His father, sensing a potential career for his son, presented young Walter's efforts to William James Linton, whose printing and engraving company was among the best in England. . . .

Because Linton had perceived Crane's talent for drawing and for inventive design, he gave the lad work to develop this talent—assignments at the zoological gardens for practice in drawing animals, and assignments to improve the faulty animal drawings of others drawn on the block, and even an occasional assignment as a press artist.

When Crane's apprenticeship ended in 1862, Linton provided him with introductions to potential clients, which landed him some respectable commissions. The following year, one of these clients introduced Crane to the man who would be responsible for establishing Crane's reputation as a children's book illustrator: Edmund Evans. . . .

Until this time, Crane had little experience with color work, but he soon adapted. On his part, Evans immediately took note of Crane's talents, with a single qualification: "The only subjects I found he could not draw," Evans wrote, "were figure subjects of everyday life." Since so many of the yellow backs portrayed just these everyday life scenes, Evans decided that the illustrator's gift for imaginative subjects would be better applied to children's books. As it turned out, Evans had already considered extending his own color printing activities to include inexpensive children's books, and so he embarked on a program of printing a new line of books, using new methods of production.

He devised a means of creating an eight-page form designed from cover to cover, and printed in color throughout, so economically planned that these slim, large-format volumes could sell for sixpence. For a toy book—as these sixpenny editions were called—the front cover was pictorial and the last page carried advertisements.

The toy-book idea was not new. Designed simply to entertain, these slender, inexpensive picture books appeared soon after the accession of Queen Victoria in 1837 and were devoured by the Victorian middle-class readers almost immediately. . . . Crane, however, did not find these early picture books terribly commendable: "They were not very inspiring. These were generally careless and unimaginative woodcuts, very casually coloured by hand, dabs of pink and emerald green being laid across faces and frocks with a somewhat reckless aim."

Working under Evans' technical direction, Crane was able to produce sixpenny toy books that were attractive and imaginative, and he created an average of three a year. His training with Linton had prepared him for these experiments, as Crane himself observed: "I consider it was an advantage to me thus to have been assisted with a definite handicraft, as well as an art like wood engraving, instead of going through the usual academic or art course." His efforts surely paid off: during the ten years he worked in tandem with Evans he became the most famous children's book illustrator of his day. Although Crane's achievements after that period extended into many other areas of design, these books he created with Evans clearly identified him as the "father of the illustrated children's book."

They made a good team. For each book, Evans handed Crane a precise layout of the entire volume, and the illustrator made his drawings following the pattern set forth in this dummy. After Evans transferred the drawing to the block, he pulled a proof and gave it to Crane for coloring. Then Evans mixed the colors with the same powdered pigment the artist had used on the colored proof. To keep down the printing costs, Evans used just three colors at first—not ten to twenty as many of the other printers did—although he increased this number with later publications. As Crane became more adept at designing with color, his books revealed greater imagination and fluency in their execution. Because the paper lacked opacity, each sheet was printed on one side only, the reverse left blank. A heavier sheet of paper was employed for the cover, pasted on both sides, and stitched through the center of the book in a single gathering. . . .

Evans contributed more than technical assistance to Crane: he acted as Crane's artistic and business adviser as well. Evans advised Crane about subject matter, about layouts and design, and he managed the business transactions with the publishers. At the outset, both Crane and Evans worked for Frederick G. Warne and for Ward Lock Publishers, but soon Routledge took over the publication of all Crane's children's books. In addition to the Sixpenny Toy Series created for Routledge, Crane also produced a Shilling Series of picture books. By 1875, Crane had created twenty-nine sixpennies for Routledge and eight shilling books, and their sales were so good that the publisher issued composite volumes of several toy books.

The variations in subject were vast: he illustrated several alphabet books and other primers and illustrated stories written by himself and in collaboration with his sister, Lucy. He illustrated the Charles Perrault stories, which were among the stories first collected in France during the seventeenth century: *Cinderella, Little Red Riding Hood, Blue Beard, Puss in Boots, Sleeping Beauty.* He illustrated traditional English tales, such as *The House That Jack Built, Cock Robin, Story of Jenny Wren;* and traditional English rhymes, such as *One, Two, Buckle My Shoe, The Fairy Ship,* and *The Three Little Pigs.* He illustrated a compendium of eastern stories called, *The Arabian Nights,* introducing Ali Baba and Aladdin. And he illustrated contemporary nursery stories, such as *Goody Two Shoes* and *My Mother.*

In 1876, Crane's contract with Routledge expired and when the publishers refused to renegotiate a contract that would give Crane royalties—instead of the flat fees they had paid previously—Crane went on to illustrate different kinds of children's books, working independently with Evans, including *Baby's Opera, The Baby's Bouquet,* and *The Baby's Own Aesop.* From 1875 to 1889, Crane also illustrated many books in black and white by Mrs. Molesworth, a popular Victorian writer for children. Although there are some fine examples in this series, the work is uneven, leaving Crane's toy books as the most enduring contributions.

Crane devoted a great deal of thought to the kind of designs that would appeal to children, and his particular style is consistent with these theories:

> Children, like the ancient Egyptians, appear to see most things in profile, and like definite statements in design. They prefer well-defined forms and bright, frank colour. They don't want to bother about three dimensions. They can accept symbolic representations. They themselves employ drawing . . . as a kind of picture-writing, and eagerly follow a pictured story. When they can count, they can check your quantities,

so that the artist must be careful to deliver, in dealing with, for instance, "The Song of Sixpence," his tale of twenty-four blackbirds.

Crane was seriously concerned with the power of the picture to educate and to inform, and he felt the illustrator had an important responsibility in shaping the child's intelligence. Long before children can read or write, children can learn "definite ideas from good pictures." Over the years, Crane created three primers, in addition to his alphabet books, which were used specifically for instruction. In 1884, for example, he collaborated with the educator J. M. D. Meiklejohn to create *The Golden Primer,* with text and illustrations designed to teach children words through their association with pictures. On the endpapers, the reader is advised: "Teach only words, teach them as wholes: never mention the names of a letter unless the child demands it."

During the first years of life, the child's imagination must be continually fresh and stimulated with bright color, sensitive line, and symbolic imagery. (In later years, Crane would be distressed by some of Arthur Rackham's illustrations of ghouls and monsters because he suspected they disturbed the child's development.) "The best of designing for children," he wrote, "is that the imagination and fancy may be let loose and roam freely, and there is always room for humour and even pathos, sure of being followed by that ever-living sense of wonder and romance in the child heart—a heart which in some cases, happily, never grows up or grows old."

Not only the content, but the very way in which the books were presented—from cover to cover—was a matter of consequence. Nothing was left to accident. Crane regarded each volume as a designed work, in which every element—text, ornaments, and pictures—was a detail that was subordinate to the whole concept. The entire volume represented a unified design, including the covers and endpapers as well. Regarding any one of these elements as simple decoration—rather than part of an organic whole—was tantamount to erecting a shanty in the woods. . . .

If Crane felt the elements within each book were subordinate to the total design concept, he also felt that book design itself was subordinate to aesthetic theories that applied to *all* aspects of design. In addition to his work as a fine artist, Crane also turned his attention to branches of the decorative arts other than books, directing his skills to the design of textiles, ceramics, embroidery, tapestries, stained glass, mosaic and gesso reliefs, wallpapers, and interiors. In each, he emphasized the importance of sound craftsmanship and a respect for the specific materials. Even his book illustrations provided a means for him to exercise his concepts in the decorative arts. ("I was in the habit of putting in all sorts of subsidiary detail that interested me, and often made them the vehicle for my ideas in furniture and decoration.") Indeed, these books were read not only by children, but by artists and architects who followed the latest modes of the reform aesthetics and who presented them to clients for decorating ideas.

At the foundation of Crane's work lay a powerful conviction that the designer's purpose ran deeper than mere decoration, that the designer's function was to rescue Victorian society from the "heavy and vulgar taste borrowed from the French empire which had for twenty years or more dominated Victorian taste in English house decoration and furniture." In elevating taste, the designer assumed a role of moral significance. According to Crane, the artist must be a reformer. . . .

Crane's training as an engraver introduced him to the plight of the laborer who, if not phased out altogether by technology, was at least the victim of the division of labor that pervaded all factory systems. His mentor, W. J. Linton, had been a socialist and had inspired Crane by his ideas. Not surprisingly, Crane became a socialist, William Morris being primarily responsible for this conversion. . . . Although Morris continued to be a far more familiar personality to the working man, Crane became the movement's most active artist. For the rest of his life, he frequently placed his versatile talents at the service of the socialist cause.

Crane's design achievements and leadership in the Arts and Crafts and socialist movements, as well as his extensive teaching and writing, propelled him into the status of international celebrity. His signature—a rebus incorporating a crane—became a familiar trademark throughout the Western world, and his work was sought from every sector. . . .

By the time of Crane's death in 1915, his work and ideas had been felt in France, Italy, Holland, Belgium, Germany, Scandinavia, and Hungary. Determined to lead his flock out of the darkness into a new era, this reformer promoted English theory and design to a wide audience, inspiring new generations of artists and designers. Yet his most ardent followers were oblivious to his polemics. Innocently turning the pages of his slender picture books, children throughout the world would remember Walter Crane not for his theories, but for his simple gift of joy, for giving them these cherished moments in an imaginary universe where reason has no place.

TITLE COMMENTARY

📖 **THE BABY'S OPERA: A BOOK OF OLD RHYMES WITH NEW DRESSES (edited with sister, Lucy Crane, 1877)**

Punch, or the London Charivari

SOURCE: A review of *The Baby's Opera: A Book of Old Rhymes with New Dresses,* in *Punch, or the London Charivari,* Vol. LXXI, January 6, 1877, p. 297.

Children are first-rate critics, and thoroughly appreciate Walter Crane's illustrations, not only in *Carrots,* but in his *chef-d'oeuvre* of the year, yclept *The Baby's Opera,* which is the cleverest, prettiest, fancifullest, and, generally, superlativest Christmas book that we've seen for a very long time. The only mistake in it is, that, in some instances, the ancient land-marks of nursery readings have been sacrificed to a sense of modern requirements. This, however, would be a subject for Shakspearian commentators; as must be evident when we question the correctness of the version as here given of the nursery song of *"Mrs. Bond and the Ducks," "Froggee would a-wooing,"* and others. Folios wouldn't exhaust the subject. But to all those interested, antiquarianly, in the rhymes of the past, and to all those interested in the happiness of the present rising generation, we say, advisedly, "Get Walter Crane's *Baby's Opera.*"

📖 **THE BABY'S BOUQUET: A FRESH BUNCH OF OLD RHYMES AND TUNES (edited with sister, Lucy Crane, 1879)**

The Spectator

SOURCE: A review of *The Baby's Bouquet: A Fresh Bunch of Old Rhymes and Tunes,* in *The Spectator,* Vol. 51, November 30, 1878, pp.1499-1500.

If this delicately illustrated little book were really meant for babies, we should be obliged to protest. It is a great deal too good for them. The babies have it all their own way, in these times, and moreover are completely unable to appreciate the high art which is devoted to their service. The true way with children is to give them plenty of scope for their imaginations, and not burden them with delicate detail. They will make as wonderful a world out of a box of ancient bricks or a book of old-fashioned woodcuts half a century old, as they can ever make out of all the elaborate mechanical toys and exquisite drawings to be found amongst the juvenile playthings of the new era. We have long been persuaded that it takes a mature eye to enter in any degree into the costly sacrifices which are now offered up to children, and that they would be happier without these sacrifices. For instance, take these delicate and humorous little illustrations of Mr. Walter Crane's, of those old and new rhymes with which, no doubt, if only on account of their simplicity, children are charmed. Will they be any more charmed with them for the elaborate help of Mr. Walter Crane's delicate fancy? Nay, but the less. They will be guided too much by it into specific modes of interpreting these nursery rhymes, whereas half their charm to children is that a child's mind vibrates in so many different directions, as it catches now one and now another note in the old strains, that it is thus stirred into an activity of fancy as pleasant as it is variable and manifold. It is for grown-up people that these pictures of Mr. Walter Crane's are really suitable and suited. They see in them particular and very happy interpretations of the old rhymes, but their fancy is too accustomed to its own independent associations with them to go into captivity even to Mr. Walter Crane; so that they have, besides the pleasure of admiring his own personal interpretation of these rhymes, the amusement of comparing them with the version of those rhymes which, to themselves, would have seemed most natural, and of canvassing the merits of each. Children indoctrinated in Mr. Crane's view of the matter would never have the same space left to their fancy again; they would cease to be fancy-free, so far as these rhymes are concerned, and would lose a great deal more in ideal liberty than they would gain in picturesque detail. For example, take Mr. Walter Crane's most humorous illustration of the rhyme:

> There was an old woman, and what do you think?
> She lived upon nothing but victuals and drink;
> Victuals and drink were the chief of her diet,
> Yet this plaguey old woman could never be quiet.

The picture is delightful in its way. A very jolly, spectacled old lady, in a very big white turban, is sitting at the head of her own table, brandishing a mighty knife and fork, while a butler of the utmost solemnity, with a napkin under his arm, and his nose in the air, is holding a bottle of wine a little behind her; an obsequious footman is taking the cover off a dish of fish; another footman is following, with the sauce; a third is going up the last flight of stairs with an *entrée;* while four inferior menials are coming along in slow procession, with decanters, bottles, and other dishes. The old lady, in fact, is a high liver. The reason she could never be quiet, is that mentally and morally, as well as physically, she lived almost exclusively in her food—not exclusively, for we are told that victuals and drink were only the *chief* of her diet; but Mr. Walter Crane evidently holds that the remainder of her diet was hope—expectation of victuals and drink not yet absolutely before her. Victuals and drink in vision fill up the hours when victuals and drink are absent from the room. She indulges in sweet musings on the *relevées,* and her reins in the night-season summon her to meditate on the flavour of the madeira. But surely this is a rather mundane and limited interpretation of the rhyme, admirably as it is worked out. The objection to Mr. Walter Crane's view, is that the gourmande would have been of a lethargic habit—far from "plaguey"—and probably would have died prematurely of apoplexy or gout before reaching old age at all, had she lived after this fashion. Our impression is that the old lady was something of a valetudinarian and a careful student of works on dietetic subjects; that she had early mastered either *Combe on the Constitution of Man,* or some earlier work of the same kind; that she rigidly limited herself to a prescribed number of glasses of wine, and weighed out her animal food with fine weights; and that what is darkly alluded to in the rhyme as something which supplemented these victuals and drink, and yet was not exactly to be included amongst victuals, was of the nature of tonic pills or powders, which could not be strictly classified as either victuals or drink. This is suggested, we think, by the double statement that the old lady *lived upon* nothing but victuals and drink—that is, that nothing else

contributed to support her vital powers—and also that it did not constitute the whole of her diet; that, in short, there was something else which was a regular part of her diet, and which did not contribute to her health, but no doubt, did contribute to her restlessness. Well, that is a different view from Mr. Walter Crane's. But no young people who had once seen his jolly old lady brandishing her knife and fork, would ever be able to take any other view of the rhyme than his. Their imagination would be possessed by his picture, and some of the available playground of their fancy would be thus lost. Or take his beautiful illustration of **"The Little Man and Little Maid"**:

> There was a little man, and he woo'd a little
>   maid.
> And he said, "Little maid, will you wed, wed,
>   wed?
> I have little more to say than will you, yea or
>   nay;
> For least said is soonest mended,—ded,—ded."
> The little maid replied
> (Some say a little sighed),
> "But what shall we have to eat, eat, eat?
> Will the love that you're rich in
> Make a fire in the kitchen?
> Or the little god of Love turn the spit, spit, spit?"

Mr. Walter Crane makes a charming little picture of it. The little man is full of genuine fervour; he clasps the little maid's hand with one hand, and puts his other arm round her. She yields her hand pensively, the other hand is pressed sadly to her lips, as she presses the prudent considerations suggested in the rhyme; and Mr. Walter Crane ekes out his impression of her thoughts, by giving us her vision of Poverty rapping at the door, as Love flies out of the window. But here again the old rhyme seems to us to admit of another interpretation. Observe the curtness, almost the sternness of the little man's offer. He declines to indulge any sentiment on the occasion, on the transparently false plea that "least said is soonest mended." He simply gives the little maid what we have, under similar circumstances, heard spoken of by a little maid as "the first refusal," and insists on a point-blank 'yea' or 'nay,' evidently intending to accept the refusal as final, if he gets it. The little maid no doubt sees perfectly well how cold his offer is, and it pains her, but she wishes to put a good face on the matter. It is she, not he, who suggests that her suitor is rich in love, but being well aware that this is a fiction of her own, she finds an excuse for declining him which shall leave it in her power to indulge the pleasant illusion for which he had given so little ground. In fact, she suggests that as there are no settlements, she is bound in prudence to decline an offer which she might otherwise have accepted; but she will not deprive herself of the power of imagining that the offer was genuine, cold and almost brutal as the succinct alternative presented had been. In her heart, she was well aware that a true lover would never have admitted that "least said was soonest mended," that he had "little more to say than 'will you—yea or nay?'" On the contrary, he would have made his offer the excuse and occasion of any amount of eloquence, and the little maid felt this most painfully. But her tact found a ready veil for his coldness, and a ready pretence for the refusal that he really wanted to elict to an offer in which he had gone too far to draw back, though he wanted to put an end to the affair. Thus, according to our view, Mr. Walter Crane should have made the little man offer himself coldly, and without the least tenderness; while the little maid, whose heart has been really touched, but has the sense to see that the matter is best ended, refers sadly to the bare pasturage before them, as the excuse—it is only an excuse—for the implied refusal which she knows is required. Here, again, the mature reader can enjoy Mr. Walter Crane's beautiful interpretation, and yet keep his own view of the transaction; but the child would be entirely prepossessed by this picture, and his ideal freedom in the interpretation of the nursery-rhyme gone. We maintain that Mr. Walter Crane's book is a book for the elders, and not for the children.

Punch, or the London Charivari

SOURCE: A review of *The Baby's Bouquet: A Fresh Bunch of Old Rhymes and Tunes,* in *Punch, or the London Charivari,* Vol. LXXV, December 14, 1878, p. 276.

[*The Baby's Bouquet* is] . . . a companion to the **Baby's Opera** of last year, or the year before that—which? No matter; that was an excellent notion, and this is a notion still more excellent. It is a fresh Bunch—not a Mother Bunch, but a young Daughter Bunch—of old rhymes and tunes, arranged and decorated in such a way by Walter Crane as only could enter into *his* (Walter) *Crani*um. English rhymes, French rhymes, and German rhymes. There is a picture of our old friend Polly [putting the kettle on, and Sukey, her twin sister, taking it off again]. Then there is *Et moi de m'en courir,* with the song of the *Cuckoo,* and the song of the *Canards,* which, by the way, is *"Cancan, cancan, cancan,"* possibly the harmless original of the dance that has brought so many gay and festive spirits into trouble with the police. We should like to have seen the *"Bonne Histoire"* there also, supposed to be the original of Mr. W. M. Thackeray's *Little Billee.*

📖 THE FIRST OF MAY: A FAIRY MASQUE (written BY J. R. de Capel Wise, 1881)

The Nation

SOURCE: A review of *The First of May: A Fairy Masque,* in *The Nation,* Vol. 33, No. 836, July 7, 1881, pp. 14-15.

The author of **The First of May** is, we believe, a young English poet, and not, as might be inferred from the title-page, Mr. Walter Crane. Mr. Crane will, however, rightly command most of the reader's attention, though

the Masque is a very pretty reflection of the spirit of seventeenth-century madrigals, has a pleasantly entertaining plot of properly insubstantial texture, and is in general of an innocent and agreeable rather than a lively interest. Much the same thing might in strictness be said of Mr. Crane's fifty-two designs which illustrate the poem, but these qualities are rarer in his art than in literature, and are consequently more noticeable. Nor do we mean to depreciate them in either of the contributors to this pretty volume. The Masque is a fairy story, and Mr. Crane has illustrated it with great copiousness, charming grace, and, within the limits imposed by the subject, great variety. Each page contains from two or three to twenty lines only, which are framed in the designs. Almost no criticism is to be made upon them from the point of view of decorative treatment of a light and fanciful fairy-tale. The drawing is very good, and if it were not, the slight conventionality which idealizes to a just perceptible degree the human figures of which the most important part of the decoration is made up, would prevent one's feeling inexactness as a defect. Some of the figures . . . are delightful, and some of the figure arrangements . . . not less so. In many the grace of individual movement and attitude is surprising, and justly to be called rhythmic. In others the mere linear scheme, independently of the interest of the figures as figures, is in the highest degree decorative.

📖 PAN PIPES: A BOOK OF OLD SONGS (composed by Theo Marzials, 1882); HOUSEHOLD STORIES FROM THE COLLECTION OF THE BROTHERS GRIMM (1882)

The Spectator

SOURCE: A review of *Pan Pipes: A Book of Old Songs* and *Household Stories from the Collection of the Brothers Grimm,* in *The Spectator,* Vol. 55, November 4, 1882, pp. 1415-16.

[In *Household Stories from the Collection of the Brothers Grimm* and *Pan Pipes: A Book of Old Songs*] we have fresh evidence of Mr. Walter Crane's peculiar, and, what is in these days a most rare power of art, expression. While it is, in its very essence, artistic, in the highest and most wholesome sense of the term, it is, at the same time, spontaneous and direct, and done apparently with the greatest ease, possessing the fresh, brilliant qualities which a full and rich invention, combined with a natural facility of execution, probably alone can give. More than ever is such direct and spontaneous art welcome. Thousands of framed pictures, more or less manufactured according to academic or specialistic schools of Art, are every year rejected from the principal exhibitions; but how few, even of those accepted, testify that the artists who produce them are born artists, more fit to work at art than at anything else. About Mr. Walter Crane's art there is an entire absence of the manufacturing element, there is very little even of the professional. Perhaps one of its greatest charms is an utter absence in it of any suggestion reminding us of the modern studio life. In his imagination there seems to be imaged a beautiful world of Nature, which is always ready to express itself in line and colour, and to add a charm of its own to the telling of any story, to decorate any incident with the loveliness and grace of fairy palaces, woods, streams, and flowers. He has a fancy which seems always ready to flow with the abundance and variety of Nature herself, not in her work-a-day, weary aspect, not with a straining after beauty under difficulties (a sense which overshadows our Art schools and studios), but as a bird sings, and as animals play when they are happy—in short, as a perfectly joyful expression of a natural condition. We cannot but feel that Mr. Crane's genius is one of the most truly poetical in the character of its art of which our age can boast. It reflects the varying and dramatic sentiment in Nature which accompanies action, growth, vitality. In his most purely decorative designs, something is always going on, some distinct action always taking place. This sense of movement creeps into his slightest decoration, into every border with which his illustrations are framed, and extends even to the fly-leaves of his books. It is the combination of this sense of the dramatic with the sense of fine balance in placing lines in original and yet satisfactory arrangements, which secures to Mr. Crane's work an unique position as illustrative decoration. His remarkable success in harmonising in an original manner and inventing combinations of flat tints of colour, is no less admirable than the distinguished grace and strength in the quality of line in his designs. Moreover, it is a combination of the dramatic with the decorative power which makes his expression of facts, in the most abstract form, entertain-

ing; while it makes his dramatic expression always agreeable as design, the most violent action in it being controlled, so to speak, by the design in which it is framed. The interest created by this power of suggesting action, and yet retaining beauty of design, is enhanced by the charm of a sense of ease in the way in which the work is evidently manipulated. The mechanical part seems to be executed with a freedom as of writing. There is an absence of all conscious effort in the work. It has a refreshing quality, suggestive of wholesome, pleasant growth and vitality. In the truest sense is Mr. Crane's work healthy. No self-consciousness is to be traced in the feeling of it anywhere.

In the illustrations to Grimm's stories and *Pan Pipes,* we have uncoloured and coloured examples of Mr. Crane's art. The engraving in line of the former is singularly good, suggesting a sense of colour, and a richness in the light and shade and tone, which are, we think, equal to anything that has ever been done in woodcutting. It would be impossible here to dwell on the many instances where there is some particularly happy sign of a rich sense of beauty, fun, and charm, in the very numerous illustrations to the old, favourite, nursery-stories. All who wish their children to make acquaintance with these in close association with a teaching to the eye of all that is most gracefully fanciful, prettily funny, and artistically good, must get the volume. Indeed, all who care for Art should get it. Particularly interesting is it to see how greatness in style can be preserved on a tiny scale in wood-cutting, as in the old Greek intaglios. In the head and tail pieces, scarcely an inch high, there are little figures which for qualities

From Beauty and the Beast, *illustrated by Walter Crane.*

of grace and beauty are beyond praise, the draperies especially being executed with the same sense of style and distinction which are so striking in all Mr. Crane's drawing of drapery. The head-pieces of **"The Frog Prince," "The Twelve Brothers," "Rapunzel," "The Three Little Men in the Wood," "The Three Spinsters," "Aschenputtel," "Mother Hulda," "Clever Else," "The Robber Bridegroom," "King Thrushbeard," "Snow White," "Rumpelstiltskin,"** are, perhaps, the most striking examples of the peculiar beauty of some of the tiny figures, whereas others are more remarkable for a delicate sense of humour and fairyland fancy, quaint and comical, but never coarse or bluntly grotesque. In the designs which are more simply decorative, there is an admirable fancy displayed, besides richness of design; for instance, in the tail-pieces of **"Hans in Luck," "Faithful John," "The Twelve Brothers," "The Vagabonds," "The White Snake," "The Six Swans."** The larger designs are all worthy of being increased in size and treated in colour, as Mr. Crane treated the **"Goose Girl,"** exhibited at the Grosvenor Gallery the winter before last.

Pan Pipes is a large, though thinner volume, suitable in shape to be placed on a pianoforte desk. Forty old English ballads are arranged in a simple pleasant way by Mr. Marzials, and encased in charming pictorial art by Mr. Crane. Here, again, the book must be seen to be appreciated, though in a slight way we can try to point out what strikes us as peculiarly admirable. Invention and fancy fly in charming line colour and tone over each page, from the cover of reeds to the last page, where Pan carries his burden of pipes, and the cranes fly, and the reed bends down to the setting sun. The page on which is "To all you ladies," opposite the preface, and the "index page," are peculiarly happy in line and fancy as introductory designs; but the design of **"The Three Ravens,"** and one or two other illustrations, pass beyond the region of inventive fancy into the dramatic pathos of truly imaginative art. Throughout the book, every page, independent of the beauty of its detail, produces as a whole a charmingly decorative effect. The ground of the space on which the music is written is toned and tinted in harmony with the design, and there are even variety and *quality* in the toning and the tinting. . . .

Mr. Walter Crane's picture-books are all distinguished by being as first-rate of their kind, as real, wholesome, and consequently beautiful, as was the sculpture of Greece in the time of Pheidias, or the painting of Italy in the time of Titian.

In Mr. Walter Crane's genius there is that which often passes beyond the purely decorative power. In all cases where the dramatic and emotional elements in art exist with any degree of fervour, full justice can be done to the artist's power only by the touch of his own hand. Therefore, though the cutting of the woodcuts by Mr. Swain in the illustrations to the Grimm stories is admirable, and the engraving and painting by Mr. Evans of the *Pan Pipes* are exceptionally good, and render the

peculiar quality of Mr. Crane's colouring with a truth which could hardly be excelled, still, it is in no work translated by any machinery, but the touch of his own hand, that we should feel the full charm and power of his gifts as an artist. . . .

[A]ll should hail with gratitude these new picture-books, which we recommend to every nursery and school-room; and not only to every nursery and school-room, but to every one who cares for good art.

THE SIRENS THREE: A POEM (1886)

The Dial

SOURCE: A review of *The Sirens Three: A Poem,* in *The Dial,* Vol. XXVIII, No. 323, December 1, 1899, p. 430.

The fine artistic fancy and skill of execution of Mr. Walter Crane are well displayed in . . . *The Sirens Three.* Script and decorations are printed in uniform light sepia on rather thick paper of medium smoothness. Mr. Crane's work is quite elaborate, and is informed, we think, with a somewhat more serious and symbolical spirit than usual. At any rate it well repays close inspection, and it makes the well-made volume containing it the choicest and most really artistic of the season's more inexpensive publications.

FLORA'S FEAST: A MASQUE OF FLOWERS (1889; reprinted, 1980)

The Nation

SOURCE: A review of *Flora's Feast: A Masque of Flowers,* in *The Nation,* Vol. 49, No. 1277, December 19, 1889, pp. 503-04.

Flora's Feast consists of forty pages of colored illustrations with verses forming a part of the design, the whole lithographed together, and printed in black lines, and in two or three colors for each page. The flowers of the year succeed one another in order. Each plate is devoted to one or two flowers, and has generally one distich describing them. The designs themselves embody a certain personification of each plant, usually by representing a young maiden, or perhaps what the author would call a nymph, dressed in the petals, the calyx, the leaves, or some other part of the flower in question. Thus [we have]

The little lilies of the vale,
White ladies, delicate and pale,

and the picture represents two maidens, drawing around themselves as a sort of outer garment a cloak of the large, enveloping green leaves of the plant, while they bend over their heads the flexible stems with their white bells. The idea of personifying the flowers in this way is not very happy. A serious effort has to be made to conceive of the plant as in any way embodied in the girl or young man who is masquerading in its spoils. The line, "The scarlet poppy-head ablaze," is illustrated by a black drum-major and black drummer, each of them in fantastic uniform, as if of the British army in some unknown period of the past, but the hats formed of the spreading blossoms; and, in order to account for the presence of the blossoms, and to give some idea of the whole plant, the drum-major has to carry the stem of the poppy as if it were his staff of office. Nor is this the most far-fetched of the fancies in the book. Perhaps the "white-flowered thorn," represented as a knight in polished armor, with a spiked mace, a crest of radiating points and exaggerated knee and elbow plates with thorny terminations, is the most disagreeable of all. But it remains to be said that the pictures have a great deal of the grace of Mr. Crane's work, and that the book is unusual in character, and, therefore, fitted to be a gratification to those who seek many Christmas gifts.

📖 *RENASCENCE: A BOOK OF VERSE* (1891)

The Dial

SOURCE: A review of *Renascence: A Book of Verse,* in *The Dial,* Vol. XII, No. 136, August, 1891, p. 108.

To the art of the designer, rather than that of the poet, we must credit the charm of Mr. Walter Crane's **Renascence.** Upon the title-page and the two score head and tail pieces, simple but exquisite in decorative effect, eye and thought are likely long to linger. Upon the verses they will linger not so long, for Mr. Crane has not the inspiration of the true singer. In fact, his work is more pleasing for its ideals than for its form. In both, it is closely akin to the work of Mr. William Morris, although distinctly inferior to that work in technical qualities. Mr. Crane is, like his friend and master, a socialist, and sings of a coming Kingdom of Man with the fervor, although not with the eloquence, of [Percy] Shelley. He thus invokes the spirit of the man to be:

> Arise, and take thy throne,
> Upbuilt in ages long by stone on stone—
> The human spirit's still aspiring stair
> Whose marble feet were laid in toil and care,
> And washed with tears, and worn in eager quest
> Of false and fleeting phantoms, seeking rest.
> But now thy feet are fledged and would aspire
> To climb the summit of thy hope's desire.
> High where in sculptured walls and towers rise
> Her architecture, white in azure skies,
> Tinged with the fire of dawn above thy head—
> Ah! there, fair soul, thy marriage feast is spread.

This is a fair illustration of Mr. Crane's workmanship, which nowhere can be said to rise above mediocrity. His diction is simple, largely Saxon in vocabulary, and marked by a touch of the pre-Raphaelite affectation. The most

important of his pieces is the allegorical poem of **"The Sirens Three"**—

> No More, and golden Now, and dark To be,
> Whose vocal harps are love, and hope, and
>   grief,—

which has been published by itself in book form. Mr. Crane's ideal of a future Golden Age, in which Art shall walk hand in hand with Toil, and life pass for all unclouded from sunrise to sunset, is very attractive, no doubt, but we fear that it is still as much a dream as it was in Shelley's time, and we doubt if its latest singer has any suggestions of practical value to offer for its realization. To the clearest vision of our age it seems farther from realization than it did sixty years ago.

The Athenaeum

SOURCE: A review of *Renascence: A Book of Verse,* in *The Athenaeum,* No. 3355, February 13, 1892, pp. 211-12.

[In *Renascence: A Book of Verse*] Mr. Walter Crane's verse has in it so much excellence of imagery and of metrical workmanship, and altogether such good poetic points, that it is vexatious not to be able to declare honest faith in him as a poet. But the truth must be said. His productions are too artfully fabricated, too ornate, too much elaborated; poetic spontaneity, if it ever existed, has become lost amid the processes of expression. The result is that the reader's mind wearies of the strain of pursuing thoughts through details and decorations, and craves, but craves in vain, for something simple to

From Mr. Michael Mouse Unfolds His Tale, *written and illustrated by Walter Crane.*

rest upon. Mr. Crane's highly allegorical method adds to this sense of mental strain in the reader. He uses allegory within allegory, and allegory to illustrate allegory. The allegories—the minor as well as the major, those which stand for metaphors and similes as well as those which are themes—show themselves, besides often being most beautiful suggestions, intelligible and true when their inner meaning has been duly followed out. But there can be few readers who will not flag sometimes if a poet keeps setting them problems: the tendency is to leave off the effort of understanding and to go on in hopes of enjoying what is beautiful without inquiring what it means. And what comes of that is that the fatigue of bewilderment takes the place of the fatigue of investigation, and is fatal to appreciation. Yet, in spite of the artificiality so detrimental to poetic quality, what is written in **Renascence** is much of it what should not pass unappreciated. Fortunately there is the help of re-reading. Not all the drawbacks will be lessened so; but that difficulty of the too great demand on the reader's research will naturally vanish when the research has been made.

QUEEN SUMMER; OR, THE TOURNEY OF THE LILY AND THE ROSE (1891)

The Nation

SOURCE: A review of *Queen Summer; or, the Tourney of the Lily and the Rose,* in *The Nation,* Vol. 53, No. 1378, November 26, 1891, p. 410.

Walter Crane's **Queen Summer; or, the Tourney of the Lily and the Rose** is a thin quarto of forty pages, each bearing a portion of text in decorative black-letter and an illustration printed in colors. The paper is folded after the Japanese fashion and printed on one side only, and the book is bound in boards with a decorative design by the author. Mr. Crane's verse is fanciful and pretty, but it is only an excuse for the forty drawings, which show endless invention, exuberance of fancy, grace of line and richness of composition, with rare delicacy and charm of color. It is as much better than any former work of Mr. Crane's that we have seen as his former work is better than that of any of his emulators in the same field, and hardly any praise can be too high for it.

AN ARTIST'S REMINISCENCES (1907; reprinted, 1968)

The Athenaeum

SOURCE: A review of *An Artist's Reminiscences,* in *The Athenaeum,* No. 4173, October 19, 1907, pp. 486-87.

Mr. Crane's autobiography [*An Artist's Reminiscences*] will be a welcome addition to the shelf of books on which is ranged the history of the men responsible for the motives of Victorian art, such as Rossetti, Burne-Jones, Morris, Watts, Leighton, and Frith. It is happily distinguished from them by the fact that its subject is still with us in full activity. His acquaintance with many of the distinguished men of the time lends the book an interest beyond that derived from his account of his own work and from the excellent illustrations with which it is enriched, and it is not too much to say that the whole of it will interest those who have ever come in contact with his circle. We are not sure, however, whether it would not have been improved, from the point of view of those who have not shared this advantage, by some judicious pruning—if it had displayed some of the power of condensed expression which Mr. Crane's verse shows him to possess. A book to be a work of art must be as well proportioned as a sonnet, and the familiar excuse for a long letter, that the writer had not time to write a short one, cannot be accepted when the work is addressed to the public. . . .

Mr. Crane's position in English art is somewhat anomalous. Here in England he occupies a well-defined place, but it is hardly likely that his name would be quoted on the spur of the moment among those of the leaders of artistic endeavour. But as we travel outside our own borders we find that the further we get from them, the more important does his work become, and that for thousands of cultivated persons Walter Crane is the only English artist. The value of this fact may be overrated—have we not been recently informed that Mr. Jacobs is the only English author known to as large and cosmopolitan a circle of admirers?—but it is to be taken into account. Mr. Crane was fortunate enough to produce a masterpiece early in his career, and has naturally developed since then; but he has developed on his own lines, and not on those the public expected of him, and the extent of its disappointment is measured by the narrow limits within which it is willing to acknowledge his mastery.

The reason is not far to seek. Mr. Crane sees things in an allegory; the public—while it loves an illustration—hates an allegory. One may paint a picture of sea-foam and call it 'Neptune's Horses,' and the public will delight in the clever way in which the shape of the horse is suggested; but the slightest suggestion of a real horse's head repels it. The popularity of Watts's allegorical pictures may be alleged to the contrary, but it is to be observed that the popular ones among them are precisely those which approach the nearest to illustration. It is therefore not surprising that students of Mr. Crane's later art must go to Germany to study its more important examples, harmonizing as they do with the Teutonic love for the discovery of a meaning in life. . . .

Another side of Mr. Crane's art . . . is exhibited by the numerous reproductions from the little sketches which adorn his diaries of travel. His more serious drawings are spirited and interesting, though we miss in the book examples of the water-colour sketches which are perhaps the most popular in England of his recent work. As a document for the student of the domestic history of our times, an agreeable, chatty volume of reminiscences for the casual reader, and above all as the monument of a delicate personality, this book has an assured place.

ROBIN HOOD AND HIS MERRY MEN (1912)

The Bookman Supplement

SOURCE: A review of *Robin Hood and His Merry Men,* in *The Bookman Supplement,* Vol. XLIII, No. 255, Christmas, 1912, p. 191.

For his material Mr. Henry Gilbert has gone principally to the older ballads dealing with Robin Hood, but he informs us in his preface [to *Robin Hood and the Men of Greenwood*] that he has also invented scenes and incidents for himself. The latter is a good deal less of a liberty than it sounds, for it must be remembered that in the casting of his chapters Mr. Gilbert has relied upon nobody's invention but his own, and the whole manner of the writing is his, and his only. Anyhow, he has written or compiled a bravely spirited book—one that will delight the heart of every boy and girl that reads it. Mr. Crane proves once again that his hand has not lost its cunning. His illustrations are full of colour, fanciful and humorous in conception, and have a good deal of the decorative effect of a piece of mediæval tapestry.

Additional coverage of Crane's life and career is contained in the following sources published by The Gale Group: *Contemporary Authors,* Vol. 168; *Dictionary of Literary Biography,* Vol. 163; *Major Authors and Illustrators for Children and Young Adults;* *Something about the Author,* Vols. 18, 100.

Ossie Davis

1917-

African-American author of plays and fiction.

Major works include *Purlie Victorious* (produced in New York City, 1961; adapted as a screenplay, *Gone Are the Days,* 1963; also released as *The Man from C.O.T.T.O.N.*), *Escape to Freedom: A Play about Frederick Douglass* (1978; first produced in New York at the Town Hall, 1976), *Langston: A Play* (1982), *Just Like Martin* (1992).

INTRODUCTION

A versatile and successful actor and director, Davis has also focused his talents on writing plays and fiction. A long-time activist for civil rights, Davis has devoted his literary efforts to dramatizing the lives and struggles of African Americans, particularly for the young adult audience. Not surprisingly, critics have praised the actor's ability to create believable characters and absorbing drama in his works, which manage to be both entertaining and informative. Davis has drawn widely on his experience with the civil rights movement to create plots that explore the lives of prominent African-American heroes from history, as well as the struggles of the ordinary people whom they have inspired. "I am essentially a storyteller," Davis once commented in *Publishers Weekly,* "and the story I want to tell is about black people. Sometimes I sing the story, sometimes I dance it, sometimes I tell tall tales about it, but I always want to share my great satisfaction at being a black man at this time in history."

Biographical Information

Davis was born in rural Georgia in 1917 to a family that valued education, preaching, and storytelling. This strong oral tradition inspired Davis to become a writer, and he entered Howard University in 1935 with that goal in mind. At the suggestion of drama critic and philosophy professor Alain Locke, he became involved in school stage productions as a means to improve his writing. Wanting to gain more experience on the stage, Davis left college for New York City in 1938. While he joined Harlem's Rose McClendon Players and earned his first role in *Joy Exceeding Glory* in 1941, success eluded him and he was drafted into the army the following year. After serving as a medical technician in Liberia, West Africa, Davis was transferred to the army's Special Services division, where he wrote and directed his first play, *Goldbrickers of 1944.* When World War II ended, he returned to New York and soon made his debut on Broadway in the title role of the 1946 play *Jeb.* While the play was not particularly successful, it was eventful

for Davis in that actress Ruby Dee was also in the cast; the couple married in 1948.

Davis and Dee enjoyed increasing success in the theater and later, in film and television, becoming known for roles that eschewed stereotypes and instead portrayed the realities of African-American life. Davis produced a second play in 1952, *Alice in Wonder,* but is perhaps best known for his first Broadway production, 1961's *Purlie Victorious.* He wrote and co-starred with Dee in this comedy, which was later made into the Tony Award-nominated musical *Purlie.* The 1960s also saw Davis's increasing involvement in the civil rights movement; he was master of ceremonies for the 1963 March on Washington and spoke at the funerals of both Martin Luther King, Jr., and Malcolm X. In the interest of keeping young people informed about black history and culture, he published two biographical plays for children: *Escape to Freedom,* about abolitionist Frederick Douglass, and *Langston: A Play,* about poet Langston Hughes. While continuing to perform with distinction on stage, screen, and television, Davis branched out yet again in 1992 with his first novel, *Just Like Martin.* His versatile career as a writer and performer, he once explained, is inextricably tied up with his interest in civil rights: "I am greatly concerned with literature, and I am deeply involved with social action, and I am fortunate enough (or, perhaps, unfortunate enough) to see no fundamental difference between the one and the other."

Major Works

Produced during the early years of the civil rights movement, *Purlie Victorious* is a comic satire which lampoons old stereotypes of African Americans. Set in Georgia after the Civil War, the play follows the efforts of the persuasive preacher Purlie Judson to purchase an old barn in order to establish an integrated church. To achieve this goal, the preacher must convince the bigoted plantation owner Captain Cotchipee that Purlie's innocent young girlfriend Lutiebelle is the college-educated woman who was left five hundred dollars by a wealthy white matron. The play received many positive notices—particularly for its use of humor—and ran for over seven months on Broadway. For his next play, Davis decided to dramatize the early life of Frederick Douglass, a freed slave who became one of the most articulate speakers against slavery in the nineteenth century. Not only does *Escape to Freedom* provide information about Douglass's early life—including an emphasis on how his ability to read made freedom possible—but it is structured in a way to make it easily performed by students. Denise M. Wilms noted that "the play has the kind of drawing power that could make it a frequently performed favorite." *Langston: A Play* uses the poetry of its subject, Langston Hughes, to help illuminate his life. While critics did not find this work as successful as its predecessor, they still observed that it had good potential as a school production. When it came time to write about activist Martin Luther King, Jr.—who the author knew personally—Davis chose to write his first novel. *Just Like Martin* does not directly portray King, however, but instead focuses on the efforts of a teenage Alabama boy to lead nonviolent protests, just as the civil rights leader did. However, fourteen-year-old Isaac Stone encounters resistance from his father, a troubled veteran of the Korean War who believes that passive resistance is cowardly and ineffective. After two of Isaac's friends are killed in a church firebombing and President Kennedy is assassinated, Isaac is left to question both his values and how far he will go to maintain them. Critics praised the characterizations and dramatic action of the novel, as well as Davis's ability to vividly re-create an era of history. As Lois F. Anderson concluded: "This work is an authentic voice of a troubled time in the history of America."

Awards

Davis and his coauthors were nominated for a Tony Award for best musical of 1969-70 for *Purlie*. In 1979 *Escape to Freedom* earned both a Coretta Scott King Award from the American Library Association and a Jane Addams Children's Book Award from the Jane

Addams Peace Association. Davis has also earned numerous nominations and awards for his performance as an actor, including induction into the NAACP Image Awards Hall of Fame, 1989.

AUTHOR'S COMMENTARY

Ossie Davis

SOURCE: "The Wonderful World of Law and Order," in *Anger, and Beyond: The Negro Writer in the United States*, Harper & Row, Publishers, 1966, pp. 154-80.

As an entertainer I'm an author. If you say that I am a writer, I will reply, "I am an actor." And if you accuse me of being an actor I will say, "No. I am a writer." If you say that I am a Negro I will escape by saying, "Of course not. I am an American." But if you accuse me of being an American, I will then dodge behind the fact that I am a Negro. Now, this kind of duplicity, this kind of double-sidedness to my character and personality is not unusual. We all know about it. We are faced with it and live with it. It is part of the Negro characteristic, and it's a major part of the basic problem that other Americans are confronted with: that is, the question of identity. Who am I? Who am I not? What do I do? What don't I do? All of these things confront us as individuals, groups and classes.

Those persons seriously involved in literature, which may be in itself a search for identity, especially in our times, will realize that though I begin in perhaps a facetious tone, I am really quite serious in my jokes. I am greatly concerned with literature, and I am deeply involved with social action, and I am fortunate enough (or, perhaps, unfortunate enough) to see no fundamental difference between the one and the other. I can appreciate and enjoy fully the literary traditions out of which contemporary Negroes and other writers have developed, and I respect and admire and enjoy their works. I have my opinions and have formed judgments as an individual and as an artist about what I consider to be their respective merits. However, though I consider myself primarily a literary man, I am also an entertainer, so, once again, if you say that I am a literary figure, I will say, "I am an entertainer." If you say that I am an entertainer, I will say, "No. I am a clown." My reason for telling you this is that these dualities are the basis of my approach toward certain important matters. One of the functions of the study of literature is to enlighten those whose interest is with the writer himself. Now, I have chosen, in my writing, to address myself primarily to those people who are living in the ghettoes of our country, who are still left on the streets, who are still down in the cotton patch, and whose literary experiences are nil because of the circumstances of their entire lives.

But does this mean that the riches of literature are to be denied this important class of Americans, white and black? I think not. I believe that the joys and the wealth of our culture belong to all. But I would like to go a step further and deliberately aim my message at the involvement of that lowest stratum in our culture and our economy, the Negro people. I would like, if possible, to carry my revolutionary message to them in a language which I think they can immediately perceive, without, at the same time, being patronizing or choosing to speak down to them from the heights of literary eminence.

By that I mean I attempt to use all of the elements of popular folk culture and try to weld them into an instrument of communication, because in addition to being the expression of what a person is, of what his personality is and what his point of view is, literature is also fundamentally communication.

More fully, it is not enough, in my point of view, merely to expose myself and all of the truth and the wonder and the awe I feel at being a person upon the face of the earth. I have, in addition, to communicate that feeling and insight to others. But even to communicate is not the final result, as far as I am concerned. I deliberately set out to communicate in order to elevate. I must clearly assume an exaggerated point of view, an exaggerated measure of my own importance to think that I have something which, when communicated to a larger mass of people, can elevate them, but without that egotism, without that assumed divine right to inform and direct and educate, I think no artist ever gets off the ground. The Negro in this country has to write protest, because he is a protestant. He can't help but be. He cannot accept the situation in which he finds himself, so, therefore, he is driven to scream out against the oppression that surrounds him, that suffocates him. So that what he writes will be in the nature of protest. The protest has been, and still is and must continue to be, loud, bitter and haranguing. It must irritate. It must shake. It must disturb. Itmust move the very bowels of compassion. It must be angry. It must be aimed at corrective action and now.

But those are not the limits of protest, and I have chosen to approach the whole problem from another direction. I say that we can protest about an unjust situation on an intellectual level by saying that in addition to being unjust the situation is also ridiculous, and that we can show that it is ridiculous, and perhaps even laughable, and, therefore, not worthy of the behavior of educated, culturally advanced human beings, such as must be the kind of people, both white and black, who inhabit America at this late date.

I have chosen to make my protest in the form of revealing the ridiculous institutions that have brought us, in our national life, to a very critical point in our cultural, economic, political and social history. And I think that such a protest is valid. The theatre, as you know, has long been given to pointing the finger of ridicule at that which it found to be ridiculous. I can imagine no other institution on the face of the earth more ridiculous than the institution of segregation, and, though it is cruel, though it is capable of committing murder and destroying me and oppressing me physically and brutally, emasculating me, still, there is a possibility that I can maintain enough of my own balance and point of view to say that in addition to being oppressive and in addition to killing me it is also absolutely ridiculous. Because, sometimes, those who will not respond to the validity of your argument as an experience in logic or rationality will respond if your argument is presented in another form, in another light altogether. And I happen to believe that one of the traditions by which my people have been able to survive in the oppressive atmosphere of American culture has been the tradition of corrective and educational humor.

We told jokes, one to another, but we weren't telling jokes for the sake of getting off fast quips and gags. That stream of humor had to carry our sense of self, our sense of history, our hope of the future, our religious concern about man's relationship to man. It had to point us to the future and tell us to "Wait, bide your time. The day is coming when you can stand up and be a man." Humor, the folk humor of the Negro people, is, of course, not the only way in which the Negro chose to stand up and assert his manhood. Those of us who were gifted enough to play trumpets and beat drums in New Orleans and other places of oppression could stand up and, with our horns, declare our manhood. We couldn't say it in the English language. We couldn't say, "I, too, am a man," because that could get you killed. But there was a chance that when you had a horn at your lips you could communicate fully the fact of your manhood, as long as you didn't do it in intelligible English. This is the nature of jazz, so far as I felt it and understand it. But I am discussing humor and I am dealing in terms that I hope are socially responsible. I would like to give back to the Negro people the humor they themselves created, give it back in the form in which they created it and let it begin, once again, to serve the function for which it was originally created.

There was a man, who has become synonymous with some of the aspects of our trouble, named Stepin Fetchit. Now, we know that Stepin Fetchit was earning a living; he almost made himself a rich man by caricaturing a certain attitude about Negro people which we know not to be true but which certain people wanted to believe, and this idea was that all Negroes were lazy and stupid and they drawled and said, "Yowsah."

This man was, perhaps, not very bright, and he became a good stereotypical justification of what was wrong with Negroes and why they lived in ghettoes and why they'd never make it. Because they just didn't have it. They were all shiftless. They were all lazy. And they never thought for themselves and always waited for somebody to do something for them. On this basis, we rightly protested the use of Mr. Stepin Fetchit and his character and his talent to demean the whole Negro race, because we realized that the community about us was drawing conclusions from his behavior which we knew to be incorrect and using his behavior to justify the continued oppression in which we found ourselves.

But let's look a little deeper into what originally was behind the meaning of Stepin Fetchit's lazy character. As you will remember, those of you who have a long memory, we were slaves in this country, and we were required to work from sunup to sundown and there was no time off, no coffee breaks, no Social Security, none of the few benefits that we have only lately acquired. Slavery was straight labor, even above and beyond the devotion required of a mule. And we were required, for the benefit of our masters, to work ourselves, literally, to death. If you could—if you were an honest man, an honest Negro, and if you had no way to escape—you would literally work yourself to death, because it was cheaper for a master to work a slave to death and get all the work out of him and later buy a replacement. Now, a slave like Stepin Fetchit, who really was a smart man, who understood the ways of the white folks, would suddenly discover that he was regarded as a very unintelligent creature, so when the master would send him to get a rope he would come back with maybe a plow, until finally the slaveowner would get the idea that this man was so dumb and so inefficient and so shiftless that nothing could be done but to let him sit under a tree.

You might ask why. Why didn't the man take Stepin Fetchit and sell him or get rid of him? Because unconsciously this behavior identified, confirmed and reinforced the slaveowner's prejudices against the possibility of Negroes being responsible, thoughtful and efficient people. So that the Negro achieved two purposes. He saved himself by being too dumb to do the work that the mules and the other slaves were doing, and therefore he survived. And he also gave the overlord the satisfaction of believing that all Negroes were dumb and lazy.

However, I must now protest against the wrong, the invalid use of a stereotype, by whites or by others, after it has been disembodied and the protest content has been removed. Most of the stereotypes we know about Negroes were invented by Negroes for the purposes of survival and social correction. We do this all the time. It is a way in which a society tries to control its members. It will criticize its leaders. It will state its aims, through stereotypes, through jokes and humor. But our humor has been taken away, emptied of its bitter protest content, and has been used against us. And this has led us, sometimes, to rebel against our own humor. In my play *Purlie Victorious* I have tried to restore the protest content of the Negro's humor. . . .

I have tried in [scene II] to sketch broadly what I knew to be the psychological and personal truths of the lives of many people and what I knew were the economic and social foundations against which those lives had, necessarily, to be lived.

Each actor, each human being . . . is caught up in a role, in a stereotype, and he behaves in accord with that stereotype. Now, I have tried to put in the stereotype what I know to be the truth of the situation out of which the stereotype grew in the first place, and I am happy to say that I think I have succeeded.

But these were not stereotypes that I created. They were created a long time ago on the plantations and then were taken by white-faced minstrels and emptied of their ammunition and protest and bite and made into something altogether different. I merely tried to bring them back where they belong.

But what is my larger intent? Is it merely to show you that we can laugh? That we look at the situations of life with more than angry eyes?

No. I have a specific reason for writing a play like *Purlie Victorious* in the manner in which it was written. To me, my intent was to have a handbook of consolation, information and struggle, which my people and their friends could use to understand, explain the situation in which they found themselves and point the way toward a possible solution.

This particular play was situated in the South, where the Negro is in economic servitude on a plantation. Now, another kind of play needs to be written about the Negro in Harlem, who is in a different kind of servitude, but nonetheless real and nonetheless disturbing and about which something must be done. That play could be done with humor, and it could point the same kind of moral and teach the same kind of lesson in the same kind of way. For it is equally ridiculous that people live in slums in this day and age of automation, when we have in our power all that it takes to create better housing and decent communities. It's ridiculous, in addition to everything else it is, that people are required to live in rat-infested decaying slum houses.

But to turn again to *Purlie Victorious.* One of the things that always intrigued me was the relationship between the iambicpentameter verse form, that came down to us through the King James version of the Bible and from Shakespeare, and the use of it, consciously and unconsciously, by the Negro ministers who wouldn't know an iambic pentameter from a hole in the ground. And yet they have adapted this particular structure to their use, and it seems to me that part of my literary job is to make conscious use of this technique.

Now, Purlie Victorious is a minister who has ordained himself. He is a stereotype of that Negro minister. If you ask him what time it is, he has to intone the answer. He can't give you a straight answer without intoning it. And Lulubelle Gussie Mae Jenkins is the updated version of Topsy, a little Negro girl who has never learned to value herself as a person and, therefore, wanders around, willy-nilly, wanting to be loved but not knowing exactly how to demand it, because she doesn't think that

she's worthy of anybody's love, especially the white folks'.

But Purlie sees her and he sees something altogether different.

Listen to this, in which Purlie Victorious, our young minister, talks about Lulubelle Gussie Mae Jenkins. He is speaking to his sister, Missy.

PURLIE: How wondrous are the daughters of my people,
Yet knoweth not the glories of themselves!
Where do you suppose I found her, Missy—
This Ibo prize—this Zulu Pearl—
This long lost lily of the black Mandingo—
Kikuyu maid, beneath whose brown embrace
Hot suns of Africa are burning still: where—where?
A drudge; a serving wench; a feudal fetch-pot:
A common scullion in the white man's kitchen.
Drowned is her youth in thankless southern dishpans;
Her beauty spilt for Dixiecratic pigs!
This brown-skinned grape! this wine of Negro vintage—

MISSY: (*Who has no tolerance for the iambic pentameter.*) I know all that, Purlie. But what's her name?

LULUBELLE: (*Looking at Missy.*) I don't think he likes my name so much. It's Lulubelle, Ma'am. Lulubelle Gussie Mae Jenkins.

MISSY: (*Gushing with motherly assurance.*) Lulubelle Gussie Mae Jenkins. My, that's nice.

PURLIE: Nice! It's an insult to the Negro people.

MISSY: Purlie. Behave yourself.

PURLIE: A previous condition of servitude, a badge of inferiority, and I refuse to have it in my organization. Change it.

MISSY: You want me to bosh your mouth for you?

PURLIE: Lulubelle. Gussie Mae. Jenkins. What does it mean in Swahili? Cheap labor.

MISSY: Swahili?

PURLIE: One of the thirteen silver tongues of Africa—Swahili, Washingo. . . . (*He names the thirteen tongues.*) A language of moons, of velvet drums, hot days, of rivers, red splashed and bird song bright. Black fingers in rice white at sunset red. Ten thousand Queens of Sheba.

MISSY: Just where did Purlie find you, honey?

LULUBELLE: It was in Dawson, Alabama, last Sunday, Aunt Missy. Right in the Junior Choir.

MISSY: The Junior Choir? My. My. My.

PURLIE: (*Carried away.*) Behold, I said, this dark and holy vessel, in whom should burn that golden nut brown joy which Negro womanhood was made to be.

Ten thousand queens. Ten thousand Queens of Sheba, Ethiopia, herself, in all her beauteous wonder. Come to restore the ancient thrones of Kush.

Parenthetically, this is iambic pentameter, if nothing else. I can attest to that. But what—what am I trying to do?

I am trying to correct a distorted image of Negro womanhood that has persisted in our culture down to this very day. I could, of course, do this clinically, by describing in ones and twos and yeses and nos, what I think happened, but I chose to do it in a poetic form, because it's more concise and it allows me to express what I actually feel and know by my senses and by my emotions to be true.

Because that is beautiful which has somewhere excited love, and this is the definition of beauty, and if a woman is loved, she is beautiful, and I must tell my women that they are beautiful, first, because I find them to be so, and, second, because they need it as an extension of my manhood and my confidence in myself.

I can say to them, "You are beautiful; you are not scrubbing the floors. That is not you. You are a queen. Ten thousand Queens of Sheba. Scrubbing floors on your knees. Get up. Walk. Talk. Be what you are. My queen. My woman, whom I will defend and fight for to the death." And this is what I tried to say in a comedy. In a farce, mind you, to Negro womanhood.

Now, you begin to get the reason for my choice of an outlandish form—because, unfortunately, I cannot express those same sentiments in realistic prose.

This is not to suggest that I have anything against realistic prose; it is merely that what I have to say creates for me a need of expression in another form, and I think that the reconstruction of the beauty of Negro womanhood will be the beginning of the emancipation of Negro manhood. This is the way I approach that particular problem.

Toward the end of the play, Purlie at last confronts his archenemy Old Captain Cotchipee, and he goes up the hill and gets the old man whipped and gets money from the old man—not by a direct confrontation—but when he comes down the hill his desire to impress his beloved gets the better of him, so he preaches a tremendous sermon of hell-fire and damnation in which he puts Old Captain on trial and consigns him to whip lashes. But this is all a sermon. It's all an extension of his need as a man to express himself, even violently. But it's done in a sermon.

Old Captain, of course, comes in during this sermonizing and there is Purlie talking to the man he has just gotten through burying as a result of his tremendous power.

After Old Captain comes in, his son, Charlie, is dragged in by the Deputy. Old Captain thinks Purlie has done some stealing, but the guilty culprit is really his own son. . . .

I've tried to sketch for you, briefly, what the content of *Purlie Victorious* is, and why I chose to express my sentiments in the style and manner that I did. Satire, farce, slapstick, but, underneath it all, a true appreciation of some important aspects of life.

In the book of the play is my apologia—the reason I wrote the book in the first place—and it reads as follows:

"Our churches will say that segregation is immoral because it makes perfectly wonderful people, white and black, do immoral things. Our courts will say segregation is illegal because it makes perfectly wonderful people, white and black, do illegal things. And, finally, our theatre will say segregation is ridiculous because it makes perfectly wonderful people, white and black, do ridiculous things. That was the point I had in writing the play and that was the point I hope I have gotten across."

But we were talking about the wonderful world of law and order. If you'll recall, in the scene between Old Captain and Gitlow and Charlie, Old Captain was defending what was, to him, ordained by God. He believed that anyone who attempted to change the world of law and order, this peaceful ordained relationship between the two groups, was threatening the very foundations of civilization. Because Old Captain believed, as quite a few of us believe, whiteliberals and black liberals, that law and order is the essence of civilization. But this is not necessarily true. Justice is the essence of civilization, and when law and order is imposed upon a basically unjust situation there is bound to be a clash, sooner or later, between law and order—no matter how respectably law and order is presented and preserved—and those forces whose cry and need for justice makes them unable to maintain a real respect for law and order.

I do not say that I have been liberated from all respect for law and order. On the contrary, I realize what chaotic conditions could come about if the skeins of law and order were to vanish, if violence and brute force were the only resort to settling our disputes.

I know what would happen. I really want law and order, but I realize that law and order presuppose justice. When we speak of young people in the streets of Harlem as having no respect for policemen we must remember that the policemen had no respect for those young people in the first place. And when we describe young people as "punks" or "hoodlums"—words I hate to use; I don't use those kinds of words because it gives permission for a policeman to shoot a human being and forget that he is a human being—who loot, break stores open and rob jewelry and socks and underwear and garments—and we deplore these things—let us not forget the other looting that goes on silently and quietly, even on the level of the policeman, who, at a certain time every week, goes to a certain store or apartment and picks up a brown paper bag filled with money.

Who is the more successful of the looters, those unfortunate young people who were out on the streets of dismal cities on hot August nights or the policeman who has, for years, made it in a middle-class society by looting every day in the black community, by turning his back on dope, by turning his back on gambling and prostitution, by not insisting upon the preservation of even the most basic rights for the members of that community? I think one should know where the looting began in the first place.

If there is to be respect for law and order it must be based upon mutual understanding and a respect for those who are under the law, and order must be maintained for the benefit of all of those who are under the law.

We face a great crisis in our country today. We have been called upon by some of our leaders to refrain from demonstrations and protest because they might be construed as an attack upon law and order. We are told that attacks on law and order might give ammunition to the white backlash, and there are those who think that this is the greatest harm that could come to the cause of the Negro people.

Now this is a debatable point. I am forced to ask, if there is a white backlash, what is it lashing back from? Where was it all the time? Am I sure that those who are lashing back were not waiting for someone to come along and give them an excuse to lash back?

I am not so certain. I fear greatly that the Negro people, after mounting a magnificent struggle for their freedom, as they have done so often in the past, will be asked, once again, in the name of some vague larger freedom, in the name of the larger community, in the name of law and order, to halt their struggle and, once again, we'll come out of that struggle, as I personally came out of World War II, to find that we have lost the war that we thought we had won. And I would hope that those who ask for patience, those who ask us to wait will meet us with a real concrete program of action, with real remedies, so we will have something to be patient about, something to wait for, something that we can understand and appreciate and explain to ourselves and our children.

We wait now, at the darkest hour of the night, in order to make it peaceable and to prepare ourselves better for the action which is certain to come at dawn.

TITLE COMMENTARY

📖 *PURLIE VICTORIOUS* (produced in New York City, 1961; adapted as a screenplay, *Gone Are the Days,* 1963; also released as *The Man from C.O.T.T.O.N.*)

Edith Oliver

SOURCE: "The Theatre Light," in *The New Yorker,* Vol. XXXVII, No. 34, October 7, 1961, pp. 129-32.

Purlie Victorious, Ossie Davis's first play, at the Cort, is a farce set on a cotton plantation, and having to do with the attempt of a Negro preacher named Purlie Victorious to get his hands on five hundred dollars that belonged to a dead cousin (female) and is now in the custody of Captain Cotchipee, the owner of the plantation and a senile leftover from the Old South. Purlie persuades an uneducated country girl to masquerade as the cousin, and also, with great difficulty, prevails on his foxy, play-it-safe brother Gitlow, a field hand, to soften up the old man while she wheedles the five hundred out of him. Purlie intends to use the cash to buy back a church for his fellow-Negroes from the Captain. Everything works according to plan until the girl innocently signs her own name on the receipt.

The play, unfortunately, doesn't seem to jell, or, much of the time, to convince, even on its own terms. Nevertheless, Mr. Davis has written some pointed, witty lines ("You're a disgrace to the Negro profession!" Purlie shouts at the girl when she tries to back out of the scheme), and the actors—among them Mr. Davis himself, in the title role—are so good that they almost save the day. I don't think I shall ever forget Purlie exploding into an eloquent sermon, speaking and chanting and singing, as he describes the way in which he has told off the Captain and then beaten him to death—all fantasy, of course, but, as he explains, "I never told a lie I didn't expect to come true someday." Ruby Dee, as expert and sophisticated an actress as we have, does some wonderful clowning as the gawky, simple-hearted hick with a cracker accent. My favorite among her scenes is one in which she reports, with professional as well as personal indignation, that the Captain has made a pass at her while she was *working* in his kitchen. The funniest performance of all is turned in by Godfrey M. Cambridge, as "good old faithful Uncle Gitlow," and he is at his best when he kneels at the Captain's feet and, with a dead pan and a mocking eye, mechanically croons "Old Black Joe."

At its worst, the play reminded me—whether it should have or not—of those clumsy left-wing shows (there were a few good ones, too) that nearly extinguished the theatre in the nineteen-thirties. Mr. Davis is, in a sense, playing it safe; if what the Negro in the South was really up against were dopey old cartoons like Captain C., then segregation could be ended in twenty minutes. He

has used humor to distort the truth rather than to point it up.

There are two questions worth asking about a first play. One is "What has the dramatist accomplished?" The answer here is that Mr. Davis has shown himself capable, at his best, of making up characters and scenes and dialogue. The other is "Is he in the right line of work?" And the answer to this one is yes.

📖 *ESCAPE TO FREEDOM: A PLAY ABOUT YOUNG FREDERICK DOUGLASS* (1978; first produced in New York at the Town Hall, 1976)

Kirkus Reviews

SOURCE: A review of *Escape to Freedom: A Play about Young Frederick Douglass,* in *Kirkus Reviews,* Vol. XLVI, No. 12, June 15, 1978, p. 641.

A free-flowing play without the standard breaks between scenes, and with one actor portraying Douglass on stage throughout as six others (three black, three white) come and go in a number of different roles. Sometimes speaking directly to the audience, more often presenting his story through dialogue, Fred starts off as a child learning the facts of slave life. He experiences as a revelation a master's explaining to his wife why slaves can't be taught to read and devotes himself thenceforth to literacy as the pathway to freedom. Punctuated with slave songs, abounding in incidents of white callousness and illogic, and emphasizing Douglass' proud determination, the dramatization is a natural choice for school and other group programs.

Paul Heins

SOURCE: A review of *Escape to Freedom: A Play about Young Frederick Douglass,* in *The Horn Book Magazine,* Vol. LIV, No. 4, August, 1978, p. 408.

First performed in 1976, the five scenes and the prologue present episodes from the life of Frederick Douglass: his childhood in a slave cabin, his zeal in learning how to read, his treatment on a slave-breaking plantation, his experiences in Baltimore, and his escape to New York. The directions for the stage production are informal and improvisational. For example, the various parts in the play, except for the role of Fred Douglass, are taken by six actors listed as Black Woman, Black Man, Black Boy, White Woman, White Man, White Boy; and the cast is responsible for rearranging the sets. To accompany the mood of the action, the scenes are interspersed with such well-known spirituals and folk songs as "Give Me That Old-Time Religion," "Go Tell It on the Mountain," and "Blue-Tail Fly." The play, which incidentally reveals the average Southern slaveholder's lack of sensitivity, celebrates—directly and naturally—the Black slaves' urge to freedom.

Helen Gregory

SOURCE: A review of *Escape to Freedom: A Play about Young Frederick Douglass,* in *School Library Journal,* Vol. 25, No. 1, September, 1978, p. 134.

Dramatically, this is the most challenging, interesting, and entertaining play for young people to appear in a long time. Ossie Davis, redoubtable actor and writer, has produced a highly imaginative and exciting tribute to Frederick Douglass in which seven characters (Douglass himself; a Black man, woman, and child; and a white man, woman, and child) take on various parts. Douglass' rise from slavery to freedom is depicted with dialog, narrative, music, and dance; simple stage effects make it possible to produce the play anywhere. The only false note is the cover design which sets Douglass against a golden oval that resembles a halo. Great people don't need to be saints.

Denise M. Wilms

SOURCE: A review of *Escape to Freedom: A Play about Young Frederick Douglass,* in *Booklist,* Vol. 72, No. 1, September 1, 1978, p. 45.

First publicly performed at New York's Town Hall in 1976, Davis's stylized dramatization of the formative years of Frederick Douglass is now available in book form. The cast is small, the action is vivid and well paced, intended to portray the trials of slavery as well as the broad development of Douglass' life. Music is not provided for the many songs and hymns, nor are there suggestions on how simple or complicated the set might be; novice directors would find such information helpful, for the play has the kind of drawing power that could make it a frequently performed favorite.

LANGSTON: A PLAY (1982)

Kirkus Reviews

SOURCE: A review of *Langston: A Play,* in *Kirkus Reviews,* Vol. L, No. 18, September 15, 1982, p. 1062.

A biographical play about Langston Hughes's early life, presented as a sort-of autobiography with Langston reminiscing to a group of actors, who in turn play the roles in the remembered scenes. Glimpsed in the process are Hughes's determination to be a writer *and* a Negro writer; his mean rich father's insistence that he study engineering; his stay in Mexico with his father; later a happier stay in Paris; his poetry prizes and struggles with poverty; his ground-down mother, a house worker with a college degree; and a strategic talk, at white-taught Lincoln College for Negroes, with a visiting black professor whose message is that "some of us have to be Uncle Toms." Frequent quotations from Hughes's poems provide the required highs, and the slipping back and forth between memories and actors gives some stage

interest to the scenes, which tend to be drawn with a heavy hand. Like Davis's *Escape to Freedom,* about Frederick Douglass, this has obvious potential for school and youth-group production.

Zena Sutherland

SOURCE: A review of *Langston: A Play,* in *Bulletin of the Center for Children's Books,* Vol. 36, No. 5, January, 1983, pp. 86-7.

This biography-within-a-play begins with a church drama group (White Man, White Woman, Black Boy, Black Girl, etc.) putting on a play by Hughes, who walks in and, having said, "I'm due up at the high school in a few minutes," then stays for the duration of the action. Thenceforth Hughes is on stage, as he and the actors dramatize scenes from the poet's life, with the characters (White Man, Black Boy, etc.) at the rehearsal playing all parts. The artifice doesn't quite work and the writing is not that of Davis at his dramatic best, but the play gives a great deal of information about the life of Langston Hughes, the genre affords intimate views of his emotions and ideas, and the incorporation of Hughes's writings adds richness and variety.

Denise M. Wilms

SOURCE: A review of *Langston: A Play,* in *Booklist,* Vol. 79, No. 10, January 15, 1983, p. 675.

Davis presents a play within a play that uses a cast of nine to portray important incidents and relationships in the life of black poet and writer Langston Hughes. The story opens with a church drama group preparing to rehearse a play *by* Hughes. They hear he is in town for a reading and hopelessly wish he would drop in; he does, and the group excitedly chats with him. That is the device for easing into what becomes a series of vignettes that sketch out his youth and development as a writer. The effect is a lively and absorbing portrait of Hughes that can be read independently as biography. Production will require a number of simple sets.

Hazel Rochman

SOURCE: A review of *Langston: A Play,* in *School Library Journal,* Vol. 29, No. 6, February, 1983, p. 87.

In a play about Langston Hughes and his struggle to become a writer in the face of poverty and prejudice, Davis combines scenes of dramatic action with monologue and Hughes's poetry. From Hughes's Kansas childhood, rich with the stories of his proud grandmother, the play moves chronologically through his life to the coming of the Depression when he was in his late 20s. Hughes's poems flash from the play: with their colloquial and jazz rhythms they speak directly to the audience, from the lyrical "A Negro Speaks of Rivers" to the angry "Clean the spittoons, boy!" But the dramatic action captures little of the authentic voice, the range and energy, that we hear in the poetry. The dialogue is often stilted, the construction awkward, the characters stereotyped. Readers will find a deeper sense of Hughes as a man and a writer in his moving autobiography, *The Big Sea,* which covers the same period.

Patricia J. Cianciolo

SOURCE: "Critically Speaking," in *The Reading Teacher,* Vol. 36, No. 7, March, 1983, pp. 712-16.

Ossie Davis has used a creative literary device to tell a fictionalized partial biography of poet and playwright Langston Hughes. In *Langston: A Play* Hughes visits a church where a drama group is rehearsing one of his plays and he recreates scenes from his early life by having these actors act them out. A generous amount of Hughes's poetry is included, giving depth to the significant aspects of his childhood, years as university student, the time he began to get recognition for his writing, and his insistence that "Black is beautiful!"

JUST LIKE MARTIN (1992)

Publishers Weekly

SOURCE: A review of *Just Like Martin,* in *Publishers Weekly,* Vol. 239, No. 39, August 31, 1992, p. 80.

Fourteen-year-old Ike Stone and his pals are thrilled to be part of the Civil Rights movement sweeping the deep South in the 1960s, but the depth of racial hatred is brought painfully home when two of their friends are killed in a bombing. The peaceful demonstration that the boy and his friends mount in response to this senseless violence forms the climax of this stirring novel. Equally moving is the subplot dealing with how Ike and his troubled father take halting steps towards making peace with each other. Noted theater figure Davis has loaded enough action and emotional energy for two novels into his tale. Even though his characterizations (particularly of the adults) sometimes blur, the book's drive and vision more than compensate. A passionate first novel.

Hazel Rochman

SOURCE: A review of *Just Like Martin,* in *Booklist,* Vol. 89, No. 1, September 1, 1992, p. 48.

Davis sets his docunovel about the civil rights movement in the crucial time of the march on Washington and the assassination of the president, when children died in the bombing of a church and their classmates studied nonviolence and overcame police dogs and clubs. The story is told in the voice of 13-year-old Isaac Stone, dutiful son, straight-A student in his Alabama school, and jun-

ior assistant pastor of Holy Oak Baptist. He struggles to keep his personal vow of nonviolence and dreams of becoming a preacher "just like Martin." Though several minor characters are vividly drawn, Isaac is more role model than person. Some of the dialogue is stiff, and there are loose ends in the story, especially in Isaac's relationship with his troubled Korean veteran father, who nurses a pistol, refuses to espouse nonviolence, and then suddenly does. This story doesn't have the lyrical power of Moore's *Freedom Songs* in showing what it was like to be young at that time. What is riveting here is the sense of history being made—of struggle and commitment in one community. Readers will go from this book to the great documentaries in book and video and to the stirring essays and speeches of the time.

Kirkus Reviews

SOURCE: A review of *Just Like Martin,* in *Kirkus Reviews,* Vol. LX, No. 18, September 15, 1992, p. 1185.

In his first novel, the actor and playwright plunges readers into the headiest days of the Civil Rights movement. Isaac, almost 14, is dismayed when his protective father refuses to let him join the great March on Washington; later, after the Young People's Bible Class at his church is bombed, he helps organize a children's march and sees his father beaten by police when the march is broken up. Davis shows how a local church could expand its role as community center to play a part in inspiring and guiding a national movement, inviting readers to consider the conflict between Isaac, who has embraced Martin Luther King's philosophy of nonviolence, and his father, who carries a pistol and promises to give as he receives. Despite witnessing racial violence and experiencing steady harassment from his peers, Isaac's convictions endure. He gets to meet his hero, Dr. King; in the end, his father, after Kennedy's assassination and some soul-searching, has a change of heart. Dramatic and simply told, with a cast of strong personalities.

Lois F. Anderson

SOURCE: A review of *Just Like Martin,* in *The Horn Book Magazine,* Vol. LXVIII, No. 6, November-December, 1992, pp. 722-23.

In a novel set in Alabama in 1963, fourteen-year-old Isaac Stone is anxious to participate in the march on Washington with a group from his church, led by their pastor, Reverend Cable. Stone—"most people call me by my family name"—greatly admires Martin Luther King, Jr., and his methods of nonviolence, but his father, Ike, feels differently and will not permit the boy to go on the march. His outlook reflects his experiences as a soldier in the Korean War as well as the discrimination and violence he faces as a black man in the South. Since his wife's death, he feels a strong responsibility to protect his son. "'I promised Lucy to look after the boy, see that nothing happened to him. . . . Somebody hurt my son, I'd have to go up there and find him, and kill him, blow Washington, D.C., clean off the map! Now you wouldn't want a crime like that on your conscience, would you, preacher?'" he says to Reverend Cable. The difficulty of maintaining a nonviolent stance in the midst of violence is clearly delineated when Stone is pushed to the limit by a young bully. The author realistically presents arguments for both sides, but non-violence wins out, even to the conversion of Ike Stone. The book incorporates three actual events that occurred in Birmingham in 1963—the children's march from the Sixteenth Street Baptist Church in May, the march on Washington in August, and the September bombing of the church when four little girls were killed—evoking memories of the tragedies of the civil rights movement with passion and drama. Martin Luther King, Jr., is always present in the background, and his "I Have a Dream" speech becomes very important to young Stone. The author is describing events he experienced personally; hence this work is an authentic voice of a troubled time in the history of America.

Publishers Weekly

SOURCE: "Flying Starts: Ossie Davis," in *Publishers Weekly*, Vol. 239, No. 55, December 28, 1992, pp. 26-7.

Ossie Davis—actor, playwright and director—has an enviable status as an American artist. He is as much admired for his ongoing commitment to the cause of racial justice as he is for his accomplishments in the theatre, motion pictures and television, including his most recent work in the television series *Evening Shade*.

The publication of his first novel *Just Like Martin,* a young adult book, presents another facet of Davis's talent and his social conscience. The book is a recreation of the civil rights movement as witnessed through the lives of the black community in a small Alabama town in 1963. Central to the story is the local black church and the young people of its congregation as they organize their own contribution to the great social changes fomented by the Civil Rights Movement and the life and oratory of Martin Luther King Jr.

While Davis has written for the stage, film and TV, he is quick to note his trepidation in taking on the YA project. "I always intended to write about the civil rights struggles," he says. "I originally hoped it would be a play about Martin, but it just wasn't working. So I tried to branch into the deep waters of the novel and I'm not entirely sure I survived." His editor, Olga Litowinsky, thinks he has not only survived but flourished. After working with Davis on two of his plays, she says, "Ossie's plays didn't require any editing. He's a master of dialogue and structure and I was absolutely convinced that he could write a novel."

Davis wrote the book in stages, Litowinsky explains,

sending in sections of dialogue. She would make notations and return them to Davis who would then fill in the narrative. "It took three passes before we had a finished manuscript; by then I knew we had something powerful and moving."

Davis attributes his need to take on new creative challenges and new mediums of expression to a deep sense of responsibility to African-American traditions of culture and a need to document the political history around it. "I can move between these differing disciplines because I am essentially a storyteller, and the story I want to tell is about black people. Sometimes I sing the story, sometimes I dance it, sometimes I tell tall tales about it, but I always want to share my great satisfaction at being a black man at this time in history."

Any book about Martin Luther King Jr. would necessarily focus on the black church, and *Just Like Martin* recreates the sense of an extended family, connected by the church community, that black people of a particular generation will recognize instantly. In particular the work focuses on the young adults of the congregation; their initiation into social protest, and the concern of church leaders and parents over the possibility of violent white retaliation that was a real and constant threat during those years.

Davis says the story is an attempt to recapture some sense of the black church as a political and moral base in the fight against racism, and to explain "to young people today about the concept of nonviolence. We used to say that if Martin Luther King Jr. had worked in the post office we'd be in trouble. That's because the black church was the only truly free institution black people had. I'm a product of the black church and it is the central theme to my thinking and my life."

Davis's book embraces the themes and issues of the Civil Rights years—racism, the beginning of the Vietnam war and U.S. domestic neglect—and illustrates how they have evolved into the urban social problems we face today. "Martin always pointed out the connection between poverty and lack of education and integration," he says.

Davis is, of course, also well known for delivering the eulogy at the funeral of Malcolm X, and when asked for his perspective on the assassinated leader, he suggests what his next literary effort may be. "I've decided to close up shop on Malcolm X," he says. "I've done a number of interviews recently because of the movie, but I've decided to stop talking about him for now because I don't know how to say what it is I want to say about Malcolm. The novel may be the way to say it for Malcolm also, I don't know, but I'm looking for a way to talk about what I think Malcolm's message to us is." Nevertheless, whether he writes another novel for young readers, or chooses once again to try a completely different medium, Malcolm's message couldn't be in better hands.

Louise Stearns

SOURCE: A review of *Just Like Martin,* in *Multicultural Review,* Vol. 2, No. 1, March, 1993, p. 67.

Noted actor Ossie Davis has written an uplifting and realistic look at the Civil Rights Movement in America. Set in Montgomery, Alabama, in the early sixties, *Just Like Martin* tells the story of a 14-year-old African American and his personal struggle to be a passive protester. Isaac Stone's greatest wish is to be "just like Martin" (the Rev. Martin Luther King, Jr.). Young Stone shares King's dream of justice for all and the desire for nonviolent demonstrations to call attention to racial injustice. Stone struggles with the recent loss of his mother and a father who is convinced that passiveness is the same as cowardice. As Stone witnesses the bombing of his church, the death of two of his friends, and the beating of his father by police, he is faced with a personal dilemma: Can he continue to turn the other cheek?

The reader grows with Stone as he reaches emotional milestones. He learns to persevere through many hardships. With the help of his friends and the wise counsel of his pastor and Martin Luther King, Jr., Stone matures and becomes a responsible young adult—a true hero of his time.

Davis's book accurately and sensitively reflects the issues facing African-Americans in the 1960s. The realistic characters experience genuine fears, friendships, and pain. The reader readily identifies with these emotions and develops an understanding of the attitudes and sensibilities prevalent at the time. *Just Like Martin* goes beyond a narrative of events; it gives the reader a deep admiration for the unconquerable spirit of the people involved in this facet of American history.

Additional coverage of Davis's life and career is contained in the following sources published by The Gale Group: *Contemporary Authors New Revision Series,* Vol. 53; *Authors and Artists for Young Adults,* Vol. 17; *Black Writers,* Vol. 2; *Dictionary of Literary Biography,* Vols. 7, 38; and *Something about the Author,* Vol. 81.

Patricia Lee Gauch

1934-

American author of fiction, nonfiction, and picture books.

Major works include *Christina Katerina and the Box* (1971), *Grandpa and Me* (1972), *This Time, Tempe Wick?* (1974), *Thunder at Gettysburg* (1975), *Dance, Tanya* (1989).

INTRODUCTION

Although her books for children range from whimsical retellings of folk songs and legends for early readers to serious treatments of painful, real-life subjects for young adults, Gauch is recognized principally for her accessible, historically based stories and picture books for primary graders. Gauch's easy-to-read accounts of historic events, such as the battle of Gettysburg and the American Revolution, and biographies of historic figures, such as Major Robert Rogers and Temperance Wick, are typically based on true-to-life experiences and told through a young person's perspective. Gauch is also recognized for her early picture books that celebrate the simple childhood pleasures of daydreaming and make believe, and feature spirited young female protagonists. Reviewers favor such characters as Christina Katerina and Tanya, who have unique, dynamic, and well-developed personalities of their own. Based on the adventures and experiences of Gauch's daughter, the Christina Katerina picture book series depicts a feisty, independent, and self-possessed child living with a loving and understanding family. In a similar vein, the stories about Tanya, rooted in Gauch's own childhood memories and experiences, feature a young girl whose exuberance and joy are not only transcendent, but contagious.

Throughout her career, Gauch's works for younger children have been praised for the quality of their prose, honest and sprightly characters, and sensitive approach to subject matter. Her young adult novels, however, have not received as much attention by reviewers. While noted for their realistic protagonists and intriguing ideas, these books have also been criticized for their weak and, at times, unfocused plots. Nonetheless, all of Gauch's books are very close to her heart, as she stated in an interview with Robert C. Small, Jr., in *Journal of Youth Services in Libraries:* "[M]y bottom line is writing and editing books that enhance a child's humanity . . . and this comes from my having been a mother, writer, teacher, editor. I don't forget the child."

Biographical Information

Born Patricia Lee in Detroit, Michigan, Gauch spent a lot of time playing and sporting near Lake Michigan. The only child of adoring parents and the darling of her

grandparents, she had a happy childhood, living in a busy suburban neighborhood full of other children. Her uncle was the city editor of the *Detroit Free Press* and later the *Detroit News*. In college, Gauch's interest in writing flourished. She decided on English as her major and, following in the footsteps of her uncle, journalism as her career goal. Gauch attended Miami University, and spent most of her time working on the college newspaper, the *Miami Student*, which claimed to be the nation's oldest newspaper. She eventually became the first woman at Miami University to be selected editor-in-chief of the paper. Her work on the *Student* also prompted her to take a writing class taught by Walter Havighurst, who Gauch credits as one of her greatest inspirations.

In 1955, during her senior year at Miami University, she married scientist Ronald Gauch, and the following year, she graduated with a Bachelor of Arts degree. When her husband was drafted, the couple moved to Fort Knox, Kentucky, where Gauch took a job as a reporter with the *Louisville Courier-Journal*. As the youngest reporter, she took the assignments no one else wanted, which brought her many valuable new experiences, covering such topics as Elvis Presley's early concerts, the Kentucky Derby, and the advent of *Sputnik*, the first space satellite launched by the Russians. She retired from her journalism career to raise her three children; during these years, on the advice of Professor Havighurst, she began writing children's books. Meeting historical biographer Jean Fritz and participating in Fritz's writers' workshop brought Gauch's talents to the fore and helped to establish her as a children's author. In 1970, she received a Master of Arts degree in teaching from Manhattanville College and published her first juvenile work, *My Old Tree*. From 1972 to 1983 she taught literature, with tremendous enjoyment, at Gill St. Bernard's School in Basking Ridge, New Jersey. She also established her own writers' workshop at Rutgers University Extension School while working on her doctorate in philosophy at Drew University, which she eventually completed in 1988. Gauch accepted the position of editor-in-chief at Philomel Books in 1985, and has continued there for over ten years, encouraging and nurturing many talented artists and writing her own stories.

Major Works

Christina Katerina and the Box is the first of a series of books about the energetic and independent Christina Katerina. Inspired by her own daughter's imaginative exploits with a large, empty box, *Christina Katerina and the Box* follows Christina Katerina through her day as she and her friend Fats invent ways to play with a refrigerator box. The children imagine the box is a castle, a club house, a racing car, a spaceship, and finally a dance floor. Christina's mother is relieved when the messy thing at last gives out and can be thrown away. The next day, however, Fats appears with *two* big boxes from his family's new washer and dryer. Gauch continued Christina's adventures in *Christina Katerina and the First Annual Grand Ballet* (1973), *Christina Katerina and the Time She Quit the Family* (1987), *Christina Katerina and the Great Bear Train* (1990), and *Christina Katerina and Fats and the Great Neighborhood War* (1996). In each of these books, Christina expresses firm decisions, makes serious choices, and learns important lessons from her experiences. Enlivened with subtle humor, the "Christina" series presents many familiar frustrations and anxieties felt by both children and parents, and depicts a loving, nurturing, and creative family environment in which a child can be completely herself.

Based on memories of time spent with her grandfather along the shores of Lake Michigan, Gauch's *Grandpa and Me* is an affectionate account of the relationship between a man and his grandson. Dubbed "a beguiling story" by a *Publishers Weekly* critic, *Grandpa and Me* follows the summer activities of the two as they arrive at a cottage at night, walk along the lake shore in the early morning, and play checkers and tic-tac-toe on the porch in the heat of the day. Gauch shifts from simple childhood pleasures to historical fiction in *This Time,*

Tempe Wick? Written for early readers, the book recounts the story of legendary figure Temperance (Tempe) Wick, a strong and strapping farm girl who lived in Jockey Hollow, New Jersey, during the American War for Independence. Tempe, an enthusiastic advocate for the Colonies, provides the American soldiers with food and support. But when the troops become cold and hungry and reinforcements fail to appear, they begin to desert and mutiny. Two try to steal Tempe's beloved horse, but Tempe cleverly hides the animal in her bedroom. Despite her politeness and efforts to help, Tempe is pushed too far and becomes "storming had-quite-enough mad," turning her gun against the soldiers and driving them out of her house with a swift kick. Anita Silvey noted, "By using simple and rustic details, the account humanizes the soldiers of the War of Independence. . . . The book presents a realistic and humane view of the war and of the people who fought it. . . ." David Willis further commented, "[O]ur children asked for [*This Time, Tempe Wick?*] almost every day for quite a while after it first entered the house. It remains a favorite."

Continuing Gauch's efforts to bring history to primary graders, *Thunder at Gettysburg* is based on the eyewitness account of 14-year-old Tillie Pierce Alleman, who was caught in the crossfire at the battle of Gettysburg. Lacking the whimsy and humor of Gauch's earlier histories, such as *Aaron and the Green Mountain Boys* (1972) and *This Time, Tempe Wick?*, *Thunder at Gettysburg* depicts vivid, dramatic, and compelling images of war and death. Sent by her father to transport her neighbor's children from their town home to the safety of a farm in the country, Tillie is horrified when she finds herself in the middle of the Gettysburg battlefield, witnessing the carnage and death of bleeding Union soldiers. She does what she can to care for the injured men—feeding them, hauling water, and tearing bandages to dress their wounds. In the end, she returns safely to her family, but she vows she will not forget her experiences. A *Kirkus Reviews* critic noted, "Some might not care to get this close to the carnage . . . but the scenes of bloodshed are handled with restraint and a minimum of sentimentality."

With a more lighthearted touch, *Dance, Tanya* introduces dear little Tanya who loves nothing in life more than dancing. Although Tanya is too little to take dance lessons with her older sister, Elise, Tanya still dances everywhere she goes to music only she can hear. The family takes great pride in Elise's performance, although Tanya falls asleep during the recital. When the family returns home, Tanya wakes up long enough to perform her special dance for them, and her aunt declares, "I think you have two dancers in your family!" In the end, an elated Tanya trots off with Elise to take her first dance lesson. *Bravo, Tanya* (1992) and *Tanya and Emily in a Dance for Two* (1994) follow Tanya as she emerges as a dancer with more imagination than precision and plenty of enthusiasm to carry her through. Denise M. Wilms commented, "[A] wholehearted respect for Tanya's earnest dedication is evident. A gentle, knowing book."

Awards

Gauch received five citations for Writers of Children's Books of the Year by the New Jersey Institute of Technology for the following titles: *Christina Katerina and the Box* in 1971, *A Secret House* in 1971, *Grandpa and Me* in 1972, *Aaron and the Green Mountain Boys* in 1973, and *Night Talks* in 1983. *This Time, Tempe Wick?* was named a Notable Children's Trade Book in the Field of Social Studies by the National Council for the Social Studies-Children's Book Council.

AUTHOR'S COMMENTARY

Robert C. Small, Jr.

SOURCE: An interview with Patricia Lee Gauch, in *Journal of Youth Services in Libraries,* Vol. 8, No. 1, Fall, 1994, pp. 27-34.

Small: *You have at least four lives, if I can put it that way: author of books for young readers, editor of books for young readers, teacher, and, well, person—wife, mother, friend, that sort of thing. How do these parts of your life relate to each other?*

Gauch: Naturally. Mary Bateson's book *Composing a Life* suggests that women "improvise a life," rather than construct a goal-centered life. That is true. I was a journalist, first, because I am inherently curious and enthusiastic; journalism made room for both. Having a young family made being a journalist difficult, but staying home with my two little girls I rediscovered picture books. The discovery was like discovering a wonderful friend I had never meant to lose. A devotee of Kurt Weise's *Ping* and Wanda Gag's *Millions of Cats,* I picked up my writing career by writing picture books. Luckily, I seemed to write with the rhythms of picture books right from the start. *Christina Katerina and the Box* was the second book I ever wrote; the story came from a chaotic box-filled day with my own five-year-old Christina. While my husband was having an orderly rise in his career as biostatistician, I was grabbing opportunity on the fly. I was lucky enough to be near Jean Fritz's writer's workshop and still luckier to talk Jean into taking me in as a writer. I went to her workshop to become a picture book writer, and learned to be an editor!

Along the way, because I was thirsty for literature of all kinds, I went back to school and became a teacher. Now I find all of these worlds relate; because I raised three children, I am close to what delights a child. I do not forget the child in my writing and editing—in the selecting of story particularly. That's easy to do in this marketing-centered world of children's books. Everyone has their bottom line; my bottom line is writing and editing books that enhance a child's humanity. That's it,

short and sweet, and this comes from my having been a mother, writer, teacher, editor. I don't forget the child.

Small: *How do you go about writing your books for young readers?*

Gauch: There is no one way. I have always loved history. I adore doing research, ferreting out the details of a historical situation that have eluded other researchers. Hmmm, that is an indescribable delight! That happened when I wrote *Aaron and the Green Mountain Boys.* I discovered the innkeeper's eight-year-old son's role at the Battle of Bennington in the local history division of the New York Public Library. And I have always seen the life in history, and have felt that historical crises, such as Gettysburg, Bull Run, reveal the human being under pressure—reveal the tragedy and wonder of us. So, there is the research first in such a book that may take a year! Then there is the writing of it.

Picture books are something else again. Generally I am piqued to do a picture book by something I see or hear. Recently, I was given a photograph that appeared in the *National Geographic* magazine, showing a life-sized granny-type woman made of wool. She was knitting a baby out of the wool unraveling from her own foot! Intriguing. I got up in the middle of the night, and the story came out almost fully written. It was as if it had a life of its own; I was just the vehicle, along for the ride. *Christina Katerina and the Box* was definitely written that way.

Novels work that way, too. When I wrote *Fridays,* I remember getting up each day at six, wandering to my typewriter and wondering where my fingers were going to take me that day. I was invariably surprised.

I am deeply respectful of the stories that seem to come to me unbidden; when they come, I follow! Whether I am on vacation, whether it's the middle of the night, whatever. I stop and write; otherwise I risk their disappearing like a dream at daybreak.

Small: *Have you always approached writing the way you do now, or did you go about it differently early on? Has your work as an editor influenced how you set about writing now?*

Gauch: Editing is a nurturing process, not unlike teaching. One of the hardest things to do when one is an editor *and* writer, is to nurture oneself as a writer. What a writer needs is support, an environment in which they create. An editor plays a crucial part in developing that environment. The biggest problem if one is both editor and writer is taking the time to create one's own writing environment. Where I used to write every morning from six until about one—every day—I now catch writing time on the fly. I write the Tanya books in the middle of the night, for example. Still, that's not all bad. I have always felt one's unconscious is a reservoir of story, and I seem to be able to get to that unconscious reservoir more quickly now in the middle of the night, or at the end of a tired day. I have edited some wonderful novels, Sally Keehn's *I Am Regina,* Brian Jacques' *Redwall;* this makes me anxious to get back to writing novels, if I can only find the time.

Small: *Do you have a favorite book of all those that you've written? Do you have a favorite character you've created?*

Gauch: I realized only recently that I have strong female characters: Christina Katerina, Tanya, Tempe Wick, Tillie Pierce (*Thunder at Gettysburg*). They are very different from one another: Christina is imaginative and determined; Tanya is an artist, looking for her own dance; Tempe is just plain strong; and Tillie is a survivor. I like these women—imagine **Christina Katerina and the Box** has been in print nearly twenty-five years!—and I like to think that each of these characters is some part of me.

Small: *Do you have much opportunity to interact with people the age of your readers? Do you have any strategies for creating that kind of contact?*

Gauch: Yes, yes, yes. I taught in the writing and literature program at Gill St. Bernard's School (Gladstone, New Jersey) for ten years, part-time, and was constantly surrounded with teenagers. During those years and since, I visit classrooms all over the United States, speaking as author mainly. Oh, I don't visit as many classrooms as I would like because editing makes its own demands, but I insist that I am in the classroom several times each semester. I want to begin a new thing: reading children stories that I am writing or am thinking about publishing. I believe we are getting too far away from what the child needs or wants. Our so-called Golden Age of Picture Books, for example, was too frequently aimed at the grandma or mother buyer. Back to kids, is what I say.

Small: *How easy is it for you to get into the mind of the male characters in your books? Do you find the female characters like Tillie in* **Thunder at Gettysburg** *easier to bring to life?*

Gauch: The dictate of being a writer is to be able to walk in the shoes of many kinds of characters; that takes study and sensitivity. Faulkner used to sit on the docks of New Orleans, just listening to the speech patterns of the people that would pass through that port. Not enough of us [writers] do that. We write from our own "voice." But I try to listen—to boys, girls, men, women, old men, old women, young, etc. Yes, I do know my female characters better. I know Tillie inside and out. But I knew Thad and Jerry in **Morelli's Game,** because I had had the real Thad and Jerry in my classes at Gill. I knew their speech patterns, their movement, their humor, goodness knows, and their dreams. But make no mistake, knowing a character outside of one's own personal experience requires ongoing sensitivity and study. I am convinced of that.

Small: *Your books like* **Thunder at Gettysburg** *show places and situations through young characters. Do you have problems keeping the characters from becoming vehicles instead of people?*

Gauch: I don't think I do. In **Thunder,** for example, I tried to look at the war from the humanity of the girl. I looked small. By using a scene-creating style, I insisted the reader walk in her shoes, feel the sweat of that hot July day, know the confusion, the uncertainty, the fear. By bringing her to the moment in the basement of the Weikert house, face to face with a dying General Weed, I wanted to test her character. I was looking squarely at her; the war was the vehicle for revealing the stuff of Tillie, first. That we saw the war because of it is not surprising.

Small: *Looking back over the books you've written, do you see a theme or set of themes that tie that work together?*

Gauch: Oh, I do. And it amazed me when I saw those themes. They are, not surprisingly, themes that celebrate the individual's own possibilities, the individual's own imagination. Particularly the female characters of my books are confronted by social or political or situational barriers—giant ones. And frequently the characters are confronted by double choices. Tempe Wick comes to mind. She has a mother who is ill and who needs her to get medicine, but she is faced with the risk of going outdoors at all because a mutiny is going on in her own apple orchard! Should she play it safe, or respond to her sense of responsibility? The tension forces an answer: she risks getting to the doctor in the face of the mutiny. All of my characters have imagination, as well as courage; theirs are not decisions that are squeezed easily from them. Decision comes through taking risks and through determination—plus imagination. Even in the littlest story these characteristics are present. In **Tanya and Emily in a Dance for Two,** for example, Emily is the perfect ballerina, and Tanya is the dancer who is more spirit than talent. But the two characters put spirit and practice together, and they dance a higher dance! They are yin and yang, picture book style. Through imagination—and, yes, energy—the heroines always win in my books.

Small: *You are both author and editor. When you are in your role as author, do you also act as your own editor? Do you have an editor with whom you work? Does the fact that you are an editor yourself make it easier or more difficult to work with an editor for your own work?*

Gauch: I have been my own editor! Not easy, and not good. Because I wrote **Dance, Tanya** for Philomel, I turned out to be my own editor. As editor, one takes on an artistic role in the production of the book, conceiving who the artist should be (along with the art director), how the story should pace, what the type should look like, and so on. It is very difficult to look at one's own work with any kind of equanimity. And yet, give the manuscript to another editor, for another list? Not in *Tanya*'s case! At the same time, the relationship with my longtime editor Margaret Frith was sacrificed when I came to Philomel because she hired me to be an editor. It was rather like losing one's creative mother. The editor-author relationship is a mysterious and profound one; if it is a longtime relationship it transcends normal business relationships. Again, it is crucial in creating a safe and supportive environment for the artist. As editor, I can help create that environment for my authors and artists, but I must create my own now.

Small: *When you are acting as editor, how do you approach the manuscript and author you're working with? Do you make specific suggestions? Does the fact that you're also an author of similar books help you know what to suggest? Does it have an impact on your relationship with the author whose work you're editing?*

Gauch: Yes. I believe having been an author has formed my editing style. I know the sensitivity of the author. I come to the author and manuscript with great respect. I do not, for example, put many editing marks on the copy itself. It is highly offensive for an author, and frequently, while perhaps more grammatical, interferes with the author's voice! The voice is often aberrant; it is risky stuff, then, for an editor to inject his grammatical construction into an author's voice. (Imagine a grammarian attacking Faulkner!) An author knows it. No wonder he or she is protective! How do I approach the manuscript? Carefully. A novel, I read twice, writing a long commentary when I am finally done. I am mainly interested in shape: Does the story move toward climax? Is there a compelling thread? Are the character and the theme that reflects character moving toward development? And so on. I always begin with specific positive comments—always. Then I suggest the changes. I walk in the author's shoes. That's important. I am not working on my story; I do not want to turn any manuscript into my story. It is not mine; it is the author's. And so my task is to see as the author sees and to ask questions—mainly ask questions—that will bring the manuscript to the point the author has intended.

With Tom Barron, author of *Heartlight* and *The Ancient One,* we begin before he writes, with a walk in the Colorado mountains. Then he writes a draft; I comment. He writes a second draft; I comment. He writes and polishes and turns the copy in. Sometimes there is a last panicky call: "That paragraph in the second chapter when Kate is in the kitchen with Grandfather, do you need it at all? I think the chapter is reading slow." "I see it," he says. "Let me think about it." Etc. We are creating a book until it is printed and on my desk. I am sure that all of the authors with whom I work would say that my being a writer has impacted my being an editor. Trust is everything in this relationship.

Small: *And, of course, the logical next question: Do you have a favorite book of those you've been the editor for?*

Gauch: I love editing novels. There is something hearty about it. Not always controllable! Because these are giant projects, and when you take a novel on you cannot always be certain your author can handle a rewrite. But there is something satisfying about editing and finally holding a book like *I Am Regina* by Sally Keehn in your hands. This was a first novel for Sally, and, fine writer that she is, she struggled magnificently to discover the emotion of her Indian captive, and to know the reality of a time that was two hundred years ago. *The Ancient One* by Tom Barron, and, of course, Brian Jacques' *Redwall* books—these books please me immensely.

In the picture book area, *Owl Moon* by Jane Yolen and John Schoenherr will also have a special place in my heart and head. It is for me the perfect union of art and text—a rare thing. Recently our art director of many years left Philomel. She asked me what had been the favorite book that we had worked on. I told her *Seven Blind Mice* by Ed Young. Like *Owl Moon,* it was a perfect union of art and text. Perfect.

Small: *You've recently written about the writing of historical fiction. Do you see these statements explaining why you write what you write the way you write? I suspect there's a lot more that explains your work. What would you add to what you've already told us?*

Gauch: I believe I am driven by passion for story. I am driven to read fine work, feeling that story drives us into a different realm of experience entirely. And since story is life controlled, aimed, formed, it can be as extraordinary as life itself—even greater than life. In its condensation, story is extraordinarily powerful. I like to read Bruce Brooks, Cynthia Rylant, Gary Paulsen, because they take me to a new place—not merely in subject matter—but through raw, word-created experience. I want a story that I write or edit to leave a reader changed. I wanted the reader to walk with Tillie, to hide with Tempe, to dance with Tanya. Don't leave me unscathed, I say to authors, artists, about their stories.

I demand the same of myself. Even the ordinary, as condensed and formed experience, is powerful through the eyes of an artist. In the articles you mention I was discussing the craft. Now I am describing the heart of story. A writer writes heart to heart. An editor selects, always searching for that same crucial connection. Perhaps that is why, at some level, the best stories write themselves. Out of what Yeats called "the rag and bone shop of our hearts" comes, not only craft, but what we know to be true, what we care about, what we want. It comes from the experience of our lives.

Small: *I understand that you have been a teacher a large part of your life. Do you find time to teach now that you are both author and editor?*

Gauch: Well, in a way I've never been a full-time teacher. I started teaching in an alternative school. I taught all day but only for four months, so I had seven or eight months to write and be a parent and so forth. I guess I was sort of a writer in residence. I have a graduate degree in teaching, and I've usually taught writing and literature classes. I taught children's literature and fiction writing for a while at Drew University. Last year I taught a course at Manhattanville College in Purchase, New York, and now I'm teaching a writing for children course at Bard College. So I guess my answer is, yes, I do find time to teach and I hope I always will.

Small: *Do you have what might be called a philosophy of teaching? How does your work as teacher relate to your roles as author and editor?*

Gauch: This is a harder question, but only because I feel that there is such an important relationship. There is some implicit idea that teaching is directed outward: the teacher knows something, the student receives it. A kind of blank-tablet teaching style. Editing proves, I believe, that the job of the mentor/teacher is to enable, to prepare a ground so rich, the child/student/writer discovers his or her own way. In editing, an editor is deeply respectful of the artist, putting notes on the page neatly and thoughtfully. The best editors it seems to me write questions directed at problems, leaving the power with the writer. T. S. Eliot said of Ezra Pound as editor: "He was a marvelous critic because he didn't try to turn you into an imitation of himself. He tried to see what you were trying to do." There you have it. Teaching informed me as editor, reminding me that the person with whom I am working is the center of the learning/creating process. Not me. Not my information. Editing informed me as a teacher, reminding me that a student, no matter how young, is as important as an author, no matter how professional. And that the highest service I can perform as editor or teacher, through my enthusiasm and support and expertise, is to enable.

Small: *I'm curious, of course, about what writing projects you have under way.*

Gauch: I am writing a story about Thomas Edison, of all people. I grew up with Tom. The train he rode as a boy to and from Detroit, went through my town. He knew the same river that I did, the St. Clair. It is his spirit that I am discovering; I feel that the books on him are too institutional, paying too little attention to his spirit and imagination. And I am researching one of the battles of the Civil War at the same time. I hate to say more, since I am a little superstitious that if I talk too much about my subject, I will dissipate my own energy to write the story.

Small: *Are you currently at work editing a book or books?*

Gauch: I have just finished editing Tom Barron's new novel, *The Merlin Effect.* What a challenge. The hardest thing about writing and editing a fantasy is the internal logic. In this book Tom connects myth, history, and science, implying that there are very real connections between these seemingly different areas; he uses Merlin's horn and DNA to develop his ideas. Writing fantasy is like creating a world—and not easy to write or edit. At the other end of fiction, Sally Keehn has just

finished writing her second novel, *The Moon of Two Dark Horses.* Her challenge in this book, as writer, is to become a Delaware boy whose white settler friend is separated from him by the Revolutionary War. It is an intense experience to edit these books; I go into a tunnel of their respective worlds. At the same time, it is a joy.

TITLE COMMENTARY

A SECRET HOUSE (1970)

Lavinia Russ

SOURCE: A review of *A Secret House,* in *Publishers Weekly,* Vol. 198, No. 11, September 14, 1970, p. 70.

This is a story with universal appeal. Maybe that's too sweeping, maybe there are girls around who never dreamed a dream. But for the lucky ones who have roamed the world over in their fantasies, here is a story of another small girl's fantasy—a story of the perfect house she would like to have and the people she would like to have live in it with her. Illustrated by [Margot Tomes] another obvious dreamer. Warning to older readers: the house is so perfect you may find yourself sighing a "too late, too late" sigh as you look at it.

Evelyn Stewart

SOURCE: A review of *A Secret House,* in *School Library Journal,* Vol. 17, No. 5, January, 1971, p. 42.

This is a happy book, good for small girls to read over and over or to share with parents, especially if the family has taken a trip to New England. The little heroine imagines what it would be like to have a grand old New England seacoast house with: her whole big family together at the dining room table; Christmas just the way it ought to be with a fabulous tree; cousins to hide with in secret rooms; and a toy-filled bedroom complete with window seats overlooking the ocean. Pen-and-ink drawings alternate with red and brown paintings, all filled with details children will enjoy searching for and pointing out. This is not a large group show-and-tell book, but teachers might use it to start children writing their own secret house stories.

MY OLD TREE (1970)

Euple Wilson

SOURCE: A review of *My Old Tree,* in *School Library Journal,* Vol. 17, No. 7, March, 1971, p. 119.

Nostalgia for childhood pervades this book about a small

boy who, like many others past and present, loves trees and tree houses. He daydreams about the kind of special tree he'll find, plans what he'll build in its branches, and wonders who he'll invite to share it with him. This is a quiet, rather intimate story, one that would be read silently by a single child rather than aloud to a group. The crayon illustrations [by Doris Burn] in soft blues, yellows and greens are capably done but somewhat old fashioned in their pastoral mood; the boy seems entirely too cute and innocent to be real.

CHRISTINA KATERINA AND THE BOX (1971, reprinted, 1980)

Zena Sutherland

SOURCE: A review of *Christina Katerina and the Box,* in *Bulletin of the Center for Children's Books,* Vol. 25, No. 2, October, 1971, p. 25.

The huge carton in which a new refrigerator had been packed is an eyesore to Christina's mother, but she agrees that Christina may keep it under the apple tree to play with for a day or two. First it is a castle; then she and her pugnacious friend Fats have a scrap and the box topples over. Mother prepares to haul it away, but Christina says, no, it is now a clubhouse; the pattern is repeated, the box serving as a racing car and a floor plan for a party. Each time Fats and Christina play, they come to some mishap. When the box is demolished, Mother is relieved, but the story ends with Fats coming over with two new boxes. The idea of imaginative play is convincing if elaborately (costumes, signs, props) pursued. . . . [T]he girl is the leader and the boy a rather spoilsport follower. . . . [The] illustrations [by Doris Burn] augment the story with visual detail (bars on the castle window, a cockpit painted on the racing car, signs on the clubhouse wall). . . .

Jean F. Mercier

SOURCE: A review of *Christina Katerina and the Box,* in *Publishers Weekly,* Vol. 218, No. 25, December 19, 1980, p. 52.

Gauch and Burns invested their story and pictures with more animation and conflicts than most authors and illustrators lend to a plot that has inspired countless variations. Christina Katerina loses no time creating a castle out of the huge box housing her family's new refrigerator. Queen CK is outraged by Fats Watson who invades her royal hideaway but pardons the boy (even though he has devoured her majesty's cookies) and they turn the castle into a clubhouse, then into a spaceship and other nifty playthings. When the carton is finally shredded, Christina Katerina's mom is relieved to get the thing out of her yard but Fats dashes over with *two* enormous boxes for more days of fun: his family bought a washer and a dryer.

AARON AND THE GREEN MOUNTAIN BOYS (1972)

Zena Sutherland

SOURCE: A review of *Aaron and the Green Mountain Boys,* in *Bulletin of the Center for Children's Books,* Vol. 25, No. 10, June, 1972, p. 155.

Large, clear print and sentences that are not too long make this historically-based fiction easy for primary-grades children to read, and the separation of the text into chapters lends it a dignity they appreciate. Nine-year-old Aaron is anxious to do his share in the fight against the British, but his dreams of glory are not realized; all his family will let him do is saw wood for the ovens that will bake the soldiers' bread. The British threaten Bennington, and the inhabitants wait anxiously for help to come from the Green Mountain Boys. When the hungry troops arrive and devour the bread, Aaron realizes that he has, indeed, done his share. The dialogue is heavily laden with exclamatory remarks and the ending of the story is weak, but it has historical interest, plenty of action, and a protagonist with whom readers can identify, since his achievements are realistic.

Booklist

SOURCE: A review of *Aaron and the Green Mountain Boys,* in *Booklist,* Vol. 69, No. 6, November 15, 1972, p. 300.

Based on a true Revolutionary War incident, this simply written, attractively illustrated story has action, excitement, and a very believable nine-year-old central character. When the Redcoats capture Fort Ticonderoga and head toward Bennington, Vermont, where supplies are stored, Aaron longs to deliver messages to the general or ride with his father and the Green Mountain Boys, but he is relegated to staying home and helping his grandfather bake bread for the army. Not until his father and the Green Mountain Boys arrive home exhausted and hungry from a long march does Aaron recognize the importance of bread to the war effort.

GRANDPA AND ME (1972)

Jean Mercier

SOURCE: A review of *Grandpa and Me,* in *Publishers Weekly,* Vol. 202, No. 12, September 18, 1972, p. 74.

"Grandpa and I like summertime best, like packing the car and squishing all in and coming to the cottage at night when the windows look yellow and warm." This is a beguiling story of a boy and the good times he has with his grandfather during summer vacation. In the mornings, they walk along the beach when no one else is out; during the heat of the day, they play checkers or tick tack toe on the porch. Sometimes they hike in the woods and find wonderful things. Whatever they do, the boy and the old man have a lovely time together.

Virginia Harman

SOURCE: A review of *Grandpa and Me,* in *School Library Journal,* Vol. 19, No. 8, April, 1973, p. 55.

Simple text superimposed on full-page wash drawings creates an intimate story of affection between a grandfather and grandson.[Symeon] Shimin's illustrations blend perfectly with the story, which is narrated by the young boy and follows typical summer days and nights spent by the sea in grandfather's company. Their mutual feelings are warmly conveyed, and both the theme and format of this book should appeal to children.

📖 *THIS TIME, TEMPE WICK?* (1974)

Anita Silvey

SOURCE: A review of *This Time, Tempe Wick?,* in *The Horn Book Magazine,* Vol. L, No. 5, October, 1974, p. 147.

Quite misnamed, Temperance Wick became a legendary figure not for her self-restraint but for her daring and nerve. The book relates the incident for which she has been acclaimed in Colonial lore—how she concealed a horse in her bedroom to protect it from mutinying American soldiers near Morristown, New Jersey. By using simple and rustic details the account humanizes the soldiers of the War of Independence, showing how they grew cold and hungry and ultimately became unheroic. The book presents a realistic and humane view of the war and of the people who fought it; and from the beginning sentence, "Long ago, when this country was just going about the business of being born," the writing is the perfect vehicle for the illustrations—in [Margot Tomes's] inimitable style—which capture the down-to-earth, unpretentious, and humorous quality of the storytelling.

Kirkus Reviews

SOURCE: A review of *This Time, Tempe Wicke?,* in *Kirkus Reviews,* Vol. XLII, No. 20, October 15, 1974, p. 1103.

In 1781, when a company of Continental soldiers mutinied against their captains, a girl named Tempe (Temperance) Wicke, so the story goes, hid her horse Bon in her own bedroom to prevent its confiscation, stood guard with a rifle over her house while unruly soldiers surrounded it, and felled one of the boldest with a swift kick. Neither the idea that one's own soldiers could be dangerous nor Tempe's big, strapping presence would have been allowable a few years back, and the results are refreshing when Tempe's polite words and strate-

gems fail and she gets "storming had-quite-enough mad." The confrontation between this staunch girl and the scruffy, squinty-eyed soldier, whom Margot Tomes draws as simultaneously threatening and laughable, makes for even more rousing action than we enjoyed in the same team's *Aaron and the Green Mountain Boys.*

David K. Willis

SOURCE: "Stories for the 6-10's: 'I Want to Read It—Now!',"in *The Christian Science Monitor,* November 6, 1974, p. 10.

One definition of high praise for a book aimed at the 6-to-10's is a penetrating whisper at first light on a Saturday morning:

"Dad! Dad! Where's Tempe? I want to read it, NOW!"

And "Tempe," otherwise known as *This Time, Tempe Wick?* is well worth waking up for. It's a charming, historical story which just happens to have a Bicentennial flavor to it, and which our children asked for almost every day for quite a while after it first entered the house. It remains a favorite.

The heroine is Temperance Wick (based on an actual character), called Tempe for short. She lived in a brown farmhouse in Jockey Hollow in New Jersey, when General George Washington camped 10,000 soldiers there in the winters of 1780 and 1781.

With a keen eye for detail and place, Mrs. Gauch tells how strong Tempe was (she could beat her brother in wrestling matches and plow a field for as long as her father could) and how she coped successfully with two hungry and disconsolate Pennsylvania soldiers who tried to steal her horse Bonny—only to find that Tempe's resourcefulness fully equalled her fortitude.

The story is well matched by the simple, sober, yet pleasant drawings of Margot Tomes, scattered profusely on almost every page.

📖 *THUNDER AT GETTYSBURG* (1975)

Kirkus Reviews

SOURCE: A review of *Thunder at Gettysburg,* in *Kirkus Reviews,* Vol. XLIII, No. 23, December 1, 1975, p. 1337.

Tillie begins and ends as a Union supporter, helping to nurse and feed the wounded soldiers at the Weikert Farm. But in between, when she's caught in the crossfire of the fighting at Little Round Top and Cemetery Hill, all she knows is the trauma of danger and death ("Two more Rebs leaped over. CAK! CAK! They crumpled like puppets") and the shock of seeing her men in blue behaving as badly as the Rebs she has come to hate. Tillie Pierce really did see the battle and wrote her own account of what went on *At Gettysburg*. Abandoning the tongue-in-cheek manner of *This Time, Tempe Wick?* and *Aaron and the Green Mountain Boys,* Gauch transcribes Tillie's experiences into breathless, free verse drama. But the result is never heavy-handed; one can believe in Tillie, and Gammell's framed charcoal sketches combine disturbing violence with a certain emotional distance. Some might not care to get this close to the carnage (and might have to read the appended note to understand why Tillie decides she doesn't "want to forget") but the scenes of bloodshed are handled with restraint and a minimum of sentimentality.

Denise M. Wilms

SOURCE: A review of *Thunder at Gettysburg,* in *Booklist,* Vol. 72, No. 8, December 15, 1975, p. 578.

At first Tillie's expressed sentiments seem like so many historical clichés: if the union wins, black men and women won't be slaves ever again and the nation won't be split; rebel soldiers are villains, stealing from the town and riding Tillie's horse Danny to death. But as the Gettysburg confrontation brews and finally explodes around the surprised townspeople, it is the trauma of battle that most impresses itself on Tillie—and readers. Sent by her father to help a neighbor shepherd her children out to a "safe" farm in the country, Tillie is caught in the battle itself; she sees union soldiers behaving not much differently than the rebels, and the free-flowing blood and bodies frighten her. The aftermath leaves her sober but hopeful and finally happy when she learns of her family's safety. As with *This Time, Tempe Wick?,* Gauch has drawn on the experiences of a real person, in this case Tillie Pierce Alleman, whose 1889 book *At Gettysburg* provided the basis of the story. [Stephen] Gammell's thorough pencilled scenes are full of atmosphere and acute emotion, their escalating drama effectively congruent with that of the story.

Joe Bearden

SOURCE: A review of *Thunder at Gettysburg,* in *School Library Journal,* Vol. 22, No. 5, January, 1976, p. 37.

The immediacy of war, the sense of loss, and the pervading feeling of death all become close companions of Tillie Pierce, as well as the other residents of Gettysburg, Pennsylvania, on July 1, 1863 when an almost accidental battle between Union and Confederate forces becomes a turning point in the Civil War. Separated from her family by a neighbor in an attempt to keep her out of the battle, Tillie is swept right into its midst, and for the next three days before she eventually rejoins her family, she becomes very much acquainted with the realities of life and death. Written in the understated manner of a young child, the horror of the situation comes through with a startling clarity. An honestly drawn, well-researched tale based on Tillie's actual account, the

layout is interesting with the verse-like treatment of the text and the realistic dimension provided by Stephen Gammell's illustrations.

Diane Roback

SOURCE: A review of *Thunder at Gettysburg,* in *Publishers Weekly,* Vol. 237, No. 23, June 8, 1990, p. 54.

Based on an autobiographical account of the Battle of Gettysburg by Tillie Pierce Alleman, Gauch's historically accurate treatment of the 14-year-old girl's experience is a welcome reissue of a book first published in 1975. Sent to a farmhouse for safety, Tillie unexpectedly finds herself in the middle of the battlefield, ducking cannon fire as she runs for water to aid wounded soldiers. The reader, like Tillie, is drawn into the sounds and sights of the rapidly unfolding events through the dramatically rendered story. In reflecting on the events, Tillie acknowledges, "It was better to win. / But look what had happened. / Dear God, look what happened." Gauch's dramatic, verse-like text and Gammell's somber black-and-white drawings evoke the horror of war with startling but not overpowering clarity.

ONCE UPON A DINKELSBÜHL (1977)

Barbara Elleman

SOURCE: A review of *Once upon a Dinkelsbühl,* in *Booklist,* Vol. 73, No. 18, May 15, 1977, p. 1420.

An old Bavarian legend tells how the children of Dinkelsbühl pleaded with the colonel of an invading army not to burn their village. " . . . take this bread . . . these shoes . . . this cloth . . . but, sir, please, sir, leave us our city, sir." Stunned by the children's appeal, the colonel agreed. In her retelling, Gauch broadens the story, develops her characters, and makes Lore, the heroic daughter of the gatekeeper, a plucky and stalwart leader; present-tense, on-the-scene coverage is used to bring an unusual perspective, along with a sense of excitement, to the tale. De Paola's chunky characters are individualistic in their conception—especially the ill-tempered colonel and spunky Lore. Gabled medieval buildings topped with turrets and tiled roofs soar over old walls; [Tomie de Paola] varies the pages with gray-shaded drawings and full-page spreads of beige, blue-green, and pink.

The New York Times Book Review

SOURCE: A review of *Once upon a Dinkelsbühl,* in *The New York Times Book Review,* June 19, 1977, p. 28.

Even first-rate talents can't make much of little Lore, a legendary heroine said to have saved the German town of Dinkelsbühl from Swedish invaders. As envisioned by Tomie de Paola, Dinkelsbühl's dumpling-faced citizens and confectionary-colored towers are a good burgher's dream of utopia. And Patricia Gauch employs considerable narrative cunning, urging readers to look here, look there and explore the fanciful setting. But the climactic scene, when Lore leads the other children in confronting the Swedish colonel, simplylacks conviction: "Whatever is he going to do? Hit them? Shoot them? Trample them?" One is cynical enough to imagine him doing just that, but these characters are so cute that the suspense is trivialized, the colonel's decision to spare the town a foregone conclusion. The result is a stick-figure exercise in patriotism. And Lore's papa's admission that "there are times when children should be seen *and* heard," though intended as comic relief, is likely to be interpreted by youngsters as an ungenerous moral.

Ethel L. Heins

SOURCE: A review of *Once upon a Dinkelsbühl,* in *The Horn Book Magazine,* Vol. LIII, No. 4, August, 1977, p. 434.

Three times foreign armies had descended on the little city of Dinkelsbühl, the soldiers shouting for bread. But each time the invaders stole much more than food, devastated houses, and took men as prisoners. The Dinkelsbühlians cowered, immobilized by depression and fear; only the children, spurred on by Lore, the gatekeeper's pertinacious daughter, kept up their spirits. When once again a party of marauding warriors swept through the town, the children boldly took matters into their own hands and saved the city—inspired, of course, by Lore's artless but determined heroism. A well-designed picture book based on a legend still told in the German town; the illustrations, some in soft color and some in white with tones of gray, are reminiscent of the artist's work in *Strega Nona.*

THE IMPOSSIBLE MAJOR ROGERS (1977)

Denise M. Wilms

SOURCE: A review of *The Impossible Major Rogers,* in *Booklist,* Vol. 74, No. 8, December 15, 1977, p. 682.

The snappy, offhand tone Gauch adopts recalls the cheekiness of Jean Fritz's biographies. Her subject, Robert Rogers, is lesser known though, an eighteenth-century character, not exactly "a good, good man" or "a terrible scoundrel," who might be termed a soldier of fortune today. He's remembered for developing the influential guerrilla style of fighting and for nerve and cleverness that led to his triumph in the face of very unfavorable enemy odds. Rogers was in and out of trouble over the course of his bumpy career: he was once the defendant in a counterfeiting trial and later in life was tried for and acquitted of treason. The War for Independence found him on the British side after being rejected by the Americans, who considered him a spy. Afterward, he drifted and drank, finally ending as "a tired and worn and

disappointed old man." Gauch includes an author's note that lends further perspective on Rogers (and the problems of researching her story).

Ralph Adams Brown

SOURCE: A review of *The Impossible Major Rogers,* in *School Library Journal,* Vol. 24, No. 5, January, 1978, p. 88.

During England's wars with France that raged throughout the late 18th Century, the American frontier "hung like a juicy plum" between these two European powers. Major Robert Rogers, ex-smuggler and counterfeiter, became a military leader at this time, exhibiting traits of ingenuity, determination, and daring that made him one of the real heroes of the frontier. Borrowing tactics, equipment, and weapons from the Indians, he captured their villages and he and his men obtained the information that made possible England's victory over France and control of the Lake Champlain region. In this slim, well-illustrated book, the author describes the exploits and conveys the spirit of this self-made scoundrel/hero in a style that will captivate young readers.

Mary M. Burns

SOURCE: A review of *The Impossible Major Rogers,* in *The Horn Book Magazine,* Vol. LIV, No. 2, April, 1978, p. 174.

A colorful and controversial figure in the annals of American history, Robert Rogers—impulsive, stubborn, impetuous—endures as a prototype of the frontiersman-adventurer. By noting in her introductory chapter that he "wasn't exactly a good, good man or a terrible scoundrel," the author underscores the ambivalence of his character, thus providing a solid framework for a vivid biographical sketch, which neither enlarges nor diminishes his personality. Organizer and leader of the intrepid rangers, a company of irregular troops who employed Indian rather than standard European military tactics, Rogers won enormous fame as an authority on frontier fighting during the French and Indian Wars, yet he died a poverty-stricken outcast in England. The circumstances of his triumphs and the reasons for his downfall are skillfully woven into the narrative; thus balance is preserved while an encyclopedic tone is avoided. The informal style permits explanatory asides without condescension; invented dialogue is kept to a minimum, so that authenticity is maintained. An excellent choice for reading aloud, the text is not difficult but sophisticated enough for a slightly older audience than the format might suggest.

ON TO WIDECOMBE FAIR (1978)

Denise M. Wilms

SOURCE: A review of *On to Widecombe Fair,* in *Booklist,* Vol. 74, No. 19, June 1, 1978, p. 1551.

An old folk song, nameless but printed in full with music at the conclusion, provides the framework for Gauch's tale of seven men who became the death of Tom Pearse's old gray mare. As the arch, tongue-in-cheek text explains, these seven were "talking men—not walking men" and the way to Widecombe was long. So it is that Tom Pearse's idle mare is a welcome sight indeed, and with his permission they one-at-a-time ride her the distance to Widecombe Fair. It's the return journey that's fatal, for having overstayed and overstuffed themselves with "goodies and brew," all seven clamber aboard to ride the mare to her death. Justice of sorts is in store, though, for Gauch assures us that "when the wind whistles cold on the moors of a night, Tom Pearse's grey mare appears, grinning ghostly and white," with seven groaning riders who cannot for the world talk themselves off. [Trina Schart] Hyman's alternating color and black-and-white spreads are sweeping and detailed with strong humorous touches; her tone here has a robustness reminiscent of Caldecott's work. The scenes are framed, the text bound off with cameo insets that spotlight some particular site. There's much to see and that's at least half the fun.

Paul Heins

SOURCE: A review of *On to Widecombe Fair,* in *The Horn Book Magazine,* Vol. LV, No. 5, October, 1978, pp. 506-07.

The story, an expanded version of the English folk song printed at the end of the book, tells how seven men of Devon borrowed an old gray mare to carry them to Widecombe Fair. The mare died on the way home and returned to haunt the moor, bearing all of the burdensome riders on her back. In the song the narrative, told in the manner of a ballad and kept to a minimum, is overwhelmed by a rollicking refrain, which lists by name the seven riders of the old mare. From these verbal hints the illustrator has created a picture book that does full justice to her talents. Not only does she devise scenes that suggest the activity and the verve of Caldecott, but she also demonstrates her skill in depicting vitally individual comic characters. In pairs of pages that alternate full color and black and white, the pictures are at once exuberant and quietly evocative of the English landscape. As in Howard Pyle's work, the book is carefully designed to allow for a subtle interplay between pictures and text, and the composition of the pages allows for a variety of vignettes, which add to the aura of abundance and good humor generated by the book.

THE GREEN OF ME (1978)

Denise M. Wilms

SOURCE: A review of *The Green of Me,* in *Booklist,* Vol. 75, No. 26, November 15, 1978, p. 545.

Feelings run deep through this novel of growing up and weathering the cuts of a first love. Jennifer Lynn Cooper is the protagonist, now 17 and riding a train to Charlottesville, Virginia, for an as yet unspecified but implicitly important purpose. She muses, "I believe everything you've ever been or done makes you what you are and what you do now," and a series of acute flashbacks proceeds to build—though sometimes disjointedly—a sensitive picture of the emotional layers that are the Jenny here and now. The person we see has been scarred by childhood hurts large and small and has savored few triumphs; still, she's a survivor, comfortable in high school and enjoying her relationship with boyfriend Chris Cochran until it goes wrong; and finally, rightly, she survives that, too, pained yet personally triumphant in the realization of her own internal strength. A special story, quiet and strong, for readers ready to settle into an uncompromisingly rendered experience.

Ethel L. Heins

SOURCE: A review of *The Green of Me,* in *The Horn Book Magazine,* Vol. LV, No. 1, February, 1979, p. 68.

Jennifer Lynn Cooper is traveling on a train to a destination which is revealed only at the end of the book. The body of the story consists of flashbacks—crucial fragments of memory from the girls' kindergarten days through her graduation from high school. Incidents and snatches of conversation reflecting her major and minor triumphs and tragedies in dealing with her parents, grandparents, friends, and teachers are presented in kaleidoscopic fashion. The tone of the narrative is never high-pitched, but it is evident that all of the bits and pieces of Jennifer's recollections—and especially those concerning her relationship with Chris, her first love—were emotional milestones in her childhood and adolescence. With her first novel for older readers the author has taken brave but somewhat tentative steps into new territory. She deals sensitively with her central character; and although the book is thoughtfully constructed, the reader is left with the feeling that it lacks a measure of vigor and substance.

Georgess McHargue

SOURCE: A review of *The Green of Me,* in *The New York Times Book Review,* March 25, 1979, p. 33.

The title refers to an incident recalled (like the rest of the book) by 17-year-old Jennifer Cooper on a train trip to Charlottesville, VA. She once showed the same green paint sample to several different people: "It's an ugly crepe-paper color." "Maybe it's like the green chlorine bottle I keep the linseed oil in." "Oh, it's a lovely green . . . it has . . . a dimension which says spring to me." What, then, is the true green of Jenny? Is she the forlorn child of 8 whose grandmother gave a coveted garnet ring to an older and prettier cousin, the one whose courage nearly failed on the half-mile swim with her father, the early teen-ager who defended the hurt gull from the boys at the beach? Or is she the Jenny who wonders if she loves Chris, the boy she's going to visit at college? Chris is warm, funny, gentle. He also lets Jenny write his English papers and invents very plausible stories about the discovery of his own remarkable talents by a jazz musician, a baseball scout, a swim coach. Which Chris do you see, and which Jenny does the seeing?

This is an ambitious and often appealing book whose ending (Jenny's realization that she has grown beyond Chris) is entirely appropriate. Why, then, does its central character somehow fail to come into focus for me? Perhaps it is simply the relatively slow pace of the opening chapters (before we learn about Chris) or the fact that some of the incidents recalled seem irrelevant. Certainly the later Jenny is more interesting and better realized than the earlier one. I wish I had come away from the book feeling that I knew the whole Jenny better. Or would another reader see a different green?

FRIDAYS (1979)

Denise M. Wilms

SOURCE: A review of *Fridays,* in *Booklist,* Vol. 76, No. 6, November 15, 1979, p. 501.

Fridays become a special gathering night for Corey and the group of girls she's become part of. Their leader is Jan, a cool, sophisticated sort the others look up to; it's Jan's house that is the setting for the group's overnighters that shape the story's development. Expectedly, these nights take on increasingly sharper edges as the girls flirt with the illicit—shoplifting for thrills, and then drinking. Corey's own feelings trouble her. She thoroughly enjoys being part of a group, but her successful shoplifting foray leaves her guilty and unhappy, and she's appalled at the way the group makes an outcast of one girl who does a striptease during a night of drinking. This victimization that Corey watches is the story's central tragedy. The outcast, a new girl whose inclusion in the group has been tenuous, is shown bitterly shifting alliances to a seedier, trouble-making crowd; by the finish she's in a stolen auto, while her ex-friends attend a long-anticipated school dance. Corey's narration is immediate and effective; descriptions of her own feelings as well as the group's dynamics allow her a unique observer/participant status that deepens the exposition and involves the reader. The picture is acute and thought-provoking.

Kirkus Reviews

SOURCE: A review of *Fridays,* in *Kirkus Reviews,* Vol. XLVII, No. 23, December 1, 1979, p. 1379.

Gauch plunges straight into a seething eight-grade social cauldron, where so many individual and group names (the Freaks, the Eight) are swirling by that a reader might feel like a new kid at school, left out and bewildered. You get the names straight soon enough, but you never lose the feeling of having your head held underwater. The story, in a series of high-intensity flashes, tells of the Friday night activities of a group of girls whipped up to a state of "heat" by their popular, glittering leader, Jan. On one occasion they drink beer, on another champagne, and on another, on the loose in a shopping center and euphoric with togetherness ("Talk about owning the world—we did"), they are egged on to a game of shoplifting follow-the-leader. One new girl, Terry, hangs on at the edges, can't bring herself to shoplift, and finally—drunk on the champagne and performing a half-nude dance in Jan's rec room—is glimpsed through a window by the eighth grade boys, who are never too far away. Suddenly Terry is a scarlet woman, the other girls shun her, and instead of showing up the next Friday at the school dance all this has supposedly been leading up to, she is hauled off by the police, apparently on drugs, from a car that her date has just stolen and wrecked. Except for Terry's melodramatic and too precipitous decline, the events are more or less credible, and kids can relate to both the girls' flushed excitement and the uneasy reservations of Corey, the narrator and one of the bunch. But the whole story has a raw, strident quality, as if Gauch is trying too hard and too heavily to share her characters' half-baked sensibility but still hasn't got it quite right.

Mary M. Burns

SOURCE: A review of *Fridays,* in *The Horn Book Magazine,* Vol. LVI, No. 1, February, 1980, pp. 60-1.

Announcement of the annual spring dance throws the eighth-graders of suburban Calvin Junior High into a state of frenetic anticipation. Hoping for her first real date and anxious to be at the center instead of on the sidelines of activity, Corey Martin becomes part of a group known as the Eight, and she seeks to win approval from wealthy, popular Jan Barrington, the leader. Their Friday night gatherings quickly escalate beyond control; the girls are impelled to seek new thrills—ignoring past conventions, friendships, and responsibilities. Events gather momentum; the relatively innocent rowdyism of the initial party is gradually transformed over several weeks until the group, befuddled by champagne and rock music, entice Terry McCue into performing a suggestive dance. The bacchanal ends abruptly with the arrival of Jan's parents; but Terry has been observed by a group of would-be gate-crashers, so that news of the event quickly spreads around school, and her reputation is tarnished. The Eight, having rationalized their own behavior, treat her as a pariah—with tragic results. Corey is left to ponder the questions of guilt and innocence, friendship and responsibility. Taut, spare, and uncompromising, the story is a compelling if unflattering portrait of a suburban wasteland without traditions or roots.

📖 *THE LITTLE FRIAR WHO FLEW* (1980)

Kirkus Reviews

SOURCE: A review of *The Little Friar Who Flew,* in *Kirkus Reviews,* Vol. XLVIII, No. 18, September 15, 1980, p. 1227.

"Across the ocean in the heel of a country shaped like a boot," a clumsy, foolish fellow who "even called himself 'Little Donkey'" takes such joy in the flowers and the birds and the statue of Our Lady in the garden that he flies a bit in their presence. Thus observed, Little Donkey is asked to join the friars in the convent, but then his more and more extended flights attract such crowds and attention that the peace-loving friars send him off to an isolated convent of his own. Still he continues to fly and feel joy because he still has the birds, flowers, and a similar statue and so is "not alone." An author's note identifies Little Donkey as St. Joseph of Copertino, a 17th-century Franciscan who became the patron saint of aviators. Gauch treats him here with benign affection, which [Tomie] de Paola matches with his old dreamy charm treatment. It's unsubstantial, but not sappy, like some of de Paola's own saintly portraits. Those so inclined might hear the little friar humming on an alpha wavelength as he glides through the pastel pages.

Barbara Elleman

SOURCE: A review of *The Little Friar Who Flew,* in *Booklist,* Vol. 77, No. 4, October 15, 1980, p. 326.

Based on the legend of Saint Joseph of Copertino, the patron saint of aviators, this story tells of simple, clumsy Joseph, called Little Donkey for his foolishness, who prefers the flowers and birds to the townspeople who scoff at him. In later years, he becomes a friar; and as the joy of the good things in life sweep over him, Joseph discovers he can fly. His reputation spreads, and soon he finds that his many friends and well-wishers also bring confusion. He retreats to his country convent, where he ends his days in quiet contemplation and joyful flying. Children who long to fly will immediately empathize with the gentle life of this happy man, reflected in [Tomie] de Paolo's muted shades and the tone of quiet amusement emanating from his handsome drawings.

Anna Biagioni Hart

SOURCE: A review of *The Little Friar Who Flew,* in *School Library Journal,* Vol. 27, No. 3, November, 1980, p. 61.

Joseph's joy is in nature. No wonder, since the townspeople (who live in "the heel of a country shaped like a boot") have made it clear that he, a.k.a. Little Donkey, is just too clumsy and foolish a fellow to live among them. The local friars don't want him either—until Joseph's aerodynamics prompt the Bishop to invite

him to join the Franciscans. Suddenly, he's more in demand than the Golden Knights. This gentle lunacy makes for a pleasant if weak retelling of the 17th-century Saint Joseph of Copertino's legend. Tomie de Paola's landscape looks Late Pastel Renaissance; page layouts are attractive; the print is good-sized. Poor Joseph, for all his joy, is curiously expressionless throughout. Airsick?

📖 *KATE ALONE* (1980)

Karen M. Klockner

SOURCE: A review of *Kate Alone,* in *The Horn Book Magazine,* Vol. LVI, No. 5, October, 1980, p. 519.

With both her fiction and nonfiction, the author is effective at capturing the immediacy of a scene through fragments of dialogue and flashes of thought on the part of characters. In a short novel she forms a collage of incidents around fourteen-year-old Kate and her dog McDuff. Duffy has just been sent to the veterinarian to be altered, and when he returns, there are noticeable changes in his personality. The lovable and energetic dog suddenly and unpredictably growls maliciously at familiar objects. Then he bites Kate's sister's boyfriend, and the family becomes seriously concerned. Although the book focuses on Kate's confusion and torn loyalties, the author also conveys the family's support and understanding during the girl's crisis. Scenes at the kitchen table or in the family den are given a natural and spontaneous quality through the playful bantering and disjointed conversations of the characters. Kate's relationships with her younger brother, her older sister, and her mother and father reveal the individuality of each character—as well as the solidarity of the family unit. Although Kate still enjoys being alone, she comes to appreciate the value of the others she had always taken for granted.

Marilyn R. Singer

SOURCE: A review of *Kate Alone,* in *School Library Journal,* Vol. 27, No. 2, October, 1980, p. 146.

This starts off like a run-of-the-mill story, of 14-year-old, introverted Kate and her beloved dog Duffy, rather irritating with its blow by blow accounts of boisterous family fun, i.e.: soccer games in the living room; wrestling matches among the house plants; etc. However, the book takes on an interesting dimension as Duffy becomes a biter, and she has to make a decision about whether to have him killed or not. The situation is complicated because the first person Duffy bit was her sister's boyfriend, whom the whole family loves. So Kate feels estranged from everyone and torn by conflicting loyalties. Her father helps her try to understand with a story about the decision he had to make at 16 about his dog, and he gives her some realistic advice: "Sometimes, there's no way to get away from something. No way."

However, after Duffy bites another person, her father's comment is clear: "sometimes decisions are taken away from us, too." And Kate stoically accedes to the inevitable.

Judith Goldberger

SOURCE: A review of *Kate Alone,* in *Booklist,* Vol. 77, No. 3, October 1, 1980, p. 250.

This is a dog story with deeper concerns than adventure; it is also about love and loss. McDuff's return from neutering surgery is heralded by the whole Arthur family, and their worry about his having the operation post-puppyhood seems unwarranted at first. Kate, whose life is tightly tied with the Scottie dog's, is last to accept the fact that McDuff is now easily threatened by what he alone interprets as danger. When he viciously attacks her older sister's boyfriend, Kate flees with McDuff and faces alone the thought of his probable death. But her family soon rallies around Kate, easing the final decision after a last, irrational attack by the dog on a neighbor woman. Beyond the characterization of Kate, which is itself intimate, Gauch's fine portrait of a close and interesting family and her graceful, image-filled writing style add considerable depth to the novel.

Jean F. Mercier

SOURCE: A review of *Kate Alone,* in *Publishers Weekly,* Vol. 218, No. 17, October 24, 1980, p. 49.

The author of *Fridays, The Green of Me* and other sensitive novels, Gauch writes here with skill and understanding about Kate Arthur, 14. Kate retreats from girls her age who, she feels, disdain her, and spends her time with the family's faithful Scottie, MacDuff (Duffy). The Arthurs' home is happy with caring parents, Kate's young brother J. and older sister Susan doing interesting things, together and on their own. When Susan's fiancé Pat McIntyre is around, he enlivens the place even more, playing rough-and-tumble games with J. Kate joins in on all the activities until the day Duffy suddenly bites Pat viciously, sending the young man to the hospital. Alone, Kate faces the inevitable. She takes her beloved Duffy to the vet for the shot that ends his life. Alone she determines to remain, pushing deep into a woods where no one can find her. But the outcome of the moving story is far different from what one anticipates.

📖 *MORELLI'S GAME* (1981)

Sally Estes

SOURCE: A review of *Morelli's Game,* in *Booklist,* Vol. 78, No. 10, January 15, 1982, pp. 643-44.

The fact that "it has to do with dragons and caves and green slime and mirkwood . . ." is the basic reason given by a Tolkien-inspired English teacher when he sends two teams of teenage boys with only five dollars apiece on a 200-mile hero's-journey bike ride from Fayette, Pennsylvania, to Washington, D.C. The narrative follows the adventures of one team—Jerry, who evolves reluctantly into the hero/leader; Thad, the map-reading wizard; Chris, the guitar strumming, humming bard; Partini, a sardonic jester; and huge Peter, dubbed Gollum after Tolkien's whiney toad. Menaced by three faceless (because of opaque helmets) motorcyclists as well as other challenging "dragons" and helped by a curiously adult 13-year-old enchantress, the five gradually work through their assorted interpersonal conflicts, each facing his own particular dragon. Each boy emerges as a sharply etched character, and the story's surrealistic quality is enhanced by the isolated setting—a hurricane-battered canal towpath. Readers will comfortably accommodate themselves to the theme, which at one point is stated by Jerry—"Is what's true always real, or what's real true?" An unusual high-adventure tale with potentially wide appeal.

Kirkus Reviews

SOURCE: A review of *Morelli's Game,* in *Kirkus Reviews,* Vol. L, No. 4, February 15, 1982, p. 208.

Morelli is a Lockwood Academy English teacher hung up on Tolkien, and his game is to send two teams of boys on bikes on a "no-race race" from their Pennsylvania school to Washington 200 miles away. On Jerry's team (which soon includes a reject from the other group) are a kid they call Gollum (the reject), another dubbed the Wizard, a bard with mandolin, and a more dominant type you suspect most of the way through who might be roughly matched with Strider. For "dragons" (Tolkien would have them goblins, but never mind), there is a menacing trio of motorcyclists who seem to be following the group and with whom Jerry has some close encounters. When the motorcyclists are not in evidence they are in the back of Jerry's mind, and it's in an ultimate confrontation with them that Jerry—*and,* unexpectedly, the group's Gollum—come through with the necessary heroism. All along, Jerry, a longtime loner who likes it that way, has been pressured into the role of "hero" (actually leader); like Frodo, he's reluctant, but he knows that anyone might be called to the test and can't refuse it. If (to their credit) neither Jerry nor Gauch is interested in heroics, Jerry does give up his loner status for commitment to the group—and that, as much as facing up to one's dragons, is about what comes of the journey. The Tolkien parallels and their implications are far from subtle, and probably about ten years late for wide recognition. (The conflict *en route* between long-hairs—the students—and rednecks is about as dated; these days the rednecks are more likely the ones with long hair.) But the fantasy references do provide a framework for the loose road-journey form, and an appropriate focus, perhaps a blotter, for Gauch's style, which has seemed in previous novels disproportionately overwrought. This time, the story takes over and everything falls into place without a grinding gear.

Ann A. Flowers

SOURCE: A review of *Morelli's Game,* in *The Horn Book Magazine,* Vol. LVIII, No. 2, April, 1982, p. 172.

Seventeen-year-old Jerry Sebastian had no feeling for team spirit; nor did he have any intention of becoming a hero. The whole idea was ridiculous—two teams of bicyclists journeying to Washington from their prep school in Pennsylvania. Even more absurd was their teacher Morelli, describing it as a hero's journey—similar to a Tolkien quest in which they might encounter figurative dragons, bards, and wizards. Right from the start Jerry and his team were faced with many problems and hazards. They were joined by a runaway girl and a monstrously fat dropout from the other team; they met a deranged hermit and were followed by a sinister motorcycle gang. Each member of the team had definite weaknesses, but the theme of the novel is their gradual coming together by trading on their strengths and by Jerry's final acceptance of his responsibilities as leader. A little heavy on the symbolism, the story is nevertheless a realistic adventure story with believable characters and a clearly discernible development.

NIGHT TALKS (1983)

Denise M. Wilms

SOURCE: A review of *Night Talks,* in *Booklist,* Vol. 79, No. 15, April 1, 1983, p. 1033.

M'Lou and her friends Laura and Anne Marie chose Camp Glenmora because they wanted to be unknown as Greenewood Pointers ("You know, the Detroit suburb: tree-lined streets, mansions on the lake, live-in maids, that kind of thing"). Though they are not wealthy in that way, they are comfortable, with backgrounds distinctly different from that of the troublesome Margaret, a bitterly defensive and aggressive (white) inner-city child who is also a Glenmora camper that summer. All four girls find themselves cabin mates after an all-knowing counselor named Nikki decides they will be good for each other. In fact they are, until the girls mistake Margaret's story of drug dealing for the truth and decide to write a well-intentioned but patronizing letter to her mother. The letter is destructive in ways they had not anticipated, and the girls are forced to confront their preconceived ideas and expectations about lives so different from their own. Gauch has provided much to think about in her characters' actions. Issues of loyalty, love, and concern versus meddling are intriguingly juxtaposed. Learning what makes each of these people tick generates a strong sense of human concern—and much to ponder about how the best intentions can go painfully awry.

Kirkus Reviews

SOURCE: A review of *Night Talks,* in *Kirkus Reviews,* Vol. LI, No. 8, April 15, 1983, p. 461.

This takes place at a high school girls' summer camp in Michigan, where Mary Lou and two others from Greenwood Pointe (read Grosse Pointe), fleeing the "rich kids" image, agree to tell everyone they're from Detroit. Popular counselor Nikki soon picks the three Pointers for her "starters," the reliable chosen ones she always uses to activate her plans. When Margaret, an inner-city problem kid, is assigned to her group, Nikki is thrilled by the challenge—and bunks Margaret in with the "starters." Margaret is sullen, silent, and terrified of woods, water, snakes, and birds. She pulls a knife on a girl who corrects her table-setting placement, and, the worst offense for her tent-mates, goes through the unusually hot summer weeks without a swim or a shower. But the three work patiently on Margaret, and she finally does come round remarkably. Then the disaster: the three Pointers, concerned about Margaret, write to inform her mother that she's a marijuana dealer—a story, it turns out, that Margaret has made up to impress them. Offended by the meddling letter, Margaret's mother yanks her out of camp just before the big canoe trip they've all planned as this year's version of Nikki's famous August Plan—which leaves Nikki the Great to face a failure and the three girls in disgrace. This never packs the intended emotional wallop because Margaret always seems an invention, as much a stranger to Gauch as to the girls; the letter is just too improbably maladroit; and the meted-out revelation that is supposed to explain Nikki is too simplistic. Still it's competently staged, recognizes the limitations of naive good intentions, and doesn't succumb to the school-spirit syndrome that infects most camp stories.

Ethel R. Twichell

SOURCE: A review of *Night Talks,* in *The Horn Book Magazine,* Vol. LIX, No. 3, June, 1983, pp. 310-11.

M'Lou has been looking forward to Camp Glenmora. She likes her tent-mates; she is prepared to adore her counselor, the charismatic Nikki, and to participate in Nikki's famous August Plan—a demanding canoe trip. But Margaret, an inner-city girl, creates a problem. Proud, ashamed of her meager belongings, and rejecting the kindness of her more affluent tent-mates, Margaret stubbornly refuses to learn to swim, thus making the August Plan impossible. Margaret's change of heart and her emerging friendships with the other girls are well-handled, although there are believable setbacks as the girls struggle with both exasperation and sympathy. As the story develops, Nikki emerges as a natural leader but is obsessed by her plans for the camp and unable to form real friendships. The story is not a conventional one about summer camp—with marshmallow roasts and canoe races. The author uses three different modes of narration—a first-person telling, the omniscient point of view, and frequent end-of-chapter italicized conversations among M'Lou and her friends. A subplot concerning a young ecologist seems extraneous, but on the whole the author has devised an interesting counterpoint of personalities that interweave and conflict with the thorny character of Margaret.

Nancy Berkowitz

SOURCE: A review of *Night Talks,* in *School Library Journal,* Vol. 29, No. 10, August, 1983, p. 76.

Having had bad experiences with reverse snobbery, M'Lou, Haze and Anne Marie make a pact not to reveal they come from a posh Detroit suburb when they go to camp. There they meet inner-city Margaret: antisocial, dirty and wild-tempered. Gradually they penetrate her defenses and a tenuous friendship develops. Then, one night, when the girls were having one of their "night talks," Margaret tries to impress the others by telling them she deals in drugs. Thinking they are helping, the girls write to her mother. The result changes all their lives—even Nikki's, their popular counselor's, in a way they would never forget. Chapters alternate between M'Lou's first person narrative and Nikki's thoughts and actions, for which the author uses third person. This contrast is not confusing; instead it provides a unique framework for the author's exceptional gift for three-dimensional characterizations—as do the short scenarios between M'Lou, Haze and Anne Marie. Nikki, the catalyst that draws the story to its inevitable conclusion, is particularly interesting. Gauch's writing is smooth and her plot original.

THE YEAR THE SUMMER DIED (1985)

Bulletin of the Center for Children's Books

SOURCE: A review of *The Year the Summer Died,* in *Bulletin of the Center for Children's Books,* Vol. 39, No. 5, January, 1986, p. 85.

In almost every childhood friendship there is the possibility that one of the two will mature faster and leave the other, saddened, behind. That's what happens to young teenager Erin, when she eagerly awaits Laurie, the summer friend who has heretofore been as eager as Erin to play their sustained game of being cowpokes. Laurie is in love, Erin is bereft; although Erin knows she no longer has her friend to herself, she tries in several ways to force herself on Laurie. There is also a running subplot about feisty grandpa, his feud with an unidentified trespasser, and the growing number of incidents—increasingly serious—that lead people to suspect the incidents may be more than teenage rowdiness. The story culminates in a storm that reveals the true culprit, gives Erin new perspective, and clears the air (figuratively as well as literally) in a manner that is just a bit pat. Gauch writes well and her depiction of the pain of

losing a friend is perceptive. It just doesn't add up to as cohesive and convincing a story as those she usually writes.

Cynthia Percak Infantino

SOURCE: A review of *The Year the Summer Died,* in *School Library Journal,* Vol. 32, No. 7, March, 1986, p. 174.

Erin, a 14-year-old girl from Connecticut, eagerly anticipates her summer visit to her grandparents' lakeside cottage in Michigan. She looks forward to the neighborhood bonfire, to sighting freighters with her grandfather and most of all, to seeing her friend Laurie. Erin's friendship with Laurie (almost three years her senior) borders on worship; as Erin imagines them replaying their Western fantasy together, she is unprepared for the fact that—this summer—she will be left behind as Laurie cultivates a romance with Matt. This, however, is not Erin's only disappointment; the bonfire turns into a beer-drinking bash for the local teens, and her grandfather becomes obsessed with protecting their cottage and pumphouse from vandalism. In order to win back Laurie's attention, Erin learns to ride, gaining self-confidence along with equestrian skills. A devastating storm creates a crisis for the cottage residents and causes Erin to reflect on her summer's experience. And yes, Erin too enjoys the awakening of a romance as the story ends. Erin's first-person narration reveals the pain and awkwardness of growing up. The underlying themes of change and growth, fantasy and reality lend depth to Erin's story.

Mary Ojibway

SOURCE: A review of *The Year the Summer Died,* in *Voice of Youth Advocates,* Vol. 9, Nos. 3 & 4, August-October, 1986, p. 142.

Summer at her grandparents' cottage on Lake Huron is always special for almost 14-year-old Erin. More than anything else, summer is best friend Laurie Kelly and their imaginative world of wild ponies and rustlers. But this year, things at the cottage are different—eccentric grandpa is making the pumphouse into a fort against the younger kids turned gang; Laurie has discovered boys—Matt Calley in particular; the bluff is threatened by break-ins falsely attributed to the kids; and Erin is chided and challenged to "Get real!"

The summer's events, a terrible storm, and a real horse force Erin into understanding what has been real all along—herself; John, the boy she's always known; and growing up means making decisions and accepting change.

Believable characters, a bit of mystery (who is breaking into the cottages if *not* the gang?) and an easy to follow plot make this a fast read.

📖 *CHRISTINA KATERINA AND THE TIME
SHE QUIT THE FAMILY* **(1987)**

Diane Roback

SOURCE: A review of *Christina Katerina and the Time
She Quit the Family,* in *Publishers Weekly,* Vol. 231,
No. 27, July 10, 1987, p. 68.

Christina Katerina, the spunky heroine of *Christina Katerina and the Box,* is back. This time, however, she
has had quite enough of her family. When she is unfairly blamed for the commotion her brother and his friends
are making, Christina decides to quit her family. "Call
me Agnes," she tells her mother. "Call me Mildred,"
her mother says. "You go your way. We'll go ours."
Agnes and Mildred divide the house—Agnes gets the left
side of the sink, one pile of clean dishes, one quarter of
the living room, three hooks in the hall and her bedroom. Mildred and the family get the rest of the house.
At first everything is perfect—Agnes can do anything
she wants, and nobody bothers her. But gradually she
begins to miss "Mildred" and the rest of the clan. [Elise]
Primavera's vivacious illustrations serve up a saucy
complement to Gauch's story about the indomitable
Christina Katerina.

Kirkus Reviews

SOURCE: A review of *Christina Katerina and the Time
She Quit the Family,* in *Kirkus Reviews,* Vol. LV, No.
15, August 1, 1987, p. 1156.

Irrepressible Christina Katerina returns, this time with a
rebellion that a patient family allows her to pursue for
a week—before luring her back with unusual tact that
allows her to come with good grace.

Christina may be difficult at times (there seems to be a
number of things her parents keep asking her not to do),
but little brother John is uproarious. When he and his
friends attack her bears one Saturday morning, in her
room, and her parents blame her—"You just can't do
whatever you please when you're part of a family"—
Christina opts out. She dresses as a bead-bedecked hip-
pie, and she and her mother divide up the house. She
enjoys her independence—leaving the crusts of her pea-
nut butter and potato chip sandwich, leaving her belongings as they fall, staying up late. By Friday she's a little
lonely, announcing to whoever might be listening that
she doesn't need anyone. Wise Mother takes the hint,
offers cake, tells her she's needed, and the family is
rejoined.

This learning experience is recounted with a wit
and verve that match Christina's own assertiveness.
The humorously realistic illustrations may reinforce
an adult's incredulity at Mom's patience, but the victory won by both sides is both healthy and satisfying.
A picture book that will also be enjoyed by young readers.

Ellen Schecter

SOURCE: "Declaring War at Home," in *The New York
Times Book Review,* November 8, 1987, p. 51.

Just about anyone who ever wanted to quit a family will
recognize the approach-avoidance impulse dramatized in
Christina Katerina and the Time She Quit the Family.
It all begins on a "perfectly good" Saturday morning
when Christina Katerina, who has been unjustly accused
of just about everything, changes her name to Agnes and
quits on the spot.

"You go your way. We'll go ours," announces Mildred
(aka Mother). And so the battle lines are drawn. Christina—I mean Agnes—ends up with the left side of the
sink, a pile of clean dishes, her own bedroom and assorted parts of the house. She eats, wears and does just
what she pleases.

This picture book grapples with a very real dilemma—
the too-much-of-a-good-thing side of family life. It's
honest about the fact that when you're feeling family-
phobic, you don't miss anyone at all—for a while. You
sing in the tub till your skin turns to corduroy, gobble
all the junk food without sharing one single chip and lick
your fingers.

I loved the wonderfully tenacious Agnes, who manages
to stay quit for almost a whole week. She's a sprightly
heroine—all too rare even now. But, unlike Agnes, the
book fizzles out. Many of the details Patricia Lee Gauch
conjures are fresh and funny, and the situation is comical, but it's too predictable and pushed too far. Elise
Primavera's illustrations are observant and contemporary, full of realistic, funny details—as long as she avoids
slipping into the too cute cartoon zone.

I certainly believe in the problem, but I can't quite buy
the resolution. On the days I'd like to quit *my* family,
reading a book this pat and predictable could push me
right out the door.

Betsy Hearne

SOURCE: A review of *Christina Katerina and the Time
She Quit the Family,* in *Bulletin of the Center for Children's Books,* Vol. 41, No. 4, December, 1987, p. 64.

The third and best of several picture books about a feisty
young character, this features a text true to the vicissitudes of child behavior along with watercolor scenes of
authentic family chaos. Feeling nagged and put upon,
Christina changes her name and defines her own auton-
omous areas of the house. Her mother wisely supports
this separation, helps label the dividing lines, and waves
goodbye. Needless to say, Christina, alias Agnes, eats
junk, wreaks messy havoc, wears mismatched clothes,
and stays up late. And needless to say, she begins to
suffer the consequences—it's a real feat to tuck yourself
in at night. Fortunately, her mother invites her back into

the family for some chocolate cake and storytelling, and Christina rejoins them ". . . because Christina liked doing what she pleased, and that's exactly what pleased her just then." The issue of control is of inexhaustible interest to young children, and this girl's carefree abandon in rebelling will be as entertaining as her return to the fold is satisfying. The art kicks up its heels as well, reveling in spirited depictions of anarchic clutter with ironically controlled line and color.

📖 *DANCE, TANYA* (1989)

Kirkus Reviews

SOURCE: A review of *Dance, Tanya*, in *Kirkus Reviews*, Vol. LVII, No. 14, August 1, 1989, p. 1156.

Though she is too young to begin ballet, Tanya loves to imitate her older sister, Elise, as she does her pliés and arabesques; Tanya is especially good as a sad swan. On Elise's recital night, while even Grandma and Grandpa and the uncle who never smiles share the family's pride in Elise's performance, Tanya falls asleep; but afterwards, at home, she wakes just long enough to do a dance of her own that convinces her mother that it is time for her to have lessons, too. The plot here is familiar, but Gauch makes it seem new with carefully selected details that give her characters individuality. [Satomi] Ichikawa's delicately painted illustrations perfectly capture the clumsy grace of the appealing little dancer in both traditional and imaginatively new positions. A lovely book.

Denise M. Wilms

SOURCE: A review of *Dance, Tanya*, in *Booklist*, Vol. 86, No. 1, September 1, 1989, pp. 70-1.

Whenever Elise practices ballet, little sister Tanya determinedly imitates her. Tanya would love to take lessons too, but her mother says she must wait until she's older. However, one night after Elise dances in a recital, Tanya takes the floor at home with so much style that Mama relents; with a gift of leotards and slippers, she signals her approval for Tanya's entrance to dance class. Gauch's sweet story gains strength from Ichikawa's soft watercolor paintings, which celebrate Tanya's enthusiasm with a sharp sense of how small children move. Even though the story and pictures are amusing (especially the tutu-clad teddy bear following in Tanya's wake), a wholehearted respect for Tanya's earnest dedication is evident. A gentle, knowing book.

Kay McPherson

SOURCE: A review of *Dance, Tanya*, in *School Library Journal*, Vol. 35, No. 14, October, 1989, p. 78.

Tanya, a vivacious preschooler, is bitten by the ballet bug before she is old enough to take lessons. She helps her big sister, Elise, practice and hangs around to watch Elise's class go through their *jetés* and *pliés*. Best of all, Tanya likes to create her own dances either alone or in a *pas de deux* with her teddy (a ballerina bear, naturally). She does a *Swan Lake* which is beyond Petipa's dreams. "You have two dancers in your family," her grandmother tells her mother after a family recital. Her mother does not forget, and sees to it that Tanya starts ballet class as soon as she is old enough. This is a charming family story, showing strong and loving relationships all around. Tanya is an engaging little heroine who does not let her size undermine her determination to have her heart's desire. Ichikawa's illustrations are especially attractive, leaning heavily on muted colors with splashes of black, red, and brown. All this is placed in a pleasing format, creating a ballet story with wide appeal.

📖 *CHRISTINA KATERINA AND THE GREAT BEAR TRAIN* (1990)

Kirkus Reviews

SOURCE: A review of *Christina Katerina and the Great Bear Train*, in *Kirkus Reviews*, Vol. LVIII, No. 16, August 15, 1990, p. 1168.

The third book about the endearingly self-possessed Christina, who now constructs a train of boxes and string for her many toy bears (she liked them "most after sugar on toast, and before her mother and father") and takes it on a neighborhood excursion—while her parents bring home her new sister. It's an eventful trip—boys throw tomatoes at them, and they get a little lost—that's warmly concluded with a hug from Dad and a new bear for the baby. An affectionate look at a small but indomitable person getting through a difficult moment in her own uniquely constructive manner. Gauch's wry, understated humor is charming; [Elise] Primavera's sturdily realistic pictures subtly deepen understanding of Christina's mixed emotions. A cheerful, wholesome addition to the new-sibling shelf.

Judith Gloyer

SOURCE: A review of *Christina Katerina and the Great Bear Train*, in *School Library Journal*, Vol. 36, No. 11, November, 1990, p. 92.

Christina Katerina will be familiar to readers of Gauch's earlier books about her as a creative and independent character. Here she is decidedly disturbed over the arrival of a new sibling. As her father wraps a present to take to the hospital, Christina gathers up her teddy bears to go on a journey. She sets out down the street, and after some small incidents she reaches a part of town she doesn't recognize. A storm threatens and breaks. Always confident, Christina marches on until familiar landmarks come into view. Then her father appears, running down the hill to hug her. The final scene has her smiling at her new baby sister and realizing that the "very best thing about going on a faraway journey was coming home." The journey and the storm provide good parallels for Christina's emotions, and Primavera's realistic watercolors capture the changing weather as well as Christina's changing moods. A book written with both skill and flair.

📖 *BRAVO, TANYA* (1992)

Luann Toth

SOURCE: A review of *Bravo, Tanya,* in *School Library Journal,* Vol. 38, No. 3, March, 1992, p. 214.

Tanya is finally old enough to study ballet, yet despite all her natural coordination, enthusiasm, and even technical mastery, she finds the structure of classes difficult and frustrating. She can't even hear the music. "She is a lovely child, and she is enjoying herself, and that is what matters" says her teacher. But Tanya doesn't experience the same joy she feels while dancing with her stuffed bear under the trees, listening to the wind. It's the helpful reassurance and gentle encouragement of her kind accompanist that makes the difference and turns the little girl into a ballerina. [Satomi] Ichikawa's fluid watercolors with finely etched pen-and-ink detail capture the action. The same lumpish little girl who is always one jeté behind in class is pure poetry in motion executing a pas de deux in the springtime meadow. Delicately expressive and infused with light, the illustrations and lilting prose are perfectly in step and gratifying.

Kirkus Reviews

SOURCE: A review of *Bravo, Tanya,* in *Kirkus Reviews,* Vol. LX, No. 7, April 1, 1992, p. 464.

The beguiling preschooler who won the right to go to dancing lessons with her big sister in *Dance, Tanya* (1989) discovers that the class poses an unexpected challenge: distracted by the teacher's claps and her loud counting voice, Tanya has trouble following the music. Fortunately, the sympathetic piano player sees her improvising as she used to, "all alone in the meadow where she could hear the music in the wind." They exchange confidences, and, later, Tanya finds she can listen to the piano and dance in time with the others. Again, Ichikawa captures the joy and energy of the dance in her sensitive paintings, contrasting little Tanya's graceful, independent style with the more practiced formality of the older girls. A lovely, warm story about dancing, learning, and respecting one's own unique identity while adapting to an activity with established rules.

Joanne Schott

SOURCE: A review of *Bravo, Tanya,* in *Quill and Quire,* Vol. 58, No. 5, May, 1992, p. 36.

Tanya also faces a clash between her style of doing things and the expectations of others. Hers is a realistic story, however, and the solution involves an understanding and like-minded adult. When Tanya (first met in *Dance, Tanya,* 1989) gets her chance to take ballet lessons, the reality is nothing like her dream. Following instructions is so difficult that she causes a disaster on parents' day. But alone by the brook, she dances beautifully to the music of the wind. The class pianist, also spending time by the brook, applauds Tanya's dancing and tells her that she, too, hears music in the wind. At the next class, Tanya finds that when she really listens to another sort of music, she can dance to that, too.

Ichikawa animates Tanya, with her mingling of grace and awkwardness and conflicting feelings about the dancing she loves, in colourful illustrations that have her characteristic lightness of touch.

Carolyn Phelan

SOURCE: A review of *Bravo, Tanya,* in *Booklist,* Vol. 88, No. 17, May 1, 1992, p. 1610.

Young Tanya and her ballerina bear, who made their first appearance in *Dance, Tanya,* dance to music that no one else can hear. Attending her first ballet lessons, Tanya's happy to don her leotard and do the barre with the older dancers. Floor exercises are her downfall, though, as she teeters in arabesque and crashes out of a pirouette. Worst of all, the teacher's insistent counting keeps her from hearing the piano accompaniment. After a few words of encouragement from the pianist, she learns to listen to the music and once again dances with joy, sometimes in class and sometimes to the music only she and her bear can hear. This sympathetic story will speak to every young ballerina whose dreams have exceeded her skill—and whose have not? The grace, joy, and poignant sadness expressed in the sunlit watercolor illustrations make this a most appealing picture book.

📖 *UNCLE MAGIC* (1992)

Kirkus Reviews

SOURCE: A review of *Uncle Magic,* in *Kirkus Reviews,* Vol. LX, No. 18, September 15, 1992, p. 1186.

At family gatherings, Uncle Roy is Jackie's favorite—with quick good humor, he can pull a walnut out of her ear or make the mashed potatoes speak, but best is the rabbit he keeps in his pocket. Jackie truly believes it's alive until the night she falls asleep in the coats on the bed and wakes to find the rabbit puppet limp on the floor; it takes all "Uncle Magic's" ample gifts of persuasion for her to see that magic is something to meet halfway by believing in it. Gauch tells her story with warmth and lively turns of phrase that recommend it for sharing aloud; Ray sets it in the 40s, when kids were more credulous—though this one looks too old to be fooled by a puppet. Still, the art [by Deborah Kogan Ray] glows with family camaraderie and is well sized for a group. An appealing portrait of a typical family character.

Sharon Grover

SOURCE: A review of *Uncle Magic,* in *School Library Journal,* Vol. 38, No. 11, November, 1992, pp. 69-70.

A young girl reminisces about the visits of her Uncle Roy, a salesman who is invariably late for family gatherings, but whose flare for magic is always welcome. He can pluck a dime out of the air or a walnut from an ear, and one day he even produces a wonderful white rabbit for Jackie to pet. Then one night, when Uncle Magic is very late, Jackie discovers the rabbit (in truth a puppet) on the floor next to the bed where she had been asleep. She is devastated and thinks that Uncle Magic is a fake. When he later explains to her that she has always helped him make magic, all is forgiven. Children may recognize a beloved relative or family friend in Uncle Roy, but the text is rather pedestrian and Ray's illustrations are a bit clumsy. Added to this is the fact that Jackie looks too old to believe that a hand puppet is a real animal, even allowing that in the era pictured (women wear full aprons and men don fedoras), children were less sophisticated than they are today. This is a look back at a more innocent period, but it doesn't quite work.

NOAH (1994)

Kirkus Reviews

SOURCE: A review of *Noah,* in *Kirkus Reviews,* Vol. LXII, No. 4, February 15, 1994, p. 225.

In a simple, invitingly cadenced retelling beginning, "Here is Noah with grace in his eyes,/Here are his sons/right by his side," Gauch adheres closely to the events described in the Bible, from God's command to Noah to build an ark to his family's planting a garden after the animals have finally left them "happily alone." [Jonathan] Green, whose debut in Lauture's *Father and Son* (1992) was widely praised, draws again on his Gullah heritage for paintings in lustrous saturated colors. He depicts most of the humans as black (though one son's wife has blue eyes), and makes creative use of the text's reiterated "two by two" in his handsome compositions. Proof positive that, when it comes to books about Noah, there is always "room for one more."

Elizabeth Bush

SOURCE: A review of *Noah,* in *Booklist,* Vol. 90, No. 13, March 1, 1994, p. 1264.

"Here is Noah with grace in his eyes." In unrhymed

verse, deftly laced with folkloric phrase repetitions, Gauch offers a retelling that is at once poetic, playful, and reverent. Although the telling itself presents no new twists, the harmony of text and illustration make this work effective. Green's Noah is muscular and ebony-skinned, not much older than his grown sons and their multi-ethnic wives. No frail, white-bearded visionary, this Noah is in command of the shipload of equally rock-solid passengers. . . . Gauch and Green leave no doubt that Noah was up to the job. And although their Noah and his menagerie live in respect on land and at sea, they are clearly glad to be quit of their close confines when the waters recede. "And Noah and his wife and his sons and their wives were happily alone, two by two."

Martha V. Parravano

SOURCE: A review of *Noah,* in *The Horn Book Magazine,* Vol. LXX, No. 4, July, 1994, p. 472.

In lyrical, rhythmic prose Gauch presents Noah as a man chosen by God for his grace and simplicity. The text—which tells the standard story of the building of the ark, the gathering of the animals, the coming of the flood, and the eventual receding of the waters—is anything but standard. Sonorous, resonant, rich, the text reads, appropriately enough, like an incantation, becoming almost hypnotic in its repetition of words and sentence structure and in its rhythm: "And soon as soon, / out came the sun, / and the waters went away, / and the earth dried up, / and God said, 'It's time,' / and Noah said, 'It's time,' / and he opened up the windows / and he opened up the doors, / and he said to the animals, / 'Go back to your fields, / go back to your mountains, / go back to your ponds. Go, / two by two.'" The remarkable telling is matched by Jonathan Green's equally remarkable illustrations. According to a note about the artwork, Green's artistic vision was inspired by his experiences growing up in Gardens Corner, South Carolina, in the Hesbah Baptist Church; the expansive, vivid oil paintings depict Noah as a strong, ebony-skinned herdsman of the African savannah—a paradise of abundant animal life and lush green fields and hills.

TANYA AND EMILY IN A DANCE FOR TWO (1994)

Publishers Weekly

SOURCE: A review of *Tanya and Emily in a Dance for Two,* in *Publishers Weekly,* Vol. 241, No. 27, July 4, 1994, p. 62.

The wiggly, petite dancer last seen in **Bravo, Tanya** continues to express her joie de ballet in this rousing encore. When Emily joins Tanya's dance class, everyone (including Barbara, Tanya's ballerina bear) recognizes that Emily is a prima ballerina: she's lithe and limber, able to execute even the difficult cabriole. At first Emily is "always alone" and Tanya "always goes her own way." But when the two girls meet by chance in the park zoo, Tanya's imitative, free-spirited ostrich dance captivates Emily, who joins with Tanya to dance the flamingo, the panther, the giraffe and the "wild leaping goat" (otherwise known as the cabriole). From then on, the two enter into a special friendship. The disciplined Emily helps Tanya refine her movements, while Tanya brings laughter to Emily. As in the other Tanya stories, [Satomi] Ichikawa applies her dexterous, empathic humor to the text through lively watercolors. With a palette varied in brightness and tone, Ichikawa evokes mood and place, whether inside the dusky dance hall or in the crisp outdoors. Even more impressively, she conveys Tanya's state of perpetual motion and Emily's unusual grace. Ichikawa and Gauch, like the girls, partner each other beautifully.

Kirkus Reviews

SOURCE: A review of *Tanya and Emily in a Dance for Two,* in *Kirkus Reviews,* Vol. LXII, No. 18, September 15, 1994, p. 1271.

The little girl first introduced in **Dance, Tanya** (1989) isn't the most talented member of her dance class, but she's the most exuberant; she dances always and everywhere, even in bed at night. Then Emily joins her class and sets a new standard: Her *arabesques,* her *pirouettes,* even her *cabrioles* are perfection. "A prima ballerina!" whispers Tanya's toy bear. Still, going home through the park, Tanya dances as blithely as ever, imitating zoo animals. Emily—also alone—is curious. Soon the two are taking turns: Tanya dances a flamingo and Emily a penguin, Tanya a leopard and Emily an antelope, then both dance giraffes, and Emily shows Tanya that a cabriole is really "a leaping, wild goat." And at the next recital, they do a spirited (if not perfectly matched) *pas de deux.* Ichikawa's rhythmic compositions subtly contrast Tanya's childish charm with Emily's more polished performances while deftly capturing the grace of both and the animals they mimic.

An unusually appealing book with an unobtrusive message: Tanya may never match Emily's achievement, but when she shows her friend the playful side of their art, both are enriched.

Hanna B. Zieger

SOURCE: A review of *Tanya and Emily in a Dance for Two,* in *The Horn Book Magazine,* Vol. LXX, No. 6, November, 1994, p. 718.

Tanya and her love of dancing have been the subject of two previous books. Now, though she is the "smallest and wiggliest" member of her ballet class and always at the end of the line, the ballet steps never stop humming in her head. She dances to them under her covers at night and all during the day. Then, one day, Emily joins their class. Emily is truly a prima ballerina. In every-

thing she does—standing, walking, exercising, and dancing—Emily is outstanding. Since both Tanya and Emily are loners, they each go their own way until they meet one day in the park. Emily is intrigued as Tanya dances like an ostrich and a flamingo and soon joins her to dance like two giraffes and two wild goats. A perceptive dance teacher, noticing the new friendship in class, adds a special *pas de deux* to the winter recital. The two friends dance, "and together they were wonderful." Ichikawa's light watercolor paintings perfectly capture the grace of the girls as they leap through the air. A delight for the dancer hidden in all of us.

Joanne Schott

SOURCE: A review of *Tanya and Emily in a Dance for Two,* in *Quill and Quire,* Vol. 61, No. 1, January, 1995, p. 43.

Tanya is back, as passionate about ballet as ever, but with enthusiasm that still outruns her ability. Then Emily joins her class. She looks like a real ballerina and certainly dances like one. In the park on the way home, Emily asks the always-dancing Tanya if she is doing a *jeté.* Tanya says she is dancing an ostrich. Emily catches the spirit and as the girls dance flamingos, penguins, and giraffes, a friendship is born. When their teacher gives them a special *pas de deux* in the winter recital, their unequal skills blend beautifully.

Author Patricia Lee Gauch keeps Tanya's achievements absolutely in perspective, doing no violence to ballet's slow discipline and developing a theme of self-esteem much better than stories about unrealistic leaps to expert performance. The integration of text and illustrations is flawless. Satomi Ichikawa's delicate and usually precise watercolours are more relaxed here than in earlier books, providing a greater sense of movement. She perfectly contrasts Emily's practiced grace with Tanya's earnest efforts while depicting their friendship with sensitivity and credibility. This is the best Tanya story yet.

TANYA STEPS OUT (1996)

Kirkus Reviews

SOURCE: A review of *Tanya Steps Out,* in *Kirkus Reviews,* Vol. LXIV, No. 17, September 1, 1996, p. 1331.

French ballet terms can be daunting for children; while this book does not provide much help with pronunciations or exact translations, it compares ballet steps to animal movements. *Jeté* is compared to an ostrich's stride; other translations are more literal: *Saut de poisson* shows the ballerina floating like a fish. Slotted windows showing young Tanya pull down to reveal the corresponding animals. Tutu pinks and toe-shoe pastels are balanced with the greens and beiges of the animals, and the slightly goofy expressions on the faces of the human dancers keep the whole thing from becoming fluff.

Joy Fleishhacker

SOURCE: A review of *Tanya Steps Out*, in *School Library Journal*, Vol. 42, No. 12, December, 1996, p. 92.

A young ballerina, first introduced in **Dance, Tanya** (1989), gracefully leaps her way through this well-designed book. When her teacher instructs her to pose like a flamingo, Tanya imitates the animal by standing on one foot and bending her other leg. Pull the tab below the picture and vertical slats move to reveal a flamingo, standing in a very similar position. This is the basic format, as Tanya jumps like a cat, runs like an ostrich, hops like a rabbit, cavorts like a goat, leaps like an antelope, and finally takes a bow. The focus here is not on plot, but on the pictures, and the simple text works well to showcase them. Ballet terms are scattered throughout, but not translated or explained. Crafted from heavy paper, the moveable sections are sturdy and easy to operate. As one picture is replaced by another, the sections separate and move like vertical blinds. Colored in gentle pinks, yellows, and greens, the illustrations [by Satomi Ichikawa] are bright, graceful, and filled with the joy of movement. A nice, but supplemental choice for young ballet fans.

📖 CHRISTINA KATERINA AND FATS AND THE GREAT NEIGHBORHOOD WAR (1997)

Christy Norris

SOURCE: A review of *Christina Katerina and Fats and the Great Neighborhood War*, in *School Library Journal*, Vol. 43, No. 3, March, 1997, p. 152.

Another installment about a feisty heroine. This time, Christina Katerina's best friend, Fats Watson, decides to side with the obnoxious Tommy Morehouse in an argument about who should be the general in a game of soldiers. Before long, the whole neighborhood is at war and the mean pranks begin. The acrylic and gouache illustrations are expressive, artfully capturing the emotions of anger and childhood revenge. The disagreement among friends is a realistic theme and the resolution is predictable but satisfying, with Fats ultimately defending Christina Katerina from Tommy Morehouse. While the girl's habit of spelling out adjectives reflects a certain arrogance prevalent in her character, it creates a stuttering effect in the text that does not lend itself to reading aloud. A nice but not outstanding purchase.

Stephanie Zvirin

SOURCE: A review of *Christina Katerina and Fats and the Great Neighborhood War*, in *Booklist*, Vol. 93, No. 13, March 1, 1997, p. 1171.

Christina Katerina shows she's no pushover when it comes to fair play or friendship. When new kid Tommy Morehouse moves into the neighborhood and shows favorites in a game, Christina objects, expecting her "true" friend Fats to stick up for her. When he doesn't, a neighborhood feud erupts, with Christina and Fats on opposite sides. Tempered with humor, [Stacey] Schuett's sturdy, brightly colored paintings catch Christina's anger and pride as she waits for her best friend to come around. Kids recognize the situation, and most will understand the messages—the main one about friendship as well as the more subtle one about gender.

Deborah Stevenson

SOURCE: A review of *Christina Katerina and Fats and the Great Neighborhood War*, in *Bulletin of the Center for Children's Books*, Vol. 50, No. 10, June, 1997, pp. 357-58.

Christina Katerina has been in a multitude of eponymous picture books, and here she's engaged in a classic neighborhood power skirmish. Obnoxious Tommy Morehouse co-opts Christina's loyal lieutenant, Fats, and then excludes her from play; Christina calls in the reserves (Doris and Joanne), so does Tommy, and the war is on. The scary ghosts and pine-cone pitching are fun, but Christina misses Fats and is hurt at his defection—until Tommy pushes too far and Fats proves true to his old loyalties. This isn't quite as snappy as some books on the subject, and the incivility-rapprochement cycle is fairly predictable. There's a nice blend of the joy and bitterness of neighborhood skirmishing, however, with Fats' refusal to come find Christina in hide-and-seek more hostile than any missile could be. The acrylic and gouache art is suburban verdant with some enlivening reds and purples; the multiracial group of neighborhood kids is lively and authentically determined. There are some good possibilities for entertaining read-aloud expression here, and kids familiar with uneasy neighborhood détente will relish a story about when it all breaks down.

📖 TANYA AND THE MAGIC WARDROBE (1997)

Dawn Amsberry

SOURCE: A review of *Tanya and the Magic Wardrobe*, in *School Library Journal*, Vol. 43, No. 10, October, 1997, p. 95.

When Tanya and her mother arrive early at the theater for a performance of *Coppélia*, the girl follows an elderly woman down a hallway and discovers a dressing room with a green wardrobe full of wonderful costumes. Tanya and the woman dress up and dance parts from *Sleeping Beauty*, *Cinderella*, and the *Nutcracker Suite*. Finally, they perform *Coppélia*, with Tanya as the magic doll, and the dressing room becomes a stage complete with scenery and beautifully costumed dancers. The book ends with Tanya sitting down with her mother to watch the ballet she has just seen in her own imagination.

Ballet fans will snap up this latest addition to the popular series and will turn again and again to the illustrations [by Satomi Ichikawa] of *Coppélia,* painted in colors just dark enough to be mysterious. The two-page spread showing all of the toys coming to life in luminous detail captures perfectly the magic of the famous ballet. The smoothly written text provides just enough narrative to keep the story flowing, letting the illustrations fill in the rest. Once again, Tanya steals the show in this well-executed picture book that pays tribute both to the beauty of dance and to the power of a child's imagination.

Carolyn Phelan

SOURCE: A review of *Tanya and the Magic Wardrobe,* in *Booklist,* Vol. 94, No. 5, November 1, 1997, p. 481.

When Tanya, her mother, and her sister arrive at the theater an hour early for a performance of *Coppelia,* they wait in the empty lobby. While the others talk, Tanya notices an old woman with her arms full of tutus and follows her into a room. When the woman learns that Tanya is a dancer, she confides that she is too. She shows Tanya a series of costumes and tells her about the ballets in which they are worn. The two dance together, imagining themselves in the stories, including *Coppelia,* which is told in abbreviated form. Besides adding to the beloved Tanya series and serving as an appealing introduction to *Coppelia,* this picture book shows that the heart of a dancer beats in people of different shapes, sizes, and ages. Ichikawa's artwork captures the grace and movement of ballet as well as the fearlessness and fascination that led Tanya into her new adventure.

Additional coverage of Gauch's life and career is contained in the following sources published by The Gale Group: *Contemporary Authors New Revision Series,* Vol. 9; *Something about the Author,* Vols. 26, 80; and *Something about the Author Autobiography Series,* Vol. 21.

Maurice (Gough) Gee

1931-

New Zealander author of fiction and nonfiction; screenwriter.

Major works include *The Halfmen of O* (1982; U.S. edition, 1983), *Motherstone* (1985), *The Fire-Raiser* (1986; U.S. edition, 1992), *The Champion* (1989; U.S. edition, 1993), *The Fat Man* (1994).

INTRODUCTION

With works typically set in his native country of New Zealand, Gee is recognized as one of the country's most popular and critically acclaimed writers. While he has written screenplays and fiction for adults and primary graders, Gee is also celebrated for his fantasies and historical fiction for middle graders and young adults featuring the unique topographies of New Zealand. His books appeal to reluctant readers seeking excitement and adventure, as well as mature teens looking for examinations of moral issues. Critics praise Gee's expertly drawn characters, his vivid New Zealand landscapes, his fast-paced and suspenseful plots, and his direct and telling writing style. Some of his works have been compared to those by such authors as Roald Dahl, C. S. Lewis, Alfred Hitchcock, Saki, Madeline L'Engle, Charles Dickens, and Nina Bawden. The theme of good versus evil figures strongly in Gee's fantasy stories. As Diane Hebley explained in *Twentieth-Century Children's Writers,* Gee "sees evil as the abuse of power, with pollution and devastation as the result." The struggle between good and evil also surfaces in his psychological thrillers and historical novels in which his young characters face challenges ranging from the extraordinary to the everyday, from the violence of war and prejudice to the problems of dysfunctional families and the embarrassments of adolescence. "Gee's kids are exactly right," Hazel Rochman concluded, "drawn with an ambiguity rare in YA books. He shows in every beautiful sentence how complicated feelings can be and how close friends are to being enemies—in the classroom, in the adult community, and on the battlefields in Europe."

Biographical Information

Gee was born in Whakatane, New Zealand, in 1931. He grew up in the small New Zealand town of Henderson, which was, during Gee's youth, a rural area providing ample entertainment for a boy, and later inspiration for the setting in some of Gee's stories. Gee once explained in *Something about the Author (SATA),* "I seem to have spent my boyhood swimming and eeling and sailing tin canoes and catching crayfish and diving from willow branches; and I suppose that's why creeks and streams

keep coming into my stories." Gee went from a small country school to Avondale College, where he received a Bachelor of Arts degree in 1949. He received a Master of Arts degree from the University of Auckland in 1953, and then studied at Auckland Teachers College before becoming a teacher in 1955. Gee told *SATA* that he became a teacher "not because I wanted to but because I couldn't think of any other way to make a living. Secretly, I wanted to write, and I did write, all sorts of things, most of them pretty awful. I didn't write anything good until my mid-twenties, and that encouraged me to give up teaching and try to earn my living as a writer." Gee held various jobs between 1958 and 1965, including working as a postman, a window-cleaner, and a hospital porter. When he married, he became a librarian in order to support his family, and eventually enrolled at the New Zealand Library School in 1966. Gee felt that the atmosphere of a library, however, inhibited him from writing, as he explained in *SATA:* "Libraries had too many books, they seemed to stop me from writing my own." Gee and his family eventually settled in Nelson, a small city in the South island of New Zealand famous for its apple orchards, when Gee began to make a living as a writer. His first writings were novels for adults, including *The Big Season* (1962), *A Special Flower* (1965), and *In My Father's Den* (1972). After publishing fiction for adults for almost twenty years, Gee launched into writing fantasy and children's books by accident. "A friend lent me Alan Garner's *The Wierdstone of Brisingamen*," he noted in *SATA*. "I read it with great enjoyment and decided it was the sort of thing I'd like to write myself. So my first children's book, *Under the Mountain,* (1979) had its beginning."

Major Works

Gee's "O" trilogy examines the corruption of absolute power in the fantasy world of O. In the first book, *The Halfmen of O,* young Susan Ferris and her cousin Nick Quinn are transported to the world of O. Their mission is to find and connect two half stones and take them to the Motherstone, thereby restoring the balance of good and evil in O. Aided by the good Birdfolk and Stonefolk, Susan and Nick travel to the dangerous Darkland, where the evil Halfmen live. Susan and Nick complete their mission, save O, and return safely home. In the sequel, *The Priests of Ferris* (1984; U.S. edition, 1985), Susan and Nick return to O to find that the High Priest and his followers have created a false religious cult with Susan as its titular head, and are using it to harbor political oppression and violence. Once again Susan and Nick defeat the priests and restore proper balance to O. The final book in the trilogy, *Motherstone,* centers around two conflicting political groups in O, both armed with weapons of mass destruction. Susan and Nick must return O to a primeval state to prevent war. Describing Gee's world of O, Marcus Crouch noted that Gee is "a remarkable writer, who uses the conventions of the outworld romance both to tell a most compelling story and to make some valid social comments. . . . Mr. Gee shows himself a master of his craft."

Gee turned from fantasy to historical fiction with *The Fire-Raiser.* Set in New Zealand in 1915, this book tells the story of four children who work together to stop a pyromaniac. Several subplots of the story, including a school pageant and a romance between two adult characters, raise issues of loyalty, prejudice, and war. A *Kirkus Reviews* critic described the book as a "well-wrought thriller that brings an entire community vividly and believably to life."

Gee's second historical novel for young adults, *The Champion,* deals with racism. Also set in New Zealand, the story takes place in 1943 during World War II and describes how a young boy's naïve expectations of heroism are turned upside down. Rex is thrilled to learn that an American soldier will be staying with his family, until the guest turns out to be Private Jack Coop, a black soldier who admits that battle frightens him. Rex's initial disappointment slowly changes into admiration for the intelligent, perceptive private; Rex also makes friends with two children of minority races. In the tragic climax, the three children help Jack when he decides to go AWOL rather than return to the war. A *Publishers Weekly*

reviewer wrote, "As it grows increasingly complex, this book sheds light onto the darkest sides of war, and the personal tragedies of its sharply defined characters will touch readers from all walks of life."

The Fat Man, a psychological thriller with several plot twists, takes place in Loomis, New Zealand, in 1933. Herbert Muskie, who has been overweight all of his life, returns home from America to seek revenge against the people who made fun of him during his youth. Colin Potter, a young man whose father tormented Herbert, becomes an unwilling accomplice in Herbert's evil schemes. Colin eventually stops Herbert, but only after Herbert has violently abused people and committed murder. "A brilliant writer," Michael Cart noted, "Gee once again demonstrates his extraordinary talent for psychologically acute characterization. Mining Muskie's past, Gee makes the fat man's motives for insinuating himself into the lives of Colin's family absolutely believable . . . and absolutely terrifying."

Gee's most recent novel for young adults, *Orchard Street* (1998), is a poignantly nostalgic tale about growing up in Loomis during the 1950s. Using the 1951 wharfie's strike as a backdrop, Gee describes the stresses and fears that Austin Dye faces as he confronts fascism, social pressures, and change. John McKenzie wrote, "This is a superb evocation of growing up in provincial New Zealand in the 1950s that brings to life for the modern young adult reader, the peculiar tensions of the time."

Awards

Gee received two Esther Glen Awards from the New Zealand Library and Information Association: for *Motherstone* in 1986 and *The Fat Man* in 1995. Gee received an AIM Award for *The Halfmen of O* in 1983, and *The Champion* won an AIM Children's Book Award, second prize in the story book category, in 1990. Gee also won the New Zealand Children's Book of the Year Award in 1982 for *The Halfmen of O* and was honored with the Sir James Waffie Award in 1993. *The Fat Man* received the New Zealand Post Children's Book Award (formerly the AIM Award) for Junior Fiction, the Supreme Award (formerly AIM Book of the Year Award), and the Esther Glen Award in 1995.

TITLE COMMENTARY

📖 *UNDER THE MOUNTAIN* (1979)

Margery Fisher

SOURCE: A review of *Under the Mountain,* in *Growing Point,* Vol. 18, No. 6, March, 1980, pp. 3652-53.

[Gee's] first novel (in the children's sphere, that is)

shows a similar disparity between the treatment of place, a familiar place undergoing violent change, and the concomitant depiction of character. *Under the Mountain* is set in Auckland and the action is plausibly linked with the extinct volcanoes which are such a feature of the sprawling, sea-bound New Zealand city. If the author had been content with a localised fantasy his plot might have been believable, but the concept of an alien galactic race, already in control of other planets, aiming to turn Earth to a desert of mud, is out of all proportion to the immediacy of the modernistic house by the lake and the red-haired twins who alone can confront the sinister Wilberforces. In a bizarre mixture of transcendental meditation and telepathy on one hand and a Blytonesque descent into underground tunnels on the other, the story reaches a climax of yet another dimension—for a volcanic explosion, the result of a momentary faltering on the part of young Theo and the age of their mentor, Mr. Jones, apparently destroys an outlying part of the city, and the story ends with that chaos of destruction whose shadow looms in so many books of this kind. In this inconsistent mixture of youthful chatter and macabre description there is a certain force in the way the author has blown up familiar and harmless creatures—slugs and worms—to produce an atmosphere of horror; but neither plot nor characters seem sufficiently well-defined to carry the invention.

Stephen Hurd

SOURCE: A review of *Under the Mountain*, in *School Library Journal*, Vol. 26, No. 7, March, 1980, p. 140.

The 11-year-old Matheson twins, Rachel and Theo, find themselves the last hope for humankind in this science fiction adventure situated in/around/under Auckland, New Zealand. Their mentor, alien Mr. Jones, places two milk-white stones in the twins' control, realizing they possess the necessary pole-like qualities, power to "pebble" (use telepathy), and red hair. Terrible symbiotic pairs (giant worm and smaller slug) of world destroying aliens constitute the threat here. Readers may well wonder how these creatures traveled through space and how they became human shaped, but the mystery and suspense are engrossing to the finish.

D. A. Young

SOURCE: A review of *Under the Mountain*, in *The Junior Bookshelf*, Vol. 44, No. 4, August, 1980, p. 189.

This splendid creepy horror story is set in New Zealand. Auckland is surrounded by extinct or sleeping volcanoes and what better hiding places could be found for the monstrous worm-like beings that await their freedom to emerge and turn the whole world to foul-smelling mud. The last survivor of a race capable of destroying this threat to our planet bears the prosaic name of Mr. Jones. For his powers to work he needs the assistance of twins

with telepathic minds. So it is that Theo and Rachel find a pleasant holiday becomes a nightmare adventure.

Afficionados of *Dr. Who* will revel in the inventiveness of the author. Even if the reader has no knowledge of Lake Pupuke or Rangitoto Island the story is so exciting and so well told that he will find it difficult to put the book down. Events move quickly and although we know that the children must triumph we are kept in suspense until the very end. The story may be full of fancied impossibilities but the skill of the author ensures a suspension of disbelief on the part of the most down-to-earth reader.

New Zealand children will appreciate a story set in a country they know rather than the home counties of Mother England, and children anywhere else will enjoy a rattling good yarn.

THE WORLD AROUND THE CORNER
(1980; U.S. and British editions, 1981)

R. Baines

SOURCE: A review of *The World around the Corner*, in *The Junior Bookshelf*, Vol. 45, No. 4, August, 1981, p. 150.

Among the goods going for auction Caroline finds a battered pair of spectacles which have magical powers. They belong to Sun and Moon elves, inhabitants of a parallel world, who wage an annual battle against the evil Grimbles. Between fights the glasses must be brought into our world. This renews their power, making them an invaluable aid to the elf selected to challenge the Grimbles' dragon.

By hiding the glasses and eventually handing them to the current Moon Girl champion Caroline plays her part in the triumph of good.

This is a well-produced book with attractive print set on excellent quality paper, and it includes agreeable black-and-white illustrations [by Gary Hebley]. The characters are credible, and Maurice Gee has a lively style. Unfortunately the basic premise that the spectacles must be brought to our world each year fails to convince. This forms the chief weakness of a disappointing plot.

Lorraine Douglas

SOURCE: A review of *The World around the Corner*, in *School Library Journal*, Vol. 28, No. 2, October, 1981, p. 141.

This gently written, brief fantasy set in modern-day New Zealand centers around the adventures of an eight-year-old after she finds a pair of magical spectacles. Caroline's new glasses give her the power to see the "world around the corner," which is threatened with destruction unless "Moon-girl" has the glasses for an annual battle with a dragon. The evil Grimbles pursue Caroline, but she eludes them and finds "Moon-girl," and the dragon is vanquished. Gee's familiar fantasy lacks interesting characters and a compelling plot. The device of spectacles with magical powers has been utilized more imaginatively in L'Engle's *A Wrinkle in Time*.

Books for Your Children

SOURCE: A review of *The World around the Corner*, in *Books for Your Children*, Vol. 16, No. 3, Autumn-Winter, 1981, p. 23.

[*The World around the Corner* is] the first book we've read by this clever New Zealand author. Here is an easy storybook that will appeal principally to girls. The nine-year-old heroine finds a pair of magic spectacles among a box of old books in her father's second hand shop. They lead her into protecting the forces of good from the forces of evil. This is an old theme but a sure one and it is given a fresh treatment here in a well written very approachable tale in big print. Very good readers of six and seven will also enjoy it.

Zena Sutherland

SOURCE: A review of *The World around the Corner*, in *Bulletin of the Center for Children's Books*, Vol. 38, No. 2, October, 1984, p. 25.

Caroline finds, in her father's antique shop, a pair of old spectacles that clearly are magical; just after finding them, she becomes aware that the evil Mr. Grimble (whose eyes, when she has the magic glasses on, are red) is frenetically hunting the glasses. Caroline learns from the old woman who had brought the spectacles into the store that there's another world from which she comes and in which the evil forces represented by Grimble can gain control if he finds the magic glasses. It is up to Caroline to thwart Grimble and save the other world—which she does, in a mildly suspenseful sequence. Set in New Zealand, smoothly written, but a bit plodding in pace and formulaic in structure.

Annette Curtis Klause

SOURCE: A review of *The World around the Corner*, in *School Library Journal*, Vol. 31, No. 8, April, 1985, p. 87.

In this pleasant fantasy set in New Zealand, eight-year-old Caroline finds a pair of magic glasses in a box left at her father's second-hand shop by a friendly yet anxious elderly woman. The glasses make the world seem brighter, more vital. While hiding in the mattress loft, she sees an odd little man below and knows right away that he is after the glasses. What follows is a series of adventures that involve guardian cats, an invisible door to another world and a hair-raising chase to the pole that

marks the center of New Zealand in order to deliver the glasses, which are vital to the survival of *The World around the Corner*. Fast-paced action, authentic characters and accessible sentence structure make this an excellent fantasy for middle elementary grades. Caroline is a perceptive, intelligent girl, and the book comes alive with her observations. The baddies are quite nasty in a Dahl-like fashion, while the goodies have an innocent, heroic appeal. The plot is almost overly simple, yet it works well.

THE HALFMEN OF O (first novel in the "O" trilogy, 1982; U.S. edition, 1983)

A. R. Williams

SOURCE: A review of *The Halfmen of O*, in *The Junior Bookshelf*, Vol. 46, No. 6, December, 1982, p. 230.

The name of half-man indicates only that the being in question lacks the balance (however imperfect) of good and evil that makes up the human psyche. By some complicated process the two halves have been separated in the World of O into which Susan Ferris and Nick Quinn are 'spirited', Susan unwillingly as one chosen to restore the balance and Nick voluntarily in the attempt to protect Susan. Both endure much danger and hardship under their pursuit by the half-men and their escapes with the humane woodlanders. If at times the action and the writing seem to incline to the melodramatic it is no bad thing in a yarn in which almost anything goes, even to escape by home-made hand-gliders. The greedy, ruthless one-time prospector, Jimmy Jaspers, responsible for the translation of Susan into an agent of redemption, is himself redeemed in the land behind the mine and remains to do good works in the heartland of his choice. The author's narrative and descriptive style keeps up well with the packed action and the running surprises.

Karen Stang Hanley

SOURCE: A review of *The Halfmen of O*, in *Booklist*, Vol. 79, No. 21, July, 1983, p. 1400.

Elements of good and evil, normally in balance, have gone awry in the world of O. Human inhabitants are either entirely good or entirely evil, but most of the former group have been slain by the cruel Halfmen who are set on conquering O. Susan, a young New Zealander, has been chosen to travel to O and restore the natural order. She is recognized by a mark on her wrist showing the interrelationship of good and evil (actually a yin and yang symbol, although it is never referred to as such). Her cousin Nick accompanies her, and their guides are two Woodland folk, Breeze and Brand. According to arrangements made long ago, Susan must journey to the Birdfolk and the Stonefolk, collect the divided halves of the yin and yang, and lay them together on the Motherstone in the heart of the Darkland domain of the Halfmen. There are dimensions of this complicated quest fantasy that are not fully developed, and the novel is fraught with violence, more spiritual than physical (such as Susan's agony in handling the evil half of the sign). The narrative is so intensely focused on Susan and her dangerous mission that other characters are vague (with the exception of Jimmy Jaspers, a rugged adventurer who follows Susan to O). Collections with heavy demand for unusual fantasy may nevertheless want to consider Gee's involving story. Unfortunately, no map is included to aid readers in tracing Susan's peregrinations.

Tony Ficociello

SOURCE: A review of *The Halfmen of O,* in *School Library Journal,* Vol. 30, No. 1, September, 1983, p. 134.

Entering a strange mine shaft, young Susan and her cousin Nick find themselves in the world of O in the middle of Halfmen, Woodlanders, Bloodcats and evil incarnate: the diabolical Otis Claw. Susan learns that because of a strange mark on her arm, placed there by the legendary, benevolent Freeman Wells, only she can recapture the Motherstone (a sort of Holy Grail) from Claw and thus reinstate goodness for the Halfmen. Although she wants to return home, a sense of moral duty causes her to stay and fight. Susan, a modern, liberated literary character, is an excellent role model of a strong, independent female. Gee has created a unique environment and his story soars with excitement.

📖 *THE PRIESTS OF FERRIS* (second novel in the "O" trilogy, 1984; U.S. edition, 1985)

Marcus Crouch

SOURCE: A review of *The Priests of Ferris,* in *The Junior Bookshelf,* Vol. 49, No. 6, December, 1985, p. 276.

This is a sequel to *The Halfmen of O.* Readers who, like myself, missed the original book need not be too much concerned, because the author provides an adequate amount of recapitulation in this second volume.

The Priests of Ferris belongs, more or less, to the 'Narnia' school of outworld fiction. It presents a picture of an alien world, that of O, which has some parallels with our world, and the similarities and contrasts are pointed effectively by the inclusion of human characters, especially Susan Ferris and her friend Nick. A year of human life has passed since they last went to O. A hundred have gone by in O, and all those with whom they had contact are long dead. Susan is still remembered, for she has passed into legend and has been made the titular head of a religious cult, devised as camouflage for a political tyranny. The priests of O rule in her name, putting down all opposition ruthlessly and destroying all alien life, like that of the Woodlanders and the Birdfolk, in true Nazi fashion. Susan returns in order to destroy the false religion, she hopes by telling the truth, not by

the use of force. But the High Priest of Ferris—a masterly portrait—is not interested in truth. He is a pragmatist, using superstition as an instrument of policy but cynically contemptuous of religion. So it has to be force after all, and in a thrilling climax the old pioneer Jimmy Jaspers, taken, literally, out of deep freeze, and his friend the giant bear, defeat the forces of evil totally. Susan and Nick go home, happy with their success and, one suspects, awaiting another call from O some day.

It is always tempting to approach this kind of book in a frivolous mood, but this would be to misjudge a formidable talent. Maurice Gee, who is from New Zealand, is a remarkable writer, who uses the conventions of the outworld romance both to tell a most compelling story and to make some valid social comments. The book is the more convincing because of the vivid portraiture of some of its principals, notably the High Priest, Jimmy Jaspers, and Soona, the visionary girl from the fishing village. As with other books of this kind, including those of C. S. Lewis, the real stumbling block is the role of the child hero and heroine. It all depends on Susan, and, cleverly as Mr. Gee shows her in her courage and vulnerability, it is difficult to accept that the fortunes of a world rest in her small hands. But in all other respects, in pace of narrative and in the painting of the topography of O, in the evocation of birds and bears and woodland creatures, Mr. Gee shows himself a master of his craft.

Margery Fisher

SOURCE: A review of *The Priests of Ferris,* in *Growing Point,* Vol. 24, No. 5, January, 1986, p. 4543-46.

A world parallel with Earth but in a different dimension had been saved from appalling enemies in *The Halfmen of O.* Now Susan Ferris, agent for good in that book, is summoned again to O, where devious men have manipulated religious enthusiasm in her name for their own evil ends. *The Priests of Ferris* again describes a confrontation between innocent people wanting to lead free lives and a vicious priesthood with ritual murder in the so-called Miracles to confirm annually their power. The New Zealand settlement where Susan lives disappears as she and her friend Nick, with the help of a magic flower, find their way through old mine-workings to the land of O and set themselves to trace old friends and allies and rescue the sad Woodlander Soona, the latest prisoner of the Temple. The image of a false religion is a familiar one, developed here with a modicum of detail of place and weather and a certain apparatus of magic with mythical associations—most notably, the terrifying pack of hounds who track the children for their sinister masters. The priests are defeated by a mixture of ridicule, trickery and cold courage entirely appropriate to the two children who, helped as they are by right-thinking friends, still carry the main burden of the fight against evil in a tale whose course, direct and telling, could hold the attention of readers around ten or so ready to appreciate action with an underlying point to it.

David Bennett

SOURCE: A review of *The Priests of Ferris,* in *Books for Keeps,* No. 47, November, 1987, p. 23.

Maurice Gee's story is a sequel to *The Halfmen of O* and has all the fast pace and gripping invention of its forerunner. Much of the first section really needs a knowledge of the earlier adventure for complete comprehension but with a bit of tenacity new readers could get by.

Susan Ferris feels drawn to return to O and when she gets there with her cousin Nick she finds that not only have 100 years elapsed, but in her name the land is gripped, vice-like, by the evil, ruthless Priests of Ferris, led by their insane High Priest for whom, 'lies are part of the system, and cruelty means fear and fear means control. Susan and her allies are set the daunting, blood-strewn task of turning that system around and restoring the truth, banishing fear. All fantasy readers will relish this one.

MOTHERSTONE (third novel in the "O" trilogy, 1985)

A. R. Williams

SOURCE: A review of *Motherstone,* in *The Junior Bookshelf,* Vol. 50, No. 2, April, 1986, p. 77.

Some acquaintance with Maurice Gee's *The Halfmen of O* and *The Priests of Ferris* would be an advantage though not an essential one to the reader of *Motherstone,* for it is easy enough to abandon oneself to the hypnotic influence of Mr. Gee's landscape as to the embrace of a well-primed bath. For the time being it does not matter where the bath is. The plot is divided between the desperately contrived escape from O of Susan Ferris and Nicholas Quinn, and the prospect of a war between two new socio-political sects both armed with a devastating weapon whose awful effects would be parallels of nuclear holocausts. The 'theology' of this suspended world may be difficult to follow or fathom but the moving stratagems are real enough and a source of nail-biting suspense and the author does excel in the creation of landscape. It is surely not everyone's idea of a relaxing read; it requires concentration, continuity and, at the end certainly some previous knowledge of the denizens of O.

Ruth S. Vose

SOURCE: A review of *Motherstone,* in *School Library Journal,* Vol. 33, No. 3, November, 1986, p. 100.

In this final volume of Gee's "O" fantasy series, Nick and Susan, before they return to earth, must once again save the Land of O, this time from self-destruction with nuclear-type weapons. Helped by old friends, including the Birdfolk, bear-like Vargs, and the great Bloodcat

Thief, they must make their way to the Motherstone and a final encounter which transforms all life on O. The story's message is a bleak one: human beings must save themselves from their own destructive natures. Gee, a New Zealand writer, excels at description of physical action; his apt choice of words sweeps the detailed plot along from one tense encounter to the next. Descriptions of characters, on the other hand, seem incomplete, as if the author expects children to know them from the previous volumes. Incidents from the past are referred to with little explanation. For this reason, the series should be read as a whole.

THE FIRE-RAISER (1986; U.S. edition, 1992)

Gerry Larson

SOURCE: A review of *The Fire-Raiser,* in *School Library Journal,* Vol. 38, No. 9, September, 1992, p. 277.

With Dickensian flair, Gee spins the tale of an arsonist whose guilt and troubled past are brought to light by a motley group of children. Lurking in dark alleyways, wearing black overcoat and red balaclava, emotionally disturbed Edgar Marwick finds release from his tyrannical mother by setting fires. The baker's adventurous children, Noel and Kitty; the mayor's pampered but frustrated child, Irene; and homeless Phil Miller band together and boldly gather evidence that indicts the guilty man. While seeking justice, they witness the prejudice against Frau Stauffel, a local German music teacher. Set in a small New Zealand town at the beginning of World War I, *The Fire-Raiser* reveals a community in which loyalties and prejudices intertwine. With the forthright support and courageous example of their teacher, the youngsters learn the power and price of fear and hatred. Well-drawn characters, steady plot development, and sharp descriptions make this novel an entertaining selection. Some questions may remain, however, about the resolution of the conflicts between Irene and her parents and Edgar Marwick and his mother. Although the setting evokes a historical time and place, the dilemmas and concerns of the townspeople and children are universal.

Hazel Rochman

SOURCE: A review of *The Fire-Raiser,* in *Booklist,* Vol. 89, No. 4, October 15, 1992, p. 424.

A scary thriller set in New Zealand during World War I dramatizes the secret fury of a pyromaniac and relates it to the mob violence let loose in the community by jingoism and war. At times, you're right there with the fire-raiser, feeling his pleasure and power ("Flame filled the inside of his head. It ran along his arteries. It licked around his bones"). At times, you're with the wise, quirky schoolteacher as he copes with meanness and cruelty, trying to give his students hope. But most of the action focuses on four town kids who start off as enemies and end up working together to stop the burning. Kitty and Noel are the children of the sensible baker; Phil's a street kid, smelly and smart; Irene's the butt of playground teasing because she's upper-class. These kids find themselves in deadly danger from a villain who is "silent, quick, and mad." Gee makes some attempt at psychologizing why the fire-raiser, Marwick, became the way he is, but, fortunately, the author leaves most of it a mystery. Marwick's mother, fierce, punishing, patrician, is straight out of old-fashioned melodrama; she's "witch and spider." What makes this story special is the combination of terror and dailiness. Gee's kids are exactly right, drawn with an ambiguity rare in YA books. He shows in every beautiful sentence how complicated feelings can be and how close friends are to being enemies—in the classroom, in the adult community, and on the battlefields in Europe.

Kirkus Reviews

SOURCE: A review of *The Fire-Raiser,* in *Kirkus Reviews,* Vol. LX, No. 20, October 15, 1992, p. 1309.

In his first children's book to be published here, a well-regarded New Zealand novelist sets a story about four children bringing a pyromaniac to justice early in WW I. From its riveting first chapter—from the point of view of the lumbering masked man who sets fire to the local livery stable because "a time had come when his fire must consume life"—the action is compelling. Noel and Kitty Wix sound the alarm in time to save the horses; knocked down by the man as he makes a hasty exit, Kitty soon realizes that he is Edgar Marwick, a reclusive, belligerent farmer. Meanwhile, Kitty's new friend is the mayor's overprotected but spunky daughter, Irene; and Noel makes an uneasy alliance with rough but intelligent Phil. Cleverly (and with a daring lack of caution), the four unearth evidence proving Marwick's guilt; meanwhile, they are involved in a jingoistic school pageant (its destructive aftermath is exacerbated by Marwick's support of local rowdies). Other subplots—a romance between their gifted, unfashionably pacifist teacher and a German-born music teacher; Phil's chance for an education—are deftly integrated. Several adult characters are as perceptively drawn as the well-realized protagonists; Marwick's madness is revealed to be the result of his mother's response to a long-ago tragedy. A well-wrought thriller that brings an entire community vividly and believably to life.

Roger Sutton

SOURCE: A review of *The Fire-Raiser,* in *Bulletin of the Center for Children's Books,* Vol. 46, No. 4, December, 1992, p. 111.

"In Dargie's Livery Stable the fires leaped and the horses screamed." While today we might call him a pyromaniac, the citizens of a small New Zealand town in 1915 are looking for the "fire-raiser," and while four teens

are convinced they know who he is, no one will believe them. That's a classic appeal, all by itself, and Gee's considerable storytelling powers turn alluring premise into absorbing narrative. The teens are a disputatious quartet: Phil, the tough, suspicious kid; Noel, the good kid not above a little troublemaking; Irene, the perfect teacher's pet; and Kitty, Noel's sister and good friend to Irene (who reveals a likeably rebellious streak when scratched). The fire-raiser is an Anthony Perkins wacko, and wait till you meet his mother: "No more fires. Or I'll let them put you in prison. You won't like that. It's dark in there."

Florence H. Munat

SOURCE: A review of *The Fire-Raiser,* in *Voice of Youth Advocates,* Vol. 15, No. 5, December, 1992, p. 277.

The year is 1915. An arsonist is on the loose in Jessop, New Zealand, and four children know who he is. Their problem is provingthat Edgar Marwick, the middle-aged son of a wealthy widow, is indeed the "fire-raiser."

The foursome (all aged about 11-13) represent Jessop's upper, middle, and lower classes: Irene Chalmers is the daughter of the rich mayor, Kitty and Noel Wix are children of the town baker, and Phil Miller lives alone in a dirty room by the docks. Thrown together by school projects and their mission to catch Marwick in an act of arson, their class consciousness becomes subordinated to their friendship.

Although the story is slow in developing (hard on reluctant readers), it becomes a gripping page-turner thanks largely to the portrayal of the sinister, demented Marwick—a villain of Dickensian stature. When the children attempt to search his house and barn for evidence, the scenes are full of tension because by then the reader knows how dangerous and violent Marwick can be. And although helpful adults are called upon when necessary, it is the children who do most of the sleuthing.

The tension is heightened by the anti-German feelings of some of the townspeople. Their jingoism gets out of control after a patriotic school pageant as Marwick leads a crowd to the home of a German immigrant music teacher. They smash her windows and burn her piano in their "patriotic" frenzy.

Confusion may arise over some New Zealand word usages. For example, when the headmaster encourages Phil to go on to "college," he is not referring to university (which would make Phil much older than he really is) but to the equivalent of an American high school. And the red "balaclava" that energizes Marwick's pyromania is more commonly known in the U.S. as a ski mask. But these differences are not significant, and may even send readers scurrying for their dictionaries. People who enjoy historical fiction will treasure this book and its unforgettable villain.

Nancy Vasilakis

SOURCE: A review of *The Fire-Raiser*, in *The Horn Book Magazine*, Vol. LXIX, No. 2, March-April, 1993, pp. 210-11.

This edge-of-the-seat story is a New Zealand import that takes place during World War I and involves the attempts of four children to discover the identity of an arsonist who has been setting buildings ablaze in their small town. Noel and Kitty Wix, together with Phil Miller, a ragamuffin who lives on his own at the edge of town, and Irene Chalmers, the mayor's daughter, develop some theories about who the "fire-raiser" might be. As the members of this motley troupe join forces to root out their suspect, they acquire a camaraderie that is born of peril. The object of their suspicions is Edgar Marwick, who lives with his mother, a disturbed, formidable woman who never recovered from the drowning death of her young daughter many years earlier. Blaming Edgar for the accident, she locked him in a cupboard, where the terrified boy, cowering in the darkness, built fires inside his head for warmth and light. The children eventually stumble onto this mad household, and Kitty is imprisoned for a time in that same dark cupboard. This smoothly constructed page-turner introduces a strong array of characters. The passages highlighting the inner workings of Marwick's sick mind are truly riveting. Another important presence is Mr. Hedges, the school headmaster with a face so ugly that "children had been known to cry at the sight of him," but whose spirited love of teaching and of the children he teaches leads him to see merit in cast-offs like Phil Miller. Two collateral events—the school's patriotic pageant and the harassment of Frau Stauffer, the Austrian piano teacher—shed light on wartime attitudes and add depth to the narrative. Such well-drawn details of time and place are woven into a narrative that will enthrall young readers from the very first page.

THE CHAMPION (1989; U.S. edition, 1993)

Publishers Weekly

SOURCE: A review of *The Champion*, in *Publishers Weekly*, Vol. 240, No. 39, September 27, 1993, p. 64.

In the vein of *Summer of My German Soldier*, this World War II novel traces the growing friendship between a young New Zealander and an American private on leave. Twelve-year-old Rex, who has spent a considerable amount of time fantasizing about battlefield heroics, is sorely disappointed to find that the soldier who is to stay in his home for two weeks is "only" a low-ranking black. Private Jackson Coop is not well received by the bigoted adults of Kettle Creek, but his sharp wit, honesty and gentle nature win him the affection of many children in the small community. After an incident at school, in which Jack gets the better of a cruel teacher, even Rex cannot help admiring the reluctant soldier from the Chicago slums. As it grows increasingly complex,

this book sheds light onto the darkest sides of war, and the personal tragedies of its sharply defined characters will touch readers from all walks of life. Particularly memorable are Rex's eccentric grandparents; his father, whose dealings with the black market are a source of humor as well as tension; and two children, Dawn and Leo, who are perhaps the most sensitive to Private Coop's deep sadness. Wrought with as much intelligence as heart, this tender story can be savored many times.

Jack Forman

SOURCE: A review of *The Champion*, in *School Library Journal*, Vol. 39, No. 10, October, 1993, p. 148, 151.

Rex Pascoe looks back on his childhood in New Zealand during World War II, when Jackson Coop, a black American soldier wounded in battle, stays with his family for two weeks as he recuperates. Rex's sister Gloria; his open-minded poet mother; and likable but scheming father welcome Jack with open arms, but it takes time for the then 12-year-old Rex to overcome his racial prejudice. The boy also resents that "his soldier" falls short of his image of a fearless hero, but he eventually joins his family and classmates in helping Jack cope with the racially motivated hostility of two American soldiers and of suspicious New Zealanders. The private finally goes AWOL, setting in motion a fast-paced, tragic climax. The man's fear of the war and his ironic views of his black identity ring true, but he's so kind, generous, and sensitive that he seems saintly compared to the mere mortals who surround him. Strong secondary characters give the story depth, and young readers are exposed to a vivid picture of another place and time. (Some may be offended by the narrator's casual use of the word "Jap," but it's historically accurate.) Readers who overlook the simplistic portrait of Jack as a veritable paragon of virtue will find an involving, action-packed novel filled with well-developed characters.

Sheilamae O'Hara

SOURCE: A review of *The Champion*, in *Booklist*, Vol. 90, No. 3, October 1, 1993, p. 341.

Twelve-year-old Rex is living World War II vicariously in Kettle Creek, New Zealand. When his mother tells him an American is coming to stay with them for two weeks to convalesce from his war wounds, Rex is thrilled. He imagines sharing his bedroom with a pilot whose plane was shot down in combat and, then, is both outraged and embarrassed when Jackson Coop arrives. Not only is Jack a mere private, but he is also a black, which means he has even less status than the Maoris and Dalmatians who are considered the lower classes. Worst of all, Jack admits to being afraid in battle. Gradually, Rex comes to see that Jack is a hero in his own way, a person who would rather avoid a fight but defends those weaker than himself. When Jack goes AWOL, Rex allies with Dawn, a girl who is part Maori, and

Leo, a despised Dalmatian "squarehead," to hide Jack. Gee fills his book with memorable characters. Rex longs for the perfect hero and has trouble accepting Jack's abhorrence of battle. Rex's father is a scoundrel, who nonetheless has his own ethical code. Dawn loves her grandmother although she drove Dawn's mother away and waters the milk she sells to their neighbors. Leo will not let the bigots grind him down, not even the tyrannical teacher. Rex's mother writes poetry; his grandmother rides a motorcycle and gardens in the nude; his grandfather specializes in flawed inventions. The ending is neither predictable nor contrived; it leaves the reader hoping to meet some of these people again.

Kirkus Reviews

SOURCE: A review of *The Champion,* in *Kirkus Reviews,* Vol. LXI, No. 19, October 1, 1993, p. 1273.

In New Zealand in 1943, wounded American GIs were invited to local homes to convalesce. Drawing on his own boyhood, Gee depicts the dramatic, ultimately tragic, events surrounding the visit of one such soldier: Private Jackson Coop. "Jack" is nothing like the enemy-destroying hero that 12-year-old Rex Pascoe has conjured up after reading simplistic pulp fiction: he's courteous, quiet, kind—and black, which elicits enmity from several locals (though their own policeman is a Maori) and especially from two other GIs, Ozark rednecks. In a skillfully plotted sequence involving two more children (half-Maori Dawn and Croatian Leo, both also butts of prejudice), Rex comes to admire and finally to love Jack; in the end, after Jack goes AWOL rather than fight the rednecks, Rex and the others try to help him escape. Jack himself comprises too many clichés to be a fully realized character (he's musically and physically gifted, with street smarts learned in a Chicago slum), but he's an admirable one, well suited to contrast with Rex's superhero ideal—as well as with his flawed father Alf ("gabby tricky Dad, my crooked dad") and his shady deals. A lively, idiosyncratic cast keeps the story moving; and while it's less intensely suspenseful than Gee's *The Fire-Raiser,* it's another likable, thoughtful examination of wartime pressures and prejudices in a small, vividly portrayed New Zealand community.

Deborah Stevenson

SOURCE: A review of *The Champion,* in *Bulletin of the Center for Children's Books,* Vol. 47, No. 3, November, 1993, pp. 80-1.

Twelve-year-old Rex, deeply involved in World War II from a safe distance, is thrilled to discover that an American GI is coming to stay with his family to recuperate in their little New Zealand village. He's dismayed, however, when instead of the dashing white lieutenant he had envisioned they receive a young black private. Jackson Coop—Jack—is quiet but sharp, and he gradually wins the respect of Rex as well as bringing the boy

friendship with two local kids, also considered "different" (one half-Maori, one the son of Dalmatian immigrants). The three form a close-knit fan club that comes to Jack's aid when he flees from attack by white GIs (and possibly from the war as well) by hiding out in the local creek instead of returning to his unit. Gee paints a vivid and detailed picture of wartime life on the antipodean homefront, with kids infected by Americamania along with local and global racism as Maori, immigrants, American blacks, and the Japanese seem equally suspect in the eyes of the town and the white American soldiers also staying there. Characterization is strong, with Rex's cheerful and law-bending father particularly convincing ("My wife didn't say you were a darkie. Say, I'll bet you could do with a beer," he jovially greets Jack); Jack himself, however, is rather too saintly to be true, even as seen through Rex's worshipful eyes. Rex's narration is touching and earnest, although the occasional interjections of Rex as adult are distracting ("This is my sixth-grade voice, not my grown up voice"). It's still an evocative tale of a world distant from that which most young readers know, but one beset with eternal and recognizable questions about hatred and loyalty.

Judith N. Mitchell

SOURCE: A review of *The Champion,* in *Voice of Youth Advocates,* Vol. 16, No. 6, February, 1994, p. 366.

Set in Kettle Creek, New Zealand, during WWII, *The Champion* is the story of what happens when a black GI intersects with a boy's dream of heroes. The boy, Rex, thinks he knows about valor; valor is something that surmounts his own sometimes uninteresting life lived with his aspiring-poet-mother and barber-conman father. He is, however, truly familiar with oppression, which manifests itself in the sadism of his teacher, Miss Betts. When Jackson Coop comes to town, all the previously drawn equations have to be reworked; Jackson turns the laughter of children against their tormentor, and he puts Rex in league with two outcast classmates.

Beautifully written, unmarred by sentimentality, *The Champion* is full of funny and haunting characters, and exudes psychological realism. I found Gee's ability to bring a place, a conflict, and a community to life reminiscent of Nina Bawden's; the only fear I have about this novel is that it will not find the readership it deserves.

📖 THE FAT MAN (1994)

Publishers Weekly

SOURCE: A review of *The Fat Man,* in *Publishers Weekly,* Vol. 244, No. 44, October 27, 1997, p. 77.

In this seamlessly crafted psychological thriller, the sins of the father are visited on the son. Years ago, Herbert Muskie was tormented for being fat by young Colin Potter's father. Now, in the year 1933, bigger (and stronger) than ever, Herbert—the fat man—has come home to New Zealand to seek revenge. Caught in the act of stealing a candy bar from Herbert's rucksack, Colin is forcibly drafted into becoming an accomplice to Herbert's evil scheme: he methodically sets out to destroy anyone who has ever maligned him, including his own feeble-minded mother, siblings and in-laws, his new bride and his stepdaughter. Next in line are two of his old classmates—Colin's mother and father. Gee gives the proverbial victim-turns-villain myth several spellbinding twists, and builds an aura of desperation around those hard hit by the Depression to make credible the psychic spell that a flush Herbert casts over the destitute town. Readers with a hearty appetite for the diabolic will get their fill here as Herbert breaks nearly every code of decency. But what is most fascinating about this horrific story is the author's ability to project Colin's pity for the evildoer. In a final chase scene, Colin catches a glimpse of the tormented fat boy beneath the fat man, and understands the cruelty he himself has suffered. Gee brilliantly allows readers to see the child within each adult, and to recognize the complexity of the consequences one's actions can yield.

Miriam Lang Budin

SOURCE: A review of The Fat Man, in School Library Journal, Vol. 43, No. 11, November, 1997, p. 118.

Times are hard in backwater Loomis, New Zealand, during the Great Depression and Colin Potter, 12, is always hungry. When a strange, fat man catches the boy stealing his bar of chocolate, he parlays his upper hand to begin a manipulation that expands to include the rest of Colin's family in ways that confuse and frighten him. For Herbert Muskie has returned to his hometown bent on revenge for his childhood of torment—and he remembers Colin's father as the ringleader in his mistreatment and Colin's mother as the unattainable prize. Soon Herbie is bootlegging with Colin's grandfather and giving his father work for unsavory purposes. Colin alone recognizes the fat man's cruelty no matter how the adults try to gloss it over. His only ally is Herbie's stepdaughter, Verna, and the two are powerless against the man's malicious intentions. At last, realizing that Muskie has killed his own mother and brutalized Verna's mother, the boy is able to admit to his mother how the process of intimidation and control began. But then, fleeing the police, the man takes the two children hostage. With its tautening tension and fascinating portrait of a psychopathic personality, this novel is definitely a page-turner. Though far from a pleasant story, it is well written and involving and should attract ordinarily reluctant readers.

Michael Cart

SOURCE: A review of The Fat Man, in Booklist, Vol. 94, No. 8, December 15, 1997, p. 693.

Meet Herbert Muskie, a mysterious fat man who appears one day in Colin Potter's small New Zealand town. The year is 1933; times are hard, and Colin's father, Laurie, is out of work. When Muskie—who had been Laurie's schoolmate years before—offers him a job, it seems like a godsend. At first. In fact, the whole town seems to welcome the prosperous prodigal back from his years in America. But the more Colin learns about Herbert Muskie, the more menacing the fat man with the wormlike scar on his face becomes. What does he really want? What hold does he have over his stepdaughter, Verna, whom Colin befriends, and over Colin himself?

A brilliant writer, Gee once again demonstrates his extraordinary talent for psychologically acute characterization. Mining Muskie's past, Gee makes the fat man's motivations for insinuating himself into the lives of Colin's family absolutely believable . . . and absolutely terrifying. Page by page, the tension builds to a climax that is at once horrifying and haunting. For mature readers, *The Fat Man* is a fascinating mixture of Saki and Alfred Hitchcock at their most artfully disturbing.

Nancy Vasilakis

SOURCE: A review of The Fat Man, in The Horn Book Magazine, Vol. LXXIV, No. 1, January-February, 1998, pp. 70-71.

Set in New Zealand during the Great Depression, this disturbing psychological thriller pits its young hero, Colin Potter, against a sadistic adult who has come back to the small town of his childhood to take revenge on those who bullied him when he was a boy. His primary targets are Colin's father and mother. When Colin steals a chocolate bar from Herbert Muskie (who in Colin's mind is always "the fat man"), he unwillingly becomes complicit in the man's evil game, too guilt-ridden to speak out when he sees Muskie drawing everyone in his family under his control. The fat man's machinations extend to his own family. He terrorizes his new wife and stepdaughter, Verna, who becomes Colin's friend. His cruelties range from the subtle to the extreme—the children suspect he has drowned his own mother. Herbert Muskie is a thief, possibly a murderer, and obviously mad. But the devastating crux of the novel is Muskie's insidious diminishing of Laurie Potter in his son's eyes. Muskie hires Colin's father, an out-of-work carpenter, for a menial job, then compounds the indignity by defeating the former boxing champion in an arm-wrestling contest, and finally tells Colin of the cruelties his father was capable of as a boy. The bullies have switched places, and it is up to Colin to make amends. So expertly has Gee drawn his characters in this twisted tale of vengeance that the reader comes to understand and even harbor some level of sympathy for the fat man by the story's end. In this world where adults come up short, Gee allows his young people to move past disillusionment to strength.

📖 *ORCHARD STREET* (1998)

John McKenzie

SOURCE: A review of *Orchard Street,* in *Reading Time,* Vol. 42, No. 4, November, 1998, pp. 32-33.

When Austin Dye meets a childhood acquaintance 'one day last summer . . . walking through the downtown square in Auckland,' a remarkable story is remembered. It is a story of the 1951 wharfie's strike, of a quiet rebellion, of the semi-rural town of Loomis, andan assortment of characters in Orchard Street. Poignantly nostalgic, we feel the peculiar pressures of growing up in the 1950s. There is the bookie who operates on the other side of the law, the fear of being arrested under emergency regulations, the downtown dances and the breaking of sexual boundaries, the struggle within a working class family of having high aspirations, the tensions between eccentricity and normality and the first awakenings of romance for the narrator, Austin. It is a story that is deftly told by a master storyteller where subtlety of point of view awakens a strong sense of empathy for the period. Behind the stereotype of the 1950s being a time of crushing uniformity, we begin to see the forces of change at work; in the promiscuity of Austin's brother Les and in the firm resolve of Mum and Dad in addressing political fascism. We see also that individuality asserts itself as one neighbour struggles with an old war wound and a problematic marriage and seeks solace in astronomy, and where Mother asserts her agnosticism in the face of religious conformity. Above all, there develops in the story a sense of community; that despite stark differences of values and beliefs, when the chips are down, the community rallies together.

This is a superb evocation of growing up in provincial New Zealand in the 1950s that brings to life for the modern young adult reader, the peculiar tensions of the time.

Trevor Agnew

SOURCE: A review of *Orchard Street,* in *Magpies,* Vol. 14, No. 1, March, 1999, p. 38.

Maurice Gee's latest novel for young readers is not really about the 51 Lockout, and in fact no wharfies appear in it at all. Rather **Orchard Street** uses this industrial and political dispute as a tension-creating background, with the fear of police reaction hanging over the street's various dubious activities (dubious by 1951 standards anyway). The result is a lively read.

Although it is set in Loomis, the same town where **The Fat Man** took place two decades earlier, this novel confines itself to the eleven houses of Orchard Street. There is hardly even a glimpse of the famous creek. Orchard Street was a busy place in 1951, but a lot of what happened there went on in the dark.

Gee gives a good picture of a post-war residential street, with its juxtaposition of old and young, rural and urban, eccentricity and respectability. Orchard Street is one of those streets where everyone knows what is going on, none more so than the narrator Austin 'Dinky' Dye. "I scuttled . . . into the dark and slid along, hearing doors open and dogs bark and bits of conversation from lighted rooms."

Readers (most will be in the twelve- to fifteen-year age range) will appreciate the romantic entanglements which keep Gee's plot moving along at a fine pace, particularly since the social pressures of the time are well outlined. There are nice touches of period detail about conformity and acceptable behaviour in the age of milkbars, shickered drivers, Sid Holland and homemade jam.

Since we are in the 1950s, the limited options facing girls are sketched in briefly but grimly. 'Dinky' Dye's mother, Lil, is a character worth studying, a woman who knows her Browning, art and music. As an Orchard Street housewife, she keeps it all stifled away. "I wondered about those things Mum kept in her head. I was glad that she had brought them out tonight, but saw that it was unlikely that she'd get the chance again . . . I wondered what use she would make now, of all those things she knew and cared about."

Orchard Street, like its setting, is not as simple as it seems on the surface. 'Dinky', the fourteen-year-old at the centre of events, doesn't always understand the significance of adults' words or actions, although he is actually retelling the tale nearly fifty years afterwards. The construction of the ending, for example, is as intriguing (and as satisfying to readers) as Gee's crafty conclusion to **The Fat Man**.

Is Gee planning a trilogy? Will Loomis have a third incarnation in the 1960s or 70s? Certainly the inventiveness and the gift for sharply sketched characters Maurice Gee has displayed in **Orchard Street** make this highly desirable.

Additional coverage of Gee's life and career is contained in the following sources published by The Gale Group: *Contemporary Authors New Revision Series,* **Vol. 67;** *Contemporary Literary Criticism,* **Vol. 29;** and *Something about the Author,* **Vols. 46, 101.**

Roberto Innocenti

1940-

Italian author/illustrator of picture books and illustrator of fiction and nonfiction.

Major works include *Cinderella* (written by Charles Perrault, 1983), *Rose Blanche* (coauthored with Christophe Gallaz, 1985; British edition written by Ian McEwan), *The Adventures of Pinocchio* (written by Carlo Collodi, 1988), *A Christmas Carol* (written by Charles Dickens, 1990), *Nutcracker* (written by E. T. A. Hoffman, 1996).

Major works about the author include *Roberto Innocenti: le prigioni della storia* (by Paola Vassalli and Michele Cochet, 1989) and *Roberto Innocenti: The Spirit of Illustration* (by Steven L. Brezzo, 1996).

INTRODUCTION

Innocenti is considered one of the finest contemporary illustrators of classic tales for children and adults. In addition, he has received both acclaim and criticism for creating *Rose Blanche,* a picture book about the Holocaust. Called "a modern-day Breughel" by Susan Perren, Innocenti is recognized internationally as an exceptionally talented artist whose detailed watercolor paintings are powerful, beautiful, and realistic. He has contributed illustrations to English, French, German, and Italian fantasies such as *The Adventures of Pinocchio,* in which he pictures scenes from author Carlo Collodi's Tuscan hometown, and Charles Dickens's *A Christmas Carol,* which he illustrates with paintings that reflect both the wealth and poverty of mid-nineteenth-century London. Innocenti has also provided the pictures for a series of informational books on ships, airplanes, and trains for Golden Press and for two volumes of "The Enchanted World," a series of fables and legends published by Time-Life Books; in addition, he has illustrated several books for Italian authors that have not yet been translated into English.

As an illustrator, Innocenti is praised for his imagination, technical skill, and extensive research. He thoroughly investigates all aspects of his subject, including interiors and exteriors, costumes, and social history, before beginning his work; as a result, according to Carla Poesio of *Bookbird,* "Innocenti's illustrations always reveal a background, a hinterland of meticulous documentation." As a stylist, he uses a classically influenced approach that has been compared to the Italian masters, combining it with innovative perspectives and unusual use of light and shadow. Innocenti characteristically illustrates his works with full- and double-page paintings in subtle yet luminous colors that feature panoramic scenes in elevated perspectives.

He is often noted for the cinematic quality of his works and for the manner in which his pictures interpret and extend the stories they illustrate. Although his art is sometimes viewed as too elaborate and self-conscious, Innocenti is usually regarded as the creator of striking, often breathtaking works that perfectly complement their texts. Writing in *Children's Books and Their Creators,* Amy J. Meeker claimed that Innocenti's style "bespeaks a scrupulous devotion to realism, a meticulous eye for detail, and a sophisticated palette and perspective"; the critic concluded that the artist possesses a "remarkable ability to create drama and story through visually eloquent yet unsentimental paintings. . . ."

Biographical Information

Born in Ripoli, a village near Florence, Italy, Innocenti has commented that World War II and its aftermath prevented him from having an enjoyable childhood and youth. When he was four, his parents hid two eighteen-year-old German deserters in the family basement; the soldiers told young Roberto several vivid stories before departing. The boy also saw Jewish villagers, including a mother and an infant, taken away by the Nazis. When he asked his father for an explanation, the man—who was normally very honest—concealed the truth from his terrified son in order to protect him. Consequently, Innocenti felt emotionally scarred by the experience, which later served as the inspiration for *Rose Blanche.* Innocenti began drawing at an early age and briefly attended a local art school, but postwar economic conditions prevented him from attending either a high school or an art institute. From the ages of thirteen to eighteen, Innocenti was employed in a steel foundry. At eighteen, he went to Rome and began working in an animation studio owned by a painter. This experience prompted his desire to create original works of his own. He studied movie cartoons, graphics, and book illustrations; when his designs for the regional government of Tuscany were published in *Graphis* magazine, Innocenti first received international attention.

In 1979, Innocenti met the American artist John Alcorn, who introduced him to the Quadrangono Libri publishing house. Innocenti was given his first assignment as an illustrator—providing the pictures for a history of the Russo-Japanese War of 1905. His watercolor paintings were praised for their drama and almost photographic realism. However, since assignments from Italian publishing houses were rare at the time, Innocenti devoted himself to graphics, working as the designer of posters for films, theatrical productions, and other projects. He was introduced to Etienne Delessert, a Frenchman who was the director of the series "Grasset—Monseuir Chat" for the Edizioni Grasset Fausquelle in Paris. Delessert commissioned Innocenti to illustrate Charles Perrault's fairy tale *Cinderella* for his series, which also included contributions by several major international artists. In evaluating how to approach the story, Innocenti decided to place Cinderella in the London of 1929, a period that he felt was not quite contemporary, but not yet antiquated. In this way, the artist felt that he could stress *Cinderella*'s timelessness by avoiding the graphic clichés of the frequently illustrated tale. He later wrote in a letter to Creative Education, the American publisher of *Cinderella,* "I wanted to make her come out of her time."

After the completion of *Cinderella,* Etienne Delessert discovered a manuscript based on Innocenti's childhood wartime experience; Delessert convinced the artist to write and illustrate his story, which had been in his desk for four years. Innocenti collaborated on the text of the book, which became *Rose Blanche,* with Christophe Gallaz, while noted English novelist Ian McEwan provided the text for the British edition. In a statement he wrote for the 1991 edition, Innocenti noted, "In this book I wanted to illustrate how a child experiences war without really understanding it." *Rose Blanche* describes how an eight-year-old German girl discovers a concentration camp in the woods near her home and risks her life by bringing food to the children there. The story ends with the death of Rose Blanche, who the reader assumes is shot during a crossfire at the end of the war,

although this is not stated directly in the text. The young girl's tragic death, plus the somber quality and sophistication of the book, caused *Rose Blanche* to be considered unsuitable for young children, an audience attracted to the story by its picture book format. However, other reviewers recognized *Rose Blanche* as the moving tale of a child's courage and compassion, as well as an effective tool for discussing important ethical issues with children. The book received a great deal of media attention in Europe, especially when President Reagan visited the Bitburg cemetery in France. Since the publication of *Rose Blanche,* Innocenti has focused on providing the illustrations for stories by other authors. His works are now considered collectors' items, and Innocenti has held several exhibitions of his paintings in Europe.

Major Works

In *Cinderella,* Innocenti relocates his rags-to-riches heroine from seventeenth-century France to twentieth-century England. The artist fills his detailed illustrations with distinctive touches: for example, he depicts the protagonist's stepsisters as self-absorbed flappers and includes postage stamps that commemorate the marriage of Cinderella and her prince. Perhaps the most unusual feature of *Cinderella,* however, is the parallel story it reflects in its closing illustration: Innocenti depicts Cinderella as a seventy-year-old woman sitting sadly with a drink and a cigarette and poring over the faded brown photo in her hand. The photo shows the happy couple standing in front of their limousine as they prepare to leave for their honeymoon.

Innocenti's next book, *Rose Blanche,* features a child who learns first-hand about the horrors of the Second World War. The title of the book is translated as White Rose, which is also the name of a Resistance movement of young Germans, all of whom were killed. Like Innocenti, Rose is denied an answer to her questions about the children she sees herded into trucks and imprisoned behind barbed wire. Each day, she brings her own food to the captives, who wear striped clothes with yellow stars pinned to their chests. At the end of the war, the villagers flee, but Rose goes back to the compound to see the children; it is empty. Before she can return home, Rose is shot outside of the camp. In the spring, flowers grow in the clearing over the barbed wire. *Rose Blanche* has been praised both as a personal statement and a universal plea for peace, and Innocenti's illustrations are commended for their realism and intricacy. Steven Heller called *Rose Blanche* "a major work of Holocaust fiction" while Marcus Crouch concluded, "Suitable for children? Why not? There is no hatred in the book, only sadness and love and a shred of hope."

In *The Adventures of Pinocchio,* Innocenti sets Collodi's story of the puppet who becomes a real boy in the place and period in which it was written, nineteenth-century Tuscany. Innocenti, filling his illustrations with panoramic street scenes and rural landscapes, is praised for capturing the essence of the tale in a definitive way. Faith

McNulty acknowledged, "This must surely be the most beautiful edition of *Pinocchio* ever seen," while Mary M. Burns concluded, "Indeed, if Tenniel is the touchstone for illustrating *Alice in Wonderland,* then Innocenti must now be considered the foremost interpreter of *Pinocchio.*"

His next book, *A Christmas Carol,* is credited with making both Dickens's narrative and the historical period in which he wrote it come alive. Acknowledged for his unsentimental depiction of the social life of early Victorian London—including the abject poverty experienced by several of the characters—Innocenti is also lauded for the book's exceptional design. Each page of *A Christmas Carol* is softly shaded, with the text framed in fine lines, and decorated by a holly sprig at the top and a medallion holding the folio at the bottom. A critic in *Publishers Weekly* noted, "Few of the many interpretations of Dickens's holiday parable can match this handsome edition for atmosphere, mood and sheer elegance," while Ilene Cooper stated, "It's difficult to believe the world needs yet another edition of Dickens's Christmas classic. But it does if it's this one." Innocenti is also the illustrator of *Nutcracker,* a fantasy by German author E. T. A. Hoffman that was originally published in 1816. The story, which outlines how a little girl breaks the spell that changes her Christmas nutcracker into a handsome prince, is illustrated with twenty color paintings that are noted for bringing out both the festive and the mysterious, even sinister, sides of the story.

Awards

Innocenti received several awards for *Rose Blanche,* including the Golden Apple from the Biennale of Illustrators Bratislava in 1985 and the Mildred L. Batchelder Award from the American Library Association in 1986. He received a Kate Greenaway Medal "highly commended" citation from the British Library Association for *The Adventures of Pinocchio* in 1988. In 1991, Innocenti received the Golden Apple, a Kate Greenaway Medal "commended" citation, and a Best Illustrated citation from *The New York Times,* all for *A Christmas Carol.*

GENERAL COMMENTARY

Carla Poesio

SOURCE: "Roberto Innocenti, Bib '85 Golden-Apple Recipient," in *Bookbird,* Vol. 24, Nos. 3 & 4, December 15, 1986, pp. 75-7.

Roberto Innocenti was born at Bagno a Ripoli, near Florence, on the 16th of February, 1940. The extremely difficult economic conditions existing just after the war

hindered him from attending an art institute; he had to work in a foundry while still very young. Thus it was as a self-taught artist that the 18-year-old without a high-school diploma was invited to work in an animation studio in Rome.

His career as an illustrator began in 1979, thanks to a meeting with the American artist, John Alcorn, who introduced him to the Quadragono Libri publishing house, where he was given the opportunity to illustrate *1905: Bagliori ad Oriente* (*Flashes in the Orient*), written by Olivo Bin on the history of the Russo-Japanese War. Innocenti's watercolour illustrations reproduced wartime moments and, above all, men in uniform with almost photographic exactitude. They were not, however, simply documents, even though the book was primarily intended to be documentary. The realism of the images indeed blended with the dramatic force of the composition, a balance and brightness of form and colour already revealing the artist's fundamental characteristic style.

Yet the situation in Italian publishing was such that there appeared to be no possibility of giving a place to Innocenti by way of steady work, and he was obliged to dedicate himself mainly to graphics (posters and graphic art publishing).

Once again it was his meeting with a foreign artist that gave him the opportunity to re-enter the publishing world. Etienne Delessert, who directed the series, "Grasset-Monsieur Chat", for the Edizioni Grasset Fasquelle, Paris, Edizioni 24 Heures, Lausanne, and Creative Education, Mankato, [Minnesota] USA—a series numbering among its contributors some of the most important names in the world of illustration—commissioned Innocenti to illustrate Perrault's *Cinderella*. The artist surprisingly set the fable in the 1920s. The *Los Angeles Times* wrote, "Perrault's version from the court of the Sun King, Louise XIV, is set in London in the 1920s, capitalizing on a sort of flapper high fashionableness which is fully in keeping with the persuasive vogueishness of the 17th century original."

Delessert at the same time tried to convince Innocenti to give him a group of illustrations along with a text that the artist had by that time kept in a drawer for four years. This was *Rose Blanche,* finally published in 1985 in an English edition for Creative Education, the French version for Edizioni Script, Neuchatel, and Edizioni 24 Heures, Lausanne. It won for him not only the BIB Golden Apple but also the prestigious Mildred L. Batchelder Award in the USA.

The basic idea of this book, in Innocenti's words: "I was a little child when the war passed in front of my door. One day two very young German soldiers, wearing grey uniforms, came to our house and begged us to hide them. They probably weren't even 18 years old. They wanted to surrender to English troops. And they kept repeating: 'Stop the war.' We were hiding them in the basement when we saw a German truck passing by, taking away a family. The mother was holding a tiny baby wrapped in a pink blanket. My father did not want to answer my questions, but I knew that something terrible was happening." And again: "In this book I wanted to illustrate how a child experiences war without really understanding it."

These declarations might make one think of explanatory subjectivism of the images, but, instead, they impress by their realism, which achieves the artist's intended effect of an impersonal chronicle without comment. As he often said, he wished to give to his story absolute simplicity, stripped of all rhetoric.

Mention has been made of "determined research" for expressions, figures, objects and details realistically reproduced. The realistic representation from time to time leads to expressionism (above all, in the martyred faces of the victims and the violent expressions of their persecutors). Watercolour, Innocenti's usual technique—often veiled in the finished work in order to achieve special chromatic patinas and lighting effects—appears here as an optimal means to express, through tints growing ever darker, the threat and explosion of the tragedy of war and persecution of the Jews. The diffused light and luminous colour are met again in the final plate, after the holocaust.

Innocenti's illustrations always reveal a background, a hinterland of meticulous documentation. The artist very carefully studies interiors, exteriors, clothes, hair styles, furnishings, history of the society of the period in which his subjects are placed.

In some plates there is also an ironic touch of personal amusement/entertainment, when the artist succeeds in creating quite unusual combinations (as in his "Cinderella of the Twenties", for example) or when he revisits illustrations in the Dorè manner or very old prints.

This trait is also evident in the illustrations Innocenti has created (and still is creating) for Time & Life Publishers (Alexandria, Virginia), producer of the Enchanted World series of fables and legends. The illustrations for each volume of the series are entrusted to a number of artists, each illustrating one or more tales. Published in 1985, with works by Innocenti, were *Spell and Bindings* and *Giants & Ogres*.

For the same series Innocenti is currently preparing his interpretation of E. T. A. Hoffmann's *Nutcracker,* to be included in a collection of Christmas stories. Next to the sheets of drawing paper on his desk can be seen piles of books on the history of costumes. The illustrations are all planned to depict interiors with meticulously portrayed figures in clothes, hairdos and attitudes, all typical of the period from the end of the 18th and the early years of the 19th centuries, surrounded by furniture, curtains, lamps and knick-knacks of the period. The rhythm of the compositions and the scenic effects are extremely suggestive. A demanding work really worthy of this artist!

TITLE COMMENTARY

📖 *CINDERELLA* (written by Charles Perrault, 1983)

Valerie F. Brooks

SOURCE: "Not the Disney Versions," in *Print,* Vol. XL, No. II, March-April, 1986, pp. 78-80, 82, 84, 86, 126-27.

Most of the treatments [of fairy tales] in "Once Upon a Time" are relatively lighthearted, as it was [Ann] Redpath's main intention to give the series a positive slant with texts that, as [Bruno] Bettelheim prefers, reassure children by ending happily. Particularly representative of that guideline are Robert Innocenti's highly detailed illustrations for Perrault's *Cinderella,* set forward in time to an English village during the Roaring Twenties. While, except for her bobbed hair, the heroine in her rags looks familiar, the vile stepsisters are portrayed as vain flappers who lounge in the garden or play silly games around the house while waiting for invitations to fashionable affairs. To further heighten the period feeling, Innocenti added such touches as postage stamps commemorating the marriage of Cinderella and the prince, and a sepia-toned photograph of the royal newlyweds stepping toward their chauffeured limousine to begin their honeymoon.

"I wanted to make her come out of her time," Innocenti explained in a letter to Creative Education from his home in Florence, Italy. Cinderella's timelessness, he felt, could be renewed for the reader by avoiding the graphic clichés of the tale. Uncertain whether to make her contemporary or to maintain a fairy-tale atmosphere, he decided that she should be 15 years old in 1929, in an era he views as "not yet modern but no longer antique." What evolved, he adds, was a story parallel to that of *Cinderella.*

This is brought home by the volume's last page, a poignant epilogue that is Innocenti's continuation of the tale, set many years after the original happy ending. On a bleak winter's day an aging woman, whom life has made into a reclusive drinker, sits staring absently out the window, a cigarette in one hand. In the other she holds a book open to a page containing a faded brown photograph. This is Cinderella at 70, Innocenti writes, "with her photograph album, her memories and even the commemorative stamps."

📖 *ROSE BLANCHE* (with Christophe Gallaz, 1985; translated from the Italian by Martha Coventry and Richard Graglia; British edition by Ian McEwan)

Publishers Weekly

SOURCE: A review of *Rose Blanche,* in *Publishers Weekly,* Vol. 227, No. 19, May 10, 1985, p. 231.

Innocenti is a gifted Italian artist, "a child when the war passed in front of my door." He says that his father told him lies about the Nazi victims in their small town, in order not to hurt his son who sensed the terror and kept wondering. To state his conviction that children must be told the truth, Innocenti composed the story of a German girl, Rose Blanche, denied an answer to her questions about the children she saw herded into trucks and imprisoned behind barbed wires. Each day, Rose brings her own food to the captives, almost starving herself. At the war's end, she is shot outside the camp by a soldier. The entire drama unfolds in the astounding pictures, wrenching in the expressions of the people, tragically contrasting with the beauties of the unscarred countryside. This is a stunning book and a forceful argument for peace.

Patty Campbell

SOURCE: A review of *Rose Blanche,* in *The New York Times Book Review,* July 21, 1985, p. 14.

It is our duty to tell children some terrible truths. If the telling causes horror and sorrow, these are appropriate emotions for certain recent historical events, and it is necessary for the young to suffer this painful learning if the future is not to repeat the worst mistakes of the past. But we must be careful to do the telling right.

Roberto Innocenti's **Rose Blanche** is a picture book that tries to give a glimpse of the Holocaust terror through a child's eyes. This Italian illustrator's skill is undeniable (his best-known previous work, a witty flapper-era **Cinderella,** has been widely admired). The intent is obviously serious. Yet this is a deeply problematic work.

The heart of the difficulty lies in the age of the probable reader. The *intended* reader, according to the publisher, is "8 up." The author agrees: the child he has drawn is about that age and his own daughter is 9. But this target is unrealistic. An 8-year-old has already graduated from the "babyish" taint of picture books. It would be comfortable to imagine that the audience might be teenagers or even adults. But the rare recent examples of picture books that have crossed over show that the essential quality is satirical or allegorical whimsy (*The Giving Tree* by Shel Silverstein, *The Motel of the Mysteries* by David Macauley). We are left, then, with the usual picture-book audience of very young children.

"This book is meant to breed questions," Mr. Innocenti says. "Fathers, mothers, and teachers can offer answers if they wish to." Most teachers and librarians would agree that his faith in the wisdom and patience of the average adult is naïve. Obviously, a very young child cannot "read" this book without the help of an adult, but although the brief text by Christophe Gallaz and Mr. Innocenti based on Mr. Innocenti's idea (and translated clearly by Martha Coventry and Richard Graglia) is evocative, it is entirely possible for a bright child to follow the narrative and sense the gloom and horror from the pictures alone.

A young child has no orientation in time, place or reality for this book, no frame of reference for understanding its broader implications. Without historical perspective, such a reader sees only the literal events and senses an implied horror too large and too vague for the fragmentary story.

In glossy, richly detailed pictures, a young girl waves goodbye to some soldiers who are getting into the back of a truck. (The text tells us her name is Rose Blanche and she lives in a little town in Germany.) Later many other trucks and tanks full of soldiers drive through the streets.

One day a truck stops for engine repair and a little boy jumps out of the back and tries to run away. The stout mayor of the town catches him and brings him back. Curious, Rose Blanche follows the truck into the woods, where she finds a clearing and a barbed-wire compound. Behind the fence stand some hollow-eyed children staring out at her. They wear striped clothes with yellow stars pinned on their chests. She gives them a piece of bread but tells no one what she has found. In the next few weeks she steals food and brings it to them. Now at night there are trucks full of weary soldiers going through the streets in the other direction. One day all the villagers flee, but Rose Blanche goes into the woods to see the children once more. The fence is broken down and they are gone. It is foggy. A soldier shoots . . . In the ruined village differentsoldiers are arriving. In the spring many flowers grow in the clearing over the barbed wire.

Powerful mythological resonances are buried here. Fairy tale is evoked in the theme of an evil thing found in the woods, the gift of a crust of bread, the title itself. (Adults will know from the jacket flap that the "White Rose" was a Resistance movement of young people.) Christian redemption through compassion is implied by the girl's martyrdom and the Easter blessing of flowers over the broken fence posts that form a cross. Jungian/Freudian symbology is suggested by the guilty adult secret discovered in a hidden place. At least some of this power may be felt unconsciously by the child reader.

Without a grounding of fact, this is a story full of puzzles and intimations of unnamed horrors. An innocent youngster who knows nothing of swastikas, Hitler and concentration camps is liable to clothe these bare bones in more personal and terrifying fantasy—a conspiracy by bad and powerful adults who are secretly cruel to children, for instance.

A comparison with *Hiroshima No Pika* by Toshi Maruki is enlightening. This picture book won many awards for its sensitive portrayal of one child's experience on the day the atomic bomb was dropped on her city. It tells the story, in the words of the text, of "something very bad that happened," which is described unflinchingly for children "in the hope that their knowing will help keep it from happening again." The facts and their meaning are simply and clearly shown with a courage that *Rose Blanche* lacks.

As a 4-year-old during World War II, Roberto Innocenti saw the war pass by his doorstep in an Italian village near Florence, and was emotionally scarred when his father would not alleviate his terror with an explanation. He has said that *Rose Blanche* is his attempt to make amends for that failure. Yet ironically, without the catharsis of confrontation with the full truth, what he has done is subject another generation to his own unexplained terror.

Julia Briggs

SOURCE: "In Time of War," in *The Times Literary Supplement,* No. 4304, September 27, 1985, p. 1079.

"When wars begin people often cheer. The sadness comes later. The men from the town went off to fight for Germany. Rose Blanche and her mother joined the crowds and waved them goodbye." So begins Roberto Innocenti's original and disturbing picture book, *Rose Blanche.* (Rose Blanche was the name of a protest group in wartime Germany.) The flat and laconic text by Ian McEwan, from a story by Christophe Gallaz, is deliberately subordinated to the large, powerful and informative illustrations which tell, in precise and highly textured detail, of Germany's aggression and defeat in the Second World War. Roberto Innocenti's pictures are conceived and executed with rare imagination: the cover shows a little girl peering through a window on to which are reflected lorry-loads of wounded and retreating soldiers. Each page uses telling angles and evocative colour: the drab red brick and dull browns of tanks and uniforms, the watery grey-blue of puddled snow give place only on the last page to the clear blues and greens of a spring landscape. Iron posts and barbed wire are wreathed with wild flowers to mark the place where Rose Blanche was accidentally shot by her retreating countrymen. "Behind her were figures moving through the fog. Tired and fearful soldiers saw danger everywhere. As Rose Blanche turned to walk away, there was a shot."

Because so much of the story is presented in pictures, some of its horror is muted. We are not told in so many words that Rose has been shot, only that there was a shot; nor are we told that the silent, hungry children behind coils of barbed wire are Jews in a concentration camp, though their yellow stars will inform the adult reader of this. Everything that the pictures show—the departing soldiers, the fat mayor with a swastika on his arm-band, the starving prisoners in the camp, the evacuation of the town—is seen through the uncomprehending eyes of childhood. The wider meaning of events will need to be explained to the young reader, who may well be more upset at Rose's mother losing her as the townspeople flee than by less familiar miseries and deprivations. How many adults will actually want to provide the necessary explanations is another question. Young children are increasingly exposed to supposedly heroic acts of brutality on films and television. By contrast Innocenti's book is an invitation to compassion—for the luckless child hustled away by the soldiers, for the camp inmates, even, latterly, for the soldiers themselves. But it does have a nightmare quality.

Roberto Innocenti's book is nowhere more perceptive than in his presentation of his heroine's courage and compassion, which acts as a counterbalance to the theme of man's inhumanity to man in war. Rose Blanche's actions, though not her fate, are full of hope. The book shows a world where individual acts still have a meaning, where moral distinctions can and must be made. It all looks very different from the world of post-war politics, where nuclear rain promises to fall alike on the just and the unjust.

Steven Heller

SOURCE: "No Bedtime Story," in *Print,* Vol. XXXIX, No. V, September-October, 1985, pp. 88-91.

By the early 1940s, when Hitler's grand plan seemed irreversible, a clandestine group of anti-Nazi German students was courageously resisting. The group was known as the White Rose, and by war's end all its members had been captured and guillotined. Their collective heroism did not die, though, and is remembered (even documented on film) by those whom they inspired.

Roberto Innocenti, a 46-year-old Florentine artist, is one such admirer. During the last days of the German occupation of Italy, his parents hid two 18-year-old German deserters in the family basement. Repulsed by the war's brutality, they told unforgettably vivid stories to the young Innocenti. But even more lasting are the memories of abruptly ended talks with his father, of whom he asked the whereabouts of Jewish school friends and their parents who had mysteriously disappeared. His father, usually forthright and honest, refused to answer.

Years later, Innocenti would conclude that his father knew—because everyone knew. That knowledge and the inability to act accordingly has repeatedly haunted Innocenti, inspiring him to make his own White Rose. The resulting *Rose Blanche* is a children's picture book of great power and artistry, and an extraordinarily moving twist to a continually retold story.

Rose is a young German schoolgirl caught up in the patriotic whirlwind of war. Like her friends, she cheers on the battle-ready troops as their tanks and lorries move in endless procession through her once-quiet village. The green and gray uniforms are familiar to Rose—they are all she's ever known. Even when she was a small child, soldiers had regularly paraded through the streets.

As the story opens, it is winter and Rose sees many more soldiers than ever before converging on the town square. For the first time she hears the faint, but ominous, sounds of distant battle. The signs are clear that Rose's own town will soon become a battleground, and that Rose will somehow be caught up in war's fury. The anticipation of the inevitable is in itself enough to build reader anxiety. However, the story takes an unexpected, even more compelling, turn.

While riding home on her bicycle, Rose witnesses a young boy jumping from a stalled truck. Running as if for his life, he plows headlong into a stout onlooker—the mayor of the town. As Rose looks on, the captive boy, hands high above his head, frozen with fear, is returned at gunpoint to the truck, which then drives on. Something compels Rose to follow. Sneaking past armed guards, she discovers a barbed-wire fence, behind which are many children wrapped in threadbare blankets and striped pajamas. Their gaunt faces show hunger and despair. What is this place? she asks herself. Why are these children here? How could it be so close to the village without anybody being aware of it?

Rose leaves, only to return the next day, and many days thereafter, sharing with the confined children small scraps of bread. One wonders how she is able to elude the guards, and one prays that she doesn't get caught. Then one day, at the point when the battle noises are at their loudest pitch, she returns to find an empty yard. A surreal gray cloud envelops her. A volley of gunfire pierces the air. Rose falls dead. The war is over. Spring returns.

Rose Blanche is destined to become controversial as much for its unique format as for its horrific theme. To read this austerely simple story, co-authored by Innocenti and Christophe Gallaz, is shocking enough, but when paired with Innocenti's detailed narrative paintings, it rises above the predictable, becoming a major work of Holocaust fiction. Although it was produced as a traditional children's picture book, the intended audience is not only children, but adults (indeed, some bookstores are putting it with their adult books). Its packager, Etienne Delessert, is convinced that if the subject is meaningful, any children's book will be appreciated by readers of all ages. However, Delessert is taking a calculated risk whichever audience he aims at: Not all children are ready to be exposed to this topic, and not all adults are willing.

Already, press attention in Europe has been overwhelmingly positive, with extended coverage on major television newscasts—specifically in France during President Reagan's visit to Bitburg cemetery. But parental reaction has been mixed, for obvious reasons. The publishers hope that the unusual story will capture the curious, and that the fine execution will overcome any concerns about theme.

The psychological complexity of *Rose Blanche* is apparent in the double-spread paintings. Washed in the gray murkiness of winter, they are nonetheless curiously soothing—like the quiet before a storm. They appear, at first, somewhat detached, but on second look, one can see that the artist is definitely in the thick of things. His obsession for detail is found in the commonplace intri-

cacies of architecture, weaponry and machines, and in the precise accuracy of uniforms and insignia. Even more importantly, he captures, through the distinctly human, though emblematic, faces of the mayor, young soldiers, schoolboys and Rose, a warped society, buckling under the twin weights of patriotism and ideology. Also notable is the lack of cliché, the only exception being an expropriation of a recognizable icon: a redrawn version of the chilling photograph of a frightened little boy being marched out of the Warsaw Ghetto, used here subtly in an ironic setting.

As a children's book, *Rose Blanche* is clearly not your conventional bedtime story, though it must be applauded for the compassion and humanism that mark any good children's tale. There is no hint of exploitation in it, no gratuitous hate, no saber rattling. In the final analysis, however, it is really less a children's book than a book about a child. It is a child's-eye view of war—a rare vantage point.

Lorraine Douglas

SOURCE: A review of *Rose Blanche,* in *School Library Journal,* Vol. 32, No. 2, October, 1985, p. 172.

During World War II, a young German schoolgirl, Rose Blanche, follows the soldiers when they arrest a boy and discovers a concentration camp in the woods. Thereafter, she takes food to the prisoners until the town is liberated. Ironically, when she travels to the camp on that day she is shot by the soldiers. The oppression of Fascism is shown through the powerful and realistic paintings. In Innocenti's large, meticulously detailed paintings, Rose Blanche is the only brightly colored individual, and her small figure is set against the drab colors of overwhelming buildings and masses of soldiers and townspeople. No skyline is shown until a radiant spring bursts forth at the site of her death after the liberation. Although the story is simply told, it will require interpretation as details such as the concentration camp are not named nor explained, and the death of Rose Blanche is implied but not stated. This is a difficult book to classify, as the text is easy enough for a young child to read alone, and it has the appearance of a picture book—but the content of the text and illustrations is full of emotional impact and subtlety.

Denise M. Wilms

SOURCE: A review of *Rose Blanche,* in *Booklist,* Vol. 82, No. 5, November 1, 1985, p. 408.

A startling, powerful picture book, but one that belongs not on the picture-book shelf but with fiction for the upper grades. It is a bleak story of the horrors of war, specifically, World War II. The story's namesake, Rose Blanche, is a young German girl who watches the escalating war activities with youthful detachment until the day she hikes out of town and discovers a concentration camp in the adjacent woods. She sees hungry children there and takes it upon herself to bring them food. One day, when the tide of the war shifts and the Germans are being routed, Rose Blanche is again making her way to the camp, only to be killed in the crossfire. The somber story is illustrated with astonishing watercolor paintings. Pictured is Rose Blanche's nameless, small German town with its narrow streets and brick and stucco buildings—the backdrop for the ebb and flow of wartime encounters. Soldiers come and go, tired looking civilians walk the cobblestones, and the occasional crystallized moment of horrible evil is caught—such as when Rose Blanche watches the town mayor grab a boy who has escaped from a truck and turns him back to the soldiers. The unstated but clearly depicted politics and the concentration camp scenarios assume a basic knowledge of World War II events. Nothing specific appears in the text; it is picture details that insinuate the developments: swastikas, German graffiti, the striped pajama uniforms of the camp victims, the red stars and steel helmets of the occupying soldiers. The story's utterly bleak finish (the spring renewal of the land is scant consolation for Rose Blanche's death at the very time of liberation) demands an older audience able to articulate the emotional overload that the story is bound to elicit and one that can discuss the lessons history has to teach.

Margery Fisher

SOURCE: A review of *Rose Blanche,* in *Growing Point,* Vol. 24, No. 5, January, 1986, p. 4557.

Drab greens and browns and stark figures set the tone of a sombre but emotionally rich picture-book demonstrating to the young in an uncertain world the cruel pressures of war. In this case the tragedy is that of a girl, sensitive and innocent, who without understanding war as a force sees it in one example when she watches soldiers forcing a boy into a lorry and follows it to a concentration camp where, ultimately, her spontaneous impulse to help leads to her own death. The book is based on the recollections of a man who in his own childhood was puzzled and distressed by evidences of war in his own streets. The bitter message is carried on a brief verbal narrative and in strong, searingly beautiful scenes in which faces and postures of figures, buildings, mist, ruined trees, all enter the reader's feelings through the eye. A personal statement that cannot be ignored, cutting across as it does the prevailing blandness of so much literature offered to the young.

Marcus Crouch

SOURCE: A review of *Rose Blanche,* in *The Junior Bookshelf,* Vol. 50, No. 2, April, 1986, pp. 62-3.

Some books demand our respect through the importance of their message. Others beguile and delight us by the beauty of their presentation. When the two come togeth-er in a single volume, then it is the occasion for special rejoicing.

I can think of nothing with which to compare *Rose Blanche.* It is surely unique. How can one bring home to today's children, living in a world in which there is much to condemn, the very special kind of evil that was Nazism? Roberto Innocenti's way is to show, in a series of exquisitely drawn and explicit drawings, the slow dawning of a realization of wickedness in the mind of an ordinary child. When the soldiers go off to fight Rose Blanche is there to wave them on with her little swastika flag. In the town goods are in short supply, but there is a cheerful mood and, for a child, much of the daily routine is unchanged. Then one day Rose Blanche sees a boy escape from a lorry. He is caught and thrown back into the truck, and it drives off. Rose Blanche knows the town well and, making use of all the short cuts, she is able to track the lorry to its destination in the woods. There, behind barbed wire, are children, dozens of them, silent and hungry. Thereafter Rose Blanche's life is changed. Even as food becomes harder to come by she hoards it up, going short herself, and going regularly to pass it through the wires to the starving children. At last, with a hostile army approaching the town, Rose Blanche makes her last visit to the camp. In the mist a single shot rings out. In a final poignant picture we see a flower hanging on barbed wire.

Suitable for children? Why not? There is no hatred in the book, only sadness and love and a shred of hope. A brief quiet text (by Ian McEwan) links the pictures but is careful not to underline their message. The points are made sufficiently, and with great power, in these remarkable watercolours. Rose Blanche's eyes, looking out from the cover with devastating candour, are likely to haunt the reader (and not only an adult reader) for a very long time.

Virginia A. Walter and Susan F. March

SOURCE: "Juvenile Picture Books about the Holocaust: Extending the Definitions of Children's Literature," in *Publishing Research Quarterly,* Vol. 9, No. 3, Fall, 1993, pp. 36-51.

Rose Blanche was published originally in the United States in 1985 and reissued in 1991. The book has won a number of awards, including a Bratislava Golden Apple for distinguished illustrations and the American Library Association's Mildred Batchelder Award for a children's book published originally in a foreign language outside the United States. Roberto Innocenti, who co-authored the text and painted the illustrations, is a well-known European illustrator. On the back flap of the 1991 edition, he writes:

In this book I wanted to illustrate how a child experiences war without really understanding it. After drawing the first page I chose Rose Blanche as its title because of the significance of the name. Rose Blanche was a group of young German citizens protesting the war. They had understood what others wanted to ignore. They were all killed. In this book fascism is a day-to-day reality. Only the victims and the little girl have known its real face.

We also learn from the book jacket that Innocenti was born in Italy in 1940 and experienced World War II firsthand as a child. The role of Christophe Gallaz in creating *Rose Blanche* is unclear; no mention is made of his contribution. . . .

The cover illustration shows a small blond, blue-eyed girl looking intently and seriously out of a window. Reflected in the window is the sight that she sees outside—wounded soldiers riding on tanks and trucks. On the title page is a small enclosed painting of a little girl running down an unpaved country road which is deeply rutted with the tracks of heavy vehicles. . . .

Rose Blanche is told in the first person in a simple narrative style. The first page begins:

> My name is Rose Blanche. I live in a small town in Germany with narrow streets, old fountains and tall houses with pigeons on the roofs.
>
> One day the first truck arrived and many men left. They were dressed as soldiers.
> Winter was beginning.

The girl goes on to describe the soldiers and mysterious military vehicles that continue to come through the town. She likes to walk along the river sometimes, and the children think that the trucks are going someplace across the river. One day a truck stops in the town and Rose Blanche sees a little boy jump from the truck and try to run away. The mayor catches him, though, and the soldiers put him back on the truck. The illustration depicting the boy's capture is a visual allusion to the well-known photo of the boy with his hands up, facing a German soldier's rifle in the last days of the Warsaw Ghetto. Rose Blanche wants to know where the little boy went after that, so she follows the truck secretly far out into the country where she had never been. There she sees a clearing barricaded with electric barbed wire. Gaunt children wearing striped prison uniforms are standing behind the wire, in front of long wooden buildings. They say they are hungry, and Rose Blanche hands a piece of bread through the wires. Times are hard in the village, but Rose Blanche continues to hide food in her school bag and take it to the children by the wooden houses, who are getting thinner in spite of her help. Spring comes, and Rose Blanche sees the soldiers coming back through the town the other way. Then one day everybody in town flees, along with the defeated German soldiers.

The narration shifts to the third person at this point and explains that Rose Blanche disappeared that day. She walked into the forest again and found that the clearing where the children had been is now empty. She dropped her satchel of food and stood still. "Shadows were moving between the trees. It was hard to see them. Soldiers saw the enemy everywhere. There was a shot." Soldiers wearing different uniforms and speaking a different language arrived. Rose Blanche's mother waited for her daughter, who did not return. The last double spread illustration shows the clearing where Rose Blanche had died, with flowers entwining the former fence posts and barbed wire of the concentration camp. The last words of the text are: "Spring sang."

The story can be seen as one of the "righteous Gentile" stories, in which a good and honorable Gentile tries to help the imperiled Jews. Perhaps this story does not even qualify as a concentration camp story, as [Eric A.] Kimmel defined it [in "Confronting the Ovens: The Holocaust and Juvenile Fiction"], because it stops at the fence of the concentration camp, with Rose Blanche on the outside looking in. The point of view is clearly not that of the Jewish victims but of the German child. It is also the point of view of "every child" in a world at war, the child who is bewildered by the events happening around her. If we had only the text to guide us, we might be as bewildered as Rose Blanche. Unlike Julie Vivas [illustrator of Margaret Wild's *Let the Celebrations Begin!*], however, who presents visual images of only what is described in the text and no more, Innocenti fills the background of the story with richly textured, detailed, hyper-realistic illustrations. Joseph and Chava Schwarcz remind us [in *The Picture Book Comes of Age: Looking at Childhood through the Art of Illustration*], however, not to be misled by the persistent photorealism of the book; in many ways, this is a highly metaphorical book about the veils of silence that cover life in this European town.

On the first page, it is the pictures that show us how happy the townspeople and soldiers are at the beginning of the war, waving swastikas and smiling. It is also the pictures that suggest that times get harder for the villagers as winter goes on, although never as hard as the conditions in the concentration camp, of course. The concentration camp inmates are not just gaunt; they are skeletal. The double-page illustration of the villagers in flight before the advancing Soviet army is full of almost Breughelian details—bandaged soldiers, people carrying belongings in bags and baskets, makeshift carts, bicycles, yoked oxen, people of all ages. The perspective, looking down on the scene, is dramatic and adds to the feeling of heightened realism.

The last illustration of the book, showing the clearing in bloom, exactly echoes the illustration two pages before, in which Rose Blanche stands in front of the empty clearing where the barracks and hungry people had been, looking down on the shattered fence, where she has placed a purple flower. Behind her in the fog we see tree stumps and the shadowy figures of soldiers firing their rifles. On the verso of the last page of text is a small square picture depicting a close-up of a shredded purple flower on a length of rusty barbed wire.

In spite of the clearly allegorical or fictional nature of this text, some libraries have catalogued it with other nonfiction accounts of the Holocaust, thus trying to ensure that its readers know what they are getting into. A child is thus unlikely to come across it while browsing in the picture book shelves. At any rate, it is not as obviously a book for very young readers . . . The illustrations are very sophisticated and dark and more likely to appeal to adults than to small children. We suspect that Innocenti and Gallaz intended this book for a somewhat romanticized, mythical "every child" much like their protagonist, a child who is also "no child."

The factual problem here of placing children in the concentration camp seems less serious here, because the concentration camp inmates are actually such a small part of the story. As a story of compassion and sacrifice, however, and as an antiwar statement, the story has considerable power. It could be used quite effectively with older children as the starting point of a discussion about a number of important ethical issues and as an example of striking book design.

📖   *THE ADVENTURES OF PINOCCHIO* (written by Carlo Collodi, 1988; translated from the Italian by E. Harden)

Publishers Weekly

SOURCE: A review of *The Adventures of Pinocchio,* in *Publishers Weekly,* Vol. 234, No. 14, September 30, 1988, p. 69.

Innocenti's luminous interpretation of Collodi's tale carves the action out of 19th century Italian landscapes. Clearly shown as a mocking marionette, this Pinocchio races through cobbled city scenes and then throws himself prostrate at the person—or fairy—whom he has most recently wronged by his hasty, thoughtless behavior. And when he becomes a real boy, the transformation is resounding: left slumped on a chair is the body of a puppet; readers may marvel that what lies so lifeless in that scene was the source of so much trouble earlier on. Enchantment reigns in the pictures, each a perfect elaboration of the text. Innocenti and Collodi are equally at home in a place where puppets have life beyond human hands, and where souls may die and live again, resurrected by the power of love.

Frances Spalding

SOURCE: "Up-to-Date Embellishments," in *The Times Literary Supplement,* No. 4469, November 25, 1988, p. 1320.

Roberto Innocenti's illustrations, inspired by Carlo Collodi's home-town in Tuscany, frequently make use of a high viewpoint in order to spread the interest across the page. When Geppetto is led away by a policeman, and Pinocchio escapes down an alley, we look down on the

From Rose Blanche, *written by Roberto Innocenti and Christophe Gallaz. Illustrated by Innocenti.*

watching crowd from the rooftops where a cat stalks some sparrows. A wealth of incident is found in this and other double-page spreads, details from which reappear like echoes on subsequent pages. Innocenti's patient delineation of detail is very absorbing, his sense of drama subtly powerful because of its restraint.

Faith McNulty

SOURCE: A review of *The Adventures of Pinocchio,* in *The New Yorker,* Vol. 21, December 12, 1988, p. 156.

This must surely be the most beautiful edition of *Pinocchio* ever seen. Roberto Innocenti has painted the Italy of a hundred years ago—its street scenes, peasants, and countryside—with a clarity and detail that are breathtaking. His strong sense of character brings out the best in Collodi's story of the naughty puppet's perilous journey along the road to moral redemption. The moral lessons no longer make much sense, but the events remain exciting.

Constance A. Mellon

SOURCE: A review of *The Adventures of Pinocchio,* in *School Library Journal,* Vol. 35, No. 6, February, 1989, p. 68.

Innocenti's dramatic illustrations, in rich, dark colors, extend and interpret the text, and the handsome design of the book is appropriate to this classic tale. The writing, in keeping with the time in which the book was written, is strongly moralistic—a far cry from the Disney version with which young children and their parents may be familiar. The long, moralistic passages may make this translation of the original tough going for modern youngsters.

Mary M. Burns

SOURCE: A review of *The Adventures of Pinocchio,* in *The Horn Book Magazine,* Vol. LXV, No. 2, March-April, 1989, p. 209.

The story of the rascally puppet who becomes a real boy after many trials and tribulations is as universally appealing as it is quintessentially Italian. Perhaps it is no mere coincidence that Florence, the principal city of Tuscany, gave the world both Dante and Collodi, for, as Martha Bacon noted in her remarkable essay "Puppet's Progress": "Pinocchio is as firmly rooted in Italian culture as Alice is in the English. He looks back to Dante and *Orlando Furioso,* forward to Pirandello and Federico Fellini. He is a descendant and an ancestor." Now another Tuscan, Roberto Innocenti, has translated the essence of that observation into brilliantly executed images. Indeed, if Tenniel is the touchstone for illustrating *Alice in Wonderland,* then Innocenti must now be considered the foremost interpreter of Pinocchio. The full-color paintings are marvels of content, composition, color, and perspective. As in stills from a motion picture, there is a sense of story informing each one. This cinematic effect is reinforced by the placement of vignettes from the single- and double-page spreads as chapter prologues or epilogues. Like close-ups, they call attention to pivotal points in the action, developing characters and situations so that the text is always extended rather than simply embellished. The picaresque style of the narrative and the improvisational elements of the plot are visually manifested in a variety of ways: the foreboding ambiance of the inn where the puppet is gulled by the villainous cat and fox; the marvelous use of light and shadow to portray the awesome interior of the great shark. The epic qualities that have made Pinocchio one of the great classics of children's literature are fully realized in this handsomely produced edition. Like a folk tale, it is immediate and vigorous, eschewing sentimentality, speaking directly to the human condition without manipulating the audience. Bravo!

📖 *A CHRISTMAS CAROL* **(written by Charles Dickens, 1990)**

School Library Journal

SOURCE: A review of *A Christmas Carol,* in *School Library Journal,* Vol. 36, No. 10, October, 1990, p. 36.

The whole of Dickens' classic text is superbly served by Innocenti's paintings of London in the mid-seventeenth century. The artist, using plenty of brown and gray in his full-color palette, depicts the streets crowded with every sort of person—emaciated, hollow-eyed, and ragged, or rich and well-fed—engaged in a multitude of holiday activities. Scrooge's ghosts and spectres, his pathetic dwelling place, and his journey through time are rendered to evoke horror and pity rather than laughter in contrast to [Lisbeth] Zwerger's much lighter and even humorous treatment. Text, generously spaced, appears framed on a white page with ochre tints; each page of the five staves or chapters is embellished with a small drawing (pinecone, candle, holly sprig), and the opening of each chapter features a small symbolic picture. A handsome example of the bookmaster's art and one that works well with Dickens's text to bring an historical period as well as the story to life.

Publishers Weekly

SOURCE: A review of *A Christmas Carol,* in *Publishers Weekly,* Vol. 237, No. 41, October 12, 1990, p. 63.

Few of the many interpretations of Dickens's holiday parable can match this handsome edition for atmosphere, mood and sheer elegance. Innocenti's full-page watercolors are striking, full-bodied evocations of 19th-century London, particularly the life and vigor of the city's streets: merchants sell their wares, urchins tumble and play, the gentry ride in their carriages, and the destitute huddle in doorways and keep warm at makeshift stoves. At the same time, the paintings' realism, dramatic intensity, occasional luminosity and almost microscopic observation of detail strongly recall the exquisite art of the Italian Renaissance. Their stateliness is carried through in the book's design: each page of text is boxed with fine sepia rules, overlaid with a delicate, gradually fading wash, and topped by a single, modest ornament. The effect suggests an old manuscript or parchment—one that, every so often, opens a splendid pictorial window on the world of this classic narrative. For all its elegance, however, this is a somber and unsentimental view of Dickens's world. The beautiful and the sordid, the good and the malevolent, are never far apart—a concept that is powerfully suggested through the frequent use of high, oddly angled perspectives, as if readers, along with Scrooge and the spirits, are privy to telling glimpses of life skimmed from above.

Edward Blishen

SOURCE: "Seasonal Stress," in *The Times Educational Supplement,* No. 3883, December 7, 1990, p 31.

If, when it comes to *A Christmas Carol,* the images in your head derive from John Leech, look at the illustra-

From A Christmas Carol, *written by Charles Dickens. Illustrated by Roberto Innocenti.*

tion facing page 36 of a new edition by Roberto Innocenti. Here, in a world of brown brick, brown cloth, brown fog, the ghosts of Marley's associates float wretchedly in Scrooge's backyard, and can do nothing to express their compassion for a ragged woman nursing her ragged child. You can smell the scene. Throughout the book it's beautifully, intimidatingly done: will be too precise for some, squalid in too theatrical and self-conscious a fashion for others. I miss Leech, and find I am unconvinced by Innocenti's surely sentimental attempt to portray the Spirit of Christmas Past, described by Dickens (who wasn't required to draw it) as "like a child: yet not so like a child as an old man". But I suspect that at inconvenient moments I shall remember Scrooge, in Innocenti's vision, climbing a mountain of brown stairs towards that at once hallucinatory and appallingly real hearse.

Ilene Cooper

SOURCE: A review of *A Christmas Carol,* in *Booklist,* Vol. 87, No. 5, December 15, 1990, p. 817.

It's difficult to believe the world needs yet another edition of Dickens's Christmas classic. But it does if it's this one. Innocenti, illustrator of such arresting books as **Rose Blanche,** has outdone himself in a glorious version of the holiday favorite. Using the original, unabridged text of the story, Innocenti illustrates it with sweeping, panoramic scenes often drawn from elevated perspectives—the way the ghosts of Christmas might view the happenings. Richly detailed in glowing colors, the pictures don't just evoke Dickens's England, they bring it stunningly to life. In fact, the whole volume is a masterpiece of bookmaking: design, paper, cover—all have been carefully chosen to make a most pleasing Christmas package.

Ann A. Flowers

SOURCE: A review of *A Christmas Carol,* in *The Horn Book Magazine,* Vol. LXVII, No. 2, March-April, 1991, p. 198.

Many an illustrator, famous and otherwise, has attempted to delineate for posterity this classic story. Innocenti, using a subdued palette of browns and grays that he combines with striking perspective, presents to perfection the picture of snowy, dirty, lively nineteenth-century London. A double-page spread of a rooftop view into back alleys shows a busy street market with apple women, a hot chestnut seller, a sick child gazing longingly from a window, and all the bustling life of a great city. The muted colors give a distinct impression of the soot and grime caused by thousands of coal-burning fireplaces. And the story itself is given its just due in an extremely handsome page design, each page lightly shaded from top to bottom within a border, altogether in keeping with both the period and the spirit of the tale. A magnificent edition.

Joan Zahnleiter

SOURCE: A review of *A Christmas Carol,* in *Magpies,* Vol. 6, No. 5, November, 1991, pp. 31-2.

[This] is a beautiful combination of high quality book design and production which does justice to the classic text and Innocenti's splendid paintings.

Infinite care and artistic skill has gone into the presentation of the text of the page. Each page features soft shading in creamy tones from top to bottom with the text framed in fine lines decorated by a spring of holly at the top and the page number in a small medallion at the bottom. An appropriate vignette is inset at the beginning of each chapter, e.g. the apparition of Marley's dead face in the door knocker at the beginning of chapter one. Fourteen full pages and three magnificent two page spreads in colour capture perfectly the mood of the story, the social life of the era, the contrast between poverty and wealth, and the bitter cold of the snowy Christmastide.

Innocenti's art work pays attention to fine detail but is suitably restrained and is never busy. It repays repeated browsing, with something more to discover each time, e.g. the face of Marley as a recurring motif in the tiles surrounding the fire place as his ghost and Scrooge have their celebrated tete-a-tete. The sombre tones of the earlier illustrations give way in the happy ending to a delightful study of Scrooge and Tiny Tim seen through an open window, in a summer garden. This magnificent production of a classic tale is a collector's item and provides an aesthetic experience which children should have.

NUTCRACKER (written by E. T. A. Hoffman, 1996)

Kirkus Reviews

SOURCE: A review of *Nutcracker,* in *Kirkus Reviews,* Vol. LXIV, No. 16, August 15, 1996, p. 1166.

This is not the *Nutcracker* sweet, as passed on by Tchaikovsky and Marius Petipa. No, this is the original Hoffmann tale of 1816, in which the froth of Christmas revelry occasionally parts to let the dark underside of childhood fantasies and fears peek through. The boundaries between dream and reality fade, just as Godfather Drosselmeier, the Nutcracker's creator, is seen as alternately sinister and jolly. And Italian artist Roberto Innocenti gives an eerily realistic air to Marie's dreams, in richly detailed illustrations touched by a mysterious light. A beautiful version of this classic tale, which will captivate adults and children alike.

Publishers Weekly

SOURCE: A review of *Nutcracker,* in *Publishers Weekly,* Vol. 243, No. 40, September 30, 1996, p. 92.

Roberto Innocenti's preternaturally crisp illustrations for *Nutcracker* bring out the sinister edge of E. T. A. Hoffman's fantastic series of stories within a story. A princely edition with 20 color illustrations, strategic spot art, elegant type and abundant use of white space, this volume will be a collector's item for followers of Innocenti's work as well as devotees of *The Nutcracker*.

Additional coverage of Innocenti's life and career is contained in the following sources published by The Gale Group: *Something about the Author,* **Vol. 96.**

Florence Crannell Means

1891-1980

American author of fiction, nonfiction, and plays.

Major works include *Shuttered Windows* (1938), *Teres-ita of the Valley* (1943), *The Moved-Outers* (1945), *Knock at the Door, Emmy* (1956), *Our Cup Is Broken* (1969).

INTRODUCTION

A pioneer writer of realistic fiction for young adults during the mid-twentieth century, Means is noted for her foresighted, multicultural approach and her insightful, sympathetic characterizations of southern Black, Native-American, Hispanic, and Japanese-American protagonists. Although she herself was white, Means sought to combat the ignorance and fear that lead to prejudice through her more than forty books for young people, including a highly regarded biography of George Washington Carver. Designed primarily for teenage girls, many of her earlier books feature female protagonists and focus on the heroine's discovery of the beauty and richness of her native heritage, finding it a source of pride and strength. Means also explored the conflicts between different cultures and the consequences when a young person is caught in the middle. Much of the power of Means's books lies in the authentic details she provides, based on interviews with individuals, time spent living among the inhabitants of the Carolina lowlands and Hopi and Navajo Indian reservations, and visits to the internment camps on the West Coast that held many American-born Japanese during World War II. Praised for her thoughtful and honest portrayals of the feelings and problems of her heroines—whether black, Hopi, Mexican, Japanese, or Jewish—Means explored social issues of the 1930s and 40s, as reflected in their lives, thus making her books still readable today even though much in society has changed. Once, when asked how she came to write books, Means replied: "For somewhat the same reason the alpinist gives for climbing the mountain: because it's there." As Peter D. Sieruta concluded in *Children's Books and Their Creators,* "Means can be credited with bringing an early social conscience to children's literature."

Biographical Information

Born in Baldwinsville, New York, in 1891, Means grew up as the privileged daughter of a Baptist minister, scholar, and poet, who served as president of Kansas City Theological Seminary for a quarter of a century and entertained people of all classes and ethnic backgrounds in his home. Means's maternal grandparents traveled from Wisconsin farm country to unsettled Minnesota in 1872, providing her with the background for her first

novel, *A Candle in the Mist* (1931). After high school, Means attended art school, studied Greek and philosophy under the tutelage of her father, and took various college extension courses. In 1912 she married a law student, Carleton Bell Means, who supported her interest in literature and the arts. Determined to fight the prejudice that existed against southern blacks and the western Chicanos and Indians, Means studied these cultures extensively, traveling to the tidal islands off the Carolinas, to the southwest to live among Native-American tribes, and to southern Colorado, where Hispanics had once been prominent. Her early books about American Indians, Mexican Americans, African Americans, and the Jewish were a novel concept as they featured ethnic minorities living in the United States, not abroad. Means also challenged the anti-German and Japanese sentiment that had escalated in America during World War II. Among the first to write about the relocation of West Coast Japanese-Americans during the war years, Means realistically described the conditions of the detention camps, and the physical hardships, the demeaning treatment that these Americans suffered, so that other young people would know and understand the consequences of war. As Siri Andrews noted, "It took courage to write of these people in the midst of war." Means and her husband had one daughter, Eleanor, and numerous "adopted" children, including several Japanese-American children, a Spanish-American boy, a Navajo "granddaughter," and children from China and Burma.

Major Works

In *Shuttered Windows,* an educated northern black teenager, Harriet Freeman, learns firsthand about discrimination and poverty when she travels to an island off the coast of South Carolina to live with her great-grandmother. Ellen Lewis Buell noted, "a very human story and one lighted by vision and understanding." In a similar vein, Teresita Martinez in *Teresita of the Valley* is uprooted from her home in a small village near the New Mexico-Colorado border, where she wants to be known as Teddy Jones; however, Teresita eventually learns to be proud of her name and heritage. Alice M. Jordan pronounced the story "vivacious and modern, as well as authentic in background." *The Moved-Outers,* a landmark story published in 1945, follows a Japanese family and their American-born high school-age children after the attack on Pearl Harbor as they are relocated to detention camps, deprived of their possessions and pride, and made victims of wartime hysteria. As Means once commented, "I think an adult reading such a book would accept its message only if he was of the same mind to begin with. But the adolescent, as has been proved by careful research, can be really moved—and changed—by it, if characters are so strong and situations so vital as to force self-identification." R. A. Hill identified *The Moved-Outers* as "not only an interesting and moving story of attractive young people who courageously faced complete upheaval of their ordered, happy lives" but "an accurate and very human record of one of our country's most tragic experiments." Siri Andrews also noted, "[*The Moved-Outers*] is a vivid and timely book, with true and detailed descriptions of daily existence . . . of the lack of privacy, the disillusionment, the physical restrictions. . . ."

Another valiant heroine is Emmy Lou, the daughter of a migrant worker, who, despite poverty, lack of a permanent home, and opposition from her own family, perseveres to earn an education in *Knock at the Door, Emmy.* Ellen Lewis Buell wrote, "Means draws a graphic picture of life among the migrant workers in this warm, thoughtful story of one girl's struggle to escape squalor and ignorance and of the people who helped her to have faith in herself." In a departure from her usual portrayals of the underprivileged and alienated, *Reach for a Star* (1957) is set at Fisk University in Tennessee, and features an immature black coed who rejects a brilliant, wealthy violinist for a kind, ministerial student and chooses social work for a career. In *Our Cup Is Broken,* Orphaned Hopi Indian Sarah returns to the traditions and security of the village she left as a child only to discover that she is no more at home in the old tribal world than in the outside American world. Sister Rita Angerman remarked, "[T]he character of Sarah is finely drawn,

and readers—particularly older, thoughtful girls—gradually become involved in her story, with its joys as well as its tragedies." As in all of her books, Means creates a memorable minority protagonist, describes social conditions with realism and accuracy, and focuses on enduring values such as compassion and understanding.

Awards

The Moved-Outers received both the Child Study Association annual award for a character-building book in 1945 and the Newbery Honor award in 1946. *Knock at the Door, Emmy* won the Nancy Bloch Annual Award in 1957 for a book promoting understanding between various ethnic and religious groups and received a churchmanship citation by the Central Baptist Seminary in 1962.

GENERAL COMMENTARY

Siri M. Andrews

SOURCE: "Florence Crannell Means," in *The Horn Book Magazine,* Vol. XXII, No. 1, January-February, 1946, pp. 15-30.

In a *New Yorker* story, William Maxwell speaks of a family's relationships as "paths crisscrossing, lines that are perpetually meeting. . . . Wheels and diagrams. . . . The patterns of love."

True no doubt of any family, but something like that had been going through my mind for days, in thinking of Florence Crannell Means; her feeling for the living past, her identification with her mother's family in Wisconsin and Minnesota, with her father's in New York State; her vivid memories of her own parsonage childhood in New York and in Kansas, and of the free outdoor life she lived in her teens in Colorado; and finally the adult life she has centered in her husband and her daughter; these form the paths and lines, the wheels and diagrams of her life. But until Mrs. Means's books are also woven into the pattern, there is still a vital thread missing. In her books Mrs. Means has recreated these experiences and re-worked all these strands, and one cannot be long with the Meanses without realizing that her books are living parts of the family life.

One of the strongest influences of her life was that of her father, Philip Wendell Crannell. Born in Albany, New York, of Dutch and English ancestry, he was graduated from Dartmouth College at nineteen, taught school in Pennsylvania and in Western Minnesota until his strong urge toward the ministry sent him to the Rochester Divinity School (now Colgate-Rochester). The rest of his life was spent in church work, as a Baptist minister—in Baldwinsville, New York, where in 1890 his second daughter Florence was born, and in Topeka, Kansas, as president of the Kansas City Theological Seminary for nearly twenty-five years, and as Head of the Department of Religion at Colorado Women's College after his retirement from the Theological Seminary.

Dr. Crannell was a scholar, a poet and a wit; he was as well a man of absolutely no racial consciousness. His daughter's earliest memories are of the men and women of many races who visited in their home, and to her a mingling of people of different colors on an equal footing has never seemed strange. But as she came to know more about racial and national minorities in our own country, she recognized the need for a wider realization of their problem, and because the foundation for racial understanding must be laid in childhood, as hers was, and must be based on knowledge as well as sympathy, Florence Means concentrated her efforts toward a better world in writing for children.

The six short books for younger children published by The Friendship Press were definitely written with this purpose in mind, with stress on Christian ethics as the fundamental element in the concept of democratic equality and opportunity. The first of these books, *Rafael and Consuelo,* published in 1929, is perhaps stronger in information than in story quality, for it is concerned mainly with the living conditions encountered by two Mexican children whose parents came to the United States for the education of their children.

Children of the Great Spirit, chronologically the second of this group of books, is about American Indians.

Of special interest is *Rainbow Bridge,* which centers around a well-educated Japanese family who settled in a small Colorado town where their Chinese, Korean, Filipino and Caucasian neighbors built a "rainbow bridge" of mutual understanding.

Across the Fruited Plain, which one of Mrs. Means's friends called "a seedless grapes of wrath," is the unhappy story of the migrant workers in the 1930's, and is a realistic treatment of a dark phase of American life which should be better known to the fortunate children who have not experienced it.

American Jewish children are the main characters in *Children of the Promise,* although their school in Denver contained a cross section of other groups of different backgrounds, including two refugee Jewish families. In this book Mrs. Means has made a definite effort to bring about better knowledge of many different religious beliefs as well as of racial origins.

The influence of the mission schools, especially the Presbyterian Mission School at Ganado, Arizona, is the theme of *Peter of the Mesa,* for it was there that Peter, a Hopi Indian boy, came to realize that the Indians must learn to stand on their own feet and not rely too heavily on the white man.

These small volumes are not great books, but they are interesting, increasingly well written and well integrated, with a unifying theme in each and great sincerity of purpose. They form a valuable part of our rather meager group of books of contemporary American life, especially in its seamier social and economic phases. . . .

Two splendid books for older boys and girls have come out of [Means's experiences at Indian missions in the Southwest], in addition to the two for younger children already mentioned. *Tangled Waters* concerns the Arizona Navajos of the present time. It is a strong story of conflict between old Indian beliefs and modern science, between strong personalities of several generations, each of which represents also a different civilization. This conflict is well brought out by the story of Altolie's desire for education in spite of her grandmother's opposition, her determination to earn money for her year at the Mission School, and her dependence on the advice, help, and moral support of The Boy. The book covers several years and so allows time for the interplay of contradictory forces and for the development of the girl's character under the impact of her grandmother's stern stubbornness, her mother's gentle sympathy, the new ideas and activities of the government hospital and at the Mission School, and The Boy, who is, after all, the real though secret force behind the girl's own determination.

A somewhat more complex story is that of the Hopi Indians, *Whispering Girl.* It presents not only the Hopi customs and beliefs, but also their attitude toward the white man, their secret amusement over some of his habits, the quiet scorn and resentment of his sometimes aggressive inquisitiveness, their bewilderment over some of "Washingdon's" regulations as to crops, flocks, sanitation, and education.

In neither book is the Indian idealized; there are honest and shifty men among the Indians as among the whites, weak and avaricious men, clear-headed, self-reliant, and intelligent ones. There is no comparison of races to the advantage or disadvantage of either; the people are all just human beings with common human faults and virtues against different ethical and economic backgrounds.

Another book of interest in this connection is *Shadow over Wide Ruin,* for it too is a story of the Navajo country in New Mexico in the 1880's. Attention centers, however, in the white family at the trading post and the Indians are seen through the white man's eyes.

Shuttered Windows, probably the finest of all Mrs. Means's books, was the result of a visit to Mather College in South Carolina for the purpose of gathering material about the little children in the Training School for a series of short stories meant for a church publication. There was at first a feeling of reserve toward the outsider on the part of the older girls in training there, but it was not long before Mrs. Means was no longer considered an outsider or intruder. In helping her with the material she had wanted, they came to recognize her warmth of sympathy, her deep sincerity, and quite spontaneously they asked her to write a story about them, just a story about them as girls at school. Mrs. Means gradually developed the story of Harriet through the reading of it, chapter by chapter, to two senior English classes at Mather, revisions and changes being made from the suggestions of the students themselves. It is a beautifully moving story, realistic in facing the economic situation of the Southern Negro, the squalor, the fanatical religious beliefs, the limitations, and yet filled with faith in the innate strength of mind and character of the Negro and in the better future which he can and must make for himself. Northern Harriet's gradual identification of herself with the Southern members of her race is a triumph of character development and maturing for her, and a tribute to the author's skill in portraying by implication a subtle change of attitude with complete sympathy and understanding. Harriet's strong sense of duty to her people is convincing; her romance is of course a satisfying and happy hint of her future.

A neglected minority group in the United States is that of the Mexicans of Spanish descent who have been residents of the West and Southwest for several centuries, many of whom have not yet been assimilated into American life, and *Teresita of the Valley* is the story of such a family in Denver. The character of Mary Aragon is based on that of a young woman who has been a friend and adopted member of the Means's household for many years.

The latest among the books about varying racial groups is *The Moved-Outers.* Written in the heat of strong conviction and sympathy, without the cooling perspective of time, this story of the Japanese and American-Japanese evacuated from the Pacific coast in the tense days of 1942 is remarkably restrained, objective, and fair. It took courage to write of these people in the midst of war, against a tide of hate which washed over even small children who did not know that they were "different" from other American children. But Mrs. Means felt that young people must somehow be helped to see what had happened, how this might affect the innocent victims and to face the possibly tragic results in a peacetime United States. It is a vivid and timely book, with true and detailed descriptions of daily existence in the temporary relocation centers and the monotonous permanent camps, of the lack of privacy, the disillusionment, the physical restrictions. This is already past history and not easily recaptured. But the bitterness remains, to be faced and if possible effaced by the generation now growing up. There is no criticism in the book of the decision which caused the evacuation, or the way in which it was carried out—only a description of the humanly tragic results. Mrs. Means has brought together Japanese of quite different temperaments and varying degrees of education and intelligence, so that we think of them as individuals, human beings, not types or unvarying members of a certain race. The book is obviously written with a purpose, but skillfully and courageously. . . .

All these books have sprung from Mrs. Means's convic-

tion that all men are brothers, one of the motivating forces of her life. But she has also written a number of other books in which this concept is incidental rather than the main theme. In her popular trilogy she has turned to the recent past, the time of her mother's childhood and youth.

Mrs. Crannell was born Fannie Eleanor Grout in Fall River, Wisconsin, in the unusual and lovely old farmhouse which Mrs. Means described, long before she had actually seen the house for herself, in *A Candle in the Mist.* Her mother's memories were so vivid and clear that there was no detail lacking, and her daughter felt herself stepping into her mother's childhood as she stepped into the glass-enclosed ombre, and recognized the stairs down which Janey (or "Fannie") had knitted her daily stint. When Fannie was still a child, the Grouts moved to a pioneer settlement of Luverne, in southwestern Minnesota, where Fannie grew up. Janey's story, in *A Candle in the Mist* and part of *Ranch and Ring,* has something in common with the life of Fannie Grout, who also taught country school at fifteen or sixteen and went to the Normal School at Mankato, but at this point their stories go their separate ways, for while Janey went to Colorado, Fannie Grout married the handsome young Dartmouth graduate who came to Luverne as superintendent of schools while she was one of the teachers, and went back to New York State with him. Mrs. Crannell, a tiny person as Janey was, in her girlhood was a tomboy whose youthful escapades were often the inspiration for Janey's; she too was quick and gay and strong-willed as Janey was.

The Grant family of the trilogy is modeled on the Grout family: Pa and Ma Grant are faithful portraits of Mrs. Means's grandparents; Lucy and Thad of a favorite aunt and uncle. Old Ingrid is based on a strange woman who came to the Grouts out of a mysterious past and lived with them for years. Inch-Along Billy was a combination of two men: one, a pack-peddler known to Mr. Means in his Ohio boyhood, and the other, a crippled Denver miner.

In *Ranch and Ring,* the second book of the series, Janey, Thad, and their grandmother go to Colorado Territory in 1874 to take up a claim near that of Haakon; and *A Bowlful of Stars* completes the trilogy. These books are very popular with both boys and girls because of their lively adventure and action.

The historical background is correct as far as reading and research can make it, even to the smallest detail of dress, food, furniture, reference to current books such as the *Rollo* books and *Little Women,* to the magazines, *Youth's Companion* and *Butterick's* and *Peterson's,* and to the popular songs of the period—realistic detail to create a real world and the atmosphere of another time. The credit for a good deal of this close attention to historical accuracy Mrs. Means gives to her husband, Carl Means, whose passion is history and who has not only insisted on correct factual background, but has often helped verify details in libraries. Mrs. Means feels that a very large part of her success is due to her husband, because of the keen interest he has always taken in her work, his active encouragement to her to carry it on, his warm pride in her accomplishment, and his care of her in her long and frequent periods of illness. There is a whole-hearted devotion, one to the other, a long sharing of books and thoughts and the great and small experiences of daily living which make them seem two parts of one whole; and although Mr. Means claims no smallest share in his wife's work, one feels that his clear thinking and his integrity have been the sort of influence which would permit of no slackening, no shallowness, no pose. Florence Crannell was still a child in her early teens when they first met in Kansas, but it was not until Mr. Means was graduated from the Kansas City University School of Law that they were married thirty-two years ago in Denver, in the charming old brick house in which they still live.

Mr. Means's leaning toward books of historical interest combined with Mrs. Means's love for the Southwest influenced the writing of *Adella Mary in Old New Mexico,* the story of a journey from St. Louis to Taos in 1846 by carriage, and of life in Taos during the following troubled winter. Such a journey had actually been made and served as the romantic inspiration for the story, although the rest of the plot and the characters are purely fictional.

There is no lack of variety in the writings of Mrs. Means, a person of many interests and great versatility. Out of her daughter's college life at the University of Redlands in California, her associations at Art School in Denver and at the Colorado Women's College have come two books, *Dusky Day* and *The Singing Wood,* although neither is in any way biographical. They are gay, light-hearted stories, meant to be truthful interpretations of modern young people with their idealism, their fumbling, their silliness, their frankness.

One of Mrs. Means's best-loved books is *Penny for Luck,* a story of the depression years and the ghost mining towns of Colorado. As a story also of outdoor life, which Mrs. Means loves, there is about it the refreshing quality of the bright clear air of the Colorado mountains. The treatment is realistic, the characters are alive, and in spite of poverty and hardship, the atmosphere is in general a happy one of unity and integrity.

During a year of illness, when writing was permitted only an hour a day, Mrs. Means relived some of the experiences of her childhood in *At the End of Nowhere.* The setting is a mountain village near Denver about 1904, about the time Mrs. Means first came to Colorado as a child. Mr. Austen in the story is mainly her father with a dash of her son-in-law, full of fun and mischief; Alice is based on her older sister, who died many years ago; Edith is more or less herself—for "Flossy" has inherited a good many of "Janey's" tomboy tendencies— and her twin is merely thrown in for good measure. In spite of a slowing down toward the end, there is probably more fun and gaiety in this book than in any of the

others, and it is a special favorite among children who want a "funny book."

Mrs. Means's books are alive with the small details of daily experience which give them solidity and a convincing down-to-earth quality in spite of the idealism which inspires them. There is frequent mention of food, and it always sounds luscious, even when it is of the simplest, as "the nutty, raisiny, cinnamony brown fragrance" of "rocks" baking in the oven. Mrs. Means seems to live with all her senses, for one feels her consciousness of odors of all kinds, of sage, of clover, of dusty roads, of the freshness after rain. Her daughter writes of her childhood memories of her mother: "Mother's intense, almost childlike, desire for richness and variety of life was not frustrated by her limitations [of health] but instead stimulated to an appreciation which valued the smallest things, though she never glamorized or mistook the truth." The consciousness of the life in little things and of the richness of the commonplace, is part of all her writing; trees and flowers and birds are mentioned by name, usually with some concrete reference as well to shape or odor or color; one feels the characteristic atmospheres of Wisconsin or Colorado, California or Arizona.

In general, the main characters of Mrs. Means's books are good and virtuous people, with only minor faults and few disagreeable traits. But on the whole the people are not idealized, and among the secondary characters there are villains and cowards and weaklings. There is never any doubt as to which are the desirable and which the undesirable traits of each individual, which is as it should be in books for young people, for they must meet evil and wrong doing in books as in life, but they must recognize it as such. To a considerable degree, the action of the stories springsfrom conflicts of character.

Also characteristic of Mrs. Means's books is a well-integrated, closely-knit quality; the plots develop logically, one incident growing out of another, convincingly influenced by the character of the people in the story.

Most of the year Mrs. Means writes at a wide flat desk in a pleasant room in her Denver home, its windows looking out into the tree tops, surrounded by such evidences of her many interests as her collection of American Indian objects, all of which have been in actual use and each of which has a story behind it, of adventure or friendship; and her collection of foreign and old dolls, among them her own and her sister's, and of special interest, "Laura," who was her mother's, and who is "Angelica" in *A Candle in the Mist.*

In the summer Mrs. Means writes at a sturdy table under the spruce trees on the hillside behind the family cottage in the mountains near Palmer Lake, where the air is light and clear and the sky unbelievably blue, and the breezes carry the sharp fragrance of pine and clover. This is perhaps the spot Mrs. Means loves best, the place which is most completely satisfying, where she is most at peace, which each year renews her strength and her faith. Every autumn when she returns to Denver, she tells herself

> I've built not over-high, but over-thin
> If my towers tremble when the world comes in.

Her deepest roots are here, for here she spent her summers as a child and through all the formative years of her life; here she has played and walked and read with her father, her mother, her husband; here her daughter and her friends have filled the cottage with activity and fun; and now a new generation is discovering the joys their mother, grandparents, and great-grandparents have known there.

Mrs. Means cannot remember when she has not tried to write and her very earliest writing was verse. Janey's poem, *A Candle in the Mist,* is actually a poem Mrs. Means wrote many years ago. Dr. Crannell encouraged his daughter in her childhood efforts, praised and criticized and gave an incentive to try again. Any emotion inspired by some beauty of nature or other experience finds with her a natural outlet in poetry.

Her urge to paint and sketch is also strong. After graduating from Denver's East High School, Mrs. Means attended Reed Art School for two years. When asked why she did not illustrate her own books she modestly and firmly said that her technique was not good enough; but in the dining room there hangs a lovely oil painting she had made of her daughter, and on the wall of her mother's sitting room there is a charming pencil portrait of her father. These talents are important in her fiction writing, for she feels with the poet's imagination and sees with the artist's eye.

Implicit in her life and in all her work is her love of books, as vital to her as the light mountain air and the sunlight she craves. She grew up surrounded by books (and *Youth's Companion,* "beloved in our home from before my birth till its own death," she says). Dr. Crannell read aloud a great deal, especially Shakespeare ("while I sat on the floor drawing or making paper dolls, which I always adored") and Robert and Elizabeth Browning and Tennyson, more poetry than prose, but much of both. The reading aloud in *At the End of Nowhere* is authentic Crannell-Means procedure. . . .

Perhaps not enough has been said about her deep religious faith which is the force behind all her actions, nor about her liberal views, her tolerance, her objectiveness, her keen sense of humor. But this is implicit in all her work, and perhaps after all Florence Crannell Means may best be described in two words—sincerity and integrity—if one reads into them also the warmth of love and understanding. Mrs. Means has never written anything except from interest and an urgent desire to express her ideas, never for any opportunist reasons, always for the joy of writing.

Florence Crannell Means is without doubt one of the most important and most influential of contemporary writers for young people. She has pioneered in a fresh field of writing, has written honestly and courageously on subjects long considered too controversial for children, or beyond their interest and understanding, and will inevitably come to be considered the leader in a new kind of writing for young people which will become increasingly important in a more mature post-war world. Mrs. Means holds a place which is unique.

Kay E. Vandergrift

SOURCE: "A Feminist Perspective on Multicultural Children's Literature in the Middle Years of the Twentieth Century," in *Library Trends,* Vol. 41, No. 3, Winter, 1993, pp. 354-77.

A number of women writers of the 1930s and 1940s made tremendous contributions to the beginnings of multicultural children's literature. Although these women could not be called feminists as we use the term today, they did exhibit many of the characteristics of feminism in their work, especially their concern for cooperation, connectedness, caring, diversity, and multiculturalism in a style that is associative and nonhierarchical. . . .

Florence Crannell Means and Ann Nolan Clark repeatedly challenged those invisible paradigms that marginalized or trivialized the lives of young people separated from the primary culture by race, class, or ethnicity. They were prolific writers who specialized in stories about "outsiders" in our society, recognizing their similarities to others while celebrating the differences. As Norma Klein said much later [in *Thoughts on the Adolescent Novel*]: "The purpose of fiction is not to force any way of life on an unsuspecting reader. It is rather to make people transcend the boundaries of their own identity to understand in an intuitive or feeling way what it is like to be someone else." Means and Clark, along with their contemporaries Marguerite de Angeli and Lois Lenski, certainly transcended their own boundaries and have helped generations of children to do the same.

Florence Crannell Means was truly a leader in introducing young readers to other cultures. Transcending one's own boundaries to view life through the eyes of another is not an unusual goal of writers, but to do so steadily, creatively, and thoroughly for one marginalized group after another, as Florence Crannell Means did for African-Americans, Japanese Americans, Mexicans, migrant workers, and various Native American peoples for more than three decades is an accomplishment worthy of note. A rereading of many of her books for young people reveals the expected datedness of terminology and tone, but these stories continue to speak to the same human concerns of society's outsiders today as they did more than fifty years ago. In 1945, Anne Carroll Moore wrote the following [in *Horn Book*]:

> It is her clear-sighted outlook upon the childhood and youth of many races scattered over this great country, her willingness to approach unfamiliar environments

and peoples, to learn rather than to contrast, to identify herself with the emotions of youth, rather than to discuss or dissect them, which set Florence Crannell Means's books apart from those written to order from racial backgrounds.

Means always referred to her childhood and the fact that her father, a Baptist minister, had "visitors of every kind and color" in their home as the beginnings of her appreciation of, and respect for, various peoples. She began her literary career writing and illustrating stories about minority children for religious presses. Her first full-length novels, a trilogy including *A Candle in the Mist* (1931), *Ranch and Ring* (1932), and *A Bowlful of Stars* (1934), tell of the life of Janey Grant, a young pioneer whose westward travels were based on the life of Means's maternal grandmother. Grant's pioneer spirit was later reflected in the more than thirty stories, biographies, and plays based on Means's yearly visits to various Native American tribes and to other remote areas in this country inhabited by African-American, Hispanic, and Asian American peoples. [As she noted in *Horn Book*] Means believed that "the writer must herself deeply know the people she's writing about. She must go to them—when they are of her day—and be of them as well as among them." In discussing what she called the "mosaic" of the United States, she began with historic groups of the past.

> Quite as vivid as the past, though, is the present with its varicolored racial groups, aboriginal and imported; and, shifting kaleidoscopically across the pattern of brights and darks, the continual trek of our migrant workers. It's since I've grown acquainted with the children of one after another of these groups that I've begun to harbor a deep desire: to fix this mosaic of American youth between booklids, one motif at a time.

For the next thirty years, Means did just that.

Means's view of multiculturalism, typical of the relatively few concerned and committed persons of that time, probably corresponded to [Peggy] McIntosh's phase two in which "others" were to be integrated into the primary culture. In a presentation to the Iowa Library Association, Means remarked:

> That brings us to the minority groups, and to the desire that has grown deep and burning in my own heart. That is the desire to present to our own white boys and girls the boys and girls of other races, other creeds and colors; to present them as just "folks," only superficially different from each other and from ourselves. To me this understanding of all peoples is the deepest need of a critical era; and, indeed, its only hope.

Today we consider "integration" to be a kind of cultural captivity in which those who are integrated give up aspects of their own identity in order to become a part of the primary culture. Now we are more likely to use

terms such as "diversity" and "multiculturalism" to indicate the need to retain one's own cultural identity in a rich kaleidoscopic mix of peoples. "The task for the 1990s was to learn to appreciate differences and yet to eliminate them as the basis for distributing power and privilege," [wrote F. Davis]. In many of her books, written in the 1930s, 1940s, and 1950s, Means did appreciate, even celebrate, differences among cultures. She also explored differences within cultures, but, as an author of realistic fiction, she also reflected the racial attitudes of those times in her work. Feminist scholars insist that a real redistribution of power and privilege will come about only when society deconstructs the white male hierarchies in which one succeeds by rising above others and reconstructs a network of connective relationships in which each member supports every other in a diverse, responsive, and inclusive society. For most people at the time that Means was writing for young people, such a society was virtually inconceivable, but she came close to achieving it in some of her stories.

Means was one of the first authors for young people to write realistically of African-Americans in America. *Shuttered Windows,* published in 1938, was certainly ahead of its time in its portrayal of class differences within racial boundaries. *The New York Times* review of *Shuttered Windows* stated:

> In this, her latest book for older girls, she [Means] has undertaken a theme which has heretofore, so far as I know, been treated only in adult fiction, that of the educated Negro in relation to the more backward members of the race, and she has handled it in such universal terms as to appeal to schoolgirls of any race.

Means frequently stated her belief that, in order to write about other races or ethnic groups, one must spend enough time in a region "so that it becomes friend rather than acquaintance; so that you know it rather than know about it." After only a few weeks in the islands off the Carolina coast, however, the Gullah girls in the Mather school she was visiting asked her to write a book about them. In order to do so, she created a protagonist, Harriet Freeman, who left her cultured and advantaged home in Minneapolis to stay with her great-grandmother who, although she could not read or write, had a strength and nobility Harriet admired. Thus her main character was of the people but also first perceived them as an outsider looking into the lives of others. The poverty, the ignorance, and the superstition of her people are gradually offset by their goodness and strength, by the beauty of the island, and by the devotion of the teachers who worked to overcome the severe limitations of the school for "colored" girls. Great-grandmother's stories of "Moses out of Arabia" and Harriet's growing friendship with Richie, the young agriculture student who wants to help his people, make Harriet realize that she too could help to open the "shuttered windows" for these people she had come to love and accept as her own. Wilhelmina Crosson (1940) wrote [in *Elementary English Review*]:

As a Negro woman, I feel *Shuttered Windows* no mere "flash in the pan" of books for young people, but a highly significant contribution to American juvenile literature. How gratifying to find a white woman who through her great tolerance has been able to treat so objectively, so sanely, and with such sympathetic understanding the life of a Negro girl. When one finishes *Shuttered Windows* one feels a piercing tenderness—an intimacy which causes one's enthusiasm to mount and to soar.

Suzanne Rahn remarks on Means being well ahead of her time when she creates a protagonist, Harriet, who is black, but also "strong, proud, and beautiful—in ways that reflect not only her individuality but her racial heritage." Rahn goes on to write [in *The Lion and the Unicorn*]: "As she talked with the students at Mather, Means must have sensed their need to find pride in their own racial heritage; in the characters of Harriet and Black Moses, she suggests—surely an unusual suggestion in the 1930s—that such pride is not only valid but necessary for their progress as a people."

One of the most interesting aspects of research into Means's work is the exchange of letters between her and Arna Bontemps in which she asks Bontemps for assistance in the creation of dialogue for her characters. The Bontemps Collection of the George Arents Research Library at Syracuse University contains approximately forty letters to and from, but mostly from, Florence Crannell Meanswritten between 1937 and 1963. The earliest of these letters from Means, dated July 24, 1937, begins with "congratulations to the writer of so charming a book as *Sad-Faced Boy*." She goes on to say:

I was especially charmed with your handling of dialogue. To avoid all the pitfalls and hurdles of contractions and misspellings and yet preserve the savor, the tempo, the rhythm—I myself have been seeking a solution of the problem which you have answered so brilliantly. I am writing a book for older teen age girls, set on the campus of one of the schools in South Carolina, largely attended by Negro girls from the coast and the sea islands.

In another letter to Bontemps in November 1937, Means writes:

If you should happen to see my *Shuttered Windows,* when it comes out, you may disapprove entirely of my use of the dialect. I did use contractions and misspellings—though I understand your decrying them and think your avoidance of them in *Sad-Faced Boy* a beautiful piece of work. My problem was a little different. In the first place, I am writing the book for teenage girls; in the second place, one of the points I want to get across is that individuals are individuals and to get that across I wanted to show that there is as much difference between the speech and custom of the Negro in Minneapolis and in Dafuskey as between any two groups anywhere. But in the third place, such rendering of the dialect as you have accomplished requires a firmer hold on it than I have on the Gullah. . . .

Bontemps was not the only one to whom Means turned for criticism prior to publication in an effort to make her books about other cultures ring true. She returned to the girls at the Mather school where she had been asked to write *Shuttered Windows* and gave prizes to those who criticized her manuscript. Her letters to Bontemps reveal that the manuscript for *Great Day in the Morning* was revised in response to the comments of three writer friends and then returned to its original state when her editor preferred the earlier version and Bontemps and Charlemae Rollins did not find fault with it.

In *Great Day in the Morning,* twenty year old Lilybelle Lawrence has to choose between teaching and nursing. She also learns that misunderstandings can cause problems between races, but that good manners and right conduct can lead to respect. In this book, even more than in *Shuttered Windows,* the use of dialect may distract or disturb readers, but it is deftly handled in this serious story of a young minority character.

In 1945, Means won the Child Study Association Award for *The Moved-Outers,* a sensitive story of the evacuation and internment of a Japanese-American girl and her family during World War II. In 1946, this book won a Newbery Honor. The author had previously written about the problems of Japanese assimilation in America in *Rainbow Bridge,* but it was the Ohara family of *The Moved-Outers* who touched the raw nerves of a war torn nation. Means met and talked with young California evacuees who were forced to live behind barbed wire fences in the Amache relocation camp near her Colorado home and wrote this story at a time when many Americans were unaware of, or unwilling to acknowledge, what was happening to these U.S. citizens.

As this story opens, Sue Ohara is looking forward to a typical teenager's weekend. Kim, her younger brother, had just won a high school debate with his fiery exhortations of patriotism, and Sue was looking forward to Christmas and then winning a scholarship and "four glorious years" in college. Both Sue and Kim were bright and popular young people, but Sue fit into high school society as an All-American girl in spite of her Japanese heritage, while brother Kim stood somewhat apart and worried about the time when they would be "out of college into real life." The first chapter ends with the author's comment: "Everyone has a shadow; everyone with substance, amounting to anything. And your shadow is as much a part of you as the shape of your eyes and the color of your hair." Unfortunately, the day was Friday, December 5, 1941, and by Sunday the Japanese attack on Pearl Harbor brought the shadow descending on even the most loyal Americans with a particular shape of eyes and color of hair.

Howard Pease, in a *Horn Book* article, praised Means's treatment of this sensitive period of our nation's history:

Young Americans will find good reading in Mrs. Means's story of a loyal Japanese-American family.

It is her best book, beautifully written, profoundly moving, yet restrained. And it possesses that rare quality of saying something about our world today, here at home. It explains and interprets, it enlarges our sympathy and understanding, and it makes plain that the story of Sue and Jiro has implications far more important than what happens to one family or to one minority group. Possibly it is already late for us to decide that from now on we must be more forthright in our treatment of controversial subjects in our books for young people. Let us hope it is not too late. The reception accorded *The Moved-Outers* will be a test of our own intelligence and our own integrity.

The reception to *The Moved-Outers* proved to be a mixed one. In spite of its literary awards, many schools and libraries did not purchase this book. Anti-Japanese feelings, even against the Nisei or those born and educated in this country, still ran high at its time of publication on February 28, 1945, especially on the West Coast where large numbers of Japanese Americans had been very successful prior to Pearl Harbor. There has always been the suspicion that it was, at least in part, personal greed and racial prejudice directed against these successful "foreign-looking" immigrants which helped to fuel the negative feelings toward these citizens. When Japanese Americans were relocated, their property was often sold to others for less than its actual value. Those more sympathetic to the Nisei were often embarrassed by the actions of this country's War Relocation Authority and did not want to expose their shameful actions to young people. For these reasons, *The Moved-Outers* did not achieve the readership or visibility it deserved and was, for a long time, one of those Newbery Honor books available but not generally known by young people.

Similar stories of Japanese-American relocation during World War II began appearing in the early 1970s and brought Means's book back into consideration by those concerned with multicultural books for children and young people. Yoshiko Uchida's (1971) *Journey to Topaz* is based on the author's own experiences during this tragic period of history. The protagonist is much younger than Sue of *The Moved-Outers,* but otherwise the parallels between these two stories are amazing. This is especially true when one considers that they were written almost thirty years apart, the first, an outsider's observations during the heat of a terrible occurrence and the latter, an adult insider's reflections on her childhood experiences. Also in 1971, Japanese-Canadian artist and author Shizuye Takashima's *A Child in Prison Camp* was released. This account of her experiences in a Canadian internment camp, poignantly presented in paintings as well as in words, was named the "Best Illustrated Book of the Year" by the Canadian Association of Children's Librarians the following year. Subsequently, *A Child in Prison Camp* (1974) was published in the United States and in many other countries and has won a number of additional awards. . . .

The Moved-Outers was a landmark book, one that dealt with this difficult topic during its own time and opened the door for these more recent books for young people. It is unlikely that any book on this subject written by a Japanese American would have been published in the 1940s or 1950s (the McCarthy period was certainly a recognizable obstacle). It was not until almost thirty years after the onset of relocation that Japanese Americans who had been children in the camps began telling their stories. Florence Crannell Means, as a sympathetic outsider, had been the first to present this injustice to young readers long before those oppressed were able to tell their own stories. This was probably true for most marginalized or oppressed peoples; someone from the outside had to tell their stories first before they were able to make their own voices heard. . . .

It is precisely this clear historical understanding that is critical to our young people. It is noteworthy that it took almost fifty years for the American government to first recognize, then admit to, and finally accept responsibility for, its actions with regard to its citizens. Children need to know such things, and it was Means who first presented this horror to young people.

Means also dedicated a great deal of time and effort to her workwith and about Native Americans. Year after year she spent as much time as possible living with the Navajo or Hopi peoples and was always very precise in distinguishing among the lifestyles and customs of various tribes. She wrote pamphlets about Native Americans for the Baptist Missionary Society, but she really brought them to life in her stories for young people. *Tangled Waters* (1936) is the story of Altolie, a fifteen-year-old Navajo who had to rebel against her grandmother's wishes to get an education in the white school. Many details of Navajo beliefs and customs are woven sensitively into this story, showing the beauty as well as the harshness of this way of life. In a winter of famine, Altolie would have married a wealthy but unpleasant young Navajo gambler if a Boy she had met at school had not come to her rescue. The Boy was trying to learn the ways of white society so that he could combine the best of these ways with the best of his own Navajo heritage. The view of white culture presented in this work would be perceived as over-romanticized today, but *Tangled Waters* was a very forward-looking book for its overall treatment of, and respect for, Native Americans at its time of publication.

A more somber view of Native American life is found in Means's *The Rains Will Come* (1954). The setting is a Hopi village in the midst of a severe two-year drought. Young Lohmay is obsessed with the thought that his irreverence toward Hopi religious symbols brought this punishment on his people. When the villagers confess their sins, however, he discovers that his own are very small. The power of this story is in its beautiful prose and in the authentic portrayal of Hopi life, especially their deep religious feelings, close-knit family life, and strength in times of trouble. There is humor here but *The Rains Will Come* also pictures a darker side of Native American life. Black and white illustrations by Hopi artist Fred Kabotic complement Means's text and add credibility to her treatment of this way of life.

Fifteen years later, Means published an even darker view of Hopi life. In **Our Cup Is Broken** (1969), Sarah left her village to live in the white world when she was orphaned at age eight. At age twenty she returns and finds that the world she remembers no longer exists. She finds it impossible to live in the white world but neither could she be comfortable with her Hopi people; she has no home. Sarah is raped, bears a blind child, marries for protection without love, and gives birth to a stillborn child. Thus, the tragedy is somewhat overstated, but Sarah is a compelling and believable character who demonstrates the personal cost of a culture that appears to be vanishing.

In addition to books about African Americans, Japanese Americans, and Native Americans, Means wrote stories about other "outsiders" in American society. Mexican Americans, Spanish Americans, Chinese Americans, and migrant workers have all been honestly and sympathetically portrayed in her work. She was a pioneer in writing realistic stories about minorities for young readers. While shevalued the uniqueness of each of these cultures, it is clear that she believed that all human beings are basically the same under the skin.

TITLE COMMENTARY

RAINBOW BRIDGE (1934)

Boston Transcript

SOURCE: A review of *Rainbow Bridge,* in *Boston Transcript,* Vol. LI, No. 18, June 23, 1934, p. 3.

Although written for children, this book has all the persuasion of actual life among the orientals who come so eagerly into our midst. A sociological study three times its length could give no warmer understanding of the apprehension, earnestness, disappointment, courage and hard work which brings the oriental into the swirl of American life. The author's vivid though delicate touch is carried into the illustrations by Eleanor Frances Lattimore, who says as much through these black and white drawings as she did in her discerning essays on Manchuria for the Atlantic Monthly.

May Lamberton Becker

SOURCE: A review of *Rainbow Bridge,* in *New York Herald Tribune Book Review,* August 5, 1934, p. 5.

Three children, well brought up and in process of being well educated, in a family of excellent social standing, are looking forward to coming to the United States of America as this story opens, and looking with some misgiving. For they are Japanese and all they have heard about the United States has led them to believe things there are very different. But the good-luck signs have said September is a propitious month for them all to start. Their father is a research physician whose special object of study must be found in a big American hospital. Their mother will go without a murmur wherever he goes, and even grandmother, who is to stay behind, shows only by the trembling of her hand how much her polite consent costs her. Even for the children there may be alleviations. Haruko, the girl, has found that girls in America do not have to study flower arrangement or the tea ceremony. It may not be so very bad, this America. So they set off, a young reader's interest with them from the start.

Through their Oriental eyes we see San Francisco and a strange new world on the way to Colorado, where their father's station will be. Then come housing troubles, difficult and humiliating, and the bumps and bruises kindly children get when first they find that other children may not mean to be kind. Though they were well along in school at home, here they must go back behind their ages. This extraordinary English comes out of Jiro's mouth more melted than it went into his ear. "I feeru pur-rity wer-ru, thank you," he replies politely to inquiries on his health, and wonders why people laugh. These American books must be read from left to right instead of going reasonably from top to bottom, and no amount of staring at *girl* on a card reveals to Harnko that it means girl. Nobody persecutes them, but nothing is easy for them. Though they gradually make friends, it is at first rather with the Chinese children, whom the young Americans seem to expect they will treat as irreconcilable foes. Japan and China may be at war, but the Miyata family is willing to waive that in the presence of Ruby Wong. Her mother may be American to the point of being president of the local Parent Teachers Association, but great-grandmother, who lives with them, is the only trousered Chinese woman left in the city, a "golden lily" woman with bound feet.

The approach of Christmas and a new teacher gives the newcomers their first chance. When all the class is making paper chains, Haruko, after an ancestral design, makes a paper bird. She makes paper dolls that every girl wants. Teacher wants to hear her read Japanese, so she brings to school a book in her own language and the children hear how well she can read it. When Jiro has trouble with *l* and *r* and Gladys giggles teacher writes on the board in German that Gladys is impolite and the German children giggle at the way Gladys pronounces it. In short, the class—composed like many American classes of specimens of different nations and races—begins to get the trick of looking at themselves through the other fellow's eyes, and the Christmas celebration is communal and friendly. Though the Miyata family has been keeping up its drooping spirits on the thought that they would be going home at the end of the year, when their father needs more time for his work each member of the family, in a secret ballot, votes to try it a little longer. Something about America has got them. It is not quite so strange after all.

This is the only one I have read of the stories for children under twelve of which this is the latest, but if the other seven serve their purpose as well the Friendship Press is doing real work for the next American generation. The gradual get-together of the children in the story is as far as possible from dubious professional "Americanization." The little Orientals win their way to acceptance on personal merits, and the little Americans learn by trial and error the rudiments of an inter-racial politeness, the fine flower of civilization.

PENNY FOR LUCK (1935)

Irene Smith

SOURCE: A review of *Penny for Luck,* in *Library Journal,* Vol. 60, No. 19, November 1, 1935, pp. 857-58.

Depression times in Colorado lurk behind this warm-hearted, natural story, which is packed to the brim with human life. Penny Adams was a shy, awkward, homely girl, running away from an orphans' home near Denver when she was picked up by a family of Smiths in an old car and taken along to their crowded apartment. The rest of the story tells how she found her own place in the "family pocket", never to leave it; but around this simple outline lies a good and wise commentary on middle-class life in America today. Mr. Smith was a hard-pressed bookkeeper, fired from his job early in the story. Mrs. Smith's beauty shop had failed. Pretty Virginia was at an expensively frivolous high school age, and there were Junior and Grandpa to provide for. So the Smiths couldn't afford to keep Penny, who adored them, until she herself suggested their camping up in a deserted mining town that summer, rent free. The author manages a very skillful atmosphere of simple life in the beautiful mountains, with leisure for the tired, harassed city family to enjoy each other and even to read. Penny was like a devoted slave, always there with the lucky suggestions, loving, humble, uneducated. That winter Penny learned of a decent birthright, and at last won "the right to starve along with her family." A book about flesh and blood people meeting their problems honestly. It comes closer to the realistic present, as young girls live it, than any recent fiction for them has done.

Alice M. Jordan

SOURCE: A review of *Penny for Luck,* in *The Horn Book Magazine,* Vol. XI, No. 6, November-December, 1935, p. 357.

This is the story of Penelope Adams, an orphan, and the family she found for herself when she ran away from the Denver orphanage and the chance for adoption by the strong-minded and psychologically wise Mrs. Hen-

ley. There is good characterization and the situation of the older people is true for these depression years. Their summer in a deserted gold-mining village of the Rockies, and Penny's part—her practical, friendly, and lucky help—is full of interest and charm. But why must there be so much dreadful English spoken? It is a blot on an otherwise good story.

TANGLED WATERS (1935)

Ellen Lewis Buell

SOURCE: A review of *Tangled Waters,* in *The New York Times Book Review,* September 6, 1936, p. 10.

Altolie, at 15, might have been any Navajo maiden, living the semi-nomadic life of her people, herding the sheep, glorying in the freedom of the desert—and hedged in by centuries-old taboos and superstitions. But Altolie had dim memories of her babyhood days when she and her mother had lived at the American mission. Those days were never spoken of in the hogan, for her step-grandmother, the powerful old matriarch, fiercely resented any influence which might turn her people from the old ways. Only Altolie's mother, gentle Bah, spoke once, wistfully, of the white people whose ways seemed straight and beautiful, who walked the world without fear of jealous spirits and evil.

Altolie was to learn the meaning of those words, for an accident to her knee took her to the American hospital, and then she entered the Indian school. Terrified at first, and humiliated beyond endurance, she would have run away had it not been for her friend, the Boy. She had met the Boy in the desert, contrary to all Navajo ideas of decorum, and in their few meetings there had grown between them a wordless understanding which ripened into something more than friendship. The Boy knew that the Indian must learn the ways of the white man to preserve his own identity, and with an understanding beyond his years he had a vision of a life which would contain the best of the two ways. From him Altolie caught the dream, but she had to use all her wits and determination to realize it. As her yearning for knowledge grow, the grandmother, the Old One, became more implacable in her opposition to the Americanization of the girl. Then came a Winter of cold and famine, and when Altolie saw how gaunt and poor her family had grown, her resolution weakened. A marriage was arranged to a rich young Navajo, a wastrel gambler, whose fortune would save the family from starvation. Altolie's last desperate device to avoid it failed and it was the Boy who came triumphantly to the rescue and bore her back to school and to a future of love and service to her people.

It is a full-bodied, well-rounded story, this tale of Altolie's gradual liberation from the fears of her people, which at the same time pictures the beauty which is to be found in the Indian way of life. Woven into the story are colorful accounts of the Navajo customs and ceremonies with realistic characterizations of patient Bah, her easy-going gambler husband, Adakai the fierce old grandmother, and in particular, the two young dreamers.

May Lamberton Becker

SOURCE: A review of *Tangled Waters*, in *New York Herald Tribune Books,* October 18, 1936, p. 9.

It takes special gifts both of judgment and of technique to write a satisfactory love-story for girls from twelve to fifteen or so. No one with experience can doubt that this age likes a good love-story, or that the right kind of one would be excellent reading matter. Florence Crannell Means has looked in a part of the country where primitive peoples live among Americans but preserve their racial and even religious independence—in Arizona among the Navajos. She has brought from the Southwest a thoroughly good Indian story for growing girls, full of rich and stately ceremonials of the tribe, showing how a living is made, and how economic stress can keep the silver ornaments of the family always in and out of pawn, showing also the good side of Indian schools, the reasons why some Indians do not see it, and some of the ways in which the wrong teacher may hurt the system. All this has been done before in books for young folks: we have now a distinguished group of stories for the teens whose heroes or heroines are young Indians of the Southwest. But all this, in *Tangled Waters,* is irradiated by the force that makes the book a novel rather than a story—the shining force of a true, honest and devoted young love, for which young creatures are willing to suffer and in whose name at last they conquer.

SHUTTERED WINDOWS (1938)

Ellen Lewis Buell

SOURCE: A review of *Shuttered Windows*, in *The New York Times Book Review,* August 28, 1938, p. 10.

Those who have followed Mrs. Means's books know of her special interest in the adjustment of the underprivileged and alien races to American life. In this, her latest book for older girls, she has undertaken a theme which has heretofore, so far as I know, been treated only in adult fiction, that of the educated Negro in relation to the more backward members of the race, and she has handled it in such universal terms as to appeal to schoolgirls of any race.

Her heroine is Harriet Freeman, whose sixteen years of life in Minneapolis had spared her some of the harder discriminations against her people and who had enjoyed the benefits of education in a large city high school. Life on a sea-island off South Carolina where Harriet went to live with her great-grandmother, her one remaining relative, was a series of shocks and painful disillusionment, intermingled with a joy in the sheer beauty of the island. Pride of family, a factor not often stressed in

stories of Negro life but here made entirely valid, was a dominant one in her life and it was a humiliation to discover that the proud old woman whom she loved on sight could not even read. There were other disappointments in store for her: the backwardness and superstition of the island Negroes, their helplessness in the face of terrible poverty in a fertile, lovely land, and chiefly the limitations of the school for colored girls which she entered.

Gradually, aided by the understanding of her teachers; by her friendship with young Richie who unconsciously did much to show her the inherent goodness and strength of their people; and by her own sense of values, Harriet overcame her resentment and discouragement, to realize not only the compensations of island life but also the opportunities for service which it offered.

The story of her adjustment is worked out on general lines which are applicable to teen-aged people of any race, but which in detail reveal much of the special problems, both large and small, of young Negroes. If it is not as rich in beauty as was *Tangled Waters,* it is a very human story and one lighted by vision and understanding.

The Booklist

SOURCE: A review of *Shuttered Windows*, in *The Booklist,* Vol. 35, No. 2, September 15, 1938, p. 31.

When Harriet Freeman, a colored girl, went to live with her great-grandmother on an island off the coast of South Carolina, she found the ways of Negro life different from those she was accustomed to in the North. A growing compassion, nurtured by the kindly wisdom of Granny, and Harriet's pride in her ancestor Black Moses, led to her decision to remain in the South and work among her own people. This is a school story for girls, yet has its social implications; the mystery is secondary and the Negro dialect may be hard for some readers.

Siri M. Andrews

SOURCE: A review of *Shuttered Windows*, in *Library Journal,* Vol. 63, October 15, 1938, p. 799.

An unusually fine and original story of an orphaned Negro girl who, born and brought up in the North, went to visit her great-grandmother on an island off the coast of South Carolina. It was Harriet's first knowledge of the South and the southern Negro, and what she learned was both a shock and a revelation to her, when instead of returning to Minneapolis for her senior year of high school, she entered a school for Negro girls near her grandmother's island home. Avoiding both preachiness and sentimentality the author shows the gradual growth in Harriet of an understanding which becomes a wide vision of service to and identification with "her people" which was unknown to her in the North. A convincing and consistent story of contemporary America and one of its serious problems presented in a form which should interest and stir both boys and girls of junior and senior high school age.

ADELLA MARY IN OLD NEW MEXICO (1939)

The Booklist

SOURCE: A review of *Adella Mary in Old New Mexico,* in *The Booklist,* Vol. 36, No. 3, October 15, 1939, pp. 74-5.

In 1846 Adella Mary, her older brother, and younger sister, set out from St. Louis for Taos with their father and a devoted colored couple to join their invalid mother; the new life proved an exciting though bewildering one. During the Mexican war Adella Mary had to run the household for her ineffectual mother, and it was through her courage and quick thinking that the family were savedfrom Indian massacre. The picture of life during a troubled period is an interesting one.

Ellen Lewis Buell

SOURCE: A review of *Adella Mary in Old New Mexico,* in *The New York Times Book Review,* October 15, 1939, p. 12.

Adella Mary's copper-colored curls belied her true nature, for she was no fighter. She was born timid—afraid of heights, lightning and Indians, but she had that finest kind of courage which carries on in the face of mortal fear, and it was this which set her on the Santa Fe Trail three years before the gold rush. Her invalid mother was in Taos and, when it seemed that the company of her children might help her to recovery, it was Adella Mary's special pleading which convinced her father to take the three children out in the wagon train.

The trip had its fearsome moments, with Indian encounters, a buffalo stampede, and a ride down the mountains behind a runaway team, but it was at Taos that Adella Mary really began to grow up. Her father was caught in the intrigue of the Mexican War and during his absence she found herself with a household of Spanish servants to manage, and with a sick mother whose comments were more frivolous than useful. She had never needed her own special brand of quiet valor more than during those days of care and suspense which came to a climax on the night that the Pueblos rose against the whites.

This story is for girls a little younger than those who enjoyed *Tangled Waters* and *Shuttered Windows,* and it is slighter in content, but it is rich in the details of a romantic period. Mrs. Means writes with sensitive understanding of the Indians who played such an impor-

tant part in the life of the sheltered little girl from St. Louis.

AT THE END OF NOWHERE (1940)

Sonja Wennerblad

SOURCE: A review of *At the End of Nowhere,* in *Library Journal,* Vol. 65, No. 19, November 1, 1940, p. 927.

The scene is laid in Apache, a small Colorado town, where a minister in search of health has brought his family. Alice, the older daughter, finds it difficult to adjust herself to hardships and strange companions, but father, mother, and the lively twins quickly feel at home in this new world. Edith and Steve not only make friends with the town's most suspicious characters, but end by reforming and taking two of them into their home. The book ends happily with Alice winning a coveted scholarship to a city school and father's health improving steadily. Wholesome, fresh picture of family life and life in Colorado in the early twentieth century, with its cowboys, wild horses, floods, etc. Rather an unpleasant portrayal, however, of unsympathetic grown people and unfortunate children.

Irene Smith

SOURCE: A review of *At the End of Nowhere,* in *The New York Times Book Review,* November 10, 1940, pp. 41, 44.

The Austins are a well-knit family, with independence of character and buoyancy of spirit. The father is a Kansas City minister recovering from a long illness. His humor is irrepressible and his religion is practical. The mother is young in heart. Alice at 16 is pretty, and the twins, Edith and Steve, are human dynamos. With these qualities and little besides in worldly goods the five land in Apache, Colorado, where Reverend Austin is to manage a small church while recovering his health.

Apache in 1904 looked to them like the end of nowhere. There is abundant human interest in the reception accorded these city folks by the local population, from the Banker Robbinses to the disreputable Finches. Yet the two Finch children became the best friends the twins had ever had, and the mutual loyalties were a benefit to the young Austins as well as to the neglected Buck and June. The elder Austins fitted themselves into the raw little town, bringing their leavening influence where it was needed.

The plot has an uncertain pattern because of slack threads. It lacks the straight dramatic interest of *Penny for Luck* and some of this author's best stories. But the character drawing and the local color have an unusually realistic quality and the whole has a liveliness and sense of fun that will hold young readers. The illustrations [by David

Hendrickson] deserve special mention for their fidelity to the times and people.

Alice M. Jordan

SOURCE: A review of *At the End of Nowhere,* in *The Horn Book Magazine,* Vol. XVI, No. 6, November-December, 1940, p. 443.

Older girls will sympathize with the sensations of Alice Austin as she looked around the squat railroad station and saw only wide stretches of prairie. The story deals with the problems of adjustment which faced a family when the health of the father took them from a city home to a crude frontier community. The twins adapted themselves easily, but it was harder for the older sister. Mrs. Means writes with full measure of awareness of the growth that comes to young people through an effort to get the viewpoint of others.

CHILDREN OF THE PROMISE (1941)

May Lamberton Becker

SOURCE: A review of *Children of the Promise,* in *New York Herald Tribune Book Review,* June 8, 1941, p. 5.

A public school in Denver has a monthly award that 6B expects to get—and doesn't. That may seem a small matter to start race trouble, until you learn that in this month the Jewish children of this class were away from school, celebrating the autumnal holidays, and though these days are not counted off in the attendance contest, they make a big difference in the grades "because those kids are some of the ones that always get the best marks." One boy asks, "Why can't all of us be satisfied with real American holidays?" and a girl says, "It does seem as if when people come over here they might—well, kind of fit into America the way it is." Some of the Jewish children "came over" from Austria and Germany, quite lately; the terror is still in their parents' eyes. Happily the teacher has a way of meeting such a situation. The class does some visiting round in each other's homes, in each other's churches and synagogues. They form a Young American League. They find it takes the strain off at certain points of tension between Jews and Christians in grade-school years.

The story is frankly educational, though the author knows how to tell a story. . . . It presupposes willingness to be reasonable, not always found in young or old just now, but the ideas it puts forth are such as should be presented to teachers of small children in cities or towns where the "refugee problem" is pressing.

The Booklist

SOURCE: A review of *Children of the Promise,* in *The Booklist,* Vol. 37, June 15, 1941, p. 496.

An idealistic but timely story of two Jewish children and of their place in school and community. A wise teacher helps the Six B's, greatly disturbed by their own racial differences, to a better understanding of themselves and each other. Religious tolerance, race prejudice, and Jewish beliefs and customs are treated in an unpretentious yet satisfactory manner for children.

SHADOW OVER WIDE RUIN (1942)

Ellen Lewis Buell

SOURCE: A review of *Shadow over Wide Ruin,* in *The New York Times Book Review,* December 27, 1942, p. 8.

There was trouble, mysterious, inexplicable, but surely trouble, hanging over the Navajo trading post at Wide Ruin when Hepzibah Plumb arrived in New Mexico from Denver in 1886 to help her uncle and aunt. Uncle Ezra was steadily losing the Indian trade, and there was a growing hostility against the kindly, honest little man and big affectionate Aunt Puss. Yet for some reasons the Indians liked Hepzy immediately. They called her Younger Sister, they gave her a horse, dressed her in Navajo skirts, called on her for aid, and Hepzy, generous-spirited and sympathetic, responded.

Under the guidance of Dolito, handsomest of all the braves, educated and wise, she learned their careful age-old etiquette, the intrinsic beauty of their ritual and beliefs, and she lost her narrowly self-righteous inclination to duty. As she threw herself whole-heartedly into the Navajo life she came to think of them not only as "The People," as Dolito called them, but as persons too.

There is much more to this story than the adventure which Hepzibah sought, for there is her own growth of character, and through her discovery and understanding of the Navajos there is made clear, with the skill of a fine novelist, the richness of their heritage and the problems of transition which they were just beginning to face as they stood between two civilizations. Mrs. Means has written excellent novels for older girls; this one, with its perception, its depth of feeling accented by humor, is one of her finest.

Alice M. Jordan

SOURCE: A review of *Shadow over Wide Ruin,* in *The Horn Book Magazine,* Vol. XIX, No. 1, January-February, 1943, pp. 38-9.

The Navajo country, with its bewildering mesas and buttes, its sparkling air and wide deserts, its hogans and camp fires, opened a new life to Hepzibah, coming from Denver, in 1885. There was adventure and a baffling secret at her uncle's trading post among the Indians, and through her experiences there Hepzy learned to respect the customs which seemed to her so strange at first. She found friendship and love at Wide Ruin and proved that the difference between herself and "the People" was one of experience and language, merely. They accepted her, too, because of the good omen in her name. Older girls, especially, will enjoy this realistic story.

📖 *TERESITA OF THE VALLEY* (1943)

Alice M. Jordan

SOURCE: A review of *Teresita of the Valley,* in *The Horn Book Magazine,* Vol. XIX, No. 6, November-December, 1943, p. 410.

The temptation which sometimes comes to young people to feel ashamed of their racial inheritance is the theme of a number of good stories for children. Mrs. Means here embodies it in an understanding book for older girls, in which she tells about Teresita Martinez, who wanted to change her name to Teddy Jones. It was after she had moved to Denver with her family, from a little Spanish village near the New Mexican border, that the idea came to her. Different persons and her own experiences brought to her finally a sense of pride in her heritage and all it had brought her. The story is vivacious and modern, as well as authentic in background.

The Booklist

SOURCE: A review of *Teresita of the Valley,* in *The Booklist,* Vol. 40, No. 4, December 1, 1943, p. 117.

A modern story of a 17-year-old Spanish-American girl in Denver, endeavoring to make a home for her family until the return of her missing father. There is much here to be commended—narrative skill, humor, feeling for the people, and treatment of the problem of racial discrimination and adjustment to a new way of life. However, the language used in conversation, a literal translation of Spanish into English, like the use of Negro dialect, will give some readers a misleading impression of the characters.

Marian Cumming

SOURCE: A review of *Teresita of the Valley,* in *Library Journal,* Vol. 68, December 1, 1943, p. 1009.

Florence Means makes another contribution toward racial understanding. Teresita Martinez and her family lose the village home, Martinez property since the old Spanish land grant, and go to Denver in search of a wandering father. The casual, crowded life in the Mexican quarter is contrasted with Teresita's ambition, which at first leads her into posing as "Teddy Jones" and denying her people. She finally finds pride in her race and a home in a rehousing project promises a combination of Spanish gaiety and the cleanliness and safety that

Teresita desires. Characters are alive and atmosphere convincing.

📖 *THE MOVED-OUTERS* (1945)

Alice M. Jordan

SOURCE: A review of *The Moved-Outers,* in *The Horn Book Magazine,* Vol. XXI, No. 1, January-February, 1945, p. 37.

Responding to the urgent need of today, Mrs. Means tells here a provocative story of a California family of Japanese origin, in the months following Pearl Harbor. No thoughtful girl can fail to be moved by the events that befell Sue Ohara in her last year of high school, when her world crashed about her. No older person should be able to read complacently of the methods by which the evacuation of citizens of Japanese background was handled. The life in the Assembly Centers and Relocation Centers is carefully described, with its effect on young people plainly indicated, the efforts of the stronger young people to adjust themselves, sympathetically treated. But this American situation is dispassionately handled in a well-sustained story interest. These are real boys and girls facing difficult problems. What effect will their experiences have upon a spirit of genuine tolerance and conquest of race prejudice?

Howard Pease

SOURCE: "Without Evasion: Some Reflections After Reading Mrs. Means's *The Moved-Outers,*" in *The Horn Book Magazine,* Vol. XXI, No. 1, January-February, 1945, pp. 9-17.

If you are a person who surveys children's books year after year, you are likely to be aware of a curious and disturbing fact. Only at infrequent intervals do you find a story intimately related to this modern world, a story that takes up a modern problem and thinks it through without evasion. Of our thousands of books, I can find scarcely half a dozen that merit places on this almost vacant shelf in our libraries; and of our hundreds of authors, I can name only three who are doing anything to fill this void in children's reading. These three authors—may someone present each of them with a laurel wreath—are Doris Gates, John R. Tunis, and Florence Crannell Means.

In 1938 Mrs. Means gave us the story of a Negro girl in **Shuttered Windows,** a story that explains and interprets a racial question on a level suitable for young people. . . . And now, just off the presses this spring, comes another book of equal importance, **The Moved-Outers** by Mrs. Means.

This new book for young people is the story of a Japanese-American family of California evacuees, or moved-outers as some call themselves. The story begins on December 7, 1941, and from that day, so tragic for all of us, it follows Sue and her family to the Santa Anita concentration camp. Here they are assigned to one of the stalls in a stable. The camp itself is surrounded by barbed wires, soldiers tramp back and forth, and at night searchlights play in circles from watch towers. From Santa Anita the family is taken by guards to a train that has its windows broken by bullets from outside as it speeds eastward to another barbed-wire camp in the desolate wastes on the eastern slope of the Rocky Mountains. The story ends when Sue is finally released to enter the University of Colorado and Jiro is allowed to join the army and fight for his country, our country.

The book is first of all a good story. It is also true to facts as I, a Californian, know those facts. It records in story form, without preaching, what I believe will be known as one of the blackest spots on the history of this State of mine, this State that my grandparents helped to found and my parents helped to build. *The Moved-Outers* is a book I should like to see in every school and library in this country. Whether it finds a welcome place on the shelves of more than half the schools and libraries on the Pacific Coast is a question—and a test especially for librarians and teachers in California.

If confusion exists in the minds of many Americans as to the exact situation on the Pacific Coast in the weeks following the attack upon Pearl Harbor, that is not surprising, since Californians themselves are only now beginning to get a perspective on that same situation. During those first terrible weeks after December 7, practically all Californians—except perhaps a few sentimentalists and some Japanese-Americans—did agree that, rightly or wrongly, something must be done and done quickly. In the first place, feeling ran high as the result of the shock we had received. Not that the attack itself was so unexpected as it apparently was to those high in command of our armed forces. What shocked us most was our own incompetency and unpreparedness. . . .

From her home in Denver, Florence Crannell Means watched our California evacuees arrive and enter another barbed-wire camp in Colorado. She learned to know these Americans with the wrong ancestors, and she learned to like them. This was no new experience for Mrs. Means. Her home has long been open to friends from here and abroad, and these friends come from many nations and from many minority groups. She learned, too, to appreciate the fine yet difficult work being done by the members of the War Relocation Authority in charge of these camps. Like so many of us, she noted with alarm the attacks upon the W.R.A. by people who, in their confusion of mind, classify all relocation centers with the notorious Tule Lake camp in California. In the Tule Lake camp are segregated all of the disloyal.

Young Americans will find good reading in Mrs. Means's story of a loyal Japanese-American family. It is her best book, beautifully written, profoundly moving, yet restrained. And it possesses that rare quality of saying something about our world today, here at home. It explains and interprets, it enlarges our sympathy and understanding, and it makes plain that the story of Sue and Jiro has implications far more important than what happens to one family or to one minority group. Possibly it is already late for us to decide that from now on we must be more forthright in our treatment of controversial subjects in our books for young people. Let us hope it is not too late. The reception accorded *The Moved-Outers* will be a test of our own intelligence and our own integrity.

Anne Carroll Moore

SOURCE: "The Three Owls' Notebook," in *The Horn Book Magazine,* Vol. XXI, No. 2, March-April, 1945, p. 108.

In his fine tribute to Florence Crannell Means and her latest book, *The Moved-Outers,* Howard Pease has revealed a concern for American citizenship that does him honor as writer, teacher and citizen.

"Without Evasion" is a contemporary human document of compelling interest. It is courageous and thoroughly informed. It points the way, I believe, to a more reflective and honest approach to the great problems of human relations which have been too long obscured by a veneer of education for democracy.

I read Mr. Pease's article before I had read *The Moved-Outers.* I share his feeling as to the importance of this true picture of a Japanese-American family living as evacuees on American soil. By its humanity and the simplicity and naturalness of presentation it should take a place of its own among the books Mrs. Means has been adding to the shelves for girls and boys of high school age since 1931.

I do not agree with Mr. Pease that *The Moved-Outers* is her "best" book. As I think of the vivid characterization, the feeling for Nature, the keen observation, the good story behind *Penny for Luck, Shadow over Wide Ruin,* and *Shuttered Windows,* I look upon *The Moved-Outers* as a timely book to be followed in her own good time by one that in development of character and relation to life may take on the stature of *Shuttered Windows.*

I know of no writer who has combined such true pictures of the West of pioneer days and of the present day with a story that stays in the mind years after the first reading. *Penny for Luck* made a special appeal to me, for I had spent some time in Colorado the year it was published, I had seen one of the "ghost towns" so vividly described, I had met and talked with Mrs. Means and realized how modestly and completely she had lived in her books. Later she came to see me in New York and I had the pleasure of taking her to visit the children's room of one of the branch libraries in Harlem; she was then hoping to write a story of a Negro girl, but she was not looking for copy that afternoon. She left with librarians and children a lovely impression of a visitor who had simply enjoyed herself and would like to come again.

Wisconsin Library Bulletin

SOURCE: A review of *The Moved-Outers,* in *Wisconsin Library Bulletin,* Vol. 41, No. 4, April, 1945, p. 48.

The author, who has done such excellent work in dramatizing the situations of other minority groups, here takes up the case of the Japanese Americans. Follows the fortunes of one family, more particularly, a sister and brother who are in their senior year in high school when the evacuation strikes them, but shows all the aspects of the problem, making especially clear the growing fear of leaving the safety and protection of the relocation centers for the uncertainties of the outside world. At the same time the story is absorbing in itself.

Ruth A. Hill

SOURCE: A review of *The Moved-Outers,* in *The Saturday Review of Literature,* Vol. XXVIII, No. 16, April 21, 1945, p. 30.

Again Mrs. Means has told us a convincing story of a group of Americans of another racial origin. It is vital because she has not only drawn material directly from our national life, but has the ability to see people first as human beings and, on that fundamental basis, to build reactions due to race, education, or background.

Sue and Kim Ohara, as integrally American as any other boy or girl in their California high school, nevertheless are aware that everyone has his "shadow," that they will have to learn to accept their special one when school days are over and they must face the world. But when the story begins they are secure, happy, popular at school, and loved and understood at home.

Then came the bombing of Pearl Harbor and the many changes that followed that disaster. For Sue and Kim were Japanese—Japanese in race only, for their home life, their education, friends, church activities were typically small-town American. There were heartbreaks for them all when their father was interned simply because his innocence of pro-Japanese activities had to be proved, when they had to give up their home, leave their friends, the college scholarships, and their bright hopes for the future and join the other evacuees. Of all the Oharas the adjustment was hardest for Kim who lacked Sue's stability and his mother's philosophy. His idealistic loyalty to America and his hot young enthusiasm for democracy received a shocking blow.

Against the background of life in an American concentration camp the people are faithfully and sympathetically portrayed, from the pathetic boy who tried to disguise his Japanese features and coloring and the Issei who have not accepted American ways to the highly educated and often delicately reared professional men's families who nevertheless accepted uncomplainingly the roughly simple ways of camp life.

This is not only an interesting and moving story of attractive young people who courageously faced complete upheaval of their ordered, happy lives. It is, too, an accurate and very human record of one of our country's most tragic experiments.

Cathi Dunn MacRae

SOURCE: A review of *The Moved-Outers,* in *Wilson Library Bulletin,* Vol. 68, No. 5, January, 1994, p. 118.

A shameful era in American history is preserved with the reprint of **The Moved-Outers** by Florence Crannell Means. This is a contemporary account published in 1945 of a Japanese-American family forced from their California home to a Colorado internment camp during World War II. One of Walker & Company's "Newbery Honor Roll" reissues, this title would now be considered a YA novel; its protagonists Kim and Sue are high school seniors. It is an affecting story of how two different young spirits cope with ethical and physical hardships.

GREAT DAY IN THE MORNING (1946)

Virginia Kirkus' Bookshop Service

SOURCE: A review of *Great Day in the Morning,* in *Virginia Kirkus' Bookshop Service,* Vol. XIV, No. 16, September 1, 1946, p. 426.

A mature, personal story of a Negro girl's adjustment to the many problems that beset her in her search for a career. Love of the land, love of her family and a deep sense of responsibility save wild, tempestuous, pretty Lilybelle and bring her to her heritage of love, work and understanding. She has a hard head and warm heart and they serve her well. The dialect, while it gives a distinctive flavor to the book, may rouse some antagonism among those Negroes among the intellectuals who are going too far in their efforts to censor books about Negroes. Watch for this reaction. But the unusual background and the good story carry conviction and feeling.

Margaret C. Scoggin

SOURCE: A review of *Great Day in the Morning,* in *The New York Times Book Review,* November 10, 1946, p. 50.

Twenty-year-old Lilybelle Lawrence had put herself through Penn School to be a teacher. When Lilybelle's progressive ideas cost her her first school she scrimped to go to Tuskegee. There she had some college fun, but she was torn between the teaching career she wanted and the nursing career for which she was naturally fitted. Only after overwork had ended her Tuskegee studies and three accidents had brought close to her the need for Negro nurses did Lilybelle write to her grandfather: "God spoke to me three times. . . . I am going into nurse training in the fall."

The dialect will bother some readers and offend others. But here is American life as it seems to a simple, ambitious Negro girl who learns the importance of good manners on both sides of the color line and the necessity for young Negroes to accept the responsibility which comes with equality. A rather serious girls' story which is also a plea for interracial understanding.

Alice M. Jordan

SOURCE: A review of *Great Day in the Morning,* in *The Horn Book Magazine,* Vol. XXII, No. 6, November-December, 1946, p. 473.

Like other of Mrs. Means's books, **Great Day in the Morning** takes up frankly and fairly the grave evil of racial hatreds. This young novel concerns Lilybelle, whose home is on one of the islands off the Carolina coast. Her ambitions and friendships, her college days and love story might be those of any young American struggling with the conflict between a wish to be counted important and the deeper urge to be of service to humanity, except over all lies the dark shadow of color. Destiny took her from the island to Tuskegee, where she was not too late to feel the personal influence of Doctor Carver, thence to Denver where the story leaves her with the determination to become a nurse finally fixed. Lilybelle's strong character, her warm nature, her Negro temperament and gifts are well drawn and the tragedy of her race's situation stands out too plainly to be missed by the most thoughtless reader. This fine story is not one-sided; Mrs. Means has a lesson for black Americans as well as for white.

ASSORTED SISTERS (1947)

Margaret C. Scoggin

SOURCE: A review of *Assorted Sisters,* in *The New York Times Book Review,* November 30, 1947, p. 47.

When the Locke family take over a settlement house in Denver's poorest section, 15-year-old Mary is terrified by the big city high school. Fortunately she finds three other girls as lonely as she and they form the "assorted sisters." There are Mei-Lee from invaded China, Mexican-American Marita, who understands how slights cause "zoot suit" riots, and a Negro girl, Carolina Collins. Together, they stand for equality of all groups in school activities; before long they are taking part in all affairs and parties; finally they win all racial groups to enthusiastic support of Friendship House. When, after

six months, the Lockes must leave or find more space, the entire community, sparked by Mary's "sisters," provides a solution.

Girls from 11 to 15 will enjoy the friendship among the sisters and their school and date problems; they will like the slight mysteries about Mei-Lee and Marita. The happy ending is too pat and the Lockes a bit too cheery but the lesson of tolerance is laudable.

Ruth Hill Viguers

SOURCE: A review of *Assorted Sisters,* in *The Saturday Review of Literature,* Vol. XXX, No. 50, December 13, 1947, p. 33.

In this story Mrs. Means accomplishes something that has seldom been done before. She pictures with complete realism and lack of sentimentality the life of a missionary family. There are many counterparts of the Reverend Mr. Locke of this story. He is not a missionary in a foreign land where physical discomfort might be offset by the glamor of strange surroundings and dramatic events, but a missionary in the United States who is so in love with the ideal of serving underprivileged people that, characteristically, he has little concern over creature comforts either for himself or for his family. The influential people responsible for the finances of his mission take his and the family self-sacrifice as a matter of course. But the Locke children were not "called" to this life, and at least one of them, fifteen-year-old Mary, had moments of rebellion. But, in spite of the fact that she did not elect a missionary career, she was born with some of the necessary attributes. She had a quick humor, high spirits, and a talent for friendship. She did not consciously select her three closest friends from three different racial groups—Chinese Mei-Lee, Spanish-American Marita, and Negro Caroline—but it was a fortunate coincidence that their loneliness at a time when Mary herself was lonely drew the four girls together. They had in common courage and initiative that could create happiness for others as well as for themselves.

Creating characters like these proves again that Mrs. Means enjoys all kinds of people because she understands all kinds. Few books with as definite a purpose as this are, at the same time, absorbing stories and convincing Americana.

Alice M. Jordan

SOURCE: A review of *Assorted Sisters,* in *The Horn Book Magazine,* Vol. XXIV, No. 1, January-February, 1948, pp. 41-2.

Mrs. Means tells another story about older girls on the theme of tolerance and friendliness between races. The scene is laid in Denver, the actors are girls and boys of high school age, with the family of the director of a social settlement in the center. In spite of entirely different backgrounds—Chinese, Mexican and American—three girls, who find they have like tastes and common points of view, draw a Negro schoolmate into their circle and the story has to do with their problems. Mrs. Means's warm sympathy and solicitude for girls shows itself in the wise, frank handling of modern manners and customs as they affect the *Assorted Sisters*. Much more than racial relations enters into the excellent story.

THE HOUSE UNDER THE HILL (1949)

The Booklist

SOURCE: A review of *The House under the Hill,* in *The Booklist,* Vol. 46, No. 8, December 15, 1949, p. 143.

With a setting of twentieth-century New Mexico against a seventeenth-century background, Mrs. Means presents the appealing story of a sixteen-year-old Spanish-American. Elena Trujillo thinks fate has singled her out for a laborious and loveless life. She longs for the glamour of the city, away from school, away from the sickness and dying of her people; but her grandmother breaks her leg and Elena's dreams of the bright world fade. Soon she forgets her troubles in those of the people around her and finds a satisfying life in the establishment of a free clinic. The gay moods, the sad ones, the hint of romance—all make a story more of a teen-age girl than one of a minority group.

Ellen Lewis Buell

SOURCE: A review of *The House under the Hill,* in *The New York Times Book Review,* December 25, 1949, p. 11.

More than anything else, Elena wanted to leave her great-grandfather's house and the tiny village where her Spanish ancestors had lived and get a job in Pueblo, where her brother and that attractive Natan work. But when her grandmother broke her knee Elena had to stay home. Rebelliously she buckled down to work and more work.

It is at this point that Elena sees how desperately the people of El Mirador need modern medicine. With very little cooperation and less appreciation she starts a clinic. In spite of her own frustrated plans, she discovers that the world outside the valley is not so rosy, especially where Spanish-Americans are concerned. And she finds that romance and fulfillment often come in unexpected ways.

That Elena does not wholly succeed in her project gives this novel for teen-aged girls an extra layer of perspective. Elena's own character is rather elementary in outline, but she is an appealing heroine and the Spanish people of New Mexico are presented with understanding and realism.

THE SILVER FLEECE: A STORY OF THE SPANISH IN NEW MEXICO (with husband Carl Means, 1950)

Virginia Kirkus' Bookshop Service

SOURCE: A review of *The Silver Fleece: A Story of the Spanish in New Mexico,* in *Virginia Kirkus' Bookshop Service,* Vol. XVIII, No. 6, March 15, 1950, p. 180.

This latest historical novel in the "Land of the Free" series is absorbing and diverting in its wealth of authentic detail about the society of the Spanish in New Mexico around 1695 when Spanish families refounded Santa Cruz during the "reconquest" of the lands the Indians had reclaimed from the conquistadors. The story of the Riveras, who take the journey to Santa Cruz provides the focus for the study of the period. Lucia, a lovely girl of sixteen, her twin brother, dashing Domingo, Signora Rivera, the twins' aunt and uncle, an old goatkeeper and an Indian slave, Gaspar, are involved in the adventures attendant upon their arrival at their ancestral home—Indian attacks, mysteries about lost property, Lucia's and Domingo's attempts to free Gaspar from their uncle's bondage, the zealous efforts of Father Antonio to root out the remains of the pagan Indian religion and the experiments to introduce a new stock of "silver" goats with superior wool in the new land. As a pageant of color and atmosphere, this book has much to recommend it, but the story itself is too diffuse—episodic on too many levels for a well-knit story. There is good material here for background reading, but the reading may be too static and rarified for many.

New York Herald Tribune Book Review

SOURCE: A review of *The Silver Fleece: A Story of the Spanish in New Mexico,* in *New York Herald Tribune Book Review,* May 7, 1950, p. 14.

Before opening this new title in "The Land of the Free" series, one wonders what aspect of Spanish colonization will be stressed, what angle taken on their religious contribution, and what will be called their gift to our present culture. After reading, one is satisfied on all scores. One feels assured that thoughtful research, and knowledge gained from living Spanish and Indians lie behind this book. A factual preface outlines the period, that around 1695.

The story tells how a Spanish family helped to resettle the section of New Mexico north of Santa Fe. They introduced a special sort of sheep which, inbred with local sheep, would produce better wool. "Silver Fleece" grew on the pet lamb which Lucia treasured and brought all the way back from Mexico. The shepherd Juan is a fine character. The action is exciting enough, with hostile Indians plotting an attack on the rancho, and the women helping to defend it, with a supposed Indian "witch-woman," and with a search for the family's hidden silver. The underlying theme is the growth in understanding and friendship between an Indian slave boy and Domingo and Lucia. They teach him to read and finally plan to buy his freedom.

It is an interesting American background, rich in colorful detail, and in showing varied points of view of priests, Spaniards, and Indians.

Siddie Joe Johnson

SOURCE: A review of *The Silver Fleece: A Story of the Spanish in New Mexico,* in *Library Journal,* Vol. 75, No. 11, June 1, 1950, p. 990.

This story, with a background of the Spanish reconquest of New Mexico at the end of the 17th century, takes Mrs. Means deeper into her field of racial roots in these United States than ever before. Her family is a pleasant one, the twins very impulsive, the girl tender, the boy brave, and the other characters life-size. Story is closely plotted, concerning danger, the search for family treasure, re-establishment of the flock, and the position of an intelligent Indian in slavery. Well done and long needed.

HETTY OF THE GRANDE DELUXE (1951)

The Booklist

SOURCE: A review of *Hetty of the Grande Deluxe,* in *The Booklist,* Vol. 47, No. 12, February 15, 1951, p. 223.

The Beaumarchand family moves from Boulder with its inspiring views, to a run-down apartment house in an unfashionable section of Denver, to the disillusionment of sixteen-year-old Hetty, ambitious and over-confident. How she adjusts to a variety of people, becomes a leader at high school, and discovers two good friends make a sound girls' story for the early teens. A trifle slow moving and introspective, nevertheless here are secure family relationships contrasted with instability in occupation, convincing characterization, and human faults, especially ubiquitous quoting and slight overtones of superiority.

Esther E. Frank

SOURCE: A review of *Hetty of the Grande Deluxe,* in *Library Journal,* Vol. 76, No. 5, March 1, 1951, pp. 416-17.

Moving to the ramshackle apartment building "Grande Deluxe" in Denver, Hetty, a normal girl, finds the neighbors in her age group to be a crippled boy of fine character and the pathetic daughter of an erstwhile sharecropper family. How she learns to appreciate the one and help the other, while making a place for herself in the mixed racial group at high school, makes an inter-

esting and very worth-while story by this excellent writer of stories of tolerance.

Siri M. Andrews

SOURCE: A review of *Hetty of the Grande Deluxe,* in *The Horn Book Magazine,* Vol. XXVII, No. 2, March-April, 1951, p. 113.

Hetty's rosy dreams about the beauty of life in "The Grande Deluxe Apartments" are swiftly crushed when she sees the rundown old building in the outskirts of Denver, and its equally unprepossessing inhabitants. She is not converted overnight for she is a normal and natural girl, but thanks to intelligent parents and the friendship of a crippled boy of her own age, she begins to see something of the tragedy under the surface of most people's lives, and to make new friends who unconsciously help her to find beauty and goodness also in unexpected places. High school classmates of many races and different social backgrounds are well integrated as part of her development. But girls will read the book because they will find themselves in Hetty and understand her, and because the story moves quickly from one situation to another and is lively and modern.

THE RAINS WILL COME (1954)

Virginia Kirkus' Bookshop Service

SOURCE: A review of *The Rains Will Come,* in *Virginia Kirkus' Bookshop Service,* Vol. XXII, No. 17, September 1, 1954, p. 585.

In a story of the Hopi Indians 70 years ago, the author returns to the Southwest region of some of her other books. Tragedy faces a Hopi settlement in the form of drought and sickness when Lohmay, the chief's nephew, commits what may be sacrilege by showing a white man their tribal ways. Then he thinks a spell is cast on his baby brother's life, a rivalry with Maqto over a girl. The continued drought in spite of the rain dances deepen Lohmay's guilt until he must make a confession of it in public. The climax lifts the weight from the boy's heart and proves his inner strength, but opens the way for change as well because the rain clouds have formed before the confession is made. Action keeps reader interest in a good picture of Hopi life that brings out their traits of non-aggression and selflessness.

Alice Brooks McGuire

SOURCE: A review of *The Rains Will Come,* in *The Saturday Review,* Vol. XXXVII, No. 46, November 13, 1954, p. 94.

A somber note pervades Mrs. Means's new book about life in a Hopi Indian village seventy years ago. Lohmay, a Hopi boy just on the verge of manhood, is caught up emotionally in the anguish and physical suffering among his people during the great drought. His guilt feeling that his own deeds of irreverence towards the symbols of the Hopi religion have caused this disaster becomes an obsession. At last, in desperation, he insists on making a public confession. To his surprise and relief his sins sound very slight when he is permitted to recite them. It becomes evident, too, that other villagers have sins to confess. Everyone feels happier when Honwi, the village's religious leader, tells them that "it is good for us to let the evil out of our hearts."

In this beautifully written novel the author portrays vividly the mores of the Hopi people—their close-knit family life, their deep religious feeling and superstitions, and their ever-present sense of humor. However, this is not a happy book! Misfortunes parade in close formation across the pages, starvation is a grim, unwelcome guest in every home—and still the rains won't come! So much unhappiness in one book makes me wonder if the slight love theme and the Hopis' pathetically brave attempts to find some humor in everything are sufficient to sustain the interest of many young readers. We hope so, because the reading of this book is a rewarding, if somewhat saddening, experience.

📖 KNOCK AT THE DOOR, EMMY (1956)

Elizabeth Burr

SOURCE: A review of *Knock at the Door, Emmy,* in *Library Journal,* Vol. 81, No. 13, July, 1956, p. 1722.

Ever since Emmy Lou could remember, the Lanes had traveled hither and yon across the western half of the country peddling and sometimes working in the sugar beets or citrus fruit crops. Even though her Pa had little use for folks or schooling, Emmy's deep desire was for an education. She graduates from high school and wins a scholarship for college against almost insurmountable odds. Here is an appealing story of the courage and fortitude of young people handled with skill and dignity.

The Booklist

SOURCE: A review of *Knock at the Door, Emmy,* in *The Booklist,* Vol. 52, No. 21, July 1, 1956, p. 466.

All her life, fifteen-year-old Emmy Lou Lane had been shuttling across the country, peddling baskets, working in the crops, and living in tent or truck. Pa, who had little use for folks, and her younger brother loved the migrant life, and ailing, defeated Ma was resigned to it, but Emmy was different. She hated the dirt and disorder, the shabbiness, and the emptiness, and yearned for an education, friends—particularly a boy who lived in Glen Lake, Colorado—and a permanent home. This is the credible story, warmly and perceptively told, of spirited Emmy's efforts to achieve her goal against almost insurmountable odds.

Ellen Lewis Buell

SOURCE: A review of *Knock at the Door, Emmy,* in *The New York Times Book Review,* August 12, 1956, p. 24.

"Andres is clean and decent and kind. And that isn't so common," said Emmy Lane of the migrant Mexican crop-worker who wanted to marry her. And that, she thought, was all that she, daughter of a free-wheeling itinerant peddler, could expect from life. Yet, as the Lanes jounced back and forth along the Western roads in their old pick-up, Emmy thought wistfully of Phil Carter, the friendly boy in Glen Lake, her mother's hometown where they stayed from time to time. In Glen Lake, Emmy first glimpsed an orderly, stable life. There she made friends and went to school briefly. Emmy was crazy about books, but sometimes she thought she would be better off without an education if she were to follow the road all her life.

In earlier novels Mrs. Means has spoken for the dispossessed and the underprivileged. Now she draws a graphic picture of life among the migrant workers in this warm, thoughtful story of one girl's struggle to escape squalor and ignorance and of the people who helped her to have faith in herself.

📖 REACH FOR A STAR (1957)

Virginia Kirkus' Service

SOURCE: A review of *Reach for a Star,* in *Virginia Kirkus' Service,* Vol. XXV, No. 15, August 1, 1957, p. 532.

Florence Crannell Means, author of other stories about Negro students, ***Shuttered Windows*** and ***Great Day in the Morning,*** sets a college love story with the Negroes of a higher economic strata against the background of Fisk University in Tennessee. Toni Deval, daughter of a Denver druggist, abandons plans to attend the University of Denver when Ferd Fenton, a rising young Negro violinist terminates their romance which had lasted for more than a year. His prosperity and social standing made him seem desirable to Toni, but on the campus she finds a new set of values. Peter, a young man preparing for the ministry, takes Ferd's place, and she resolves to enter the field of social welfare. A sympathetic projection of the snubs, social distinctions and glimmering hopes of young Negroes today.

Augusta Baker

SOURCE: A review of *Reach for a Star,* in *Junior Libraries,* Vol. 4, No. 3 November 15, 1957, p. 40.

Third in a group of Negro school stories by Mrs. Means, this is set at Fisk University. The characters are more economically privileged than those of the previous books.

This campus story presents the usual problems of freshman life, new friendships, dates, broken romances. Interracial problems are minor, and ordinary life on a large Negro campus appears quite like life on any other campus.

The Booklist and Subscription Books Bulletin

SOURCE: A review of *Reach for a Star,* in *The Booklist and Subscription Books Bulletin,* Vol. 54, No. 7, December 1, 1957, p. 204.

Set against the background of Fisk University and its traditions this college romance focuses upon Toni Deval, a somewhat self-centered and snobbish Negro girl from Denver. As Toni comes to understand and respect students less fortunate than she during an activity-filled freshman year, her values change. She develops an interest in social work and rejects the wealth and prestige offered by a selfish though talented young violinist for the devotion of Peter, a kindly and generous boy studying for the ministry. Sensitively and sincerely written for teen-age girls.

BORROWED BROTHER (1958)

Virginia Kirkus' Service

SOURCE: A review of *Borrowed Brother,* in *Virginia Kirkus' Service,* Vol. XXVII, No. 15, August 15, 1958, p. 609.

Jan Pratt, a sixteen-year-old only child, envies her distant cousins, the Averys. For theirs is a lively, large family and their bustling home in Colorado Springs seems to Avery a panacea when compared to her orderly but quiet Boulder home. When she and her cousin Molly agree to exchange homes for a month, Jan is delighted, particularly because her feelings about her cousin Mark have taken a decidedly romantic turn. Baffled by Mark's moodiness, she does not learn until she is ready to leave, the reason for his depressions. But despite her concern over Mark, it is a lively time for Jan, who, while making a happy adjustment to the Avery home, learns to appreciate the advantages her own family offers. She returns home, enriched and happy, particularly because Mark, freed from his moods, promises that he will come to visit her even if he has to "hoof" it all the way. Florence C. Means, author of *Reach for a Star* and other popular teen-age novels, writes of American family life with a warm enthusiasm, turning day to day incidents into dramatic situations without sacrificing verisimilitude.

The Booklist and Subscription Books Bulletin

SOURCE: A review of *Borrowed Brother,* in *The Booklist and Subscription Books Bulletin,* Vol. 55, No. 4, October 15, 1958, p. 106.

Sixteen-year-old Jan Pratt, an only child, eagerly agrees to a month's exchange of homes with her distant cousin Molly Avery, one of a family of ten. Jan's experience in the lively, haphazard household so different from her own quiet, well-ordered home is a happy and rewarding one: she shares in the normal give and take of a large family, gains an even better appreciation of her own home, and learns the reason for the changed attitude and moodiness of the oldest Avery boy in whom she has a romantic interest. While not the author's best work, the story is worthwhile and enjoyable.

Ruth Hewitt Hamilton

SOURCE: A review of *Borrowed Brother,* in *The Saturday Review,* Vol. XLI, No. 44, November 1, 1958, p. 56.

Jan, only daughter of the Pratts, who lead an orderly and predictable life, changes places with her friend Molly Avery for a month and finds herself catapulted into unexpected adventure. Molly's four brothers and sisters, her parents and grandparents, lead lively, free-wheeling, and independent existences. Jan finds this a very realistic taste of what it is like to be the member of a large and energetic family. Mark, the oldest brother, provides a touch of romance and a thread of mystery to the story.

This is a pleasant book and a welcome change from the "social problem" theme.

Ruth Hill Viguers

SOURCE: A review of *Borrowed Brother,* in *The Horn Book Magazine,* Vol. XXXV, No. 1, February, 1959, p. 55.

Jan, an only child, by exchanging homes with Molly Avery for one month, had the chance to experience all the fun, confusion and excitement of big-family life. In addition, she could help seventeen-year-old Mark (to her the most appealing of all the attractive Averys) weather an especially stormy interlude in the process of growing up. Interesting as good family stories are, this is particularly notable for the complete normalcy as well as liveliness of its characters. It is easy to see that the wisdom and understanding of the Avery parents is the result of self-discipline and the inevitable smoothing of corners that comes from living with diverse personalities. The Colorado background is very real.

TOLLIVER (1963)

Ruth Hill Viguers

SOURCE: A review of *Tolliver,* in *The Horn Book Magazine,* Vol. XXXIX, No. 5, October, 1963, p. 510.

The depth of Mrs. Means's feeling for justice and human rights is very evident in this book. It begins with a tragic incident on Tolly's graduation day at Fisk University, which focuses attention on the core of the problem which America faces today. Tolly, after feeling that Sojer, the boy she loved, had tossed away his future, which she herself had sacrificed to help him make possible, determined never again to become involved with the troubles of others. When her impulsive, spoiled, and adored younger sister announced that she was going on a Freedom Ride, Tolly went along and, in subsequent disastrous and shocking events, her fine resolutions were swept away. Occasionally in recent books this author has appeared to be trying too hard to bring home her message. Here her involvement with her characters is so complete that self-consciousness does not cloud the drama of the story. The writing may lack the restraint of two of Mrs. Means's other books with Negro heroines, **Shuttered Windows** and **Great Day in the Morning,** and her very important **The Moved-Outers,** but it is warm and real. A timely, stirring, and moving story.

Best Sellers

SOURCE: A review of *Tolliver,* in *Best Sellers,* Vol. 23, No. 18, December 15, 1963, pp. 341-42.

It was a shock and a disappointment to Tolly to find out that Sojourner Pratt, whom she had so industriously helped for four years, had cheated on his final examination and would not graduate with the rest of his class. Promising herself that she would not become involved in the personal affairs of anyone else, Tolly spent the summer with her family. With each exciting happening she realizes that she cannot ignore the feelings and needs of those around her. Participating in a Freedom Ride with other Negro students, she suffers physically and mentally from the injustice of race discrimination. A well-written story. The author clearly presents the race problem, without malice or bitterness.

Ellen Rudin

SOURCE: A review of *Tolliver,* in *The New York Times Book Review,* February 2, 1964, p. 24.

Nineteen-year-old Tolly Tolliver is disillusioned when her boyfriend Sojer is caught cheating and is thus denied his diploma and a chance at med[ical] school. She picks up her marbles and Phi Beta Kappa key and goes home to teach in South Carolina, vowing never to become involved again with anyone or anything. It's an impossible pledge to keep, of course, especially for a young woman like Tolly with a strong, if selfish, love of family and community and an inbred, if vague, wish to do something for "our people," the Negroes. She involves herself with the problems of many people and takes part in a Freedom Ride—during which the unforgotten Sojer again enters the story.

One really grieves less for Tolly than for this book which aims so tall yet falls so short. The plot is grossly

episodic, the scenes badly balanced, the characters lack bulk or depth. Worst of all is the author's thick, clumsy prose style (except for the St. Helena's Island dialect which rings true, though is sometimes inconsistent and could prove offensive).

The proud, gentle-eyed Tolly looking out in wordless accusation from the dust jacket makes the book inviting to today's civil-rights-minded teenagers but, colored or white, if they expect substance they are in for disappointment.

US MALTBYS (1966)

Zena Sutherland

SOURCE: A review of *Us Maltbys,* in *Bulletin of the Center for Children's Books,* Vol. 20, No. 6, February, 1967, p. 95.

Mary Jane Maltby and her younger sister, Sylvia, are stunned by the news that their parents have decided to take in foster children. Not only that, but five teenage girls with problems! First Bobbi, tough and cynical, then two sisters whose mother is in a mental hospital and whose father is an alcoholic; the last two are Spanish-American sisters. The family adjusts to their new members slowly; the newcomers adjust even more slowly. One of the problems is the town's prejudice against Prudencia and Letitia. There is a town rule that no Negro may stay over night, and Mrs. Maltby decides to test this rule, too; she has become enamored of a deserted baby boy who is Negro. With family agreement, tiny Jamie is taken in; the Maltbys give a party, hoping that Jamie will charm people into acceptance, and that's just what happens. The ending is a wee bit pat, but the characterizations, the relationships of the characters and the shifts in those relationships, are excellent. Mrs. Maltby, an effusive woman given to cute speech ("a mell of a hess" or "One sell fwoop") is particularly well-conceived, since her gay, childish, affectionate and energetic personality is one that provides good motivation for her actions.

Agnes Gregory

SOURCE: A review of *Us Maltbys,* in *School Library Journal,* Vol. 13, No. 6, February, 1967, p. 82.

At the beginning of the book Us Maltbys consists of Mum, Dad, and two teen-age daughters, Mary Jane and Sylvia, but, suddenly, five teen-age foster sisters, including Mexican twins, are added to the family, and later, a Negro baby boy. How the family adjusts to this unusual situation in modern-day Scotia, Colorado, a town noted for its conservatism and restrictions, forms the plot of the story. This is a timely subject, but the author has not been as successful in telling this story as with some of her former books. Too much seems to be accomplished in too short a time when, in a period of a few months,

Scotia citizens accept this mixed family with very little protest. The young people are rather too good and noble, and the exemplary mother's use of outmoded slang such as "kiddoes, duckies, etc" becomes very annoying.

📖 *OUR CUP IS BROKEN* (1969)

Sidney D. Long

SOURCE: A review of *Our Cup Is Broken,* in *The Horn Book Magazine,* Vol. XLV, No. 3, June, 1969, p. 311.

Twenty-year-old Sarah returns to the Hopi village she had left as an orphan eight years before, determined to rejoin the Indian world. She is driven not only by a broken love affair with a white boy but also by her hunger for the ways of her childhood—the wide spaces of the mesa, the traditions of her people. Nurtured by modern America and the ancient world of the Hopi, Sarah is a victim of both. Her story is compelling because although the way of life she remembers has vanished, it still exists within herself—and is at once her great strength and the cause of much of her sorrow. The author has written a serious and absorbing novel about the slow disintegration of a culture, and about the bewilderment and pain that it causes to the people involved.

Zena Sutherland

SOURCE: A review of *Our Cup Is Broken,* in *Bulletin of the Center for Children's Books,* Vol. 23, No. 2, October, 1969, p. 29.

A story about the tragedy that can ensue from intercultural conflict. Sarah's parents had both died when she was twelve and she was taken from her home in a Hopi village to live with the school principal and his wife, who took her with them when they moved to Kansas. Thus for nine years Sarah lives in a white community, returning in heartbreak and disillusionment to her home village when the parents of the white boy who is in love with her hasten to break up the attachment. Revolted by some of the mores she had once taken for granted, Sarah finds that she is no more at home in the tribal culture than she is in the white world. Raped by a Hopi boy, she turns all her love toward her baby. Her child is blind. When she does marry, Sarah has a still-born child. There is a note of hope at the close, when Sarah and her husband decide to move to a newly-formed community, but the total effect of the book is grim and depressing. It is candid and realistic, with strong characterization; it has the strength of a documentary film in depiction of the plight of the individual who is torn between two worlds and belongs to neither.

Sister Rita Angerman

SOURCE: A review of *Our Cup Is Broken,* in *School Library Journal,* Vol. 16, No. 2, October, 1969, p. 152.

The themes of self-identification and cultural conflict are represented here in this sensitive, honest novel about a Hopi Indian girl, Sarah, who spends eight years with a white family after the death of her parents, is hurt in her love for a white boy, and runs home to her reservation at the age of 20. Determined to forget the boy, she tries to immerse herself in the Hopi way of life, but finds it difficult to accept the living conditions and some of the customs. After much personal suffering—an unwanted, husbandless pregnancy, the blindness of her baby, the still-birth of a second child—she eventually finds happiness with her Indian husband, with whom she's about to begin a new life in a settlement away from the reservation. She has realized that primitive Indian life, for all its peculiar beauty, is doomed. The story is slow-moving in the beginning, but the character of Sarah is finely drawn, and readers—particularly older, thoughtful girls—gradually become involved in her story, with its joys as well as its tragedies.

📖 *SMITH VALLEY* (1973)

Mirel Touger

SOURCE: A review of *Smith Valley,* in *School Library Journal,* Vol. 20, No. 4, December, 1973, p. 55.

An unbelievable story of life as it once was, which sweeps through a quarter of a century of straight-laced, upright living in middle America from the end of the 19th century to the World War I Armistice period. At 15, Laurie Ford is a carefree daydreamer trying to translate her feelings into poetry. When she inadvertently overhears neighbors refer to her as "one of those shiftless Fords," the shock causes Laurie to embark on a lifetime plan of rigid discipline and self-abnegation. After suffering through years of family drudgery, a loveless marriage, the influenza epidemic, and sudden widowhood, the now "old" heroine, suffering "change of life" melancholia (at forty!), finally gets a chance at happiness. The characters are stick figures who move inexorably toward their just deserts—unfortunately without the capacity to inspire reader empathy.

Booklist

SOURCE: A review of *Smith Valley,* in *Booklist,* Vol. 70, No. 13, March 1, 1974, p. 737.

Initially this appears to be a light, predictable romance, but as readers wade deeper they will discover a full-bodied, full-blown narrative that involves a goodly segment of Smith Valley Colorado society. At fifteen Laura Ford determines to prove to the gossipy town that the heretofore lackadaisical Ford family can repair their claim to respectability. Duty sends her to a Denver high school and then bids her forego a coveted college scholarship to care for her motherless nieces. Her penchant for respectability plays a strong role in her dutiful marriage to Earl Scofield at the cost of happiness with warm, exuberant Dan Wyckliffe. Efficiency dominates Laura's 25 years of marriage until her husband's death, when she perceives that her single-mindedness has left her an essentially empty life. Of course her long-ago sweetheart Dan returns to reawaken Laura's interest in life. Occasional florid prose and over characterization of Laura in her iron-willed quest are weaknesses, but some strongly etched emotional scenes generate enough strength to hold reader interest.

Additional coverage of Means's life and career is contained in the following sources published by The Gale Group: *Contemporary Authors New Revision Series,* Vol. 37; *Major Authors and Illustrators for Children and Young Adults;* and *Something about the Author,* Vol. 1.

J(ohn) R(onald) R(euel) Tolkien

1892-1973

English author and illustrator of fiction and nonfiction; philologist.

Major works include *The Hobbit, or There and Back Again* (1937; U.S. edition, 1938), *Farmer Giles of Ham* (1949; U.S. edition, 1950), *The Lord of the Rings*, Volume 1: *The Fellowship of the Ring* (1954), Volume 2: *The Two Towers* (1954), Volume 3: *The Return of the King* (1955), *The Father Christmas Letters* (1976), *The Silmarillion* (1977).

Major works about the author include: *J. R. R. Tolkien: A Biography* (by Humphrey Carpenter, 1977), *A Guide to Middle-earth* (by Robert Foster, 1971; revised as *The Complete Guide to Middle-earth: From The Hobbit to The Silmarillion*, 1978), *J. R. R. Tolkien: Six Decades of Criticism* (by Judith A. Johnson, 1986), *The Hobbit: A Journey into Maturity* (by William H. Green, 1995).

The following entry presents criticism on Tolkien's *The Hobbit, or There and Back Again.*

INTRODUCTION

Recognized as the originator of modern fantasy and an esteemed scholar of language, Tolkien has pleased countless readers and fascinated critics with the originality and literary depth of his Middle Earth stories. While his *The Lord of the Rings* trilogy claims the highest place among avid fans, it was its predecessor, *The Hobbit, or There and Back Again,* that first established Tolkien's reputation as a storyteller and mythmaker. *The Hobbit* has generated frequent comparisons to Lewis Carroll's *Alice's Adventures in Wonderland* and Kenneth Grahame's *The Wind in the Willows* and, in more recent years, the work has perhaps enjoyed more attention than these two masterpieces. Tolkien's imagined world of Middle Earth, first introduced in *The Hobbit* and further expounded in *The Lord of the Rings* trilogy and *The Silmarillion,* retains a strong appeal to child and adult readers alike. So powerful was Tolkien's hold over readers who entered his world of hobbits, elves, dwarves, and dragons that he is credited with inspiring many fantasy writers to create their own worlds via trilogies and sprawling epics, attempts that are now practically *de rigueur* in the genre. Drawing considerable inspiration from Norse mythology and *Beowulf,* Middle Earth is a world complete with its own history, myths, legends, epics, and heroes. *The Hobbit*'s structure draws a good deal from the fairy stories and fantasies that Tolkien loved. According to Augustus M. Kolich in *Dictionary of Literary Biography,* the book's structure demonstrates that fairy tales are "worthy of serious attention," as Tolkien implies in his essay "On Fairy Stories." "Fairy tales were

fantasy," Kolich argued, "allowing their hearers or readers to move from the details of their limited experience to 'survey the depths of space and time.'. . . The successful writer of the fairy story 'makes a Secondary World which your mind can enter. Inside it, what he relates is 'true': it accords with the laws of that world.'" Reviewers have further remarked that *The Hobbit*'s Middle Earth and its inhabitants seem more real than many other children's—or adult's—literary inventions. Writing in *Mythlore,* Mitzi M. Brunsdale noted that Tolkien's work, starting with *The Hobbit* but including the later trilogy, "exhibited a universe that seemed to exist in history rather than one merely an invention of Faerie." Owing perhaps to the believability of the fantastic creatures and settings, reviewers such as John Rowe Townsend, in his *Written for Children,* continue to celebrate *The Hobbit* as "[t]he most remarkable fantasy of the 1930s" and, as Anne T. Eaton termed the work, "a glorious account of a magnificent adventure."

Biographical Information

The eldest of two sons, Tolkien was born in 1892 in

Bloemfontein, South Africa, where his father worked as a bank manager. In 1895, his mother Mabel, brother Hilary, and young John moved to England, near Birmingham, after John began experiencing health problems. His father stayed behind, planning to join his family in a year or so, but died of rheumatic fever in 1896 before rejoining his family. Tolkien's mother introduced her eldest son to two of his strongest loves—the Catholic Church and the study of languages. In 1904, however, Mabel died from diabetes, leaving her two sons in the care of her friend, Father Francis Xavier Morgan. Morgan provided Tolkien with a father figure and helped finance his studies at King Edward's School in Birmingham and later at Oxford University. Tolkien's interest in languages flourished at King Edward's and he added to his curriculum not only the mandatory Latin and Greek, but also Welsh, Old and Middle English, and Old Norse. This burgeoning love of language would have an enormous impact on Tolkien's future as a writer. While at school, he also met his future wife, aspiring pianist Edith Mary Bratt, who was five years his senior and an orphan. Fearful their relationship would interfere with Tolkien's studies, Morgan forbade Tolkien from continuing his relationship with Bratt, who was not a Catholic. Tolkien uneasily complied and did not communicate with Bratt for three years. On his twenty-first birthday, however, he proposed to her and the couple was married in 1916. Meanwhile Tolkien began his studies in comparative philology at Exeter College, Oxford University. He graduated with honors in 1915 and joined the army during World War I, although illness kept him out of combat much of the time.

When the war ended, Tolkien took a position with the Oxford English Dictionary for a couple of years and then at Leeds University as an Appointed Reader in English Language before being appointed professor of Anglo-Saxon at Oxford University. During this time, Tolkien started writing *The Book of Lost Tales,* which later developed into *The Silmarillion,* published posthumously in 1977. By that time, he and Edith had three sons—John, Michael, and Christopher—to whom he wrote "Father Christmas" letters, fictional accounts of a harried Father Christmas and various North Pole activities. In 1926 Tolkien joined The Coalbiters (later The Inklings), a small group of Oxford professors who would meet to discuss their respective works-in-progress; C. S. Lewis was also a member. In 1929 his daughter, Priscilla, was born, and about one year later Tolkien started writing his first children's book, *The Hobbit, or There and Back Again,* which he did not finish until 1936. "Tolkien often recorded how he began the story," wrote Douglas A. Anderson in his introduction to *The Annotated Hobbit.* "One hot summer day [Tolkien] was sitting at his desk, correcting student's examination papers. . . . He told an interviewer, 'One of the candidates had mercifully left one of the pages with no writing on it, which is the best thing that can possibly happen to an examiner, and I wrote on it, "In a hole there lived a hobbit." Names always generate a story in my mind: eventually I thought I'd better find out what hobbits were like.'" Tolkien began using the hobbit—now named

Bilbo Baggins—as the basis for stories. Much like his Father Christmas letters, Tolkien's initial audience consisted solely of his children. In a 1964 letter published in *The Letters of J. R. R. Tolkien,* he once explained: "I had the habit while my children were still young of inventing and telling orally, sometimes of writing down, 'children's stories' for their private amusement. *The Hobbit* was intended to be one of them."

Tolkien's audience would not be limited for long, however, and *The Hobbit* was published in September, 1937. The book encountered almost immediate success, selling out the first edition before Christmas. Certainly aiding the book's sales were glowing reviews by C. S. Lewis—first in *The Times* and then in *The Times Literary Supplement*—who had seen a completed typescript of an early draft in 1932. Tolkien quickly started work on a sequel; however, it took seventeen years before the hobbits returned in *The Lord of the Rings,* a trilogy consisting of *The Fellowship of the Ring, The Two Towers,* and *The Return of the King.* Though his bibliography contains a great many works, including the posthumously-published *The Silmarillion,* a collection of *The Father Christmas Letters,* and scholarly works on both *Beowulf* and Middle English, the four books—*The Hobbit* and *The Lord of the Rings* trilogy—represent the heart of Tolkien's literary accomplishments. His wife died in 1971; Tolkien died in England on September 2, 1973, of a perforated ulcer.

Plot and Major Characteristics

In an early review published anonymously in *The Times,* C. S. Lewis characterized *The Hobbit* as a book in which "a number of good things, never before united, have come together: a fund of humour, an understanding of children, and a happy fusion of the scholars with the poet's grasp of mythology." The influence of texts that Tolkien studied throughout his life, especially *Beowulf* and Northern epics, can be seen in *The Hobbit*'s adventurous episodes and in the nature of the tale, a quest by, in this case, hobbits, for "gold, revenge, justice, and death." In the story, Bilbo Baggins lives a quiet, comfortable, and respectable existence in a hobbit hole, smoking his pipe and drinking pots of tea. His home is not luxurious, nor is it dirty, damp, nor bare, but a many-roomed underground home with "panelled walls, and floors tiled and carpeted, provided with polished chairs, and lots and lots of pegs for hats and coats—the hobbit was fond of visitors." One day Bilbo is unwillingly summoned by the wizard, Gandalf the Grey, to join a party of dwarves searching for a long-lost treasure stolen by Smaug the dragon. Although the dwarves hesitate to accept the hobbit, the equally reluctant Bilbo proves to be a valuable companion, as he gets the dwarves out of many mishaps, and seemingly has the luck of providence on his side. Along the way, Bilbo discovers a magical ring in a goblin tunnel, thus establishing the link with *The Lord of the Rings* trilogy; however, it later proved necessary for Tolkien to rewrite chapter five in order to establish continuity between the two works over the significance of the powerful ring. A new edition of *The Hobbit* incorporating the revised chapter was published in 1951. Bilbo eventually brings the dwarves to their treasure, only to find that the dragon has died while attacking a nearby town. Having seen the results of greed, Bilbo gives up his own share of the gold and he and Gandalf journey home.

Although *The Hobbit*'s legend-like adventures, "deft scholarship," and mythological elements have found favor among adult audiences, it is generally believed that Tolkien originally wrote the story as a "tea time read" for his children. Critics have noted that this is especially apparent when the narrator breaks into asides during the action to directly address the reader. While Tolkien grew to dislike these narrative interruptions—they seemed to him too much like "talking down" to his young audience—he could not very likely remove them without debilitating the novel. The obtrusive narrator is not the only evidence of the tale's oral-storytelling heritage; throughout *The Hobbit*, sound effects are embedded within the prose and the poetry. Paul H. Kocher, in *J. R. R. Tolkien: Master of Middle-earth*, catalogued a few such sounds: "Bilbo's doorbell rings *ding-dong-a-ling-dang*; Gandalf's smoke rings go *pop!*; the fire from his wand explodes with a *poof*; Bombur falls out of a tree *plop* onto the ground; Bilbo falls *splash!* into the water, and so on at every turn."

Kocher continued with the poetry: "One prime example is the song of the goblins underground after their capture of Bilbo andthe dwarves with its *Clash, crash! Crush, smash!* and *Swish, smack! Whip crack* and *Ho, ho, my lad*. The elves' barrel-rolling song has all the appropriate noises, from *roll-roll-rolling* to *splash plump! And down they bump!*" Furthermore, hobbits, diminutive in stature, are frequently referred to as childlike. As Tolkien describes: "Hobbits are (or were) small people, smaller than dwarves—and they have no beards—but were very much larger than Lilliputians." Children can readily identify with hobbit Bilbo Baggins and his initial hesitancy and subsequent maturation, both physically, as he learns to throw stones and move about quietly, and psychologically, as he develops the inner fortitude to see himself through to the end of the adventure.

Despite the appeal that the book has held for more than fifty years, *The Hobbit* does not enjoy as positive a critical reception as the trilogy it preceded, owing perhaps to its status as a children's book or to the trilogy's sprawling epic look and feel. Celebrating the fiftieth anniversary of *The Hobbit*, Brian Aldiss and David Wingrove, writing in *Punch*, characterized *The Hobbit* as a book that "lies in the shadow of the greater work," referring to *The Lord of the Rings*. In *The Master of Middle-earth*, Kocher wrote, "[M]any potential readers approaching Tolkien for the first time have inferred that they must tackle *The Hobbit* first. Unfortunately that work often puzzles, sometimes repels outright." Algis Budrys, reviewing *The Hobbit* in *The Magazine of Fantasy and Science Fiction*, dismissed Tolkien with a backhanded complement as "[t]he most successful gifted amateur of our time." Indeed, even Tolkien himself did not generate a great deal of critical enthusiasm when the subject is *The Hobbit*, as he once explained, "*The Hobbit* was written in what I should now regard as bad style, as if one were talking to children. There's nothing my children loathed more. They taught me a lesson. Anything that in any way marked out *The Hobbit* as for children instead of just for people, they disliked—instinctively. I did too, now that I think about it. All this 'I won't tell you any more, you think about it' stuff. Oh no, they loathe it; it's awful." Throughout all of the criticism and ugly-duckling comparisons to *The Lord of the Rings*, however, *The Hobbit* retains a substantial presence in both children's and adult's literary circles, owing not only to its storytelling prowess, but also to its (or, perhaps, readers') adaptability as the years pass. As Lewis remarked in *The Times Literary Supplement* shortly after *The Hobbit*'s publication, "[I]t must be understood that this is a children's book only in the sense that the first of many readings can be undertaken in the nursery."

Awards

The Hobbit, or There and Back Again received *The New York Herald Tribune* Children's Spring Book Festival Award in 1938.

COMMENTARY

The Times Literary Supplement

SOURCE: A review of *The Hobbit, or There and Back Again*, in *The Times Literary Supplement*, No. 1861, October 2, 1937, p. 714.

[The following review, originally published anonymously, was later attributed to C. S. Lewis.]

The publishers claim that **The Hobbit,** though very unlike *Alice* [*in Wonderland*], resembles it in being the work of a professor at play. A more important truth is that both belong to a very small class of books which have nothing in common save that each admits us to a world of its own—a world that seems to have been going on before we stumbled into it but which, once found by the right reader, becomes indispensable to him. Its place is with *Alice, Flatland, Phantastes, The Wind in the Willows*.

To define the world of **The Hobbit** is, of course, impossible, because it is new. You cannot anticipate it before you go there, as you cannot forget it once you have gone. The author's admirable illustrations and maps of Mirkwood and Goblingate and Esgaroth give one an inkling—and so do the names of dwarf and dragon that catch our eyes as we first ruffle the pages. But there are dwarfs and dwarfs, and no common recipe for children's stories will give you creatures so rooted in their own soil and history as those of Professor Tolkien—who obviously knows much more about them than he needs for this tale. Still less will the common recipe prepare us for the curious shift from the matter-of-fact beginnings of his story ("hobbits are small people, smaller than dwarfs—and they have no beards—but very much larger than Lilliputians") to the saga-like tone of the later chapters ("It is in my mind to ask what share of their inheritance you would have paid had you found the hoard unguarded"). You must read for yourself to find out how inevitable the change is and how it keeps pace with the hero's journey. Though all is marvellous, nothing is arbitrary: all the inhabitants of Wilderland seem to have the same unquestionable right to their existence as those of our own world, though the fortunate child who meets them will have no notion—and his unlearned elders not much more—of the deep sources in our blood and tradition from which they spring.

For it must be understood that this is a children's book only in the sense that the first of many readings can be undertaken in the nursery. *Alice* is read gravely by children and with laughter by grown-ups; *The Hobbit,* on the other hand, will be funniest to its youngest readers, and only years later, at a tenth or twentieth reading, will they begin to realize what deft scholarship and profound reflection have gone to make everything in it so ripe, so friendly, and in its own way so true. Prediction is dangerous: but *The Hobbit* may well prove a classic.

The Times (London)

SOURCE: A review of *The Hobbit, or There and Back Again,* in *The Times (London),* October 8, 1937, p. 20.

[*The following review, originally published anonymously, was later attributed to C. S. Lewis.*]

All who love that kind of children's book which can be read and re-read by adults should take note that a new star has appeared in this constellation. If you like the adventures of Ratty and Mole you will like *The Hobbit,* by J. R. R. Tolkien. If, in those adventures, you prized the solidity of the social and geographical context in which your small friends moved, you will like *The Hobbit* even better. The hobbit himself, Mr. Bilbo Baggins, is as prosaic as Mole, but fate sets him wandering among dwarfs and elves, over goblin mountains, in search of dragon-guarded gold. Every one he meets can be enjoyed in the nursery; but to the trained eye some characters will seem almost mythopoeic—notably lugubrious gollum the fish-man, and the ferociously benevolent Beorn, half man, half bear, in his garden buzzing with bees.

The truth is that in this book a number of good things, never before united, have come together: a fund of humour, an understanding of children, and a happy fusion of the scholar's with the poet's grasp of mythology.

On the edge of a valley one of Professor Tolkien's characters can pause and say: "It smells like elves." It may be years before we produce another author with such a nose for an elf. The Professor has the air of inventing nothing. He has studied trolls and dragons at first hand and describes them with that fidelity which is worth oceans of glib "originality." The maps (with runes) are excellent, and will be found thoroughly reliable by young travellers in the same region.

Eleanor Graham

SOURCE: A review of *The Hobbit, or There and Back Again,* in *The Junior Bookshelf,* Vol. 2, No. 2, December, 1937, pp. 93, 95.

The Hobbit is a strange book. It has in it the makings of a very good story, or perhaps a book of short stories for children, but it is marred, in my opinion, by some reflection of the author's attitude to the world. A sort of "Aunt Sally" spirit replaces the benevolence which is notable in the most loved books for children. Instead of natural obstacles in the path of achievement, the journey of the Hobbit and his companions is interrupted by obstructions which somehow give the effect of deliberately intentional setbacks and not of natural developments.

Nothing could be more attractive than the opening picture of the Hobbit himself and his home with its "perfectly round door, like a porthole, painted green with a shiny yellow brass knob in the exact middle." He was a friendly sort of creature who enjoyed hot buttered toast with his tea and lots of bacon and eggs and coffee for breakfast. His comfortable life was broken in on, however, by a visitor called Gandalf, who might be called the spirit of adventure except that the courageous freedom of real adventure doesn't appear. There is instead an uneasy sort of compulsion and the Hobbit never really resigns himself to his exile or his long journey.

While making these criticisms, I must also say that there is a strong sense of reality in the writing and real distinction, and that those people who like it, will like it very much indeed. They will enjoy the involved plot and the rather frightening scenes and the ogre-ish atmosphere of much of the story.

Richard Hughes

SOURCE: A review of *The Hobbit, or There and Back Again,* in *The New Statesman and Nation*, Vol. 14, December 4, 1937, pp. 944, 946.

[I] am tempted to say that all children will enjoy *The Hobbit.* That of course would be nonsense. But a very great many will; and though the ages for which it is written range roughly from six to nine years, you may expect very considerable extensions at both ends of that period. I myself have tried it on a four-year-old with marked success; and I have tried it on myself with marked success also. The author is a professor of Anglo-Saxon; and because the author of "Alice" was also a professor the publishers are tempted to compare the two books. Actually, they are wholly dissimilar. There is no philosophical fantasy in *The Hobbit.* But they are alike in this, that in both cases the author is so saturated in his life-study that it waters his imagination with living springs. Professor Tolkien is saturated in Nordic mythology: so saturated that he does not rehash this mythology and serve it up at second-hand, rather he contributes to it at first hand: and thus his wholly original story of adventure among goblins, elves and dragons, instead of being a *tour-de-force,* a separate creation of his own, gives rather the impression of a well-informed glimpse into the life of a wide other-world; a world wholly real, and with a quite matter-of-fact, supernatural natural-history of its own. It is a triumph that the genus *Hobbit,* which he himself has invented, rings just as real as the time-hallowed genera of Goblin, Troll, and Elf.

One word of warning, though. Some adults may think parts of this book rather terrifying for bedside reading (although, however fearful the adventure, things always turn out right in the end). I myself think this caution is a mistaken one. For a child has a natural capacity for terror which it is next to impossible to curtail; and if you withhold from him such proper objects of terror as goblins, trolls, and dragons, he will work himself just as frantic over an odd-shaped bed-post—or the overhearing of such a frightful piece of news as that *there is a barrister pleading in the court.*

J. R. R. Tolkien

SOURCE: "On Fairy Stories," in *The Horn Book Magazine,* Vol. XXXIX, No. 5, October, 1963, p. 457.

[The following excerpt is from Tolkien's essay, "On Fairy Stories," originally published by Oxford University Press in 1938.]

If fairy-story as a kind is worth reading at all it is worthy to be written for and read by adults. They will, of course, put more in and get more out than children can. Then, as a branch of a genuine art, children may hope to get fairy-stories fit for them to read and yet within their measure; as they may hope to get suitable introductions to poetry, history, and the sciences.

Very well, then. If adults are to read fairy-stories as a natural branch of literature—neither playing at being children, nor pretending to be choosing for children, nor being boys who would not grow up—what are the values and functions of this kind? That is, I think, the last and most important question. I have already hinted at some of my answers. First of all: if written with art, the prime value of fairy-stories will simply be that value which, as literature, they share with other literary forms. But fairy-stories offer also, in a peculiar degree or mode,

these things: Fantasy, Recovery, Escape, Consolation, all things of which children have, as a rule, less need than older people. . . .

Fantasy is a natural human activity. It certainly does not destroy or even insult Reason; and it does not either blunt the appetite for, nor obscure the perception of, scientific verity. On the contrary. The keener and the clearer is the reason, the better fantasy will it make. If men were ever in a state in which they did not want to know or could not perceive truth (facts or evidence), then fantasy would languish until they were cured. If they ever get into that state (it would not seem at all impossible), Fantasy will perish, and become Morbid Delusion.

For creative Fantasy is founded upon the hard recognition that things are so in the world as it appears under the sun; on a recognition of fact, but not a slavery to it. So upon logic was founded the nonsense that displays itself in the tales and rhymes of Lewis Carroll. If men really could not distinguish between frogs and men, fairy-stories about frog-kings would not have arisen. . . .

Fantasy is made out of the Primary World, but a good craftsman loves his material, and has a knowledge and feeling for clay, stone, and wood which only the art of making can give. By the forging of Gram cold iron was revealed; by the making of Pegasus horses were ennobled; in the Trees of the Sun and Moon root and stock, flower and fruit are manifested in glory.

And actually fairy-stories deal largely, or (the better ones) mainly, with simple or fundamental things, untouched by fantasy, but these simplicities are made all the more luminous by their setting. For the story-maker who allows himself to be "free with" nature can be her lover not her slave. It was in fairy-stories that I first divined the potency of the words, and the wonder of the things, such as stone, and wood, and iron; tree and grass; house and fire; bread and wine.

May Lamberton Becker

SOURCE: A review of *The Hobbit, or There and Back Again,* in *The New York Herald Tribune Books,* February 20, 1938, p. 7.

At this time of writing, still under the spell of the story, I cannot bend my mind to ask myself whether our American children will like it. My impulse is to say if they don't, so much the worse for them.

For the world from which, on closing the book, one emerges, is peopled thickly with tribes, not one of them human and each with its own sharply defined characteristics to which each specimen is consistently true. That is the reassuring quality of all true fairy tales like this. A goblin, for instance, is always a goblin from head to feet and you know on which end to stamp to get results: George Macdonald told us when we were little. Through other such sources we learned no trolls were ever to be trusted, even the one-headed ones, but if you could keep them above ground till after daybreak you could strike them with a word into perpetual stone. On the other hand, dwarfs are friendly, good miners and workers in metal; there were many friendly tribes in our forests and the unfriendly ones were always at our mercy because we knew their vulnerable points. The most timid of children go not only unscathed but unscarred through a true fairy tale; they know the right magic, their nimble minds have Jack's way with giants and other one-track folk; they are safe.

So a child who goes with the hobbit—a creature new to folklore but familiar from the first—on a crusade against a proud and greedy dragon, even though he passes every night, as his mother reads out a chapter, through scenes of immediate peril, will sleep in reasonable peace. His dreams will not be haunted by clutching fingers of pursuit; he will be safe; he is on the good side. Into these pages a world is packed, an odyssey compressed, as adventures on the road to the dragon's ill-got treasure thicken. I do not know how our children will like a story so close-packed, one of whose chapters would make a book elsewhere; they may think they are getting too much for their money. But dwarfs have come this year into fashion in America; perhaps these will benefit from the Disney boom.

Like the learned Charles Dodgson, the author is an Oxford professor, his specialty being Anglo-Saxon; like "Alice," the story has unmistakable signs of having been told to intelligent children. But its style is not like Lewis Carroll's; it is much more like Dunsany's.

Anne T. Eaton

SOURCE: A review of *The Hobbit, or There and Back Again,* in *The New York Times Book Review,* March 13, 1938, p. 12.

This is one of the most freshly original and delightfully imaginative books for children that have appeared in many a long day. Like *Alice in Wonderland,* it comes from Oxford University, where the author is Professor of Anglo-Saxon, and like Lewis Carroll's story, it was written for children that the author knew (in this case his own four children) and then inevitably found a larger audience.

The period of the story is between the age of Faerie and the dominion of men. To an adult who reads of Smaug the Dragon and his hoard, won by the dwarves but claimed also by the Lake men and the Elven King, there may come the thought of how legend and tradition and the beginning of history meet and mingle, but for the reader from 8 to 12 *The Hobbit* is a glorious account of a magnificent adventure, filled with suspense and seasoned with a quiet humor that is irresistible.

Hobbits are (or were) small people, smaller than

dwarves—and they have no beards—but very much larger than lilliputians. There is little or no magic about them, except the ordinary everyday sort which helps them to disappear quietly and quickly when large, stupid folk like you and me come blundering along, making a noise like elephants which they can hear a mile off. They are inclined to be fat in the stomach; they dress in bright colors, chiefly green and yellow; wear no shoes because their feet grow natural leathery soles and thick, warm brown hair; have long, clever, brown fingers, good-natured faces and laugh deep, fruity laughs (especially after dinner, which they have twice a day, when they can get it).

Bilbo Baggins was a hobbit whom we find living in his comfortable, not to say luxurious, hobbit hole, for it was not a dirty, wet hole, nor yet a bare, sandy one, but inside its round, green door, like a porthole, there were bedrooms, bathrooms, cellars, pantries, kitchens and dining rooms, all in the best of hobbit taste. All Bilbo asked was to be left in peace in this residence, known as "Bag-End," for hobbits are naturally homekeeping folk, and Bilbo had no desire for adventure. That is to say, the Baggins' side of him had not, but Bilbo's mother had been a Took, and in the past the Tooks had intermarried with a fairy family. It was the Took strain that made the little hobbit, almost against his will, respond to the summons of Gandalf the Wizard to join the dwarves in their attempt to recover the treasure which Smaug the dragon had stolen from their forefathers. Bilbo has an engaging, as well as an entirely convincing personality; frankly scornful of the heroic (except in his most Tookish moments), he nevertheless plays his part in emergencies with a dogged courage and resourcefulness that make him in the end the real leader of the expedition.

After the dwarves and Bilbo have passed "The Last Homely House" their way led through Wilderland, over the Misty Mountains and through forests that suggest those of William Morris's prose romances. Like Morris's countries, Wilderland is Faerie, yet it has an earthly quality, the scent of trees, drenching rains and the smell of woodfires.

The tale is packed with valuable hints for the dragon killer and adventurer in Faerie. Plenty of scaly monsters have been slain in legend and folktale, but never for modern readers has so complete a guide to dragon ways been provided. Here, too, are set down clearly the distinguishing characteristics of dwarves, goblins, trolls and elves. The account of the journey is so explicit that we can readily follow the progress of the expedition. In this we are aided by the admirable maps provided by the author, which, in their detail and imaginative consistency, suggest Bernard Sleigh's *Mappe of Fairyland.*

The songs of the dwarves and elves are real poetry, and since the author is fortunate enough to be able to make his own drawings, the illustrations are a perfect accompaniment to the text. Boys and girls from 8 years on have already given *The Hobbit* an enthusiastic welcome, but this is a book with no age limits. All those, young or old, who love a fine adventurous tale, beautifully told, will take *The Hobbit* to their hearts.

The Christian Science Monitor

SOURCE: A review of *The Hobbit, or There and Back Again,* in *The Christian Science Monitor,* Vol. XXX, No. 105, March 31, 1938, p. 13.

A priceless tale of wonder and enchantment which has just made its way from England to America, is *The Hobbit,* by J. R. R. Tolkien.

When Mr. Bilbo Baggins, of Bag-End under the Hill, was chosen by Gandalf, the wizard, to be the fourteenth for luck to go on anadventurous expedition with the dwarves—Thorin and Company—to recover ancestral treasure from Smaug the fire-belching dragon who was guarding the plunder at the deepest roots of the far distant Lonely Mountain, we find ourselves introduced to the hero while he is the bewildered host at a veritable mad tea-party.

Gandalf had put strange marks over the round green door of the hobbit hole, and tales and adventures sprouted up all over the place, as was usual wherever he went in the most extraordinary fashion. Extraordinary is a mild word to express the fashion, however, in which the hobbit found himself somewhat reluctantly involved, for the dwarves wanted no less than an expert treasure-hunter for the job they had on foot.

The expedition almost departed without the hobbit but, fortunately enough for the dwarves, he reached the appointed place in time. In the encounters with the trolls, elves and goblins in the escape from the lake monster and later from the wild wangs, and in the hurried journey from elfin dungeon caves where magic closed the gates, and in the final success of obtaining inside information about Smaug, and his piles of treasure, the little hobbit with his heroism and resourceful wit became the mighty treasure-hunter like the mighty warriors of old, "Forever at your services" thus did the dwarves acclaim their imitable champion.

All who enjoy a well wrought tale of originality and imagination will revel in the adventures of the hobbit.

The Saturday Review of Literature

SOURCE: A review of *The Hobbit, or There and Back Again,* in *The Saturday Review of Literature,* Vol. XVII, No. 23, April 2, 1938, pp. 28, 30.

The Hobbit: whose little hobbit people and their strange land is as remarkable a work of imaginative literature for children to have come from a professor of Anglo-Saxon at Oxford as was *Alice in Wonderland* to have come from such a mathematician as the Reverend Dodgson. *The Hobbit* is both prose and poetry and, above all, gorgeous fancy.

The Booklist

SOURCE: A review of *The Hobbit, or There and Back Again,* in *The Booklist,* Vol. 34, No. 16, April 15, 1938, p. 304.

Small Mr. Bilbo Baggins, the hobbit, who liked his hobbit-hole and his singing tea kettle, is inveigled by Gandalf the wizard into an expedition to help the dwarfs win back their treasure from Smaug, the dragon who guards it. Grim and even horrible adventures beset them and pleasant ones, too. The well-sustained plot maintains its interest in spite of its length and the style is easy yet properly serious. The interspersed songs really sing. The book will appeal to children who like tales of goblins and trolls and adventures, and will be enjoyed by many others if read to them by their parents. An integral part of the story are the black-and-white illustrations and three colored ones. Appeared first in England.

Mary R. Lucas

SOURCE: A review of *The Hobbit, or There and Back Again,* in *Library Journal,* Vol. 63, May 1, 1938, p. 385.

"Its place is with *Alice* and *The Wind in the Willows.*" That statement needs considerable amplification, it seems to me. The book has some of the same underlying adult philosophy as the two mentioned. The Hobbit, a new creation—neither elf nor dwarf—is to the adult mind an excellent example of the smug, self-satisfied middle class individual, who is suddenly dragged out of his complacent way of living and thrust into adventures which demand the use of his brain. This upsets him. Such is the Hobbit to the adult, and believe it or no—he is called Mr. Bilbo Baggins. To children, the Hobbit is something else. He is a rather interesting small person, who lives in a delightful manner in a hole in the ground. One day the Wizard comes along and by his spells, forces Bilbo Baggins, the Hobbit, to go with the dwarfs to recover a hoard of long forgotten gold. Their adventures and mishaps are numerous, too numerous in fact for really enjoyable reading. The book would be better read aloud in small doses, or the child should be advised to read it that way, himself. It will have a limited appeal unless properly introduced and even then will be best liked by those children whose imagination is alert.

The Catholic World

SOURCE: A review of *The Hobbit, or There and Back Again,* in *The Catholic World,* Vol. 147, July, 1938, p. 507.

Do you know the difference between a goblin and an elf, a dwarf and a hobbit, a troll and a lilliputian? If not, we would advise you to read this book to your boy of nine. Bilbo Baggins, the hobbit hero of this entrancing tale, leads a number of his friends the dwarfs on an adventurous journey to the Mystic Mountain, over enchanted forests and rivers in search of the enormous treasure of gold and gems guarded by the cruel dragon Smaug. More than once disaster would have been the lot of the venturous fourteen, were it not for the magic wand of the wizard Gandalf and the magic ring of Bilbo. We guarantee that you will enjoy this stirring tale as much as your boy. Make him solve the riddles of Gollum and Bilbo. They alone are worth the price of the book.

Marcus S. Crouch

SOURCE: "Another Don in Wonderland," in *The Junior Bookshelf,* Vol. 14, No. 2, March, 1950, pp. 50-3.

Professor J. R. R. Tolkien is no joke, as anyone who has grappled with *Beowulf,* not to mention *Gawaine and the Green Knight,* must know. After a career of very great distinction this 57-year-old scholar is now Merton Professor of English Language and Literature in the University of Oxford. His published works are considerable both in number and in weight of scholarship; for the most part they suggest a bias towards the earliest period of our literature and to the unwritten lore which preceded the written word. A significant pointer towards his private interests is the essay **"On Fairy Stories"** which is included in the presentation volume to Charles Williams.

Any consideration of Professor Tolkien's work in the pages of *The Junior Bookshelf* would have been a gross impertinence, but for the kind of accident which sent a Don of an earlier generation sculling down stream to Wonderland. A young family had to be entertained, and to do this Professor Tolkien dipped into an imagination deepened and enriched by a lifetime of study in the literature and legend of the Dark Ages. The result was *The Hobbit,* which was published in 1937. The passage of a dozen years, and the recent publication of a new, and slighter, work of imagination, will perhaps justify some reconsideration of this most remarkable book.

The Hobbit had a mixed reception, as do most books of marked originality. It has been, I believe, no more than a moderate success in the bookshops, and librarians who have had the courage to buy it in suitable quantities cannot claim that it rivals the popularity of current mass-produced goods. It seems to me, however, to possess in a high degree some of the qualities which make for endurance. I know of no children's book published in the last twenty-five years of which I could more confidently predict that it will be read in the twenty-first century.

First, *The Hobbit* is a great story. There are plenty of books which are strings of exciting incidents. In few do

all the episodes add up to one tremendous total. *The Hobbit* is a very long story, but only the most blundering of editorial blue-pencils could make it shorter. There are no digressions. The suspense is handled in masterly fashion. With what architectural skill is each episode fitted into place, interesting in detail and still contributing to, and not detracting from, the general effect. Professor Tolkien has followed the model of Homer and the author of *Beowulf* and built outwards from the middle. His book is in effect a Northern epic. Like the best of such stories, and like so many of the finest children's books, it is the narrative of a quest. The dwarves set out in quest of gold, revenge, justice, and death, all of which objectives they attain. It is the core of the book's genius that their nobility and greed, selfishness and courage are set against the matter-of-fact commonplace of the Hobbit, Mr. Bilbo Baggins, surely one of the most endearing of the creations of modern fiction. Mr. Baggins is a lover of home and comfort who is taken out into the hard and comfortless world; he is a man of peace who goes from one battle and peril to another; he is the common man who beats the politicians and strategists at their own game. There is no hero like the hero malgré lui, and that is the secret of the Hobbit's charm.

Who can say when memory ends and invention begins? This book is the product of an imaginative conception of life in the far distant past. It may have been written for fun and to amuse children; the writer may not believe in his own invention but the book nevertheless carries conviction. For the period of reading, the world in which these dwarves plot and fight to regain and retain their gold is a living world. The reason for this mastery of conviction is, I imagine, that the book is the work of a man whose natural powers of invention have been reinforced by vast stores of learning. Professor Tolkien knows what men have thought and written about the forces of nature from the earliest times; for him the words "elf," "dwarf," "goblin," are not vague synonyms for indistinct airy-fairy creatures; they are precise terms connoting beings of clearly defined characteristics. So throughout the book, there is no loose thinking or writing. The result is a picture of a world immeasurably remote but seen clearly and in detail. There are numerous examples of this conviction, none, I think, more moving than that interview between the hobbit and a wet, cold, colourless, primeval being at the root of the mountain and the ancient and magical riddle-game which they play there. Is this writing for children? The psychologist may not agree; I feel that it is the kind of magical story which has been told to children since the beginning of the world.

Warmth and nobility and lofty imagination are not common qualities of modern writers of fantasy, most of whom prefer to chase the frail moth of whimsy. These qualities, however, produce in *The Hobbit* a story which is profoundly imaginative and yet firmly based on truth. It is a convincing answer to those who find fantasy "escapist." Here is no escape from, but an interpretation of, reality.

It will, I hope, be clear that I think this a very fine book indeed. It is likely to be an isolated phenomenon. The professional writer's job is to produce a regular supply of books and to maintain a high standard throughout. . . . Professor Tolkien is, in this field, an inspired amateur, and I cannot but hope that he will not be cajoled against his judgment into the publication of a series of books for children. On the strength of one book, his position is secure. I for one am abundantly satisfied.

Marcus S. Crouch

SOURCE: "Renaissance," in *Treasure Seekers and Borrowers: Children's Books in Britain, 1900-1960,* The Library Association, 1962, pp. 55-86.

The Hobbit was written for children (the author devised it originally for the amusement of his own family) and taken over by adults. This was partly because J. R. R. Tolkien, having undertaken his story lightly, seems to have been taken by surprise by it and to have found successive layers of meaning in it. This is not uncommon—there are depths in *Alice* and *The Wind in the Willows*—but only Tolkien has made his children's book the starting point of a great fantastic and romantic allegory [*The Lord of the Rings,* 1954-55]. *The Hobbit, or There and Back Again* appeared in 1937. It was the work of a Professor of Anglo-Saxon at Oxford. Tolkien had made the early literature and still earlier traditions of England (and the countries from which the English came) particularly his own, and it was his scholarship that helped to give authority to his story about the hobbit's quest, for he could define with great precision the differences between dwarves, elves, goblins and trolls and describe the society in which each lived. *The Hobbit* carries great conviction; it reads more like history than romance. It also blends the heroic and the homely with extraordinary skill. Bilbo Baggins, the Hobbit, who liked comfort and staying at home but who became a great traveller and nearly a hero, is a most subtle character. So too is the dragon Smaug who stood guard over the treasure of the dwarves. *The Hobbit* is an exciting story of adventure, a tragedy with comic episodes, a picaresque romance with strands of magic in it, an historical novel about the remote past which, by the author's craft, becomes more real than the present. It is better to use superlatives sparingly, but this, by any standards, is a great book.

The Use of English

SOURCE: A review of *The Hobbit, or There and Back Again,* in *The Use of English,* Vol. XIV, No. 3, Spring, 1963, p. 198.

Professor Tolkien's *The Hobbit* is suitable for children of all ages from eight to hundred-and-eight. Mr. Bilbo Baggins, like Alice, Pooh, and Toad, is a character of whom one can never tire; with him and the twelve dwarfs we are transported by Gandalf the magician over the Misty Mountains to a strange land of trolls, goblins and Waugs to win back the treasure of gold from Smaug the Dragon. My favourite chapter is 'Riddles in the Dark' in which Bilbo has to play the ancient fairy-game of exchanging riddles with the absurdly comic monster Gollum to avoid being eaten by him. This enchanting tale is ideal to read to young children and is also very suitable for class-reading aloud.

Paul H. Kocher

SOURCE: "The Hobbit," in *Master of Middle-earth: The Fiction of J. R. R. Tolkien,* Houghton Mifflin Company, 1972, pp. 19-33.

The beginning of wisdom in understanding *The Hobbit* is to think of Tolkien, or another adult, in a chair by the fireside telling the story to a semicircle of children sitting on the floor facing him. From the opening paragraphs hardly a page goes by in which the narrator does not address the children directly in the first person singular. Since the breed of hobbits has just sprung freshly minted from his brain, he loses no time in telling his young listeners about how they look and behave, notably their shyness "when large stupid folk like you and me come blundering along," and he ends his description by, "Now you know enough to go on with. As I was saying . . ." Sometimes he uses the direct address technique to create anticipation, as in introducing Gandalf: "Gandalf! If you had heard only a quarter of what I have heard about him, and I have only heard very little of all there is to hear, you would be prepared for any sort of remarkable tale." Sometimes his remarks to the child audience take on a genial, joking tone, as in pointing out the flaw in Bilbo's plan for freeing the captive dwarves by putting them into barrels (his inability to put himself into one): "Most likely you saw it some time ago and have been laughing at him; but I don't suppose you would have done half as well yourselves in his place." Then, there are jocular interjections of no special moment, but aimed at maintaining a playful intimacy: "If you want to know what *cram* is, I can only say that I don't know the recipe; but it is biscuitish . . ."

Tolkien also makes the technique work for him expositorily in making clear to the youngsters important shifts in the plot sequence. Normally he describes every scene from Bilbo's point of view, and describes none in which Bilbo himself is not present. . . . This care in keeping the plot crystal clear is adapted to the possible squirmings and short attentiveness of the children he is speaking to.

Also for their benefit is Tolkien's method all through *The Hobbit* of prefacing the introduction into the story of each new race with a paragraph or so setting forth in plain words whatever needs to be known about its looks, its habits, its traits, and whether it is good or bad. He has started this practice off with the hobbits. He extends it to trolls, dwarves, goblins, eagles, elves, and lakemen as each of these makes its entry. These little capsules of racial qualities are enlivened usually with personal interjections: "Yes, I am afraid trolls do behave like that, even those with only one head each"; or "Eagles are not kindly birds," but they did come to the rescue of Bilbo's party, and "a very good thing too!" Goblins are wicked and bear a special grudge against dwarves "because of the war which you have heard mentioned, but which does not comeinto this tale." Elves are hunters by starlight at the edges of the wood and are "Good People." After such set pieces no small auditor will be in any doubt as to which people he should cheer for. The whole tale gives him a very firm moral framework by which to judge.

Another minor but persistent device in the manner of its telling likewise is meant to delight childish ears. The prose is full of sound effects, which the eye of the reader might miss but the hearing of the listener would not. Bilbo's doorbell rings *ding-dong-a-ling-dang;* Gandalf's smoke rings go *pop!;* the fire from his wand explodes with a *poof;* Bombur falls out of a tree *plop* onto the ground; Bilbo falls *splash!* into the water, and so on at every turn. Nor are these sound effects limited to the prose. Many of the poems are designed more for onomatopoeic purposes than for content. One prime example is the song of the goblins underground after their capture of Bilbo and the dwarves, with its *Clash, crash! Crush, smash!* and *Swish, smack! Whip crack* and *Ho, ho, my lad.* The elves' barrel-rolling song has all the appropriate noises, from *roll-roll-rolling* to *splash plump!* and *down they bump!* Tolkien knows that up to a certain age children like their stories to be highly audible.

But the question as to what age Tolkien is addressing cannot be long deferred. Probably he himself had no precise answer in mind, but the very nature of the tale and the methods of its telling draw the principal parameters. The children listening to its recital must be young enough not to resent the genial fatherliness of the I-You technique, the encapsulated expositions, sound effects, and the rest, yet old enough to be able to cope with the fairly stiff vocabulary used on many occasions and to make at least something of the maturer elements that keep cropping up in what they hear. For, although *The Hobbit* is predominantly juvenile fiction, it is not all of a piece. Much of the confusion about it arises from the fact that it contains episodes more suited to the adult mind than the child's. . . .

In truth, *The Hobbit* is seldom far from comedy. Tolkien begins by making Bilbo the butt of Gandalf's joke in sending the dwarves unexpectedly to eat up all his food, proceeds on to the lamentable humor of the troll scene, hangs his dwarves up in trees, rolls them in barrels, touches the riddle scene with wit, makes the talk between Bilbo and Smaug triumphantly ridiculous, and tops it all off with Bilbo's return home to find his goods being auctioned off and his reputation for respectable stupidity in ruins. It must be acknowledged that the comedy is not invariably successful and that Tolkien's wry paternal manner of addressing his young listeners

does not always avoid an air of talking down, which sets the teeth on edge. Nevertheless, *The Hobbit* was never meant to be a wholly serious tale, nor his young audience to listen without laughing often. In contradistinction, *The Lord of the Rings* does on occasion evoke smiles, but most of the time its issues go too deep for laughter. In the interval between the two stories the children are sent off to bed and their places taken by grownups, young or young in heart, to hear of a graver sort of quest in which every human life is secretly engaged.

Alan Chedzoy

SOURCE: "Who Reads Tolkien—and Why?," in *The Manchester Guardian,* Vol. 106, No. 5, January 29, 1972, p. 2.

[Critic] John Ezard's article on the work of J. R. R. Tolkien gives some indication of the qualities that promote its popularity, particularly among young people. It has something in common with *The Wind in the Willows,* but is, of course, much more pretentious in its aspirations. What Mr. Ezard does not consider is the significance of its becoming a cult among students.

Children at a pre-adolescent stage need to live partly in fantasy, to create and inhabit imaginary worlds which are both refuges from and responses to their everyday lives. Fiction which helps them to give unconscious symbolisation to their most deeply felt concerns has great value in the reading of the 9-to-12-year-olds, even if it derives from the very conscious working out of adult prejudices as in the C. S. Lewis "Narnia" books.

The Brontë children created such worlds for themselves as an escape from the hopelessness of Haworth, but, of course, they did not choose to remain in them. They then moved on to the fictional exploration of human relationships with all the pains and dangers that these involved.

In my work I meet a number of young students who profess an admiration—even an adulation—for Tolkien's writings. Such students, and I understand that there are many of them in England and the United States, share certain personality traits, in my observations. On the whole they are rather timid in human relationships, rather orthodox in attitude. They prefer escapism to genuine emotional self-exploration. They usually do not like literature; the articulation of mature experience, whether by Austen or Joyce does not appeal to them.

Frequently they are scientists or mathematicians with a preference for crossword complexities within a firm frame of traditional values. According to Mr. Ezard, the germ of all Tolkien's writing comes from a period of "solitary frightened adolescence" and it is certainly to this state in young readers that the books appeal.

When I meet intelligent young students who, apart from

their 'A' level set books, have read little but Tolkien I reflect upon what they could have read in his place. When we have votes at eighteen and a greater and greater participation by young people in the shaping of their own education (both of which I think to be good things) the cult of a literature of arrested sensibility is an alarming phenomenon. One suspects that it is the coterie qualities of the books that give them their appeal but that it is other qualities which leave their mark, the escapism, the conservatism, the prissiness, and the knowingness which make Tolkien the supreme ostrich writer of our time.

Some years ago an educational journal had a correspondence on how to wean young children from Enid Blyton. Perhaps we need to think how to wean students from Tolkien. After all, education is supposed to be a preparation for life.

Margery Fisher

SOURCE: "Bilbo Baggins," in *Who's Who in Children's Books: A Treasury of the Familiar Characters of Childhood,* Holt, Rinehart and Winston, 1975, pp. 44-5.

Bilbo Baggins, when his great adventure with the dwarfs is some years behind him, sets to work on his memoirs, which he thinks of calling 'There and Back Again, a Hobbit's Holiday'. If the title has an ironical ring, in view of the terrors of Mirkwood, the rigours of the Lonely Mountain and the devastation left by the Five Armies, the irony does not come from Bilbo. He does not return from the adventure any less warmhearted and ingenuous than he is when he sets out. He has changed, all the same. The strain of adventurousness he has inherited from his famous mother Belladonna Took has come to dominate the sober, cautious Baggins side of him, and the comment of the dwarfs that he is more of a grocer than a burglar proves untrue, for he has undoubtedly acted the burglar, and successfully.

When Gandalf the Wizard visits Bilbo's comfortable burrow-home at Hobbiton he fixes a notice on the door which indicates to the thirteen dwarfs that if they want to recover their long-lost treasure from Smaug the dragon, the hobbit is their man. The dwarfs annoy Bilbo from the start. They crowd into his house, command their favourite dishes for supper and breakfast, start on the journey without him and use him as a scapegoat for everything that goes wrong. All the same, as one danger after another (capture by trolls, near-suffocation by the hideous spiders of Mirkwood, imprisonment by elves, the blasting breath of Smaug) is escaped partly, if not wholly, because of the hobbit, they begin to realize that Gandalf was right in his assessment of this small, determined creature.

The scene of the exchange of riddles with Gollum by the underground lake is crucial to the story, for it is here that Bilbo picks up the little gold ring, Gollum's most precious possession, the ring that confers invisibility and thus gives Bilbo confidence and makes many of his later exploits possible. The confrontation with Gollum has a mystery and terror unlike anything else in the book. Whether or not Tolkien already had it in mind to develop this character further when he wrote *The Hobbit,* he chose a different way of describing him from the few but explicit classifying details with which he introduced the hobbit and the various beings he meets in the course of his adventures. Gollum is either described in negatives ('I don't know where he came from, nor who or what he was') or with phrases that stir imagination strongly (he has 'pale lamp-like eyes' and long fingers, he rows a boat on the cold lake where he lives on a 'slimy island of rock'). Then, too, as though evading identification, Gollum alludes to himself as a third person, 'my precious', a term he also uses for the ring of power which holds him in thrall to evil and with which he is associated so significantly in *The Lord of the Rings.*

The riddle contest he and Bilbo hold further deepens Gollum's character by linking him with one of the great languages of myth. Finally, the innocent, warm response of the hobbit towards life is evoked most of all by Gollum. Having defeated the creature by sheer luck and persistence, the hobbit suddenly has 'a glimpse of endless unmarked days without light or hope of betterment, hard stone, cold fish, sneaking and whispering'. The pity he feels adds a new, important element to the story, and it gives a final, sharp picture of Gollum, that unrealized and superbly real character.

Bilbo Baggins has no wish to be conventionally heroic; indeed, during the final, fierce battle of the Five Armies he uses the ring to help him, for if a magic ring is 'not a complete protection in a goblin charge . . . it prevents your head from being specially chosen for a sweeping stroke by a goblin swordsman'. The deflationary remark is typical of the hobbit. Just so he counters the ceremonial farewell of Balin—'If ever you visit us again, when our halls are made fair once more, then the feast shall indeed be splendid!'—with the characteristic answer 'If ever you are passing my way . . . don't wait to knock. Tea is at four, but any of you are welcome at any time!' Moderate, too, but unmistakable, is the change in Bilbo's behaviour in Hobbiton after his return, but it is enough to isolate him somewhat from his neighbours. Because he is often visited by dwarfs and wizards, he is held to be 'queer', especially as he has taken to writing poetry. All the same, though his neighbours pity him, he 'remained very happy to the end of his days, and those were extraordinarily long'. If ever there was an autobiographical note in a book, this is surely one of the most endearing, in a story which Tolkien told by instalments to his children long before he put it into book form; there is surely a wry, urbane self-portrait in Bilbo Baggins.

Paul Kocher, in his book *Master of Middle-earth,* rightly calls *The Hobbit* a quarry for *The Lord of the Rings* rather than the book for which the later epic was a true sequel. Certainly the humorous, intimate, relaxed tone of *The Hobbit* is entirely different from the orotund, concentrated magic of the saga of Frodo Baggins, who as hero bears a far heavier burden than Bilbo ever did. All the same, Mr. Kocher hardly allows enough credit for the skill and the subtlety with which the character of the hobbit is drawn and the very mature attitude that lies behind his seemingly comic, even clownish behaviour in the story. The characters in the epic may stand taller, their words may carry further, but the hobbit is a personality as vivid and as recognizable.

Margery Fisher

SOURCE: A review of *The Hobbit, or There and Back Again,* in *Growing Point,* Vol. 15, No. 6, December, 1976, pp. 3014-15.

When *The Hobbit* was first published in 1937 it was received as a very personal recension of an old tradition, magic adventure in its own right but one that played cunningly on associations deep in the mind of anyone brought up on folk-tale, legend and balladry. Much later it was categorised by some critics as a kind of rehearsal for *Lord of the Rings.* Certainly the trilogy was tangential to the earlier tale, the whole business of the Ring harking back to Bilbo Baggins' encounter with Gollum and the acquiring of his "precious". But *The Hobbit* is something far more than a rehearsal. It is a richly varied, intimately narrated adventure obviously directed at children—the whimsical asides and stage properties suggest this, among other things. This sumptuous boxed edition, [with illustrations by the author] with its dignified black cover embellished with a dragon in crimson and gilt, its maps and runes, extra illustrations and other decorations, is something for the connoisseur: the Puffin paper-back, usefully pocket-sized, is more accessible to the young.

The Hobbit has one quality (apart from links in plot and setting) in common with the longer books, which were not specifically "for children"—the element of domesticity. One of the hitherto unpublished illustrations found in the new edition makes this very clear. The coloured frontispiece "The Hill: Hobbiton-across-the-Water" shows a serene and prosperous landscape conspicuously different in atmosphere from the picture (also new) of "Rivendell", with its springlike, magic beauty. "There and Back Again" has its significance as the book's sub-title; the last illustration (one that has been published before) depicts "The Hall at Bag-End, Residence of B. Baggins Esquire". There is a demure humour in the very masculine, bourgeois furnishing of the tunnel-room, with its circular doorway opening on to a gentle landscape. Here Bilbo is at home, shown in his normal size, whereas on all the other occasions on which he appears he is minute, almost microscopic; in another illustration (now first published), "Conversation with Smaug", he is a tiny figure bowing respectfully to the dragon in a vast cavern heaped high with treasure. Tolkien was wise not to show us Bilbo as an individual, for each of us must be free to form our own image of him, but he did in his pictures underline what is obvious in the story—Bilbo's diminu-

tive size and sheer ordinariness. *The Hobbit* has a touch of the parody, the ironic reservations, of *Farmer Giles of Ham;* the little man is hero.

There are all together six illustrations in the new [1976] edition which did not appear in the original one. All these were coloured by Tolkien, while seven more which do appear in the earlier editions were coloured by H. E. Riddett. Of the "new" illustrations, "The Misty Mountains looking west" has been enlarged to full-page from its original state as a small end-piece. "Bilbo woke with the early sun in his eyes" shows the hobbit, again dwarfed by his surroundings, lying on a rock in the Misty Mountains beside the Lord of the Eagles—another example of the defenceless physical state of the hero. The same diminishing effect is found in "Bilbo comes to the Huts of the Raft elves", which shows him riding downstream on a barrel. In all these pictures (especially in "Rivendell") and in those already published, there is a pleasantly literal quality, a very circumstantial handling of landscape or interior, always corresponding closely to the text. Exciting though the episodes of the story may be, there is nothing either deeply alarming or artistically subtle about the illustrations. While they are not self-consciously naïve, they put into visual form the kind of magic world which a child might well have imagined. This artless quality of fireside, family fairy-tale reminds me of Masefield's incomparable fantasies, which have the same tone; certainly Masefield was telling his stories not to particular children but to the child in himself but then perhaps Tolkien was satisfying himself as well as his children when he related and illustrated *The Hobbit.*

William H. Green

SOURCE: "The Four-Part Structure of Bilbo's Education," in *Children's Literature: Annual of the Modern Language Association Group on Children's Literature and The Children's Literature Association,* Vol. 8, 1980, pp. 133-40.

The Hobbit, J. R. R. Tolkien's fantastic quest-tale, traces the maturation of a timid hobbit named Bilbo after he reluctantly joins a company of dwarves on an expedition to take a dragon's gold. Bilbo, described in the beginning as a "little fellow bobbing and puffing on the mat," looks "more like a grocer than a burglar." But he later steals a cup from the dragon and a gem from the leader of the dwarves and discovers an unarmored spot beneath the dragon's left shoulder. Though Bilbo is half a century old, his hobbit stature and innocence suggest childhood, and he matures like Perceval through a series of hardships and tests. At first a sheltered innocent, he becomes a proven hero—an adventurer uncowed by dragons and uncorrupted by gold.

The story of Bilbo's education has four parts: first, the departure from the Shire, second, the adventures in the Misty Mountains, third, the adventures in Mirkwood, and fourth, the adventures at the Lonely Mountain. Though they are links in the chain of a single, coherent story, the four parts are clearly divided from each other. Structurally similar, they each begin with a well-equipped journey into the wilderness and move through want, danger, captivity, and unlikely escape to a hospitable house where the expedition rests and obtains new supplies. The four sub-tales are four turns in the spiral which is the hobbit's education.

Bilbo's double nature—what he is at first and what he later becomes—is suggested by a likely derivation of his name, a compound of two Middle English words suggesting his initial immaturity and subsequent heroism. *Bil-boie,* "sword-boy," is a suitable name for the hobbit because a sword is central to his development. A small sword from the trolls' cave is his reward for his first heroic effort. With this sword he resists Gollum and the spiders and, ultimately, assumes leadership over the dwarves. With the sword Bilbo grows from a boy in deeds as well as size to a knight "more worthy to wear the armor of elf-princes than many that have looked more comely in it." The boylike hobbit becomes a military hero. Though it may be accidental that the days of the meeting with Gandalf, of tea with the dwarves, and of the departure for Wilderland—the three days which begin Bilbo's adventure—are Tuesday, Wednesday, and Thursday, the three days which are named after Norse gods of war, it is difficult to believe that anything Tolkien does is accidental when it involves Germanic philology. The name *Bilbo* is foolishly hobbitlike on the surface, but underneath there are intimations of the military hero or the knight.

The Hobbit is cyclical, beginning and ending with an unexpected visit from Gandalf. Emphasizing this cyclical structure is Bilbo's tentative title for his memoirs—the pseudo-historical source of *The Hobbit*—which he plans to call "There and Back Again, A Hobbit's Holiday." Gandalf and the dwarves initiate the action, and the action ends with a visit from the wizard and a dwarf. Bilbo is smoking "an enormous long wooden pipe" at the beginning when Gandalf appears, and at the end Bilbo laughs and hands Gandalf a tobacco jar. Again, the cycle is not a simple return—it is a spiral. Bilbo's adventure has been productive, for his waistcoat is "more extensive" and has "real gold buttons," and the dwarf has a longer beard and a magnificent jeweled belt. The good people around the mountain, we are told, have prospered, and Bilbo has become cosmopolitan, at least in the eyes of his provincial neighbors. He has "lost his reputation" and taken to "writing poetry and visiting the elves." The final scene of *The Hobbit* is a positive echo of its beginning.

But the beginning of the story is also echoed, however negatively, by the climactic events at the dragon's lair in the Lonely Mountain. In opposition to the hobbit smoking at the door of his burrow under the Hill, there is the dragon (Smaug, whose name J. S. Ryan derives from OE *smeocan* 'to emit smoke') fuming in his cave under the Mountain. In order to mature Bilbo must leave his ancestral home, the womblike hobbit-hole, and pass uncorrupted through the tomblike dragon lair, the moun-

tain tomb which is the womb of heroic rebirth. He must confront and negate the dragon, a vast incarnation of the infantile selfishness which Bilbo has been outgrowing throughout the story and which is manifest in his peevish irritation with the dwarves in the first chapter. The hobbit's Hill and the dragon's Mountain are congruent but opposite and are connected in the text. *The Hobbit* begins with Bilbo standing by his door, and a chapter title identifies the rock shelf beside the tunnel into the dragon's lair as "the doorstep." As Bilbo enters the heart of the Mountain, he wishes that "I could wake up and find this beastly tunnel was my own front hall at home." In effect, the tunnel is a negative version of his own front hall, but he cannot awaken from the negation merely by wishing it away. The importance of Bilbo's decision to face the dragon is emphasized in the text: "Going on from there was the bravest thing he ever did." In view of the connection between Bilbo and Smaug, implicit in the connection between their homes, it is interesting that when the hobbit returns to find his home (like Smaug's) being plundered, he takes the loss of "many of his silver spoons" much more gracefully than Smaug takes the loss of his two-handled cup. It is Bilbo's high resistance to greed—called "dragon sickness" by Tolkien—which lets the hobbit remain "very happy to the end of his days."

Underlying *The Hobbit,* then, is a structure combining *opposition* and *return:* opposition between the Hill and the Mountain and return to the Hill when opposition is overcome. A similar structure is found in each of the four parts, which may be read almost as distinct tales in their own right. In all four parts Bilbo sets out from a homelike refuge, is opposed by monstrous foes, and ultimately arrives again at a homelike refuge. In the subtales, of course, he does not return each time to his own home, but to a surrogate home where he is a welcome guest. There are, in fact, only three houses visited in *The Hobbit,* and all three are places of rest, resupply, and song, havens of consolation after the danger and suffering through which the company has passed. The last haven, the lake-town of Esgaroth, is shattered by the dragon's attack; but it is significant that Bilbo and Gandalf stop at the other two houses—those of the good animals and of the elves—to rest on the return journey. The return visits emphasize the structural function of the houses, which divide the story into its four distinct parts.

Part I, an account of Bilbo's journey to the "Edge of the Wild," is the briefest of the four parts and sets a pattern for the others. Said to have inherited domesticity from the Baggins branch of his family, adventurousness from the Took branch, Bilbo is at first a complete Baggins—timid, fussy, and agreeable, but a little peevish at the upset in his domestic routine. Then the dwarves awaken "something Tookish" inside him and thus initiate his growth toward heroism. Once awakened, Bilbo's Tookishness is overcome by Bagginsish hysteria as he shrieks and faints at the suggestion that he "may never return." The struggle between Baggins and Took personalities will continue until the climax of the book, until finally the two will be integrated by Bilbo's brave self-sacrifice under the Lonely Mountain. Though the half-Tookish Bilbo does leave home for unknown dangers, he does so reluctantly, and at the onset he is still a middle-aged child: "My boy," Gandalf calls him; and Tolkien apologizes for Bilbo's ignorance of the dragon's hugeness: "He was only a little hobbit you must remember."

The journey in Part I moves quickly with the dwarves losing their baggage and being shut in bags by giant trolls, the foes in this part. Here, for the first time, the motif of *bagging* occurs—a motif with ample medieval analogues and psychological overtones. The dwarves are repeatedly trapped in **The Hobbit,** twice in bags and three times in tunnels. These accidents presumably symbolize breaks in the maturation process or, in terms of comparative mythology, absorption into the passive female principle. Bilbo—born Mr. Baggins of Bag-end—achieves heroism because he repeatedly avoids being "bagged" by his foes. In Part I, when he is sent ahead to steal food, Bilbo may seem to have accomplished nothing, but actually his efforts lead directly toward his future self-integration and toward his later successful rescues. Though Gandalf, not Bilbo, saves the dwarves, Bilbo's attempted burglary is a remarkable adventure for the homebody hobbit, and he does steal the key which opens the trolls' treasure cave. From this cave come the swords which are so important in Part II, and with a knife from the cave Bilbo later saves his life and acquires the magic ring which is the key to his later success. After turning the trolls to stone, Gandalf leads the company across the river Loudwater and to the house of Elrond, an elf-man who rules the hidden vale of Rivendale.

Part II, treating the adventures between Elrond's house and Mirkwood, is longer and more complex than the previous section. The entire company is threatened by two sorts of foes; and Bilbo, divided from the company for many hours, faces a third species of danger underground. The knife from the trolls' cave, the prize he won in Part I, saves his life, and his solitary valor wins a valuable prize, the ring of invisibility. In Part II, for the first time, Bilbo is called upon to combine Baggins virtues with the Took virtues which were awakened in Part I; he does so by risking his life to avoid killing the villainous demi-hobbit, Gollum. In Part II, also, there is moral ambiguity; Gollum, though very dangerous, is pitiful and human; and the dwarves' new friends, the Eagles and Beorn, seem alien and dangerous. But the ambiguity is slight. The Goblins and Wargs which threaten the company as a whole are, if possible, more darkly evil than the trolls of Part I. In any case, after losing their baggage and surviving the attacks of monsters both animal-like and manlike, the dwarves cross the Great River and take refuge in the home of a benevolent bear-man at the end of Part II.

Moral ambiguity deepens in Part III. In the first two parts, the dwarves were threatened only by obvious villains—dastardly, quarrelsome cannibals who hated the sun—and took refuge with orderly and helpful non-hunters. In Part III, however, the dwarves are imprisoned by hunting elves who are, nevertheless, Good

People; and they take refuge with foolish men who have corrupt leadership. Dwarfish greed makes enemies of the greedy elves, and human greed welcomes the dwarves at Esgaroth. Structurally, Part III resembles the other parts. Again the dwarves run short of food in a dark tunnel, this time an overgrown road through the forest. Approaching a fire beneath the trees as they did in Part I, the dwarves are drawn away from the road and eventually trapped in bags by giant spiders. In Part III, Bilbo's Tookishness is dominant. Bilbo alone engineers the dwarves' escape. When it is discovered that Thorin is missing, the leadership of the company devolves upon Bilbo, who leads the dwarves into an elvish ambush. The dwarves are trapped underground, and, as de facto leader, Bilbo arranges their escape, this time by concealing them in floating barrels. So, once again enclosed in containers, the company drifts down the river Running to the lake-town. Here again they enjoy the consolations of rest, food, shelter, and song in a hospitable house; but the lakemen, unlike Elrond and Beorn, have dwindled in the shadow of their enemies. Their leader is a selfish and cowardly merchant, a sort of Kay without an Arthur, who helps the dwarves only because his people demand it. Symbolic of the town's corruption and, generally, of the ambiguity which pervades Part III, is the town's location on piles in a broad portion of the river. In the previous two parts, the company's passage over a river before reaching a house of refuge implied a sort of baptismal grace, a barrier dividing the house from the peril behind. But the lake-town, mid-way in the river, offers no such grace. Ambiguity is building toward the climax.

Because Part IV, as the final part, must resolve the total story and balance Part I, it is longer and more complex than the others. Two of Part IV's eight chapters are devoted to consolation after the real peril is past. Indeed, though evil could triumph any time before chapter 18, in a sense everything after Smaug's death in chapter 14 is dénouement. After the dragon's death, though, the treasure remains, testing the victors, ready to destroy them unless they overcome their greed. The moral structure here resembles that in *The Song of Roland*. There are two armies, one good, one evil, but there is also evil within the good army—selfishness and distrust which only the onslaught of evil and a battlefield full of deaths can purge. In the welter of temptations, Bilbo maintains his integrity and prospers.

Again, in Part IV, the dwarves are trapped underground, and Bilbo is separated several times from them. His first separation is the ultimate test of Tookish bravery, walking alone into Smaug's lair. Finally, by passing this test, Bilbo becomes a hero and gives Smaug dreams of "a warrior, altogether insignificant in size but provided with a bitter sword and great courage." The prize won in Bilbo's first penetration of the mountain is a two-handled cup, symbolic of the dwarves' disputed treasure; and his second visit is more important, for he observes the flaw in Smaug's armor, information which allows a heroic lakeman to kill the beast as it attacks the lake-town.

Bilbo's third separation is most important in that it shows the full moral development of the hobbit, but it has little effect on the greater events of the story. The dwarves' greed has grown with their approach to the treasure, and within the treasure cave it becomes absolute. The chief dwarf, Thorin, refuses to share with anyone and lusts especially for the famous Arkenstone, a jewel which Bilbo has secretly found. Bilbo's will to risk all for the jewel may seem pure Tookishness, the will to take and hold, but Bilbo is not pure Took. Alone in the deepest sense, alienated from the greed-crazed dwarves who are themselves alienated from elves and men, Bilbo decides that peace is more important than the two ends for which he has been ostensibly working up to this point—the friendship of the dwarves and a portion of the treasure. But, curiously, this transcendent expression of Bilbo's maturity—his integration of Bagginsish love of peace and Tookish courage by giving up the Arkenstone as his portion of the treasure—is utterly ineffectual. Though Bilbo's sacrifice expresses his hard-won identity and wins the respect of Gandalf, the conflict at the Lonely Mountain is too great for one hobbit to resolve. Having found himself, Bilbo finds himself swept along, like everyone else, in uncontrollable currents, Baggins becomes baggage. The victory of the allied Good People occurs while he is unconscious and invisible, and the rest of the story is an uneventful ride back to Bag-end with accumulated prizes, a ring, a byrnie, and chests of gold. The story ends where it began.

As a scholar Tolkien is conscious that he is only adding a few leaves to "the countless foliage of the Tree of Tales;" and, as a story-teller, he intimates a vast history of which his tales are only fragments. In *The Hobbit,* which may be read as prologue to *The Lord of the Rings,* there are hints of goblin wars in the mines of Moria and of the Necromancer driven from his tower to the south of Mirkwood. These places and the results of these events are shown at first hand in *The Lord of the Rings,* where there are scores of additional "historical" allusions. Sam and Frodo discuss the Tree of Tales at a dark moment in *The Two Towers.* Noticing his connection with an ancient legend, Sam asks if the "great tales" ever end. "No, they never end as tales," Frodo answers. "But the people in them come, and go when their part's ended." Bilbo's own part, which is told mostly in *The Hobbit,* becomes part of other tales when he carries the One Ring of Sauron. In the words of an early reviewer, the book is "crammed with episodes that will obliterate need for meals and bed," but it is not loosely episodic. Patterns of opposition and return submerge the four tales, each dependent on the others, in a coherent and relentless narrative flow.

Lois R. Kuznets

SOURCE: "Tolkien and the Rhetoric of Childhood," in *Tolkien: New Critical Perspectives,* edited by Neil D. Isaacs and Rose A. Zimbardo, The University Press of Kentucky, 1981, pp. 150-62.

If there is anything left to say about *The Hobbit,* it is this: no matter how Tolkien wished to deny it, to repudiate those very qualities that confirm it, his first novel is solidly based on the great tradition of the British children's classic. For that reason above all, Tolkien's *The Hobbit*—like Lewis Carroll's *Alice's Adventures in Wonderland,* George Macdonald's *The Princess and the Goblin* and *The Princess and Curdie,* and Kenneth Grahame's *The Wind in the Willows*—still deserves critical consideration.

My aim here is to show how, in *The Hobbit,* in contrast to *The Lord of the Rings,* Tolkien employs a "rhetoric of childhood" highly influenced by these writers, Grahame and Macdonald in particular. I use the word "rhetoric" as Booth does in *The Rhetoric of Fiction,* to designate the means that the literary artist uses to persuade the reader to dwell, at least momentarily, within a "realistic" or "fantastic" world totally created and controlled by the writer. The writer exercises rhetorical control largely through means technically known as voice (that is, point of view or narrational stance), but also through style in general as well as through choice of character, characterization, and manipulation of time and space.

The classic rhetoric of childhood combines the following characteristics: an obtrusive narrator, commenting, addressing the reader, and using richly descriptive prose; characters with whom pre-adolescent children can comfortably identify and who develop and change as they do; an emphasis on the relationship between time and development within a compressed narrative time scheme; a circumscribed geography and a significant concern with the security or danger of specific places in the setting.

I will discuss these rhetorical devices beginning with time and space, moving on to the more problematic point of view and associated stylistic matters, and ending with the complexities of characterization and their implications.

The Hobbit covers about a year and emphasizes seasonal change; movements in space are also correlated with changes in season. Baggins, Thorin, and company make major changes in position on solstices and equinoxes. Simple age-old seasonal associations are conventionally exploited: spring is the time of hopeful starting out; summer signals the ripening of adventure; autumn brings despair; winter is total war and death; spring is peace and joyful return. Generally, in children's literature, seasons are also specifically equated with developmental cycles: spring is associated closely with growth and exploration of the outside world, winter with a kind of hibernation or growth plateau. Sharing this common pattern are the openings of *The Hobbit* and *The Wind in the Willows.* Bilbo and Mole emerge from their respective holes in the spring of the year; they return only after much growth and development have taken place. Their spring beginnings contrast with the autumn beginning of *The Fellowship of the Ring,* which heralds another kind of development in Frodo that leaves him without the impulse ever again to respond to spring in Middle-earth.

The three-volume "interlaced" *The Lord of the Rings* covers about one year too, but in *The Hobbit* Tolkien tells the story straightforwardly and quickly, in digestible portions, with a feeling of some closure at the end of each incident. Children, like adults, are capable of delight in suspense and the unexpected, but they cannot for long patiently sustain a sense of incompleteness. Bilbo, in very childlike fashion, having already traveled for months, can hardly stand the short wait (in days) "on the doorstep"; child readers have barely a page of waiting before the light beams on the keyhole. As in this instance, children's literature both divides and compresses time and, therefore, good children's books are episodic despite their underlying unity.

Again in contrast with the trilogy, Tolkien's landscape in *The Hobbit* is a circumscribed bifurcated one with lowlands to the west and forested lands to the east of the central and longitudinal mountains and river. This spatial representation quite neatly divides the world into safe and dangerous sides. Grahame's geography in *The Wind in the Willows* is roughly similar, if less graphic; there the safe field and rich river cultures oppose the Wild Wood, which lies on the other side of The River. Such simple geography not only emblematically indicates outside good and evil but also represents inner states and relative psychic disturbance. So Mole is threatened and experiences sheer psychological "Terror of the Wild Wood" just as Bilbo and the dwarves experience Mirkwood.

Superficially, Merry's and Pippin's first impression of Fangorn is similar, but Fangorn is an ambiguous, paradoxical place, unlike most places in children's literature. In children's books, dangerous forests remain dangerous, unless they are directly tamed through the characters' development and change. Safe places remain safe, a source of comfort in tribulation (Toad's homesickness in prison is much like Bilbo's on the journey). Sometimes, however, characters have to fight to regain their safe places, once they have ventured "across the river and into the trees." Both Toad, in *The Wind in the Willows,* and Bilbo have their homes invaded during their absence and must confront the invaders. Usually the characters, like Bilbo, have been so strengthened by their adventures that they are well able to do so. The trilogy differs in spatial quantity and quality. Places are more ambiguous; safe places are more seriously threatened or polluted; they can be cleansed only at great cost.

In the matter of maturing adventures underground, Carroll's *Alice* is the recognized children's literature exemplum and is, like *The Hobbit,* amenable to both Freudian and Jungian interpretation. *The Hobbit* is also much like other children's classics in its depiction of this highly significant space. On the one hand, no one—certainly not Tolkien—beats Grahame in the detailed description of what one might call the secure "domestic underground": comfortable accommodations for gentlemen of limited (Mole) and extensive (Badger) means. On the other hand, Macdonald shares with Tolkien a fascination with the dangerous "foreign underground": the wonder of mountain caves, their terrors, treasures, and the characteristics of their degenerate inhabitants. The following passage, for instance, is part of Macdonald's long introductory description of the "beautiful terror" of mountains:

> But the inside, who shall tell what lies there? Caverns of the awfullest solitude, their walls miles thick, sparkling with ores of gold or silver, copper or iron, tin or mercury, studded perhaps with precious stones—perhaps a brook, with eyeless fish in it, running, running ceaselessly, cold and babbling, through banks crusted with carbuncles and golden topazes, or over a gravel of which some of the stones are rubies and emeralds, perhaps diamonds and sapphires—who can tell?

As Robert Wolff points out in his study of Macdonald, this passage from *The Princess and Curdie* (1882) and others like it from the totally cave-oriented *The Princess and the Goblin* (1871) closely resemble the writings of the nineteenth-century German Romantics Novalis, Hoffmann, and Tieck. Tolkien's cave descriptions, both in *The Hobbit* and in *The Lord of the Rings,* belong to a long literary line which Macdonald, not Tolkien, introduced into children's literature. Tolkien does, however, combine and relate the safe with the dangerous undergrounds as Grahame and Macdonald do not.

In point of view as in use of time and space Tolkien, in *The Hobbit,* belongs with these writers. The rhetorical element that distinguishes *The Hobbit* most immediately from his later books is the obtrusive narrator. In *The Hobbit,* the narrator is constantly addressing the reader and is thus involved in a kind of "talking to children," as Tolkien himself regretfully points out. This is, indeed, the most usual voice in all the great classics of British children's literature. A rhetorical convention like any other, the obtrusive narrative voice can be used well or badly. When it is well used, the voice can steer the child along the course of a complicated narrative, Socratically raise certain questions in his or her mind, and point to implications beneath the surface of behavior or events. Abused, it can be cloyingly didactic.

In the work of better children's writers, the obtrusive narrator is the instrument of emotional sensitivity, moral perception, andplayfulness. Lewis Carroll is working within this convention when he writes: "'Well!' thought Alice to herself, 'after such a fall as this, I shall think nothing of tumbling downstairs. How brave they'll all think me at home! Why I wouldn't say anything about it even if I fell off the top of the house.' (Which was very likely true.)" C. S. Lewis, who readily admits the influence of the rhetoric of childhood, also uses that convention. He writes, in *The Lion, the Witch and the Wardrobe,* after the sacrifice of Aslan: "I hope no one who reads this book has been quite as miserable as

Susan and Lucy were that night; but if you have been— if you've been up all night and cried till you have no more tears left in you—you will know that there comes in the end a sort of quietness. You feel as if nothing was ever going to happen again." Tolkien uses it particularly skillfully when he comments dryly, "You are familiar with Thorin's style on important occasions, so I will not give you any more of it, though he went on a good deal longer than this", or notes about Bilbo's approach to the dragon's lair: "Going on from there was the bravest thing he ever did. The tremendous things that happened afterwards were as nothing compared to it. He fought the real battle in the tunnel alone, before he ever saw the vast danger that lay in wait."

The continued practice of reading aloud to children partly accounts for the persistence of the obtrusive narrator, with its explicitly oral quality. But this convention has always been more than just mechanical; it can be a special gift from adult author to child reader. The obtrusive narrator implicitly promises protection and companionship even when one is reading alone (or when childlike characters are left without protectors like Gandalf). One trusts the voice, at least, to desert neither the characters nor the reader, to say when one should be afraid and therefore alert and prudent and when one— either character or reader—can safely venture on or lay oneself down to sleep. This voice is the voice of a benevolent anthropomorphic god—not only the creator but the guardian of the imaginary universe in which it persuades the reader to dwell.

Tolkien on occasion used this voice awkwardly, but naturally turned to it because he was composing a work directed toward children. When he abandons this voice in *The Lord of the Rings,* he abandons it for reasons that really have little to do with theories of what children feel as readers being so addressed. His particular and growing strengths in "showing" rather than "telling" work together with esthetic preferences and theological constructs to change his rhetorical stance.

In **"On Fairy Stories,"** Tolkien expresses in passing his dislike for frames and machinery that get between the reader and the reality of the fantasy. His own "subcreation" of the Red Book of Westmarch might have become such a frame had he elaborated on it more than half-heartedly or attempted really to keep up the pretense that he was translating Bilbo's or Frodo's words. His true esthetic preference clearly lies in the omniscient, *distant* narrator who comes as little between the reader and the experience as possible. This "subcreator" as Tolkien calls him, seems modeled on Tolkien's Creator—non-anthropomorphic, surveying the world from afar, more the pure Word than any other manifestation of divinity. "He" is certainly not the obviously intervening and comforting god, on whom the obtrusive narrator is modeled.

The obtrusive narrator, whom Tolkien explicitly disliked, is, nevertheless, so ingrained in *The Hobbit* that to edit him out would deplete the book fatally. Yet other aspects of Tolkien's style, of which he was less aware, reveal that the rhetoric of childhood did not come as naturally or as richly to him as to some of his predecessors. Particularly noticeable to the reader of other great children's books is Tolkien's lack of sensory detail. In *The Hobbit,* characters like to eat but when they get a chance to do so they never seem to taste or smell their food; it's all dreams of bacon and eggs. Contrast Tolkien's eating dreams or scenes with Grahame's evocative prose: "When the girl returned, some hours later, she carried a tray, with a cup of fragrant tea steaming on it; and a plate piled up with very hot buttered toast, cut thick, very brown on both sides, with butter running through the holes in it in great golden drops, like honey from the honeycomb. The smell of that buttered toast simply talked to Toad." The visually intriguing sport of smoking pipes and blowing smoke rings is conveyed by Tolkien with far more reality as an oral satisfaction than is eating. The sense of touch, exploited by Macdonald and C. S. Lewis after him is not indulged; sensory discomforts—with which children are unfortunately very familiar—are mentioned but minimized.

Tolkien thought of himself as having "a very strong visual imagination" that was "not so strong in other points." He revealingly doubted "if many authors visualize very closely faces and voices." This suggests not only that lack of sensory imagination already noted but also the nature of Tolkien's visual imagination: he doesn't see things close up very clearly—unlike many children and writers for children—but has a much longer visual span; he is able to reproduce total landscapes and see relationships among landmarks; he is basically uninterested in interior or decorative details. Tolkien is figuratively farsighted rather than nearsighted.

Tolkien's lack of sensory detail and his long view are not particularly characteristic of the rhetoric of childhood, but in other stylistic matters, he is again among the masters. In *The Hobbit,* there is plenty of one thing Carroll's Alice wanted: "conversation." Characters talk to each other naturally and with differentiation among their speech patterns. They do not make speeches much or tell seemingly interminable "digressive" tales, as they are wont to do in the trilogy. They also make up words, like "bebother" and "confustication," and use constructions like "miserabler" as Carroll does. They engage in verbal trickery and combat, riddle games, and raillery— remnants of ancient verbal pastimes that also appear in Macdonald's and Carroll's works. Neither of the latter has characters play the riddle game as straightforwardly as Tolkien does in the Gollum chapter; however, Macdonald's Curdie taunts the goblins in much the same way that Bilbo taunts the spiders in Mirkwood. Another of Macdonald's characters, Diamond in *At the Back of the North Wind,* brings back poetry from other worlds and spiritual experiences, inspired in a Caedmonian fashion, as many of Tolkien's characters are. The general interspersion of verse and song in the prose narrative is another remnant of an earlier tradition that has remained longer in children's fiction than in adult and is exploited by all of the authors mentioned. Tolkien's most original touch in the matter of dialogue and the like is to have Gollum talk the true "rhetoric of children," narcissistic baby talk; one wonders whether children don't catch on to this faster than adults.

The physical and emotional traits of Tolkien's characters and the relationships among them are well within the rhetoric of childhood. The invention of the beardless, three-to-four-foot-tall hobbit is especially so. In beardlessness and size (roughly the height of the four-to-seven-year-old child), the hobbit evokes the most primitive type of identification on the part of children. Children's literature abounds with characters from Tom Thumb to Alice whose size is in some fashion contrasted with the demands of the world around them. These characters have, in various ways, to use the power of the psyche to overcome or to take advantage of the limits of their physical power (which is reflected, on a deeper level, by the male characters' lack of a beard).

Significantly, the other notable characteristic of the hobbits, their hairy feet, is virtually ignored in the trilogy. These feet symbolize a relationship to the animal kingdom that often appears in children's literature—where childlike characters are animals, or where children have special relationships with animals from whom they receive uncritical affection and toward whom they can feel superior and grown-up. The hobbits' hairy feet are, however, a vestigial trait related to much less conscious identification with animals on the part of children. Bettelheim, in *The Uses of Enchantment,* describes a whole cycle of animal transformation stories as having a repulsion-recognition-integration theme, through which the child first tries to rid himself of his "animal" instincts, especially sexuality, then recognizes them as part of himself, and finally integrates them into his personality and so controls them. The hobbits' hairy feet are constant reminders of both the good and bad aspects of one's relationship to animals; hairy feet are somewhat repulsive but also allow more freedom of self-expression than even bare feet do. The child in me is both repelled by the grotesquerie and attracted to the freedom of those hairy feet. After all, to wear shoes is one of the continuing restraints and privileges of being grown-up and "civilized."

The hobbit species is truly an original and inspired subcreation. Certain other creatures or features seem less original when one compares, for example, Tolkien's wily chatty dragon with Grahame's "reluctant dragon." And Gollum of *The Hobbit* is preceded by strange, degenerate animal creatures that live in the caves of Macdonald's *The Princess and the Goblin* and *The Princess and Curdie.* The conception of physical and moral degeneration of both species and individuals living away from fresh air and light is also a prominent theme of the two *Princess* books. Macdonald too uses savior birds and in the great battle at the end of *The Princess and Curdie* a battalion of pigeons rescues the outnumbered forces of good.

The character of the hero or heroine is a central issue

in the rhetoric of childhood. In contrast to Frodo, Bilbo is the typical hero of children's literature with the typical quest. Bilbo and Frodo are exactly the same age at the beginning of their respective quests, but Bilbo is youthful and inexperienced, Frodo much more mature and relatively learned. In addition, the nature of Frodo's quest is not to find himself but to lose himself and so to find himself on another, other-worldly level. Self-integration of Bilbo's type, not self-transcendence of Frodo's type, is *the* quest of children's literature.

More specifically, Bilbo, like many heroes of children's literature, displays all the outer traits and needs of the period that Freud designates as latency, when Oedipal and sexual conflicts are temporarily at rest. This period corresponds roughly to the elementary-school years. Erikson identifies it as the "fourth age of man" in which the main conflict is one between "industry and inferiority." This is the period when the child must learn the "fundamentals of technology" and become "ready to handle the utensils, the tools, and weapons used by the big people." That is, among other things, what Bilbo is doing: discovering that he has not only inner resources but outer skills—seeing clearly, moving quietly, throwing stones, as well as developing power to wield the sword—that make it possible for him to function in a world less protected than his home.

The break at that particular period of life from home to public school was the most significant trauma for many an English schoolboy, as we see not only in adult memoirs but in children's literature of the schoolboy variety (slang from which sometimes surfaces in the prose of *The Hobbit*). The struggle to become one of the boys is present in *The Hobbit* although not so blatantly as in these realistic novels.

Present too, in the fantasy element of the work, is the desire to *repress* rather than express competitive conflict and much of the other psychological conflict of childhood. This repression is characteristic of another kind of children's book: Lili Peller, a child psychologist, calls it "the early tale." The stories that she so designates have in common a denial of conflicts inherent in the dichotomies of male-female, old-young. She notes:

> In each story we find a group of loyal friends and we find a Protector who can work magic. . . . Every member of the group has unique gifts and skills and foibles. . . . The magician-Protector stays offstage or near the wing and the friends' actions and their feelings really carry the story. . . . Family relations of all kinds are nonexistent or they are at the very fringe of the story. . . . Most of them [the characters] belong to different species. Who will compare a monkey with a toad?

Tolkien's story exhibits many of the repressive elements of "the early tale." One might note especially here the absence of contact with "the opposite sex,"—a trait that *The Hobbit* shares with the major portion of *The Wind in the Willows.* Without reference to the clear misogyny of *The Lord of the Rings,* even a feminist might find Bilbo, as a character in *The Hobbit,* androgynous rather than misogynous in his bachelorhood. Either male or female children may, therefore, finally come to identify with him.

One element of Peller's early tale that Tolkien does not replicate is a static quality in terms of the growth and development of the characters. This growth and development in Bilbo is the major theme of the story. But what Tolkien regarded as the end product of that growth and development in 1937 is quite different from what he tried to make it later, by changing the Gollum chapter after he began the trilogy. In the early version, the high point of Bilbo's moral development can only be construed as an expanded concept of *justice* that goes beyond selfish desires to acknowledge Bard's claims: "Now these were fair words and true, if proudly and grimly spoken; and Bilbo thought that Thorin would at once admit what justice was in them."

Bilbo's subsequent renunciation of the Arkenstone perhaps foreshadows his later renunciation of the ring but is well within the morality of fairness and sharing inculcated in children at an early age. This morality is synonymous with justice to them; therefore, a child might be capable of what Bilbo is capable of at the high point of his moral development in *The Hobbit.*

Mercy, however, is not a concept of childhood, as many, including Tolkien himself, have been at pains to point out. Tolkien attempted to write the concept of mercy into Bilbo's development when he revised *The Hobbit* in the 1950s. The moment in "Riddles in the Dark" when Bilbo has a flash of understanding of Gollum's fallen state—"a glimpse of endless unmarked days without light or hope of betterment, hard stone, cold fish, sneaking and whispering"—is not part of the original story nor of the usual rhetoric of childhood.

The "mercy passage" is really connected with the very unchildlike sacrificial development of Frodo's personality and his acknowledgment of his relationship to "it," his shadow, Gollum. In *The Lord of the Rings,* Frodo practically goes mad and the three small creatures—Frodo, Gollum, and Sam—who move across the devastated landscape are emblematic not only of man's state in general, but also of the struggle in the divided psyche among superego, id, and ego. Sam, the ego figure, survives, but he is not, after all, prominent even among the several "heroes" of the narrative.

Bilbo's resourcefulness and basic sanity are honored in *The Hobbit,* not overshadowed by saintliness, as Sam's similar qualities are in the trilogy. The contrast between Bilbo and Frodo as heroes recalls Chesterton's distinction: "In the fairy tales, the cosmos goes mad, but the hero does not go mad. In the modern novels, the hero is mad before the book begins and suffers from the harsh steadiness and cruel sanity of the cosmos." In most good children's literature, as in fairy tale, the hero or heroine appears to represent the healthy developing

ego with its capacity for just action and for survival in *this* world. Bilbo lives. And Bilbo joins Alice, Curdie, Mole, Rat, and Toad in the gallery of such sane and down-to-earth protagonists. In this way, as in others, *The Hobbit* belongs to the great tradition of "the rhetoric of childhood."

Mitzi M. Brunsdale

SOURCE: "Norse Mythological Elements in *The Hobbit,*" in *Mythlore,* Vol. 9, No. 4, Winter, 1983, pp. 49-50, 55.

Andrew Lang, the Scottish nineteenth-century collector of fairy tales, believed that "Is it true?" was "the great question children ask." But J. R. R. Tolkien declared (**"On Fairy Stories,"** 1938) that children had asked him far more often, "Was he good? Was he wicked?" Tolkien concluded, "they were more concerned to get the Right side and the Wrong side clear. For that is a question equally important in History and in Faerie."

First in his children's book *The Hobbit* and later in the trilogy *The Lord of the Rings,* Tolkien exhibited a universe that seemed to exist in history rather than one merely an invention of Faerie. Much of Tolkien's ability to convince his readers of the "real" existence of the Middle-earth he created seems to stem from the conviction he shared with Chesterton, that children "are innocent and love justice: while most of us are wicked and naturally prefer mercy." Tolkien drew upon a child's stern perception of right and wrong, in which "mercy untempered by justice" leads to "falsification of values" and turned for the basis of his Middle-earth to a world he had loved since his own boyhood, "the nameless North of Sigurd of the Volsungs, and the prince of all dragons [quoted in Edith Hamilton's *Mythology.*]"

Since that somber Northern atmosphere is illuminated only by human heroism in the face of inevitable defeat by the forces of evil, and "the hero can prove what he is only by dying," hero and dragon inthe great Germanic myths are as intimately bound together as the child's Right and Wrong, one unable to exist without the other. Conventional explanations for children's fascination with fantasy and adventure maintain that [as quoted in Robert Scholes's *Elements of Fiction*] "the child lacks the experience that would make realism meaningful to him, and he lacks the learning which is necessary for the interpretation of allegorical fiction." Tolkien, however, broadened "children's literature" by building not on the child's inabilities but on children's positive—if rigorous—Northern moral sense, unclouded by softer virtues of mercy and forgiveness.

The Hobbit centers on a decidedly Northern quest for dragon's gold, culminating in the slaying of the dragon Smaug by Bard, a human hero, and the ensuing Battle of the Five Armies, pitting the forces of Good against those of Evil, with the prize the freedom of men, elves, and dwarves—and hobbits, the utterly new beings Tolkien created to witness the quest and to act out its principal role. Tolkien's gently rounded little protagonist, the hobbit Bilbo Baggins, half human size, brightly clad, and good natured, dwells at first in the epitome of creature comforts: "a very comfortable tunnel without smoke, with paneled walls, and floors tiled and carpeted . . . and lots and lots of pegs for hats and coats" and dinner "twice a day when they can get it." But Bilbo's mother, "the fabulous Belladonna Took" gave her son an unhobbitlike yearning for adventure that draws him, willynilly, into accepting the wizard Gandalf's invitation to join Thorin's band of dwarves in seeking out Smaug's lair. Aside from the hobbit himself, though, Tolkien bases each of the major elements of the quest on an identifiably Northern mythological source.

Gandalf the wizard displays each of the three manifestations of the Scandinavian god Odin. Odin is said [as quoted in H. R. Ellis Davidson's *Gods and Myths of Northern Europe*] to have appeared to Harald Wartooth, King of the Danes, in pre-Christian times as "an old man of great height, . . . clad in a hairy mantle," rather like Gandalf, famous in hobbit lore as a magician, who one day turned up from his wanderings at Bilbo's door as "an old man with a staff, . . . a long grey cloak, and a white beard." In Norse myth, Odin primarily appears as a god of battle and giver of victory, choosing slain warriors to live with him in Valhalla until they join in the last great battle between the gods and evil forces, when Odin's special adversary is the great wolf Fenris. Gandalf too at first seems only an old wanderer, but once on the way, he soon uses his magical power, like Odin's, to speak with beasts and birds like the King of the Eagles, who saves Bilbo and the dwarves from the wolfish Wargs beyond the Edge of the Wild. The eagles, sacred in Norse myth to Odin, help preserve the forces of Good Gandalf guided at the Battle of Five Armies. Odin was also known as a shaman, especially able to bring ecstasy in battle and poetic inspiration, with sacred ravens to bring him news, like the ravens who attend Gandalf. Gandalf's strange friend Beorn, who rescues Bilbo and the dwarves from goblins and at last wins the Battle of Five Armies for the forces of Good in the shape of a great bear, is reminiscent of the berserker warriors consecrated to Odin, who fought with superhuman strength in the intoxication of battle and could reputedly assume the shape of fierce animals. Odin's third function, as God of the Dead, also underlies Gandalf's inability to change Man's mortal fate, just as Odin had to bow to the earthly death of his warriors.

The other two non-human races portrayed in *The Hobbit,* the elves and the dwarves, are similarly closely related to Northern mythology. Tolkien's elves have nothing but their name in common with the amusing but ineffectual pixies of folklore. The inhabitants of the Old Norse Alfheim, one of the three divisions of the Scandinavian mythological universe, were impressive, powerful beings with a special power of healing. Ceremonies honoring them continued until the late Viking period, around 1018 A.D., when animal sacrifices were made at burial-mounds in which elves were supposed to reside. The fey elves of Tolkien's Mirkwood are beautiful and dangerous, inhabiting forests the Hobbits normally fear and avoid, and their powers involve healing and magical regeneration. The Last Homely House of Elrond Halfelven at Rivendell where Bilbo and the dwarves recuperate after the first part of their journey is permeated with such redoubtable magical lore that "Evil things did not come into that valley." Tolkien's dwarves also strongly resemble their Old Norse forebearers, "creatures with strange names, who bred in the earth like maggots, and dwelt in hills and rocks. These were skilled craftsmen, and it was they who wrought the great treasures of the gods," among then the great gold ring Draupnir from which eight other rings dropped every ninth night. Once Tolkien's dwarves had wrought equally splendid wonders, but, like so many other of his folk, Evil has driven them from their lands. Lacking "a mighty Warrior, even a Hero, Gandalf has chosen Bilbo to help steal the dwarves' treasure back from Smaug the dragon. Like the Germanic hero Beowulf, Bilbo is thus engaged to help a people not his own. Echoing the traditions of the Germanic warriors, too, when the dwarves' leader Thorin falls in battle, a victim of his own lust for gold, his two nephews also die defending him, exemplifying the strong relation between a Northern chieftain and his sister's sons as well as the Germanic code of the *comitatus.*

One of the Norse dwarves' mightiest artifacts was the gold ring in the story of Sigurd the Volsung. This ring brought only destruction on those who wore it, even Sigurd, who killed the dragon Fafnir and took over his hoard of treasure. When little Bilbo, certainly no hero in the stamp of Sigurd, is separated from the dwarves and finds a strange creature, Gollum, they play one of the primitive riddle games beloved of early Germanic tribes. The prize is Gollum's "precious," a ring that enables its wearer to be invisible. Bilbo knows the riddle game binds even wicked creatures, and so Gollum must unwillingly yield it up when Bilbo wins. The ring enables Bilbo later to carry out his mission in the dragon's cave, but by doing so it brings about the climactic battle of the story. In giving this ring so much power in *The Hobbit* (to say nothing of his later trilogy), Tolkien is employing the long tradition of Old Norse ring-magic. In the old temples of Thor, silver or gold arm rings were kept to swear sacred oaths and magically protect their wearers from sword-blows. Germanic tribes offered brides their wedding-rings on a sword, linking marital with military fidelity, and the ring-hilts of Viking and Germanic swords testify to the sacred reciprocal bond between the lord (ring-giver) and his *heoroweard.* The ring in Tolkien's work as well as in the Germanic mythological tradition which inspired it encircles the universal dualistic principle of Good and Evil.

The evil fiery dragon who guards the mound of burial treasure stolen from the tomb of a dwarf king, Thorin's ancestor, is another of the strongest motifs of Northern myth, as in *Beowulf,* where the theft of one of the dragon's gold cups brings on the vast devastation of the countryside that forces the aged hero to battle for his people's lives. When Bilbo removes one cup—all that the little hobbit can carry—to prove to Thorin that Bilbo has indeed been inside Smaug's lair, Smaug's vengeance is just as harsh: "Flames unquenchable sprang high into the night" from the town of Dale. The human hero Bard eventually faces and slays Smaug, even though Bard apparently dies, like Beowulf, in the effort. But Tolkien does not allow Bard to die, a departure from the tradition. An old thrush carries Bard a message from Bilbo, revealing the one vulnerable spot in Smaug's bejeweled armorplating. In the Norse myth, the dragon, as the symbol for the law of mortality exemplified in the devouring flames of Northern funeral ritual, represents the force of death which neither heroes nor the gods themselves could conquer. Bard's success, however, admits humanity in Tolkien's universe to a kind of heroic immortality, only possible through the small but essential role of the hobbit. The heroic act for Tolkien, in fact, could only exist in the presence of a catalytic witness, here the hobbit, one who had overcome his own fears in order to persevere.

At the same time when he was writing *The Hobbit,* Tolkien enunciated the harsh but necessary lesson of maturity in the essay **"On Fairy Stories"**: ". . . that on callow, lumpish and selfish youth peril, sorrow, and the shadow of death can bestow dignity, and even sometimes wisdom." Bilbo had to face not only the outward perils of unknown regions, fierce beasts and evil sorcery, but far worse, faced the inward danger most perilous to the Northern soul: that he would prove a coward. Bilbo fought his real battle with himself in the tunnel leading to Smaug's lair, "before he ever saw the vast danger that lay in wait. At any rate after a short halt go on he did." Bilbo also experiences sorrow by Gandalf's shaming him out of his despair as Gandalf leaves the party at the edge of Mirkwood: "You must either go through or give up your quest. And I am not going to allow you to back out now, Mr. Baggins. I am ashamed of you for thinking of it. You have got to look after all these dwarves for me!" Bilbo experiences an even greater sorrow, however, at the loss of his frequent dream of being back in his safe hobbit hole. His sorrow is necessary to know himself, though, and recognize his illusions for what they are. By the time the Battle of Five Armies seems lost, Bilbo has achieved a Northern stoicism, regretting only the lack of glory in the defeat:

> Really it is enough to make one weep, after all one has gone through. I would rather old Smaug had been left with all the wretched treasure, than that these vile creatures should get it, and poor old Bombur . . . and all the rest come to a bad end; and Bard too, and the lake-men and the merry elves. . . . I have heard songs of many battles, and I have always understood that defeat may be glorious. It seems very uncomfortable, not to say distressing. I wish I was well out of it.

Thus following the *Weltbild* of the pagan Northern peoples, the greatest danger to the characters of **The Hobbit** is not the shadow of physical death but the threat of a

death that will not allow them to prove themselves. Bilbo won the beginning of his personal dignity, even acquiring the Germanic warrior's right to name his sword, in a lonely battle deep in the fearsome forest:

> Somehow the killing of the giant spider, all alone by himself in the dark without the help of the wizard or the dwarves or of anyone else, made a great difference to Mr. Baggins. He felt a different person, and much fiercer and bolder in spite of an empty stomach, as he wiped his sword on the grass and put it back into its sheathe. "I will give you a name," he said to it, "and I shall call you *Sting.*"

Bilbo has thus changed considerably by the time he arrived at the entrance to Smaug's cave:

> He was trembling with fear, but his little face was set and grim. Already he was a very different hobbit from the one that had run out without a pocket-handkerchief from Bag-End long ago. He had not had a pocket-handkerchief for ages. He loosened his dagger in its sheath, tightened his belt, and went on.

Even trapped in Smaug's tunnel with the dwarves despairing around him, Bilbo is strengthened, feeling "a strange lightening of the heart, as if a heavy weight had gone from under his waistcoat."

Bilbo's hard-won self-knowledge allows him to recognize Thorin's destructive obsession with gold even when Bard the dragon-slayer cannot. Bilbo tells Bard, ". . . you don't know Thorin Oakenshield as well as I do now. I assure you, he is quite ready to sit on a heap of gold and starve, as long as you sit here." Bilbo averts suicidal war between dwarves, men and elves by giving Thorin's great desire, the Arkenstone, to the Elvenking, and even Thorin, dying, comes to praise Bilbo's wise decision: "'There is more in you of good than you know, child of the kindly West. Some courage and some wisdom, blended in measure. If more of us valued food and cheer and song above hoarded gold, it would be a merrier world.'"

Tolkien's "merrier world" of Middle-earth surely provides children a rousing adventure tale, but **The Hobbit** is also a tale about the child at the heart of most of us, perceiving Right and Wrong as sternly as did the heroes of the North. Perhaps Tolkien's "child" is another name for an acute moral sense impossible to achieve in comfort and security and the certainty of salvation. If humble little witnesses may win the right to perceive and assist the noble act through their-own suffering and trials, their world necessarily appeals to all of us, young and old, who want to believe in the existence of a child-like and yet immortal father to the man.

Algis Budrys

SOURCE: A review of *The Hobbit, or There and Back Again,* in *The Magazine of Fantasy and Science Fiction,* Vol. 67, No. 4, October, 1984, pp. 45-7.

The most successful gifted amateur of our time in SF is, of course, J. R. R. Tolkien. He was 45 in 1937, when *The Hobbit* was published; a good age for fantasy writing, especially if one is going to use the avuncular voice.

The Hobbit [has]. . . an air of slight detachment between the narrator and story, creating the sense of a kindly relative or close friend enthralling the children at bedtime with a told tale. Fairly often in traditional kidlit this feature is additionally glossed by overt tones of salutary instruction . . . what James Blish mock-apothegmised with "Remember, in the days of Ancient Rome, dear children, there were no motorcars at all."

Puritan Ethic accounts for such impositions on the canon in general. What's interesting about Tolkien . . . is that when he spun *The Hobbit* into being, he incorporated that mode wholeheartedly, retaining not only the sense of Uncle in the chair with the book in his lap but the didactic intrusions. While it is true that the subjects of the didacticism are invented and need exposition—the ethnography of *genus Hobbit,* for one—I think we have here a clear case of an amateur's creating a story feature because he hasn't even thought about any other way of performing that particular function; he simply did what was "natural."

Similarly, *The Hobbit* abounds with intrusions of song . . . outbursts of onomatopoeic, not to say echolalic, doggerel poetry that works quite indifferently as written verse and often constitutes a seemingly pointless and redundant interruption in the flow of the prose narrative. Uncle is literally telling the tale aloud, responding to private melodies no one out of hearing can share.

Furthermore, Uncle dawdles shamelessly through passages any conscious professional would have paced far more expeditiously. Gandalf's wizardly recruitment of Bilbo Baggins as the dwarves' burglar hardly requires the sorts of self-indulgent detail Tolkien dwells on. It's enough we know that Bilbo loves living smugly in his Hobbit-hole and that he has equipped it with comestible treats to a fare-thee-well; no pro would have given these scenes the sort of overkill their author fondly lavishes upon them. Nor would a professional storyteller have taken so long to get the tale of the dwarves' quest into motion . . . a characteristic which, infuriating as it is here to the sophisticated reader, pales by comparison to the molasses-in-January opening of Tolkien's next work in his cycle, as we shall see when I get around to reviewing that.

In fact, except for a few outstanding sequences—Bilbo's acquisition of Gollum's ring, and the lingering tinge of that poor dread creature's horripilating enmity—the intervention of the eagles—the intervention of the were-bear—the surreptitious entry into the lair of Smaug, the dragon, and the subsequent dialogue exchanged with him, as well as the scenes of his wrath—the passage through the Elven forest—the return home—there isn't much here that's done with particular or recognizable skill. Even in the memorable scenes (when one thinks about it, there

are quite a few of them, aren't there, and the more one thinks, the more of them emerge back into the forefront of the mind) the writing seems hardly dramatic enough. Meanwhile, in general the story is far shorter than its manuscript, and . . . well, I could go on for quite some time to list the technically flawed or at least technically dubious aspects of this work.

But perhaps that's not always what matters. Do we know what matters?

Rayner Unwin

SOURCE: "The Hobbit 50th Anniversary," in *Reading Time,* Vol. 31, No. 2, 1987, pp. 8-10.

The fiftieth anniversary of the publication of J. R. R. Tolkien's *The Hobbit* will be celebrated in March 1987 and throughout the rest of the year, but for me the anniversary is now. On 30 October 1936 I had just supplemented my pocket money by reading and reporting on the manuscript of a book called *The Hobbit.* My father believed that children were the best judges of children's books and one shilling was his standard fee. I liked this particular book, and although my report was not a model of perceptiveness (I conceded, with the superiority of a 10 year old, that the book "should appeal to all children between the ages of 5 and 9") it was good enough to ensure publication, and the reader's fee was probably the best investment my father ever made.

From the start, *The Hobbit* was a success: not such a runaway success as it has subsequently become, although there were two reprints before and during the war. It was after 1945 and especially after *The Lord of the Rings* was published in 1954/5, that the number of reprints escalated. It is hard to calculate how many copies have been produced to date—8 million in English alone is an informed guess—and there have been editions in some fifteen languages.

The word "Hobbit" started life as a scribble in the margin of an exam paper that Tolkien was correcting, and has become so much a part of the language that it now has its place in the *Oxford English Dictionary.* The book itself is generally accepted to be a classic; one of those rare children's books (*pace* my original comment) that adults are not ashamed to be found reading. Over the years Bilbo Baggins has manifested himself in a variety of media—on radio and film, as figurine and jigsaw, in theme park and restaurant. Fan clubs have sprung up in many countries, each publishing its own journals, replete with technical observations by dermatologists about the hair on hobbits' feet, recipes for their favourite meals, or speculations about why the author insisted on spelling the plural of dwarf as 'dwarves.' A crop of children are now growing up with strange Christian names, derived from their parents' devotion to characters in *The Hobbit,* and living in houses called "Rivendell."

In the end, it is the book itself that matters most, and there are not many books—let alone 50-year-old books—that provoke such popular manifestations. It is indeed a very remarkable book—a splendid, original story, witty, exciting and imaginative in its own right, and fundamental to the unsuspected potency of Gollum's Ring. Without *The Hobbit,* the infinite complexity and riches of Middle-Earth might never have been revealed. Yet, for many readers, this deceptively simple story, written for his own children's winter "Reads," is Tolkien's greatest achievement of all.

Brian Aldiss and David Wingrove

SOURCE: "A Comfy Chair in Middangeard," in *Punch,* Vol. 292, No. 7633, April 15, 1987, pp. 52-3.

Tolkien was rather an ordinary Oxford don, learned, opinionated, fond of his own cronies, far from fond of modern civilisation. What was extraordinary about him was his imagination.

On its first publication in September 1937, *The Hobbit* was received with great enthusiasm by readers and critics. It was something new, and read like a genuine folktale. The edition sold out by Christmas and a second edition with coloured illustrations was rushed through. As might be expected, Tolkien's publisher, Stanley Unwin, pressed Tolkien for a sequel, "a new Hobbit". The "new Hobbit" did not emerge until the fifties—as the three-volume *Lord of the Rings.* It was, of course, larger, darker, and more serious than its predecessor. And both were part of a shadowy greater work, *The Silmarillion.*

On this fiftieth anniversary, about which Tolkien's publishers are rightly more excited than we mortals, we can see what was different about *The Hobbit.* Before it arrived on the scene, there had been numberless stories crammed with the creatures of Faery—dragons and dwarfs, elves and trolls, wizards, wolves and necromancers. Tolkien owed something to his favourite childhood tale—first encountered in Andrew Lang's *Red Fairy Book*—of the heroic Sigurd and Fafnir the dragon, as well as to the Curdie stories of George MacDonald and the fantasies of William Morris.

Two factors, above all, separated Tolkien from this older tradition. In both *The Hobbit* and the greater work to come, they were to change the nature of Fantasy itself. The first was to do with the character of Tolkien's "hero," Bilbo Baggins, the second with the care with which he had created his world of Middangeard—Middle Earth.

Bilbo Baggins is the eponymous hobbit, a kind of manchild, less than four foot tall and furred, but in most other respects a comfortably well-off, unmarried bourgeois male in his fifties, partial to good food, good ale, and a pipe of fine tobacco. Into his well-ordered, self-satisfied world—in effect the world of pre-Great War rural midland England—comes Adventure, in the form of thirteen dwarfs, a wizard, and a map of a dragon's hoard far to the East. From that moment on the story is concerned with the gradual changes in Bilbo's character—the shedding of complacency and fear in the face of a hostile environment.

Unlike previous models of "the hero" in such fantasies, Bilbo is a complex, "double" creature. There is the Baggins side of him, the side we first encounter in the tale, which, as Tolkien emphasises, "means comfort". But there is also his mother's side, the Took side to his nature, which emerges only slowly. The conflict between these sides of Bilbo's nature heightens the tone of the simple and colourful story-line and engages the reader more fully. The quest is both inner and outer—for the treasure in oneself as well as the treasure hidden in the cave of the Lonely Mountain, guarded by a dragon. In this lies much of the work's power. The second area from which it derives its imaginative potency is Tolkien's Middle Earth.

Tolkien became a Professor of Anglo-Saxon. His first love was philology—and for an examination of the complex ways in which philology shaped his life, one must turn to T. A. Shippey's absorbing *The Road to Middle Earth.* As a boy, Tolkien was fascinated by words and invented his own languages. On sick leave after the Battle of the Somme in 1917 he decided to use one of these languages, Quenya (or High-Elven)—a language based on Finnish—as the basis for the creation of another world. He had his language. But what kind of people spoke it? What kind of land did they live in? What did they think? What was their history? From such speculations grew **"The Book of Lost Tales,"** Tolkien's overall name for his conception of Middle Earth and its history. Chief of these tales was to be the history of the three great elven jewels, **The Silmarillion.** Between 1917 and 1937 Tolkien spent a great deal of energy inventing—or, as he put it, "discovering"—Middangeard and its peoples. When he came to write *The Hobbit* in the early thirties it was only natural that he should use the setting of his greater work for the landscape of the lesser. Unlike all previous fantasies, the world of *The Hobbit* was not invented as the tale unfolded, but was there, solid in its existence, in Tolkien's mind as he wrote. Tolkien drew upon the wealth of northern mythology for his "sub-creation," and the power of myth transforms his writing.

The Hobbit lies in the shadow of the greater work, sharing not merely a setting, a history and more than a handful of characters, but also a number of plot elements. The ring, discovered by Bilbo in *The Hobbit,* must, in *The Lord of the Rings,* be returned to chaos, to the Crack of Doom, by Bilbo's nephew, Frodo. All that was peripheral in *The Hobbit*—the elves of Rivendell; the ancient tales of war between dwarfs, elves, orcs and men; the Necromancer and his evil empire—becomes central in the later book. In effect, the ancient past becomes the present. But most significant is their difference of tone. *The Hobbit,* for all its refinements on juvenile fantasy, is still a children's book, with elements of the tall tale (as in the story of Bullroarer, the giant hobbit, who knocked off the head of the goblin king, Golfinbul, and invented the game of golf). It addresses its young reader in familiar terms, conscious that books are read more often in a comfy chair before a roaring fire than in the midst of dark, enchanted woods. *The Lord of the Rings* takes that comfy chair and sets it down in Middangeard itself.

The first chapter of *The Lord of the Rings,* written in December 1937, is delivered in the same light tone as *The Hobbit.* But by the time Tolkien had written two more chapters in early 1938 he had begun to realise that the new work was different in kind from *The Hobbit*: a continuation but not a sequel. Its concerns were more adult, its tone was darker, nastier, altogether harder. An element of what might almost be called realism had entered. A war had intervened. Moral issues had grown large. The element of comfort, ever-present in *The Hobbit,* is absent from *The Lord of the Rings.* Even the Shire, the very heartland of comfort, is subject to violent, discomfiting change. We are often on the edge of our comfy chair—or behind it. Vicarious adventure has become moral confrontation.

Tolkien has his critics. Most complain that the ethos of his Middle Earth is unrealistic, externalising evil, making the moral issues too overtly black and white—Gandalf versus Sauron. This is to forget that at its deepest level *The Lord of the Rings* is myth, just as the *Mabinogion* or the *Kalevala* are myths, and it was Tolkien's intention to create a myth for England. This said, it is true that Tolkien as a man profoundly rejected the modern world. He was oblivious to the leaps of understanding made by Science in his lifetime, remaining rooted in words and myth and in what he instinctively *knew* from personal experience. In some respects, therefore, his critics are justified in viewing him as a kind of well-educated barbarian; not a Renaissance man but a relic of the pre-war Oxford academic system, with its snobberies and limitations.

In a way, Tolkien reminds us of another great storyteller of his generation, P. G. Wodehouse; both were born in the later Victorian Age and brought up to a large extent by aunts; both looked back to a lost childhood world. The Drones Club is analogous to the all-male company of the hobbits, with the martini replacing ale, far from the depraving company of women. Lord Emsworth's rolling acres have a parallel in the Shire. But there similarities cease. Wodehouse's brilliant prose is designed to be seen and heard; Tolkien's prose is the sometimes laboured medium through which we view Middle Earth.

Whether we accept Tolkien or not, the common readers as defended by Dr. Johnson and Virginia Woolf are surely vindicated. They took to Tolkien's greatest work in their millions because his world was thoroughly imagined; his holistic view was to be preferred over all imitations.

The influence of Tolkien has not been confined to fantasy alone. Science fiction in particular was changed when *The Lord of the Rings* appeared in the mid-fifties. World-building is one of the great games of SF. Here was a prime example. The elves, dwarfs, and orcs are, in effect, people like us in higher or lower states of being—not unlike the standard SF alien. Indeed, on its first publication, Naomi Mitchison perceptively referred to *The Lord of the Rings* as "super-science fiction".

The very existence of Middle Earth, an enormous and deeply imagined world, subject not to whim or fancy but to consistent laws (even though those laws contain "magic") has determined that all subsequent models have had to measure themselves against Tolkien's achievement. Whether those subsequent models have accepted Tolkien's philosophy or not, they have often produced work of superior quality, such as Ursula Le Guin's *Earthsea* trilogy. A vast hinterland has been created between SF and fantasy, science fantasy, which has a wide if sometimes uncritical following. . . .

Fifty years on, Tolkien's Middle Earth, and his small, bourgeois hobbit, are as much a facet of modern life as Chernobyl, and as pervasive in their after-effects. He was the man who created a new taste in literature.

Tolkien once said he wanted to dedicate his legends "simply to England: to my country". As it has turned out, the Americans have been more grateful for the gift than the English. We still have some genius; but enthusiasm is now an American virtue.

Catherine Bennett

SOURCE: "In the Beginning, There Was Bilbo," in *The Times Saturday,* August 22, 1987, p. 13.

From its small beginnings, with a print run its publishers recall only as "modest," *The Hobbit* has not merely become standard children's reading: it has sold more than eight million copies and has spawned a massive escapism industry in books, board and computer games. . . .

It was at Inkling meetings in the early thirties that Tolkien first began to air parts of *The Hobbit,* the story of a prosaic, comfort-loving creature coerced into a quest for Dragon's gold, which he had first devised as bedtime entertainment for his children. The landscape of *The Hobbit,* and the tribes and terrors beyond Bilbo Baggins's untroubled Shire, were drawn from *The Silmarillion,* the invented mythology of Middle-earth, which he began after the First World War, as a background for his made-up languages.

His complex runes and myths lent a sense of depth and importance to a simple story, whose prose style often strayed into the nannyish. Amid the slaying of giant spiders and the encounters with man-eating trolls, there are still babywords like "misrabler"; cosy asides—"just imagine his fright"; and 1930s' slang—"Certainly Bilbo was in what is called a tight place."

The story appealed to the Inklings, but it was left unfinished, until a chance meeting with a publisher from Allen and Unwin, Susan Dagnall. In 1936 she asked Tolkien to complete the work, which was passed to Stanley Unwin's 10-year-old son, Rayner, for a reader's report. "This book, with the help of maps, does not need any illustrations. It is good, and should appeal to all children between the ages of five and nine," Rayner concluded, thereby earning a shilling, and unleashing fantasy from its confines in comics and science fiction.

After favourable reviews, including two fulsome tributes by C. S. Lewis, sales of *The Hobbit* were at first encouraging rather than extraordinary. Under pressure for a sequel from his publishers, Tolkien returned to the obscurity of his Oxford study, where he finally devised *The Lord of the Rings,* which would take the children's story on into a world of dark, heroic romance—so dark that he worried it might be "quite unsuitable".

It was only after the trilogy was published, 12 years later, and began to attract a cult following, that readers looked for further tales of battling Hobbits, and discovered Bilbo, quietly opening the saga in Bag End. In 1961, Kay Webb, doyenne of children's publishing, brought *The Hobbit* out as a Puffin paperback. "It seemed to me to satisfy everything in children's imagination," she says. "Children like journeys, and they like them to be mystical and a bit removed from themselves. It had this quest aspect to it that children always like, and a combination of fantasy and humour." Within a year, *The Hobbit* sold out its 30,000 imprint.

At the same time, Alan Garner, the children's author, found his first novel compared to Tolkien and began, irritably, to read the work meant to have inspired him. "I can't stand it," he says now. "I think it's dreadful. I think it's phoney, and I think it's escapist in the worst sense. It's the result of a man running away from life." A few years later he was unimpressed when a man arrived on his doorstep, announcing: "I've just travelled 3,000 miles to meet the second greatest writer of fantasy."

His visitor was the founder of the Tolkien Society in America. . . .

To the fury of his fans, academic respect has yet to be accorded to Tolkien in Britain. Anne Barton, Regius Professor of English at Cambridge, has no wish to see him studied in universities, although she considers *The Hobbit* "an absolutely enchanting children's book. . . ."

Gene LaFaille

SOURCE: "Science Fiction Universe," in *Wilson Library Bulletin,* Vol. 64, No. 6, February, 1990, pp. 91-2.

Of interest to Tolkienians is the reissue of *The Hobbit, or There and Back Again,* illustrated by Michael Hague. This 7¾-by-10-inch version retains all of the delightful text of the authorized edition as it recounts the adventures of Bilbo Baggins, a hobbit, as he joins the wizard Gandalf and a party of dwarfs on a quest to regain stolen dwarf treasure. The forty-three single-page and five double-page color watercolors add much pleasure and increase the reader's interest in the story, especially in the stirring battle scenes. Hague's illustrations offer fine detail without being busy and make the work more exciting for storytelling purposes. Tolkien's two drawings (the Wilderland map and Thror's map) are included for reference purposes.

Daniel Grotta

SOURCE: "The Professor: 1925-1937," in *The Biography of J. R. R. Tolkien: Architect of Middle Earth,* Running Press, 1992, pp. 72-90.

In the summer of 1928, while marking an especially boring lot of examination papers, Tolkien came across one with a blank page in it. "One of the candidates mercifully left one of the pages with no writing on it—which is possibly the best thing that can happen to an examiner—and I wrote on it 'In a hole in the ground lived a hobbit.' Names always generate a story in my mind and eventually I thought I should find out what hobbits were like. But that was only the beginning; I spun the elements out of my head; I didn't do any organizing at all."

Tolkien was never certain how he came to invent the word "hobbit." It was more spontaneous generation than calculation; certainly, not the combination of "rabbit" and (Thomas) "Hobbes," as the eminent American critic Edmund Wilson speculated. "I don't know where the word came from," admitted Tolkien. "You can't catch your mind out. It might have been associated with Sinclair Lewis' *Babbit.* Certainly not rabbit, as some people think. Babbit has the same bourgeois smugness that hobbits do. His world is the same limited place." Another theory on the origin of the word hobbit is advanced by Paul Kocher, author of *Master of Middle-earth.* According to Kocher, the Oxford English Dictionary defines the Middle English word "hob" (or "hobbe") as a rustic or a clown, a sort of Robin Goodfellow (the English equivalent of the "little people" of Celtic mythology). Since hobbits seem to display many of the characteristics of hobs—small size, simple nature, love of countryside—then perhaps Tolkien unconsciously transformed a word with which he was undoubtedly familiar into a new creature. In any event, the word "hobbit" is uniquely Tolkien's invention, like "pandemonium" in Milton's *Paradise Lost* and "chortle" in Carroll's *Alice in Wonderland.*

For Tolkien, stories germinated from words, and the word "hobbit" stimulated the beginning of a tale following in the best tradition of the old Norse sagas. In those days, Tolkien had no idea of his story's plot or probable ending; his method was improvisational, and the story grew in the telling. He said later that *The Hobbit* was really a distillation of several ideas that had occupied his professional mind for some years and that he merely adapted those ideas to children. But he emphasized that *The Hobbit* was *not* simply a children's book. When an interviewer asked him if he had only written *The Hobbit* to amuse his children at bedtime, Tolkien replied, "That's all sob stuff. No, of course, I didn't. If you're a youngish man and you don't want to be made fun of, you say you're writing for children. At any rate, children are your immediate audience and you write or tell them stories for which they are mildly grateful: long, rambling stories at bedtime." When confronted with the suggestion that *The Hobbit* reads like a children's tale with a somewhat paternalistic narrator who uses the simplest language, Tolkien admitted that "*The Hobbit* was written inwhat I should now regard as bad style, as if one were talking to children. There's nothing my children loathed more. They taught me a lesson. Anything that in any way marked out *The Hobbit* as for children instead of just people, they disliked—instinctively. I did too, now that I think about it. All this 'I won't tell you any more, you think about it' stuff. Oh no, they loathe it; it's awful."

Since Tolkien denied he wrote *The Hobbit* solely to amuse children, then precisely why did he write it? At one time, Nevill Coghill thought he had done it for the money. After all, Tolkien frequently complained about his uncomfortable financial position, and everyone knew he was always in need of money. For that reason, when the book was published in 1938, Coghill refused to read it, and only picked it up years later when he discovered it at a friend's house on a bedroom bookshelf. He read the book through, quickly changed his mind, and declared it a wonderful tale with elements—like the riddle game with Gollum and the dialogue with the dragon Smaug—right out of the Norse sagas.

But the real reason Tolkien wrote *The Hobbit* can be found in a statement he made about *The Lord of the Rings,* which applies equally to his earlier work: "In *The Lord of the Rings,* I have tried to modernize the myths and make them credible." Both as mythmaker and as philologist, Tolkien knew the importance of mythology to language and culture. Myths develop a link with the past, a continuity that helps people weather the present and look forward to the future. In an era of unprecedented change, the links to the past are stretched to the breaking point, and a people without roots are likely to become, analogously, a people without branches or flowers. The roots of the past—mythology—are no longer acceptable in their traditional form and have to be recast in a more contemporary, relevant mode. *The Hobbit, The Silmarillion,* and *The Lord of the Rings* are Tolkien's contributions to modern mythology. Tolkien once commented that it was unfortunate there were virtually no native English fairy stories (with the exception of *Jack and the Beanstalk*), and that he had written *The Hobbit* in order to help fill this vacuum.

As chronicler of a modern myth, Tolkien borrowed heavily from the myths and sagas of the past, with which he was intimately familiar. He never claimed originality for either his names or plots. Only his most devoted readers later disputed and denied any attempts to establish wellsprings from which many of his ideas flowed. The names of the dwarfs in *The Hobbit,* for example, were not invented by Tolkien, but lifted intact from *The Elder Edda,* a series of old Norse poems taken from a thirteenth century Icelandic text. In that work, the dwarfs' names were Durin, Dwalin, Dain, Bifur, Bofur, Bombur, Nori, Thrain, Thorin, Thror, Fili, Kili, Fundin, Gloin, Dori, and Ori (there was even a Gandalf)—the same as those of the dwarfs with whom the hobbit Bilbo and the wizard Gandalf went on their adventure to recover the dragon's gold. "This particular lot of dwarfs are very secretive," Tolkien once explained, and since in the book they came from the extreme north, "I gave the dwarfs actual Norse names which are in Norse books. Not that my dwarfs are really like the dwarfs of Norse imagination, but there is a whole list of attractive dwarf names in one of the old epic poems." The name for the forest of Mirkwood also appears in an Icelandic saga, *King Heidrek the Wise,* which Christopher Tolkien translated in 1960. Gandalf is mentioned in the saga of *Halfdan the Black,* and the term Middle-earth comes from an obsolete phrase describing our own world. Each name Tolkien used was carefully constructed or selected to describe the individual bearing it. His fantastic ability to give attractive, descriptive, and unusual names is one of the most appealing aspects of his works. Being a philologist and knowing the importance of words and titles meant that this name-giving ability was important to Tolkien. He said, "In the writing, I always begin with a name. Give me a name and I'll produce a story—not the other way about."

In writing *The Hobbit* and *The Lord of the Rings,* Tolkien applied his talents as a professor of language and a lover of mythology. "I used what I knew" he said. "Every human being has an individual character, just as everyone has an individual face. I think people have linguistic predilections, but like one's physical characteristics, they shift as you grow, also as you have more experience. In language, I've tried to fit my actual personal predilection or pleasure."

Tolkien probably produced a handwritten draft of *The Hobbit* in the early 1930s. It was written late at night in an attic at 20 Northmoor Road. He worked sitting on the edge of a camp bed, writing on a late nineteenth century English oak keyhole desk that his wife Edith had given him in 1927. This handwritten manuscript of *The Hobbit* was never intended for publication, but was circulated privately among friends and students. C. S. Lewis encouraged Tolkien to submit it to a publisher, but he refused. Nor would he listen to other friends who suggested he seek publication. Why Tolkien was uninterested in having the book published is not clear. There are a few possible explanations, though they are not particularly convincing. One is that he feared the ridicule the public might have heaped upon an Oxford professor writing a children's book, or the disapproval of his colleagues for writing such a frivolous, time-wasting work when he could have been engaged in much more serious scholarship. Another possibility is that as a truly modest man who sought privacy and anonymity, he feared that publication might inadvertently bring popularity, and put him in the limelight. Still another explanation may be the fear of rejection. Tolkien apparently never recovered from the humiliation he suffered when some of his poems were rejected by Sidgwick & Jackson in 1916. Several of his early stories, later incorporated into *The Silmarillion,* were similarly rejected.

There is one more possibility that may explain why *The Hobbit* was not offered to a publisher before 1936. In 1934, Tolkien was awarded a Leverhulme Fellowship, which enabled him to pursue a scholarly subject of his own choosing. . . . Tolkien received a Leverhulme for the years 1934 through 1936; in all probability, he used the grant to do research on *Beowulf.* . . .

The story of how *The Hobbit* came to be published is interesting because it reveals Tolkien's reliance upon others to recognize and support his genius. The manuscript was known to a small but select circle of friends and colleagues. One of these was Elaine Griffiths. She tried to persuade Tolkien to let a publisher look at the manuscript, but he preferred to leave it in his desk drawer. Shortly afterwards, Griffiths happened to meet an old friend and fellow undergraduate, Susan Dagnell, who had taken a position at a small but distinguished London publishing house, George Allen & Unwin. She mentioned that her former professor had a wonderful children's story in manuscript that would make a smashing book—if only he could be persuaded to part with it. "Susan had a delightful voice," recalled Griffiths, "And if anyone could get it out of him, it was her." Apparently, Susan Dagnell succeeded, for in autumn, 1936, he first allowed *The Hobbit* to be considered for publication.

Susan Dagnell gave the manuscript to Sir Stanley Unwin, chairman of George Allen & Unwin. Sir Stanley, judging himself incompetent to evaluate children's books, turned it over to his ten-year-old son Raynor. Young Unwin had an arrangement with his father in which he was paid between one shilling and a half crown for reading and reporting on each children's book given him for consideration. Of *The Hobbit,* Raynor Unwin wrote to his father on October 30, 1936:

> Bilbo Baggins was a hobbit who lived in his hobbit-hole and *never* went for adventures, at last Gandalf the wizard and his dwarves persuaded him to go. He had a very exciting time fighting goblins and wargs. At last they got to the lonely mountain; Smaug, the dragon who guards it is killed and after a terrific battle with the goblins he returned home—rich!

> This book, with the help of maps, does not need any illustrations. It is good and should appeal to all children between the ages of 5 and 9.

Many years later, Raynor Unwin said, "Some publishers get their lucky break at a very tender age. At the age of ten I was handed the manuscript of a children's book called *The Hobbit,* and promised the fee of one shilling for my report on it. My father, Sir Stanley Unwin, reckoned children the best judges of juvenile books, and I think he was right. I earned that shilling. I wouldn't say my report was the best critique of *The Hobbit* that has been written, but it was good enough to ensure that it was published."

Despite Raynor Unwin's advice that the map Tolkien had drawn to go with the manuscript made illustrations unnecessary, Tolkien wanted the book to include his own drawings (he was an inveterate doodler and enjoyed painting water colors). The map, however, was absolutely vital to the story, and it is likely that, as with *The Lord of the Rings,* it had been drawn up long before the book was written. Tolkien once advised that in an adventure story it is essential for the author to draw a map first; otherwise, he is likely to encounter great discrepancies.

The Hobbit was published in autumn 1937, and for the most part received excellent reviews. . . .

The London *Observer*'s reviewer spoke of "Professor Tolkien's finely written saga of dwarves (sic) and elves, fearsome goblins and trolls, in a spacious country of far-off and long ago . . . a full length tale of traditional magic beings . . . an exciting epic of travel, magical adventures . . . working up to a devastating climax." And *The New Statesman & Nation* concluded that "his wholly original story of adventure among goblins, elves and dragons . . . gives . . . the impression of a well-informed glimpse into the life of a wide other-world; a world wholly real, and with a quite matter-of-fact, supernatural natural history of its own." W. H. Auden (who was a friend, colleague, and former student of Tolkien's) called it "the best children's story written in the last fifty years," and when *The Hobbit* was published in America by Houghton Mifflin the following year, it won the prestigious *New York Herald Tribune* prize as the best children's book of 1938. After World War II, *The Hobbit* was placed on many approved reading lists in elementary schools, and was (and still is) a highly recommended children's classic in thousands of libraries in both England and America.

Curiously enough, despite the reviews, the book did not sell well initially. It barely went through one edition; a second edition was destroyed in 1942 in the London Blitz. Tolkien did not realize any significant financial rewards from his book until much later, but he lived to see the day when well over a million copies of *The Hobbit* would be sold in the United States alone. But then, Tolkien once admitted, "I never expected a money success." . . .

It is probably not a coincidence that the hobbit, Bilbo Baggins, happened to have been just about the same age as his creator, Professor Tolkien, when he embarked on his great adventure with Gandalf and the dwarfs. Perhaps it might even be said that they were traveling in roughly the same direction.

William H. Green

SOURCE: In *The Hobbit: A Journey into Maturity,* Twayne Publishers, 1995, 145 p.

The Hobbit is important as a suspenseful and original story synthesizing existing material in an utterly new way to support an archetypal theme. It is the flagship of all of Tolkien's popular writing. His adult masterpiece, *The Lord of the Rings,* was planned as a sequel, a second "hobbit book," and grew magnificently out of control. The hobbit books imprinted college student culture in the 1960s and became models and inspirations for a revival of heroic fantasy, a vast expanse of postmodern fiction that Tolkien still rules.

The Hobbit is a variation on the archetypal story of apprenticeship in which an inexperienced hero goes out into the world and discovers himself through adventures and hardships. *Tom Jones* and *Treasure Island* are classic examples of the pattern—as old as the stories of Joseph in Genesis and Telemachus in *The Odyssey*—a staple of fairy tale, romance, and popular fiction.

Typically the protagonist of these tales is young, of course, but Tolkien manages an interesting variation: his hero is a middle-aged gentleman who has stayed too close to home and become spiritually stagnant. Like the heroes of Hesse's *Steppenwolf,* Goethe's *Faust,* and Cervantes's *Don Quixote,* Bilbo is some fifty years old when he answers a call to step from his womb-like home into a magical otherness. This is normally not material for juvenile fiction, this dangerous flight from second childhood, but Tolkien makes it work by inventing a diminutive hero who has avoided worldly experience. Not only is Bilbo small, but boyishly open and aimless, much like a good-natured adolescent whose parents are on extended vacation. No reference is made to ravages of age in Bilbo (wrinkles or loss of stamina), and he is much younger than the long-lived, bearded dwarves he accompanies. So, by omission and contrast, Tolkien achieves indirectly what Goethe must use the machinery of a witch's potion to achieve in *Faust:* he creates a male-menopausal protagonist endowed with the energy and appeal of youth, a children's-book hero.

In this juvenile masterpiece that hides, like a Trojan horse, an adult story, Tolkien reinvents traditional heroism for his century. The myths of northern Europe and the old heroic poetry he loved were composed within a military aristocracy, where the bravado of Beowulf and Sigurd made sense. With the postmedieval rise of the middle class, the emergence of merchants and artisans as the patrons of books, the type of the aristocratic swordsman grew more and more remote; and the twentieth century nearly lost belief in traditional heroes, substituting antiheroes, superheroes, and doomed vic-

tims. Tolkien skillfully wove motifs from medieval myth into *The Hobbit* to explore and demonstrate how a hero who is timid, bourgeois, and ethically Christian might achieve at his own level feats comparable to Beowulf's. The book is a narrative position paper in the debate between nihilistic relativism and traditional values. Monsters still exist: fighter bombers, if not dragons; bigots, if not goblins. Moral good and evil exist, and heroism is still needed. However inexperienced and small we are, like Bilbo we can show courage and make a difference.

Such idealism struck a resonance with students in the 1960s. As much as Tolkien disagreed with "hippies" about drugs and sex, Bilbo's message of idealistic simplicity and hope—the ultimate triumph of young courage against the dragons of a corrupt establishment—spoke to the generation that protested racism, fascism, pollution, and war. Bilbo's "sit-in" on a dragon's doorstep, putting himself at its mercy until he found its weak spot and forced an uncorrupted remnant of the establishment to act, seemed a practical model for social reform. . . . And somewhere between Bilbo's hole by the Water and the elvish community at Rivendell, young adults found paradigms for their communes and universities. By the end of the decade, Tolkien was unofficial required reading for American college students, and his books were best-sellers. In 1972, Tolkien discovered that the "main business" of his British publisher was marketing his fiction. Sales of his thirty-five-year-old children's book were "rocketing up to hitherto unreached heights." . . .

Had *The Hobbit* not successfully penetrated the juvenile-fiction chink in his era's anti-fantastic armor, Tolkien would never have begun the trilogy that possessed the imagination of a decade and, along with the magical realism of Gabriel García Márquez, trumpeted the death of modern realism.

The Hobbit is, as Randel Helms has demonstrated [in "Tolkien's Leaf: The Hobbit and the Discovery of a World"], *The Lord of the Rings* "writ small," the prototype for all that followed. Writing it, Tolkien discovered harmonious relationships between several existing literary genres that happy coincidence threw together in his life: medieval narratives, fairy tales, classic children's fiction, and popular adventure stories. Tolkien's emulation of "escapist" fiction, particularly late-Victorian boys' books, explains hostile reactions from critics such as the high-modernist Edmund Wilson [in "Oo Those Awful Orcs"], who called Tolkien's work "juvenile trash," and medievalist Burton Raffel [in *The Lord of the Rings as Literature*], who marginalized it as not "literature." But the success of the Middle-earth books depended on Tolkien's discovery that serious themes and heroic motifs could be popularized by orchestrating them in the "escapist" mode represented by Alexandre Dumas, Jules Verne, Edgar Rice Burroughs, and H. Rider Haggard. It was while writing *The Hobbit* that Tolkien made this discovery and a major postmodern movement began, though its promise was not to be recognized for almost half a century.

Published in Great Britain on 21 September 1937, *The Hobbit* sold so well that a new printing was needed before Christmas. The presence of positive reviews was assured by Tolkien's close friend C. S. Lewis, who in early October published anonymous raves in the *Times Literary Supplement* and in the *Times* itself, influential publishing addresses. Lewis called attention to the "deft" scholarship behind the story, its appropriateness for a wide range of ages, and its bringing together good things "never before united." He predicted that *The Hobbit* would become a classic. Though one anonymous review in *Junior Bookshelf* found Bilbo's adventures "contrived," nearly all the early reviewers, British and American, displayed enthusiasm that forecast a place on juvenile booklists.

Though Tolkien began *The Hobbit* for the amusement of his children, he denied that it was especially intended for young readers. Of course, early reviews were typically buried in columns bothering over illustrations and age suitability, back alleys unlikely to attract an adult audience, so it was not until the eruption of Tolkien fandom in the 1960s that Bilbo's quest attracted many adult readers. Still, early reviewers noticed a potentially wide age appeal. A review published in New York twelve days before the American release asserts that "if the book does not please American children, so much the worse for them." And C. S. Lewis had already asserted that, though *The Hobbit* will amuse younger readers, only adults reading it repeatedly "will begin to realize what deft scholarship and profound reflection have gone to make everything in it so ripe, so friendly, and in its own way so true." It is no hollow sales slogan that the story appeals to "all ages."

Richard Hughes, a perceptive early critic, identified what Tolkien called "the Richard Hughes snag": the likelihood that he would overshoot his young audience if he wrote any more about hobbits (as, of course, he did overshoot them). Hughes, in a letter to the publisher, called *The Hobbit* "one of the best stories for children I have come across for a very long time" but also mentioned the "snag"—that parents might find some parts "too terrifying for bedside reading." In his published review, confined under the heading, "Books for Pre-Adults," Hughes noticed the difficulty of assigning a book's appeal to a specific age group—a point Tolkien acknowledged a year later in his Andrew Lang lecture, **"On Fairy Stories,"** where he disputed the idea that fairy stories were particularly suited for children. Hughes notes that Tolkien is "so saturated in his life-study that it waters his imagination with living springs." *The Hobbit* is "Nordic mythology" rewritten by a man so intimate with it that he does not merely rearrange, but "contributes to it first hand." In April 1938 the book won a *New York Herald Tribune* cash prize as best juvenile story of the season.

In the seventeen years between publication of *The Hobbit* and the renewed interest provoked by its sequel, the book remained in print in England and America. It secured early and without controversy a niche it occupies today in histories of children's literature. In his two histories of children's books in Britain, Marcus Crouch sets the highest literary standards—books must be good books first, for children second—and lavishes unmixed praise on *The Hobbit* as "an exciting story of adventure, a tragedy with comic episodes, a picaresque romance with strands of magic in it, an historical novel about the remote past which, by the author's craft, becomes more real than the present. . . . By any standard, [it] is a great book." Crouch's 1972 history observes that Tolkien's original achievement has been blurred by *The Lord of the Rings* "cult" and praises *The Hobbit* as a different sort of success from its sequel, less apparently allegorical, more about character development than good and evil, more friendly and humorous, yet "a story of high adventure, with vividly imagined episodes, funny, grotesque, sad and noble, all sustained and given continuity by the writer's scholarship and his command of every detail of his created world." I have cited Crouch for his evocative style, but *The Hobbit*'s rank as classic children's book is uncontested. Comparable praise appears in Judith Saltman's *Riverside Anthology of Children's Literature* and in Zena Sutherland and May Hill Arbuthnot's *Children and Books*—virtually anywhere juveniles are surveyed.

Critical reception has been less consistent in the field of Tolkien studies, where critics are obliged, sometimes grudgingly, to read *The Hobbit* as the first of a four-volume set, overture to *The Lord of the Rings.* Here Bilbo sits in the shadow of Frodo and is occasionally seen in a dim light, particularly by those who dislike the paraphernalia of classic children's fiction: cute verses, clarified good and evil, and asides to small readers. We read, as it were, sitting in Papa Tolkien's tobacco-scented lap, and some find that lap uncomfortable. A strong instance is Paul H. Kocher, whose analysis of *The Lord of the Rings* [in *Master of Middle-earth: The Fiction of J. R. R. Tolkien*] is perceptive and enthusiastic but whose response to *The Hobbit* is to argue circular proofs that the children's book is more childish than the adult one. His avowed purpose is to reassure would-be readers of *The Lord of the Rings* that they don't have to "tackle" *The Hobbit* first—a work that "often puzzles, sometimes repels outright." Fans of Bilbo might say the same thing about Kocher's humorless complaints.

Typically, however, major critical treatments of Tolkien's fiction have given *The Hobbit* respectful attention as precursor of the trilogy, usually devoting a chapter to it as prelude. Early reviews by insiders such as C. S. Lewis and W. H. Auden set the tone for criticism that analyzed Tolkien's work as folklore and myth, with particular attention to the quest and to the obvious echoes of medieval literature and Victorian medievalism. Later came serious analysis in terms of depth psychology, twentieth-century popular fiction, and philology. Most long studies of Tolkien have some value for a student of *The Hobbit,* but many assume that children's books are inferior books, the attitude that inspired Francelia Butler to subtitle her first issue of *Children's Literature* "The Great Excluded." Typically, the adult story is the "masterpiece,"and students of children's literature must gather the crumbs that fall from its table. . . .

Many other critics have seen *The Hobbit* as a symbolic story of growing up, a basic theme in children's fiction. . . .

In contrast to chapters that either attack the story as juvenile or defend it as fit for adults, Lois R. Kuznets's 1981 "Tolkien and the Rhetoric of Childhood" analyzes *The Hobbit* as a contribution to "the great tradition of the British children's classic." In her view, the book's excellence as a juvenile is the chief reason it deserves attention. Using *Alice's Adventures in Wonderland, The Princess and the Goblin,* and *The Wind in the Willows* as touchstones, Kuznets lists a catalog of traditional traits: the obtrusive narrator, characters appealing to pre-adolescents, maturation within a short time span, dialogue and verse, circumscribed geography, and concern with safety or danger. Traits that earlier critics have called weaknesses become strengths within this tradition. The obtrusive narrator, Kuznets finds, is skillful at maintaining a thematic focus. She praises Bilbo as an androgynous childlike hero who appeals to both boys and girls in elementary school, the period of sexual latency. His incremental self-integration and "basic sanity" are held up to admiration, not twisted into wounded saintliness as Frodo's character is in *The Lord of the Rings.* "Bilbo lives. And Bilbo joins Alice, Curdie, Rat, and Toad in the gallery of such sane and down-to-earth protagonists." . . .

Since the long-awaited 1977 publication of *The Silmarillion* and subsequent publication of stories and fragments from the private papers, emphasis in Tolkien studies has necessarily shifted away from *The Hobbit* and *The Lord of the Rings.* The excitement of new ground to break is elsewhere—with the elves of the First Age. For instance, in the two volumes of *The Book of Lost Tales* (1983-84), we read directly about the goblin wars and the fall of Gondolin often mentioned in *The Hobbit.* The volumes of new material make Bilbo's adventure a smaller piece of a larger mosaic, but a piece of unquestionable importance, a point of origin. As high-quality children's fiction the book's status is uncontested, and many adult critics have discovered in it workmanship worthy of serious study and comment, both in the framework of Tolkien's other work and as a free-standing story. . . .

The Hobbit begins with three pages in the author's voice introducing us to Bilbo Baggins, a well-to-do bachelor from a family of conservative hobbits. Hobbits, by the way, are a fictional branch of humanity, not a mythical species. Their definitive traits of hairy feet, sharp senses, and small stature, as well as their conservatism and common sense, may occur in people today. Bilbo's quiet strength, his point of view close to theground, and his vulnerability among "big people" echo universal facts of childhood and speak to adults who feel small in the world of global media.

Though Bilbo may remind us of Winnie-the-Pooh with his frequent daydreams of food, his nearest counterpart in A. A. Milne's stories is Piglet, always fearful because he is a Small Animal, yet rising to heroism and generosity beyond his size. For instance, Piglet allows himself to be raised by a string on a rescue mission out of Owl's fallen house, and he donates his own house "in a sort of a dream" to the homeless Owl. Milne's tiny hero inspires the longest and grandest "Hum" from Pooh, the poetic Bear of Very Little Brain (seven whole verses), and is cheered to discover in Pooh's naive parody of heroic song that he, Piglet, is brave. Such a comic textual hero Bilbo Baggins becomes—a hero who repeatedly models his action on stories and ends up writing the story of his own adventures, humorously titled "A Hobbit's Holiday." Even Piglet's pride in his imaginary grandfather "Trespassers William" parallels Bilbo's pride in "Old Took's great-grand-uncle Bullroarer, who was so huge (for a hobbit) that he could ride a horse." Like Piglet, Bilbo is a comic figure who must assert himself bravely to earn an identity in a world where he is almost beneath notice, even among undersized companions.

At first, Bilbo is a generic hobbit. In the first two paragraphs he is called simply "a hobbit" as attention is given to his comfortable underground home like the furnished holes of Mole and Rat in *The Wind in the Willows.* Tolkien begins in a fanciful world reminiscent of Grahame, Milne, and Carroll, with more attention to setting than to character and no hint of heroism. In the third paragraph we learn that our hobbit is a Baggins, member of a wealthy family that is respected "because they never had any adventures or did anything unexpected."

Finally, deep in the fourth long paragraph, a rambling discussion of Bilbo's mother and hobbits in general, Tolkien offhandedly drops Bilbo's name—a short name in a long sentence characterizing his mother's people, the Tooks. Clearly, though he has prominent family connections, Bilbo is not a prominent person. Like a child, he is defined as an offshoot of his family, his "house." He is undifferentiated, absorbed (the terms here are Jung's) in mystical participation with the hobbit community. Bilbo behaves "like a second edition of his solid and comfortable father." He has not found himself. When the action finally begins three pages into the book, we understand that Bilbo is a late bloomer, a middle-aged child whose identity is submerged in generic hobbitness and shaped by his dead father's heritage.

This may not seem bad. Certainly, Bilbo appears to live a stable life and enjoy creature comforts, and there is no obvious surface reason why he could not live like a happy child until he dies. Nevertheless, the wizard's benign intervention and a great deal of psychological theory suggest that Bilbo's nervous passivity may read as depression. Something like the miserable little underground creature Gollum may be festering at the roots of his personality, in the early stages of transforming him into a bitter little Scrooge. In fact, Bilbo is in no danger of becoming a cannibal like Gollum but of becoming like his grasping, materialistic cousins, the Sackville-

Bagginses, who personify Baggins traits in negative purity at the end of the book. Marie-Louise von Franz puts the case forcefully when she refers to the "human psychological fact . . . that evil entails being swept away by one-sidedness, by only *one single* pattern of behavior."

Between his paternal and maternal families, the conservative Bagginses and the adventurous Tooks, Bilbo is suffering an unrecognized crisis because he has lost the Tookish half of his character. His life is aimless and stagnant because of his one-sided habit of avoiding risks. Because he had shut off the Took half of himself, the Baggins half has become a sterile re-enactment of the dead paternal past. Ironically, Bilbo has also reenacted the choice of his mother, who lost her Took name to become a Baggins. Perhaps for her this was a rash decision, an adventure, but for Bilbo it is a passive birthright. He is his father and his mother but not himself. The elder Baggins at least married an exotic woman, had a son, and built a home; but Bilbo has only slept, eaten, kept house, and taken walks. In fifty years he has accomplished nothing worth mention. When a wizard appears at his doorstep to give him what he "asked for," the hobbit is arguably at a crossroads, destined either to wither and die or to break into new life.

Bilbo's situation can be compared to that of Don Quixote, another stagnant fifty-year-old who embarks suddenly on an adventure. But Bilbo's departure, unlike the Don's, is a sane act, however mad it seems to the neighbors. Clearly, though he parallels Don Quixote, Bilbo is also much like Sancho Panza, the sensible peasant whom Don Quixote drafts as his "squire." Bilbo combines in a single not-yet-integrated whole the foolhardy gentleman and the practical bumpkin: the dreamer of adventures and the "solid and comfortable" Baggins. Loosely speaking, Don Quixote is a Took, Sancho Panza a Baggins, and Bilbo is both. Physically, of course, he resembles the short, potbellied peasant, and like Sancho, he is insular and naive, fond of food and comfort. Repeatedly during his adventure, more than a dozen times, Bilbo is said to long for food and home, like Sancho mourning over the empty wine bottle. Unlike Don Quixote, Bilbo thinks about creature comforts. His concern over going off to fight a dragon without his handkerchiefs contrasts with the Don's forgetting to pack money and clean shirts.

But a more important contrast is the fact that Bilbo's call to adventure comes from a compelling authority outside himself, from a quixotic wizard who summons him suddenly to discover his buried potential. Sancho, an unschooled peasant, accepts his call to adventure because it comes from an educated gentleman, and Bilbo receives his call from an even higher authority. In *The Hobbit,* Gandalf is a legendary wizard, but in Tolkien's later accounts, he is no less than an angel. As orthodox angel, Gandalf has a limited mandate to interfere in human affairs. He can function only as a catalyst to provoke and guide the faithful. He sets events into motion and then must leave them to unfold in accordance with moral character and free will.

As Gandalf's allusion to prophecy on the final page suggests, *The Hobbit* is about a man's discovering his vocation, discovering his true self. Though Bilbo seems at first to be only a literate Sancho, a comic "little fellow bobbing and puffing on the mat," he is "Belladonna Tooks's son," heir to a family acquainted with elves. He is a hero called to change the world. By the end of the story Bilbo is quixotic in the highest sense: he has dared and succeeded beyond all sane expectations. A pot-bellied, middle-aged child has imitated Sigmund and Beowulf, faced a dragon and contrived its death.

Tolkien explains in a later retelling of the story that Gandalf does not transform Bilbo supernaturally. The old wizard merely remembers a young hobbit's "bright eyes, and his love of tales, and his questions about the wide world outside the Shire," and calls out a heroic inner child, a lost vocation. In *The Hobbit,* as in classical tragedy, character is destiny. Gandalf understands and teases into action Bilbo's latent heroic desires, "dwindled down to a sort of private dream." Tolkien makes his design explicit in a 1966 letter to his publisher: hobbit heroes are "ordained individuals inspired and guided by an Emissary to ends beyond their individual education and enlargement."

The Hobbit is a fairy story: its world a world where things are broken open alchemically to show what they really are. Inside the half-witted third son of the tale is the future king. Inside the frog is a prince. And inside the selfish little Baggins is a noble Took "more worthy to wear the armour of elf-princes than many that have looked more comely in it."

The narrative is not only linear, a story of forward progress, but cyclical. *The Hobbit* begins and ends with a visit from Gandalf, and Bilbo gives his adventures the cyclical title "There and Back Again." Gandalf starts the action by visiting with dwarves, and the action ends with a visit from Gandalf and a dwarf. Pipe smoking, a standard ritual of bonding in the male adventure stories of Jules Verne and Rider Haggard, ceremonially opens and closes the book. Bilbo is on his doorstep smoking a large pipe when Gandalf first appears, and at the very end Bilbo laughs and hands the wizard a tobacco-jar. In their communal smokes, the men create and compare symbols of completion and repetition, smoke rings.

Northrop Frye's description of the typical "quest romance" [in *The Secular Scripture*] fits *The Hobbit* exactly: it "takes on a spiral form, an open circle where the end is the beginning transformed and renewed by the heroic quest." The hobbit has returned at a higher level, and recapitulations within the last scene show this. Bilbo's discovery of his inner heroism, his hand in the death of the dragon, his self-sacrifice—all of this has been productive. His waistcoat is larger and has "real gold buttons," and the dwarf has a longer beard and a magnificent jeweled belt. The folk around the once-desolate Mountain, we are told, have prospered, and Bilbo has continued his heroic life-style into the less hazardous arena of hobbit social life. He has become a nonconformist—a cosmopolitan, at least in the eyes of his rural neighbors. He has "lost his reputation" and taken to "writing poetry and visiting the elves." In short, he has found himself. Bilbo has become a complete person separate from his benighted community. The final scene of *The Hobbit* is a positive echo of the beginning.

But the beginning of the story is also echoed, however darkly, by Bilbo's encounter with the dragon at the Lonely Mountain. This is the turning point of the book, a terrible parody of home at the place farthest from home, a sort of fun house mirror at the edge of the world. In opposition to the hobbit's round front door under the Hill, where he blows rings of smoke, there is Smaug's round Front Gate under the Mountain, out of which issue smoke and steam. To mature, Bilbo must leave his ancestral home, the womblike hobbit-hole, and pass uncorrupted through the tomblike dragon lair, the mountain tomb that becomes the womb of heroic rebirth. This is, by the way, his third dangerous underground journey from east to west, the night sea journey of the archetypal solar hero, and in each case Bilbo must make important parts of the journey alone and in darkness. The hobbit hero must confront and overcome the dragon, a vast incarnation of the infantile state that he has been outgrowing throughout the story.

The two ends of Bilbo's adventure, the hobbit's Hill and the dragon's Mountain, are congruent but opposite and are connected in the text. The action begins with Bilbo standing by his door, and a chapter title identifies the rock shelf that leads into the dragon's lair as "the Doorstep." As Bilbo leaves this doorstep to enter the heart of the Mountain, he wishes that he could "wake up" and be back home in his own front hall. The tunnel is, of course, a negative double of his front hall, but he cannot awaken from its dark negativity except by going forward, facing the dragon who is snoring up ahead, sounding like a pot boiling on a fire. The reference to a cooking pot establishes a connection, for it echoes the kettle that Bilbo rushes to set on the fire in his own hole when unexpected guests arrive for tea—a grisly doubling, of course, because, when Bilbo arrives as an unexpected guest, he expects to be eaten, not to eat. The importance of the hobbit's decision to face the dragon is emphasized in the text: "Going on from there was the bravest thing he ever did."

Given the connection between Bilbo and Smaug, implicit in the connection between their homes, it is interesting that when the hobbit finds his home (like Smaug's) being plundered, he takes the loss of silver spoons much more gracefully than Smaug takes the loss of the two-handled cup. It is Bilbo's high resistance to greed, a vice Tolkien calls "dragon-sickness," that permits the hobbit to remain "happy to the end of his days." In coming to know himself, he learns how to be happy within his limitations.

The movement from the Hill to the Mountain and back

again, the book-length story, is made up of five parallel parts, five component tales. In each of the five parts Bilbo sets out from a homelike refuge, is opposed by monstrous foes, is saved by a *eucatastrophe* ("a sudden joyous turn"), and then arrives at another homelike refuge. In each component tale he faces the foes in tunnel-like darkness after touching or passing over a body of water. The foes are deadly, but, oddly, they do not immediately kill their victims. Rather, they trap victims in bags or blind tunnels, to starve or be eaten later. Food is the theme sounding constantly under the narrative, like a drone string, the cycle of hunger and gratification. And there is always a lack of good food associated with Bilbo's perils—almost as if as long as there is an ample supply of delicious food, no monsters can come near. The hospitable homes that end each component tale, arrived at after passage over a second body of water, offer resupply of food. In each of these refuges, or Homely Houses, a host sets retrospectively the tone of the component tale, reflects the type of perils that have been overcome, and sets the next component tale into motion.

These parallels are strong, but not monotonous, because of many variations: sometimes perils come in clusters, and the last two tales are melded together by a major shift in point of view and a narrative flashback, which prevents the slackening of narrative tension occasioned by the earlier Homely Houses and drives the story toward its climax. Still, however transformed, the component tales are remarkably parallel in their parts, like seasonal variations on a familiar ritual, an oft-told tale.

Also, in each of the component tales, Bilbo experiences an initiation, enacts progressively a pattern of testing and reward. He is placed in situations where he must choose to act, and when he acts appropriately, he is rewarded with a prize—in all but one part a physical object, and in one part (the third) promotion to a position of leadership of the company that at first only grudgingly accepted him as a follower. When the company is in danger, Bilbo tries within his limited but growing abilities to save it. And in each of the component tales, a savior does appear to work a *eucatastrophe* at the moment of direst peril. Bilbo participates in this pattern progressively: in the first part he is saved by luck and watches as Gandalf saves the others, in the second he saves himself but cannot save others, in the third he saves himself and others, in the fourth he contributes a collective effort of salvation, and in the fifth (a strange culmination suggesting a complex moral or theological position) he makes great sacrifice and is honored for it, but is unable to affect the outcome. Salvation comes, so to speak, from unearned grace, from the sudden arrival of forces beyond human prediction or control.

In each part Bilbo is rewarded for service, for growing unselfishness, but perhaps more for a willingness to act decisively, to move outward from the passive stance in which Gandalf finds him in the beginning, smoking by the door of his well-stocked hole.

Zena Sutherland

SOURCE: "Modern Fantasy: Fantasy with Folktale Elements: J. R. R. Tolkien," in *Children & Books,* ninth edition, Addison Wesley Longman, Inc., 1997, pp. 232-33.

No other fantasy of our time has appealed to as broad an age range of readers as has *The Hobbit;* children are enthralled by it, and adults probe and discuss the inner meanings of the book and of its companion tale, *The Lord of the Rings,* a complex three-volume sequel. Professor Tolkien was an eminent philologist and an authority on myth and saga, and his knowledge provided so firm a base for the mood and style of his writing that there is no need for scholarly demonstration. Middle-earth *is.* Tolkien wrote of it as easily as one writes about one's own home, and the familiarity of approach lends credence to the world he created.

The hero of *The Hobbit* is Bilbo Baggins, a little creature who is neat and quiet, who loves his material comforts, and who has no desire to do great deeds. When he is tricked into going along on a quest, however, the little hobbit rises to the occasion, showing that even the common person (or hobbit) is capable of heroism.

There are several qualities that contribute to the stature of *The Hobbit.* The adventures are exciting, the characters are differentiated and distinctive, and the book bubbles with humor. One of the amusing qualities is the aptness of the invented personal and place names. Bilbo's mother's unmarried name was Belladonna Took, perfectly in accord with her reputation as a hobbit who had had a few adventures before she settled down as Mrs. Baggins. And what an admirable name for a dragon—Smaug, and what an equally appropriate name for his lair—the Desolation of Smaug. Perhaps a special appeal lies in the very fact that Bilbo Baggins is a quiet little creature whose achievements are due to a stout heart, tenacity, and loyalty to his friends rather than to great strength or brilliance. He puts heroism within the grasp of each reader. Many folktale elements are present—the human-beast, elves, the enchanted artifact—all woven naturally into the tale.

Yoshiko Uchida

1921-1992

Japanese-American author of fiction and nonfiction and author/illustrator of fiction.

Major works include *Journey to Topaz: A Story of the Japanese-American Evacuation* (1971), *Journey Home* (sequel to *Journey to Topaz*, 1978), *The Best Bad Thing* (sequel to *A Jar of Dreams*, 1983*), The Two Foolish Cats: Suggested by a Japanese Folktale* (1987), *The Wise Old Woman* (retold by Uchida, 1994).

For more information on Uchida's career prior to 1983, see *CLR*, Vol. 6.

INTRODUCTION

Uchida is respectfully considered one of the most important pioneers of Japanese-American literature for middle-grade readers. A writer of picture books, short stories, folk tales, historical fiction, and contemporary fiction, Uchida strove to advance an understanding of Japanese life and increase the pride of Japanese-Americans in their heritage. She is the author of nearly three dozen books, including masterful retellings of Japanese folk tales, autobiographical and fictional interpretations of the Japanese-American relocation camp experience during World War II, and stories about pilgrimages of the world seen through the eyes of Japanese and Japanese-American pre-teens. An American of Japanese descent, Uchida drew from her own experiences in the United States and Japan to write brilliant stories that delight children of all nationalities. Her writings are generally set in Japan and feature Japanese youngsters, or focus on Japanese-American youth living in the United States. Her early works allow readers to see what life in Japan's cities and countryside is like, as well as observe the ancient traditions and the modern, post-war culture. Uchida turned to the Japanese-American experience after becoming convinced that she should share her own recollections as an internee at a government camp during World War II. In *Major Authors and Illustrators for Children and Young Adults*, she explained, "I want to dispel the stereotypic image still held by many non-Asians about the Japanese and write about them as real people. . . . I write to celebrate our common humanity, for the basic elements of humanity are present in all our strivings."

Often historically based, her books have been described as well researched and faithful in details of the period and setting, while her prose is regarded as simple, charming, and smoothly written. Her heartwarming stories also incorporate universal themes such as interacting with parents and friends, assuming responsibility, and gaining self-confidence. Uchida's goal when writing for a young

audience is clear, as she once commented, "Although all my books have been about the Japanese people, my hope is that they will enlarge and enrich the reader's understanding, not only of the Japanese and the Japanese Americans, but of the *human condition*. I think it's important for us each to take pride in our special heritage, but we must never lose our sense of connection with the community of man. And I hope our young people will, through the enriching diversity of books they read, learn to celebrate our common humanity and the universality of the human spirit."

Biographical Information

Born in 1921 in Alameda, California, Uchida was the younger of two daughters born to Japanese immigrants. When Uchida was a child, the family moved to Berkeley, California, where they lived for nearly twenty years before the beginning of World War II. Uchida was interested in writing and books from a young age, and kept a journal in order to, as she stated in *Something about the Author Autobiography Series (SAAS)*, "hold on to and somehow preserve the magic as well as the joy and sadness of certain moments in my life." She attended the University of California and, during her senior year of college in 1942, she and her family, along with thousands of other Japanese Americans, were transported to U.S. internment camps after the bombing of Pearl Harbor. *The Invisible Thread: A Memoir* (1992) is Uchida's stirring account of her childhood and the impact her experience in the prison camps had on her writing. "My whole world fell apart," she recalled in *SAAS*. For five months, Uchida and her family lived in a horse stall at the Tanforan Racetrack in California. During this time she taught second grade in a makeshift school until the family was moved again, with all the internees, to a larger camp called Topaz in the Utah desert. With the help of the American Friends Service Committee, Uchida and her sister were able to leave Topaz in order to do graduate-level work on the East Coast.

Uchida left the camp in 1943. "It had been a devastating and traumatic year," she recalled in *SAAS*, "which left a lasting impact on my life, but it was many years before I could write about the experience." In 1944, Uchida received a master's degree in education from Smith College. In addition to being a full-time writer for a number of years, Uchida also taught school at the Frankford Friends' School in Philadelphia. In 1952, Uchida received a Ford Foundation research fellowship that allowed her to visit Japan for two years. "[M]y years in Japan had made me aware of a new dimension to myself as a Japanese American and deepened my respect and admiration for the culture that had made my parents what they were," Uchida explained in *Authors and Artists for Young Adults*. Three collections of Japanese folk tales resulted from her research there, including the works featuring Sumi, an "appealing little girl of modern Japan," wrote a *Virginia Kirkus' Service* reviewer. Uchida's best-known books, however, are her five historical novels about Japanese Americans, including *Journey to Topaz, Journey Home, A Jar of Dreams* (1981), *The Best Bad Thing*, and *The Happiest Ending* (1985), all written for middle-graders. Uchida's memories of the past inspired her work all her life; she continued to "find bits and pieces of [her] child self turning up" in her writing as an adult. Uchida died of a stroke in 1992.

Major Works

Uchida retold Japanese folktales and wrote stories about children living in Japan in an effort to share the spirit of Japan's culture with Americans and to dispel stereotypes about the Japanese. She wrote historical fiction about Japanese Americans to give children of Japanese descent pride in their ancestry and to educate children of all nationalities about the past. She shared her experiences during World War II as a testimony to those who survived the internment and to help prevent the same suffering from being repeated. In all of her works, Uchida attempted to show that people are the same, no matter where they live or what they look like—a goal, most critics agree, she has admirably fulfilled. The death of her mother in 1966 prompted Uchida to write a book for

her parents "and the other first-generation Japanese (the Issei), who had endured so much," she commented in *Contemporary Authors*. The outcome was *Journey to Topaz: A Story of the Japanese-American Evacuation* and its sequel, *Journey Home*. Based on her own experiences, these books marked a shift from an emphasis on Japanese culture to the Japanese-American experience in the United States. The stories tell of eleven-year-old Yuki Sakane, her father, mother, and eighteen-year-old brother Ken and their internment in the relocation camps during World War II, and how their lives changed after the war. Both works educate young readers on the fundamental values of a Japanese-American family. *Journey to Topaz*, written for an eight-to-twelve-year-old audience, uses a remarkably light and positive tone to tell the story, despite the harsh circumstances. At the beginning of the story, the FBI takes Yuki's father away from the family because of his prominence in the Japanese-American community. Yuki's brother, Ken, replaces the father as the head of the household and, as the story unfolds, the reader witnesses Ken's increasing bitterness about the way the Japanese are being treated. Yuki's mother is a strong and noble character who admirably keeps a positive attitude about life throughout the tragic ordeal and refuses to submit to despair. Uchida carefully balances good and bad characters and events, describing several acts of kindness shown to the family throughout this otherwise devastating time. The American friends who visit the Sakanes, bringing delicious food with them, remind the audience that not all Americans were prejudice against the Japanese. Ester Mikyung Ghymn remarked, "The author does not dramatize events to evoke pity or anger. Instead she reveals the circumstances through the innocent eyes of a child. This perspective draws a child's emotional response from the adult reader." *Journey to Topaz* conveys the quiet dignity and strength demonstrated by the prisoners, especially the Issei. "Young Japanese-Americans could benefit considerably from reading this work, for it would enable them to come to grips with an experience their parents, grandparents, and others in their families lived through. Others, neither Japanese-Americans nor young, should find Miss Uchida's work a moving experience," marveled Laurence Smardan in *Journal of Home Economics*.

Journey Home depicts the hardships that individuals and families faced while rebuilding their lives in a harsh environment of distrust, fear, and hatred. "This sequel to *Journey to Topaz* offers a realistic picture of the domestic cruelty governments and people—including the American—have been capable of in wartime. The persecution of the Nisei during the 1940s will open the eyes of many young readers," writes Sharon Spredemann Dreyer in *The Bookfinder: A Guide to Children's Literature about the Needs and Problems of Youth Aged 2-15*. Now twelve years old, Yuki Sakane still thinks about the horrid time she spent with her family in the Japanese relocation camp during World War II. Although the Sakanes were still fortunate to have been released, the harsh anti-Japanese feeling makes earning a living a great challenge. The Sakanes return to Berkeley and, in time, work with other Japanese Americans to open a grocery store. After returning home from the war with a broken leg and a shattered spirit, Ken suffers post-battle emotional agonies. Yuki watches his anguish with sadness and grapples with her own feelings of loss and change, as the world they once knew no longer exists. "Though one wishes that relationships and characters were more fully explored and developed, there are many sensitive touches and interesting glimpses into a largely ignored but important historical episode," noted Judith Goldberger. Dora Jean Young remarked that "[a]s in other Uchida books, including the one to which this is a sequel . . . family tradition and loyalty overcome all problems. This book fills a great need in describing the cruel treatment inflicted upon Japanese Americans during World War II by their fellow Americans."

Every book Uchida wrote after *Journey to Topaz* responded to the growing need for identity among third generation Japanese Americans. Uchida wrote in *SAAS*, "I wanted not only to reinforce their self-knowledge and pride, but to give them and all young people a sense of continuity and kinship with the past." The trilogy—*A Jar of Dreams, The Best Bad Thing,* and *The Happiest Ending*—studies Japanese-American life during the Great Depression of the 1930s. The second novel in the trilogy, *The Best Bad Thing,* finds eleven-year-old Rinko Tsujimura dismayed at the thought of spending the rest of her cherished summer vacation with Mrs. Hata, a recently widowed friend of the family, as her mother has requested. Although Mrs. Hata has two young sons, her broken down house has no phone or electricity, and everyone claims Mrs. Hata is "a little crazy." Rinko, however, soon fits into the household and even grows to enjoy the company of the somewhat eccentric Mrs. Hata. However, Mrs. Hata faces one devastating catastrophe after another: her son, Abu, is seriously injured while hopping a train, her much-needed truck is stolen, and Rinko discovers that the mysterious man who lives in the barn is an illegal immigrant who fears discovery and deportation. These events, however, eventually lead Rinko to realize that things are not always as bad as they seem. Anne Okie noted that "the details of Rinko's Japanese-American family life make fascinating reading and Rinko's occasional references to the prejudice she encounters provide some gentle messages." Okie concluded, "The rich warmth and complexity of family and community life that radiate from this story make a refreshing change from the relentless trivialism of much modern fiction."

In *The Two Foolish Cats,* Uchida entertains readers with this English adaptation of a Japanese folk tale about a big cat, Daizo, and a little cat, Suki. After a day of unsuccessful hunting, the cats stumble across two rice cakes by the edge of a stream; they begin to hiss and spit at each other to determine which deserves the larger rice cake. This noisy episode draws the attention of a kimono-clad badger, who advises that they consult the wise monkey of the mountain to settle their dispute. The monkey, a type of trickster figure, attempts to solve their problem by eating bits and pieces from each cake in order to make them equal sizes. Of course, both cakes manage to disappear during this process, and the cats are left greatly embarrassed by their behavior. A *Publishers Weekly* reviewer noted that "Uchida's telling is as lyrical as that of her longer novels."

The Wise Old Woman, also a retelling of a Japanese folktale, is set in medieval Japan where a young farmer lives with his elderly mother in a village ruled by a cruel young lord. The lord has decreed that all people who reach the age of 70 are useless and must be abandoned in the mountains and left to die. When the farmer's mother turns 70, she tells him to take her away, but he cannot bear the thought of leaving her alone to die. He digs a hidden room in his house, where the old woman lives undiscovered for two years. One day, the powerful Lord Higa threatens to conquer the village unless its cruel young lord can pass a test. Higa gives the lord three seemingly impossible tasks, but the wise men in the village are unable to solve them; likewise, gods do not answer the invocations of the people. The farmer's mother, however, is able to solve all of the tasks, and the cruel young lord, after hearing who saved his village, reverses his decree and declares that from now on elders "will be treated with respect and honor, and will share with us the wisdom of their years." A *Kirkus Reviews* critic noted that "Uchida tells this folktale with simplicity and grace. . . . A wonderful way to explain respect for the elderly." John Philbrook further hailed the story as "[v]erbally and visually elegant, emotionally touching, with a timeless moral."

Awards

Uchida has received countless awards and honors during her years as a writer. Among them are a 1976 citation from the Contra Costa chapter of Japanese American Citizens League for outstanding contribution to the cultural development of society and twoChildren's Choice citations from the International Reading Association, for *Journey Home* in 1979 and for *The Happiest Ending* in 1985. Uchida received a Distinguished Service Award from the University of Oregon in 1981 for significant contribution to the cultural development of society. She also received an award from the Berkeley chapter of the Japanese American Citizens League in 1983 for "her many books which have done so much to better the understanding of Japanese culture and Japanese American experiences in America."

In addition, Uchida was bestowed the Friends of Children and Literature Award in 1987 for *A Jar of Dreams. Journey to Topaz, The Best Bad Thing*, and *The Happiest Ending* were all ALA Notable Books, and *Journey Home, A Jar of Dreams, The Best Bad Thing,* and *The Happiest Ending* were all Junior Library Guild selections. *The Best Bad Thing* received several Best Book of the Year citations, including one from *School Library Journal*. Uchida also was honored in 1988 by the Japanese American Citizens League with the Japanese American of the Biennium Award for outstanding achievement.

GENERAL COMMENTARY

Cathryn M. Mercier

SOURCE: "Yoshiko Uchida (1921-1992)," in *Writers of Multicultural Fiction for Young Adults: A Bio-Critical Sourcebook,* Greenwood Press, 1996, pp. 423-35.

Yoshiko Uchida draws widely upon her personal and family experiences in all her fiction. She was born in Alameda, California, and was the second daughter of Iku (née Umegaki) and Dwight Takashi Uchida, Japanese immigrants to the United States. Uchida claims the stories of her parents' lives were integral to her own growth and identity as a Japanese-American. She outlines their history in the young adult/adult autobiography *Desert Exile: The Uprooting of a Japanese American Family* (1982) and touches upon it in her memoir for children titled *The Invisible Thread* (1991). Elements of their courtship and marriage appear in *Picture Bride* (1987). Uchida's individual and collective relationship with her parents serves as a model for the parent-child dynamics in her thirty-six books. . . .

Even though she began writing at the age of ten, her first book was not published until 1951. Yoshiko Uchida received a two-year Ford Foundation Fellowship in 1952 which enabled her to visit Japan for the first time. While discovering new aspects of herself in her parents' native land, she researched Japanese folk arts, documented the lives of a well-known potter and a poet, and collected the folk tales which she would retell and publish later. She completed a series of articles about Japanese folk arts and crafts for the *Nippon News* (1953-1954) and later became a regular columnist for *Craft Horizons* (1955-1964). She wrote regularly for children and young adults from 1951 through 1987, with two newly illustrated folk tale picture books published posthumously in 1993 and 1994; she published a single novel for adults in 1987 and four works of nonfiction between 1953 and 1982. For *The Happiest Ending* (1985), she received the Bay Area Book Reviewers Award for Children's Literature. In 1981 the University of Oregon honored her life and work with its prestigious award. Her manuscripts and papers are housed at the Kerlan Collection at the University of Minnesota, the University of Oregon Library, and the Bancroft Library at the University of California at Berkeley. Uchida died in her childhood— and adulthood—hometown of Berkeley, California, in 1992.

Yoshiko Uchida believed that "a sharing of ideas will someday bring about the kind of peaceful world we all hope for" (*Magic Listening Cap*). Clearly, her experiences of harsh institutionalized and governmentally perpetuated racism fuel this drive. All her writing speaks to the humanitarian necessity of personal cultural identity and the possibility of a heterogeneous, complementary human community.

Yoshiko Uchida best states the unifying theme of her

work: "I hope to give young Asians a sense of their own history, but at the same time, I want to dispel the stereotypic image held by many non-Asians about the Japanese-Americans and write about them as real people. I also want to convey the sense of hope and strength of spirit of the first generation Japanese-Americans. Beyond that, I want to celebrate our common humanity" (*The Dancing Kettle*). Uchida accomplishes these goals in four distinct genres of writing for children and young adults: folk tales, including the picture book retellings as well as volumes of collected tales; stories for the young reader; historical novels; and autobiography.

Uchida's best-known volumes of Japanese folk tales fall within the earlier part of her career. The collection *The Dancing Kettle and Other Japanese Folk Tales* first saw publication in 1949 with Harcourt Brace and was reissued with a new cover, but with Richard Jones' original illustrations, in paperback in 1986 by the Creative Arts Book Company in Berkeley. These fourteen tales establish Uchida as a skilled reteller. She does not translate the stories directly from their Japanese source; rather, she adapts them to meet a contemporary and largely Americanized, if not American, audience. In this volume, too, Uchida provides a glossary and a pronunciation guide. This tactic enables her to use original Japanese words throughout the stories, resulting in a natural flow and ease of language. In addition, these appendixes also encourage unfamiliar readers to discover items, foods, places, or characters specific to Japanese culture; the pronunciation guide especially educates them in a new way of speaking and of sounding. *The Magic Listening Cap: More Folk Tales from Japan* (1955) also contains Uchida's original, simple illustrations to fourteen tales. *The Sea of Gold and Other Tales from Japan* (1965) adds twelve more tales. It echoes the other two volumes in their vivacity and freshness. Uchida's voice in all three captures the humor and color of Japanese folk characters. Uchida briefly establishes a Japanese setting in these three volumes as she describes rice fields, flower gardens, high mountains, and the ever-present sea. These three collections stand not only as authentic in their voice and research, but also as authoritative in their unique contribution of Japanese folklore to children's literature. Perhaps their importance is just now being understood as Japanese and non-Japanese artists return to these sources to select individual tales for picture book-length versions. Margot Zemach illustrated *The Two Foolish Cats* in 1987; Keiko Narahashi chose *The Magic Purse* for a 1993 book; and Martin Springett painted scenes for *The Wise Old Woman,* a 1994 publication.

Though not a folk tale in origin, *Rokubei and the Thousand Rice Bowls* (1962) takes its pattern and characters from folklore. Rokubei works in the rice fields all day but enjoys making pottery rice bowls in his free time. Soon the hundreds of rice bowls overwhelm his studio and threaten to push his wife and two children out of their home. Just as the family is about to revolt, a wealthy lord buys all of the bowls and appoints Rokubei as chief potter. Uchida's direct, simple telling of the story makes its ending, Rokubei's return to his beloved country home, not only predictable but also deeply satisfying.

By far, the largest and most inclusive group of Uchida's fiction falls under the category of books for young readers. The earliest of these publications was illustrated for and addressed to an audience of children ages five to eight. They contain straightforward stories told with wit and humor; they focus on a single event in a young protagonist's life. Though the setting may be Japan or the United States, though it may be ancient times or the modern day, Uchida instills the book with a profound sense of community and the underlying, sustaining potential of family. Like Rokubei, these characters discover the wonder and tranquillity of home.

Takao and Grandfather's Sword (1958) features one of Uchida's few male protagonists. At ten years old, Takao yearns to help his father make the twenty-five tea sets just ordered by a prominent shopkeeper. It is unfortunate that Takao seems to create havoc wherever he goes, no matter how good his intentions. When his best efforts result in ruination of the kiln, Takao sells his treasured legacy, his grandfather's sword. Uchida's appreciation for the potter as artisan infuses this book and underscores Takao's respect for his talented father. A forgiving family and a village wise man help Takao restore his own pride as he helps his father rebuild from disaster.

Uchida combines the Christian celebration of Christmas with the Japanese winter in *The Forever Christmas Tree* (1963). In Sugi Village in Japan, bored Takashi and his school-aged sister Kaya venture into the backyard of the annoying Mr. Toda to decorate the only appropriate tree for Christmas. The children's daring eventually brings them the friendship of the old man. As she did with Takao, Uchida keeps the world of these two children limited to their immediate family at first, then she slowly expands that world to include an elderly man from the village. The children grow beyond their original expectations as they cross intergenerational boundaries with their respect and friendship.

Seven-year-old Sumi in *Sumi's Prize* (1964), *Sumi's Special Happening* (1966), and *Sumi and the Goat and the Tokyo Express* (1969) has one best friend in all of Sugi Village: its oldest resident, Mr. Gonzaburo Oda. In the first book, Sumi's father helps her to design and construct the most beautiful butterfly kite for entry in a contest. In this story, Sumi crosses an unspoken gender boundary to become the only girl entered in the contest. Rather than chastising her, the community welcomes her and recognizes the uniqueness of her contributions. This departure from gender-defined expectations of female characters appears in many of Uchida's books. As she discovers cultural differences in the treatment of gender, Uchida devises female characters who push the confines imposed by a Japanese perspective; however, she does not reconfigure completely the Japanese girl into a liberated American female. Thus, Uchida boldly exposes Japanese attitudes without merely replacing them with an American counterpart. She creates a tension between the two cultures which resides within the emerging personality of the female protagonists.

In the second book, Sumi's relationship with Mr. Oda develops. She yearns to give him an exciting, meaningful ninety-ninth birthday present. With the help of her schoolteacher-mayor, she takes him on a ride in the village's first fire engine. The third book once again starts at Sumi's school. However, Sugi Village undergoes change when the Tokyo Express extends its line along the edge of town. As Uchida introduces subtly the implications of this event, she holds true to the child's perspective and shows the school children's curiosity in the train and its passengers on the day Mr. Oda's red-hatted goat stops the train in its tracks. Uchida enlarges the tight circle of Sumi's family to include the larger community, and, through the symbolic train, to places beyond the familiar village.

Two of Uchida's picture books fall toward the end of her career, though they continue the themes she invokes in earlier books for young readers. In *The Birthday Visitor* (1975), Emi Watanabe wants to protect her seventh-birthday celebration from the intrusion of yet one more in her parents' long line of visitors from Japan. Emi's birthday turns out to be a fine party not just because her special friends the retired Wadas come, not just because five-year-old Benji stays, but especially because the visiting Reverend Okura appreciates a seven year old's perspective. Once again, Uchida combines children, adults, young, and old in joyful ways. Similarly, *The Rooster Who Understood Japanese* (1976) shows the reassuring results when a young child helps an older friend. Mrs. Kitamura's neighbor called the police to cease the disturbing daily cock-a-doodle-dooing of her rooster. Miyo devises a plan and finds the perfect home in the country for this beloved pet. The young characters operate within a safe, loving environment which instills self-esteem and makes success possible.

Large, bold print and small page decorations point to the older intended readership for *Makoto: The Smallest Boy* (1970). In the third grade, Makoto already feels a failure because others excel in ways he cannot. Uchida extends the special relationship between old and young explored in the Sumi books as Mr. Imai directs Makoto to discover his hidden, distinctive talent as an artist. Family and friends remain the central empowering components for the young artist.

Children ages seven to eleven can learn much about the city of Tokyo in *In-Between Miya* (1967) and *Hisako's Mysteries* (1969). Twelve years old and the middle child, Miya feels caught "in-between" and trapped by her plain house, family, and friends. She quickly accepts an invitation to do chores and household duties for her sick aunt and struggling uncle living in Tokyo. Miya expects more fun than work; she discovers she just may be too young to cope with the demands of running the house. Miya returns to her family with appreciation of them and their quiet, simple lifestyle. It is Hisako's curiosity about a mysterious birthday and about life outside her grandparents' house, her home since her parents' deaths, that prompts her to accept an invitation to visit her cousins and a friend in Tokyo. Hisako learns that her father is alive; yet, like Miya, she also finds that she may be too young to accept the full implications of some secrets. With these two books, Uchida's characters begin to venture outside their immediate families and towns into an extended family and into a larger sphere of activity and expectation.

Throughout these books, Uchida depicts a childhood of comfort and safety. Like Sumi, Takao, Miya, and Makoto, these children grow up within firmly identified, traditional families. Elders within the family and the community are respected and even befriended. It is this world that shifts dangerously when Uchida crosses the ocean to set her stories in America. That effect began in *Samurai of Gold Hill* (1972), and escalates in the Topaz books. This change also defines a change in Uchida's audience. As she tackles material of increased emotional complexity, she turns to an older audience and more intricate storytelling in slightly longer novels. The characters in these books are older, ranging in ages from eleven to fourteen, and they assume significant responsibilities within the household as they grow in independence and reliability.

The Promised Year (1959) signals Uchida's interest in stories of immigration. For middle readers, she describes Keiko's journey across the ocean to live in California with her Aunt Emi and Uncle Henry. Keiko decides she can endure her visit with this difficult uncle because of its limit to a single year. Uchida uses that time frame to demonstrate the tremendous growth that can occur. In that short time, eleven-year-old Keiko helps to run the household during her aunt's hospitalization, and she risks Uncle Henry's displeasure when she warns him about an oncoming smog that threatens his carnation business. Keiko goes well beyond her desire to be accepted as she assumes the role and the trust of an older child.

Samurai of Gold Hill (1972) also moves from Japan to America. Living in a historically distant Japan of 1869, Koichi yearns to be his father's companion and apprentice. When his father joins with other men in town to pool their funds to emigrate to America, Koichi wonders what will happen to his dream of continuing the family tradition of samurai. Their life in California becomes less peaceful than imagined as the Japanese fall under racist attack and Koichi devotes his best, most noble samurai efforts to ensuring peace and goodwill in the Wakamatsu colony on Gold Hill. Koichi moves from his self-centered wishes into full participation as a reliable community member.

Somehow, *Journey to Topaz* (1971) and *Journey Home* (1978) never betray Uchida's domineering belief in hope

as they shape fiction around a bleak episode in America's history. Despite the shameful treatment of the Japanese-Americans during World War II, Uchida's two novels demonstrate a pervasive trust of and loyalty to the American government. The novels hold tenaciously to an eleven-year-old child's perspective as they describe the prisoners' existence: Uchida speaks of inadequately met basic needs of shelter, clothing, and food. She traces the four Sakane family members' evacuation from their beloved, cultivated Berkeley home to the Tanforan Race Track Assembly Center and then to the windy, dusty, incomplete relocation center in the Sevier Desert at Topaz. Father eventually joins them from his location in Montana while older brother Ken answers the army's call to join a special Nisei, second-generation Japanese-American unit. Uchida describes the concentration camp in all its dispiritedness and gloom. Yet, both novels simultaneously depict resilient characters whose constant tie to family and willingness to reach out to others allow them to persist and even to flourish.

Twelve-year-old Yuki makes a lifelong friend in Emi; the neighbors on the other side of the Sakane's barracks share despair and happiness; a community builds itself up, complete with schools, dances, funerals, and weddings. The move home proves nearly as devastating as the journey to Topaz. Once again, the family surrounds itself with good friends, with others in need, and they organize a solid foundation from which to build a future. Uchida does not shy away from showing the historically accurate hate crimes and resistance to the released Japanese; however, she uses the opportunities to bind together further the tight community. Most importantly, Uchida contrasts those who continue to hate with those who start to see individuals beyond appearance. When Ken returns, injured and broken, from his army service, only the Olssens can free him from his emotional pain—they understand because their only son died fighting against Japan. Uchida resists overplaying these moments. She inserts them into the fabric of the fiction, presents them with understated subtlety, and invites the reader to determine their magnitude.

The Topaz books certainly offer the generational "link to the past" and provide young readers "with the cultural memory they lack" (*Desert Exile*). Noting Uchida's desire to convey to "Japanese-American young people an understanding of their own history and pride in their identity" [in Karen Nelson Hoyle's *Twentieth-Century Children's Writers*], her final trilogy of novels makes a fitting conclusion to her fictional work. In these books, Uchida continues to portray the closely knit Japanese family, to examine how it nurtures its young, and to envision a future of promise and hope. Uchida departs from her characteristic third-person narrator to develop the first-person voice of eleven-year-old Rinko in *A Jar of Dreams* (1981), *The Best Bad Thing* (1983), and *The Happiest Ending* (1985). Rinko's adventures in just over a year immerse the reader in Japanese traditions. Rinko's favorite foods and festivals are given full description here. Additionally, Rinko feels the pull between her

Japanese heritage and her American culture. She discovers no easy answers, but learns to look at and to listen to individuals. Here, Uchida truly realizes her goal to expose a common humanity. For example, Rinko resists the idea of the arranged marriage of an acquaintance and tries to make a match for romantic love. Only when she sees the intended bride and groom as complex people, truly capable of independent choice, can she forgo the American romantic ideal for the better advised Japanese tradition. Throughout these three books, Rinko emerges as a typical, and an exceptional, Uchida character. She defeats stereotypes, both those she holds and those others cast her in, to materialize as an individual thinker and confident young woman with a firm sense of her own identity. That identity combines the dual cultures which shape her personality in original, exciting ways.

Uchida's narrative skills and her interest in personal life stories combine in a very early book, *The Full Circle* (1957). Umeko Kagawa, a teenager growing up in Japan, feels burdened by the celebrity of her father, a world renowned Christian leader. His popularity disturbs her quiet time, often makes him unavailable, and sometimes challenges her with insurmountable expectations. In this fictionalized story of the daughter of Dr. Toyohiko Kagawa, Uchida enters fully the reality of an adolescent girl. Readers quickly sympathize with Umeko's difficulty in part because they also recognize the fun and the joy characterizing her life. Umeko's mother and her friends help her to see past her own, at times, selfish need to recognize the contributions made by her father, and to see what individual attributes she shares.

In her two autobiographies, *The Invisible Thread* (1991) for children, and *Desert Exile: The Uprooting of a Japanese American Family* (1982) for young adults and adults, Uchida continues to explore a momentous, defining experience of being Japanese-American: the 1941 forced internment. Both books detail the full range of Uchida's life experience. *The Invisible Thread* follows Uchida's childhood and includes the internment episode: it focuses on her life within a stable, strong family. In contrast, *Desert Exile* turns explicitly on recounting the tragedy of the Japanese-American internment. A search for truth, a prevailing desire for understanding an incomprehensible historical reality, and the triumph of resilience, fortitude, and hope distinguish the books. Readers will find many biographical facts which Uchida reforms into story elements or into aspects of a character in her fiction. Young readers, especially, delight in this overlapping of fact and fiction as they discover the person who also is the author.

Picture Bride (1987) fits neatly into none of these genres. While published as an adult novel, *Picture Bride* could be read by a young adult audience, too. Though requiring greater reading skill than Umeko's story, adolescents, particularly adolescent females, will take immediately to the urgency felt by the twenty-one-year-old Japanese woman Hana. The match-making of Hana with Taro Takeda and her need to relocate to the United States will pique their romantic curiosity. Even more so will the irresistible attraction Hana feels to Taro's best friend. Hana's and Taro's marriage sustains; they fall in love slowly as they develop a life together. Adolescent readers will see in the Takedas' daughter Mary, who wants to forget her Japanese roots and become a fully integrated, fully accepted American, their own struggle for personal identity. And, like the Topaz books for younger readers and the autobiography *Desert Exile*, this novel recounts the Japanese-American internment experience; however, here Uchida adopts the more controlled, patient, yet equally confused perspective of two mature first-generation Japanese-Americans.

Yoshiko Uchida has won citations from prestigious professional organizations such as the National Council of Teachers of English, the American Library Association, the California Association of Teachers of English, the Japanese-American Citizens League, the International Reading Association, the National Council for Social Studies, and the Children's Book Council.

Uchida's work continues to receive critical applause. Her work consistently garners favorable reviews in journals such as *School Library Journal, The Horn Book, Kirkus Reviews, The Bulletin for the Center of Children's Books, Booklist,* and the *New York Times Book Review*. Her work is praised for its age-appropriateness: Uchida speaks to her different audiences in ways which respect their emotional and intellectual maturity even as she asks them to grow beyond themselves as a result of reading. Crafted stories and well-developed characters who lead complex lives and whose decisions are often difficult continue to earn the admiration of reviewers, educators, and children alike. Uchida's willingness to explore the rich theme of cultural identity makes her a daring author, and one of the first authors to break the boundaries of stereotype. She manages to describe the ceremonies, traditions, and customs of each culture without diminishing the other. Reviewers generally applaud the central place of the family in Uchida's work; some comment upon the distinct sense of morality and living a morally responsible, humanitarian life which define the core of Uchida's work.

While no definitive critical, or biocritical, study of Uchida's work has been published, she does earn substantial attention in both *Major Twentieth Century Writers* and *Twentieth Century Children's Writers*. These essays remark upon Uchida's accomplishments as storyteller, be it in retelling Japanese folk tales or in writing original fiction. They note her ability to establish character through description and through a masterful use of dialogue. They compliment Uchida's success in depicting Japanese and American settings. Karen Nelson Hoyle honors Uchida's writing from a multicultural perspective when she states that the "author has worked diligently in describing an ethnic group and interpreting cultural patterns as a step toward the 'creating of one world.'"

TITLE COMMENTARY

📖 *THE BEST BAD THING* (1983)

Kirkus Reviews

SOURCE: A review of *The Best Bad Thing,* in *Kirkus Reviews,* Vol. LI, No. 17, September 1, 1983, p. J-167.

In her stories of the Berkeley Tsujimuras in the 1930s, pursuing their own, Japanese-and-American life, Uchida is opening long-closed doors for children, just as Maxine Hong Kingston did for adults with her mysterious, earthy tales of California's Chinese. It is the summer after *A Jar of Dreams* (1981), and almost-twelve Rinko does not want to go to stay with newly-widowed, slightly "crazy" Mrs. Hata, and help her pick cucumbers, do housework, watch over "two pesky boys" like younger brother Joji. But Mama and Papa make her feel "it was my Christian duty to go." Auntie Hata, at any rate, is not uninteresting; and if eccentric, not crazy. As Papa has remarked, she may be the only Japanese lady to drive a truck—and she drives fast, like Papa. Though she understands English, it makes her uncomfortable to speak it: "Like I've put my undershirt on backwards. You know?" That's the way Rinko feels about speaking Japanese. Rinko learns other intriguing things. Auntie Hata isn't Buddhist or Christian. She hasn't electricity or a single clock—sons Zenny and Abu time themselves by the nearby trains. Baths are taken in a tub set outdoors, under the stars. An elderly, reclusive man, Mr. Yamanaka, lives in the barn. Then the "bad things" start happening, one after another. Instead of preventing Zenny and Abu from hitching rides on the trains, Rinko tries it herself—and sprains her ankle. In his kite-filled barn, Mr. Yamanaka applies a poultice—but she's not to tell anyone but her parents about him. Little Abu, hitching a train ride, is severely hurt; Auntie Hata's truck, the mainstay of her livelihood, is stolen. Are still more bad things in store? Not really. Mr. Yamanaka, an illegal immigrant, leaves when the welfare lady comes poking around—but it is good (as he writes) for him "to go home and to stop living in fear." Auntie Hata stupefies and routs the welfare lady (with some help from new "medium" Rinko); and Mama and Papa get her a job—keeping house for the Japanese bachelors in the church dormitory. "A brave lady" and a likable, live-wire girl—both with depths.

Denise M. Wilms

SOURCE: A review of *The Best Bad Thing,* in *Booklist,* Vol. 80, No. 2, September 15, 1983, p. 174.

Rinko, last seen in a *A Jar of Dreams,* here finds herself dispatched by Mama to spend a month with Mrs. Hata, whose husband has died and who needs help harvesting the cucumber crop and taking care of her house and two sons. Rinko is less than thrilled; Zeni and Abu, Mrs. Hata's sons, aren't her favorite people, and Mrs.

Hata herself is something of an eccentric. But Rinko does as she's told, and shortly comes to feel at ease with both the boys and Mrs. Hata. Then bad luck strikes the Hatas: Abu's habit of hopping freights lands him in the hospital with a serious injury; Mrs. Hata's precious truck is stolen, and a welfare worker shows up trying to get the Hatas to move to town and accept aid. Also, Rinko learns that the recluse who lives in Mrs. Hata's barn and who has helped her and the boys on several occasions is an illegal who fears discovery and deportation. Mrs. Hata shows signs of being beaten, but her faith and an opportune directive from Rinko save her from giving up. Thanks to a job found by Rinko's parents, Mrs. Hata's independence and well-being is a surer thing than before. Rinko's personality makes her a lively narrator, and her view of things will make readers sympathize with Mrs. Hata as much as she does—which makes for an absorbing, satisfying story.

Kate M. Flanagan

SOURCE: A review of *The Best Bad Thing,* in *The Horn Book Magazine,* Vol. LIX, No. 5, October, 1983, p. 578.

The sequel to *A Jar of Dreams* takes place in 1936, one year after the first book about Rinko Tsujimura and her family. With the summer almost over, the eleven-year-old girl was dismayed to learn that her mother wanted her to spend the rest of her vacation with a recently widowed friend. Mrs. Hata had two young sons, but she needed help with her housework and with her cucumber crops. Rinko hated to admit that she was "sort of scared about going to Mrs. Hata's." Her dilapidated house had no phone or electricity, and everyone said that the woman was "'a little crazy.'" But cheerful, forthright Rinko soon fitted into the household, even coming to like and admire Mrs. Hata, a strong and independent, if somewhat eccentric, woman. And the girl was intrigued by the mysterious, reclusive old man who lived in the barn. Then "the bad things started to happen"; as Mrs. Hata faced one trial after another and the old man's unhappy secret became known, Rinko learned about courage and dignity and how "'sometimes what you *think* is a bad thing . . . turns out to be a good thing.'" Rinko's chatty, first-person narrative is candid and often amusing. And while the book reveals some of the problems faced by Japanese Americans in prewar California, it is essentially about an appealing young girl's unique way of interpreting life's vicissitudes.

Anne L. Okie

SOURCE: A review of *The Best Bad Thing,* in *School Library Journal,* Vol. 30, No. 3, November, 1983, pp. 83-4.

When her parents ask her to spend a month helping Mrs. Hata, whom she believes is crazy, Rinko is sure her summer vacation will be ruined. One disaster follows another during her visit, but Rinko discovers that things are not always as bad as they seem. Set in California in the 1930s, the details of Rinko's Japanese-American family life make fascinating reading and Rinko's occasional references to the prejudice she encounters provide some gentle messages. Style and characterization are both excellent. The first-person narrative of this sequel to *A Jar of Dreams* is simple and direct, yet full of variety and imagination. Rinko's personality is so clearly communicated that the book will be of general interest, despite the unfamiliar setting. The rich warmth and complexity of family and community life that radiate from this story make a refreshing change from the relentless trivialism of much modern fiction.

📖 THE HAPPIEST ENDING (1985)

Bulletin of the Center for Children's Books

SOURCE: A review of *The Happiest Ending,* in *Bulletin of the Center for Children's Books,* Vol. 39, No. 2, October, 1985, pp. 38-9.

A third book about a Japanese-American community in California during the Depression Era is also narrated by Rinko, now twelve, and romantic enough to overcome her usual diffidence and determined to take a hand in an arranged marriage. What Rinko plans is stopping the union, since she feels the groom is too old for his bride. What she learns is that one shouldn't make hasty judgments and that admitting one's mistake can be a sign of maturity. Like the other books, this is convincing as a document by a child, it's faithful in its details to the period and the setting, and it's a warm, smoothly written story about family and family friends.

Phyllis Ingram

SOURCE: A review of *The Happiest Ending,* in *School Library Journal,* Vol. 32, No. 3, November, 1985, p. 92.

Rinko Tsujimura is a 12-year-old Japanese-American girl. When forced by her mother to take Japanese language lessons from Mrs. Sugino, she meets Mrs. Sugino's three boarders, one of whom is to marry Teru, an American-born girl of 19 who has been raised in Japan. Rinko is outraged by Teru's arranged marriage with a stranger and promptly finds a more handsome and youthful bridegroom. The Japanese community in Oakland, California, is a closely-knit one of mutual support and assistance, and when Mrs. Sugino's irresponsible husband loses the money that a boarder had given him to invest, her friends contribute their help and support. Most important, Rinko learns a valuable lesson in growing up and redefines her expectations regarding personal relationships. Rinko is an attractive heroine—bright, active and caught between the divergent cultures of Japan and America. Young readers may be confused by the attitudes expressed and the vocational and educational re-

strictions imposed upon the Japanese-Americans, for the fact that the story takes place in 1936 is not well integrated into the story. However, this is a good, comforting rite-of-passage story which will be particularly appealing to those who have read the previous two books about Rinko: *A Jar of Dreams* (1981) and *The Best Bad Thing* (1983).

Denise M. Wilms

SOURCE: A review of *The Happiest Ending,* in *Booklist,* Vol. 82, No. 5, November 1, 1985, p. 415.

Rinko is upset when she learns that Mr. Kinjo is the man who will be marrying the daughter of her friend Mrs. Hata. "You're too old for her!" she blurts and privately vows to find Teru a more suitably matched fiancé. What Rinko discovers, though, is that appearances can be deceiving and that Mr. Kinjo is a kind, honest, generous man who without a doubt will make Teru a wonderful husband. Set in the 1930s, the story highlights the blending of American and Japanese cultures. What Rinko observes in the adults around her are facets of shifting values. Her brother Cal is seriously dating a girl he has chosen himself; Teru, on the other hand, is happy to be matched to a good man who is paying her ticket from Japan. And then there is Rinko's Japanese-language teacher, who is the victim of a bad match and who decides to divorce her husband after he disgraces the family. As the title implies, Uchida fashions happy endings for nearly everyone, plus some definite growth on Rinko's part. Readers who have enjoyed the characters and stories in *A Jar of Dreams* and *The Best Bad Thing* will find further satisfaction here.

Patty Campbell

SOURCE: A review of *The Happiest Ending,* in *The New York Times Book Review,* February 9, 1986, p. 32.

In the dark purple shadow of the sheer eastern face of the Sierra Nevada, near the hamlet called Independence, Calif., lies a desert plain. It is baking hot in summer, swept by freezing winds from the mountains in the winter and barren except for brittle clumps of tumbleweed. Here and there, half hidden by the blowing sands, are flat stretches of concrete, sealed-off drains, scraps of rusted barbed wire. At a discreet distance from the highway that passes through this stark landscape is a monument erected by the California State Park Service. "May the injustices and humiliation suffered here as a result of hysteria, racism and economic exploitation never emerge again," it proclaims in bronze letters which have been nearly obliterated by vandals intent on denying our national disgrace. For this is the site of Manzanar, one of 10 relocation camps in which Americans of Japanese descent were interned during World War II.

Denial is an expensive attitude to hold toward history. Appropriately, the literature of the Japanese relocation is extensive on both adult and juvenile levels. . . . In fiction, the graceful and lively books of Yoshiko Uchida have drawn on the author's own childhood to document the Japanese-American experience for middle-grade readers. Two of these, **Journey to Topaz** and **Journey Home,** deal directly with the internment years. Her latest book, **The Happiest Ending,** is set in Berkeley, Calif., in the mid-1930s and continues the adventures of spunky Rinko Tsujimura so engagingly begun in **A Jar of Dreams** and **The Best Bad Thing.**

Rinko is now 12½, and still getting into trouble for saying exactly what she thinks. "I want to be like every other American," she sulks when Mama insists that she take the streetcar on Saturday afternoons to Mrs. Sugino's house for tutoring in Japanese. But Mrs. S., as Rinko calls her, turns out to be nicer than expected, and when she breaks her wrist chasing her bratty young son Boku, Rinko is glad to be delegated to help out. At Mrs. Sugino's supper table the middle-aged boarder, Mr. Kinjo, jubilantly announces that he has sent for and is planning to marry 19-year-old Teru, just as soon as she arrives from Japan. Rinko is appalled and says so, much to her own and everybody else's embarrassment. Nevertheless, she and her best friend, Tami, plot to prevent what seems to them an unsuitable match. But Teru, when finally told of their plan, is unimpressed, and when Mr. Kinjo shows his sterling character by saving Mrs. Sugino's honor with a generous sacrifice, Rinko has to admit that she has been wrong.

Yoshiko Uchida has a gift for humorous twists and vigorous narrative, and Rinko even at her most pig-headed is immensely likable. The canvas is filled in richly with details of Japanese-American life in the 30s: the furniture, clothes, food, social patterns and manners of a culture balanced between two identities. Over these cheerful daily events falls the shadow of the virulent anti-Japanese prejudices that were to be the foundation for the relocation. In **A Jar of Dreams** Rinko and her little brother are chased by a bigot who calls them "No-good Jap kids!" and who kills the family dog to discourage Mama from setting up a home laundry business. (Actually, the Anti-Japanese Laundry League was a fact of San Francisco life for several decades.) Rinko's older brother, Cal, studies hard at college, but often is discouraged because, as he says, "Who's going to hire a Japanese engineer?" Papa's profound pride in his Armistice Day display of the American flag is full of irony. Rinko herself, in her rejection of things Japanese, typifies the energetic Americanization of the second generation. But in five years the Nisei were to find that no amount of patriotic avowal could earn them trust from their native land.

Valerie Ooka Pang

SOURCE: A review of *The Happiest Ending,* in *Interracial Books for Children Bulletin,* Vol. 17, No. 1, 1986, p. 7.

This is the third novel in a trilogy about spunky Rinko Tsujimura, who lives in Berkeley, California, during the 1930s.

Rinko, like any other twelve year old, has many romantic notions about love. She puts her "foot in her mouth" when she finds out about an arranged marriage between Teru Sugino, only nineteen, and Mr. Kinjo—twice Teru's age. Rinko doesn't mean to hurt Mr. Kinjo by telling him he's too old for Teru, but she believes in this country women should be able to choose their own husbands. Rinko dreams about playing matchmaker between beautiful Teru and young and handsome Johnny Ochi. In the process, she learns people are not always what they seem to be.

Uchida, author of **Best Bad Thing** and **A Jar of Dreams,** has written another winner. She is a master at weaving Japanese American culture and values into her stories. **The Happiest Ending** carefully presents the delicate balance between old country values and U.S. culture and shows how Japanese America is not only a blend of both, but a dynamic community creating its own unique perspectives. The California setting provides all children with much-needed literature about Asian Americans, including information about U.S. racism during the period. (For example, Rinko's older brother, Cal, keeps encouraging her to be a teacher because he says maybe by the time Rinko grows up Japanese American teachers will be hired.) Educators can use sections of the book to stimulate classroom discussion about racism and cultural differences. This is an excellent novel not only for its literary merits but also for its social statements.

THE TWO FOOLISH CATS: SUGGESTED BY A JAPANESE FOLKTALE (1987)

Kirkus Reviews

SOURCE: A review of *The Two Foolish Cats: Suggested by a Japanese Folktale,* in *Kirkus Reviews,* Vol. LV, No. 8, April 15, 1987, p. 646.

Adopting a Japanese folk tale into casual, readable English, Uchida brings us an entertaining tale, reminiscent of Will and Nicolas' *Finders Keepers,* brought to vibrant life by [Margot] Zemach's glowing watercolors in an updated style suggestive of Japanese landscape painting and inhabited by delightful animals. A big cat, Daizo, and a little cat, Suki, have their tempers frayed by unsuccessful hunting, but discover two rice cakes lying on their path. They argue noisily over who gets the larger cake, and on the advice of a kimono-clad badger they consult the wise monkey of the mountain. The monkey solves their problem by eating from each cake in an attempt to make them equal. Naturally, both cakes disappear, and the cats are shamed by their foolishness.

Children will delight in the illustrations, finding amusing details such as the monkey's teapot and the dancing mice. The book could also serve as a fine introduction to the Japanese arts of brush and watercolor painting.

Publishers Weekly

SOURCE: A review of *The Two Foolish Cats: Suggested by a Japanese Folktale,* in *Publishers Weekly,* Vol. 231, No. 16, April 24, 1987, p. 68.

Uchida tells the story suggested by a Japanese folktale of two cats who are friends. The small birds and animals living in the Japanese pine forest fear the cats because they consume prey in a mouthful. One day the cats are having no luck finding a meal. In the forest they see two rice cakes, one larger than the other, and argue over who should have it. The cats go to a wise old monkey to settle the dispute, but he whittles the cakes down, trying to make them the same size, and eventually finishes both rice cakes himself. Uchida's telling is as lyrical as that of her longer novels. Zemach, with her marvelous versatility in depicting various cultures, triumphs with these Japanese-style watercolors.

Mary M. Burns

SOURCE: A review of *The Two Foolish Cats: Suggested by a Japanese Folktale,* in *The Horn Book Magazine,* Vol. LXIII, No. 3, May-June, 1987, p. 351.

"Long ago, at the edge of a dark pine forest in Japan, there lived two cats named Daizo and Suki. Because Daizo was big and fierce and had seven toes on each paw, he was called Big Daizo. Because Suki was small and skinny, he was called Little Suki." Although different in size, they are alike in one respect—their greed—and that is their downfall. One day, when their predatory skills fail, they discover two rice cakes. Unable to resolve their differences over the ownership of the larger viand, they consult the wise old monkey of the mountains, who offers to make the cakes equal in size by nibbling the excess from each in turn. Of course, he never quite succeeds, thus outwitting the pair while satisfying his own hunger. Shamed before all the other animals, the two "never quarreled again," having paid dearly for their folly. Based on a Japanese folk tale, the text flows smoothly with a rhythmic pace well suited for storytelling or reading aloud. Zemach's illustrations, executed in watercolor, reflect the humor of the story as well as its country of origin. Less flamboyant in portrayal of character, more delicately colored than her work for tales from the European tradition, they utilize motifs from the Japanese idiom—bamboo, iris, definitively limned branches—to create gracefully framed pages for the type. Yet, the principals, while carefully delineated to conform to the setting, reflect her genius for capturing the essence of a personality.

Kay E. Vandergrift

SOURCE: A review of *The Two Foolish Cats: Suggested by a Japanese Folktale,* in *School Library Journal,* Vol. 33, No. 11, August, 1987, pp. 75-6.

In this story suggested by a Japanese trickster tale, two cats, Big Daizo and Little Suki, are unsuccessful at finding breakfast. On their way home, they find two rice cakes in the reeds by the edge of the stream. Of course, one is big and plump and the other very small. The snarling, hissing, spitting fight over which cat should have the bigger rice cake draws the badger from the forest to scold the cats and send them to the wise old monkey to settle their quarrel. In typical trickster fashion the monkey ends the dispute by weighing and munching, weighing and munching until both rice cakes are equally gone. This telling just misses that magical quality of language which creates vivid images, and Zemach's illustrations do not give the story the life that it deserves. The soft tones of the watercolors at times seem overburdened with the dark outlines of trees, drawing attention away from the main action, and the details do not always match the text. Children will search in vain for the seven toes on each of Daizo's paws and will wonder why the birds and mice who are supposed to be frightened by the cats follow them so closely or why the cats do not appear wet as they emerge from the stream. The main characters are more crudely drawn than the portly robed badger and the mischievous monkey. On some pages Suki looks as much like a dog, a rodent, or a rabbit with a long tail as a cat. Overall, the illustrations lack the humor which is the essence of the trickster tale.

THE INVISIBLE THREAD: AN AUTO-BIOGRAPHY (1991)

Zena Sutherland

SOURCE: A review of *The Invisible Thread: An Autobiography,* in *Bulletin of the Center for Children's Books,* Vol. 45, No. 7, March, 1992, p. 195.

Photographs of the author and her family are included in the moving autobiography of a child who was born in this country, treated like an enemy during World War II, and only slowly—as maturity has lent perspective—able to accept the values of the Japanese culture that was her heritage, the culture to which she is tied by so many invisible threads. Many readers will be familiar with the horrors of relocation camps through reading *Journey to Topaz* and its sequels. Here is a sharper focus on those horrors and on the emotional anguish that accompanied physical stress and deprivation. Uchida is open about her feelings in a way that will make admirers feel they are friends; as always, she writes with mastery of style and an implicit respect for her readers. A list of Uchida's published works is provided.

Kay Weisman

SOURCE: A review of *The Invisible Thread: An Autobiography,* in *Booklist,* Vol. 88, No. 13, March 1, 1992, p. 1272.

Children's author Uchida, whose works include *Journey*

to Topaz and *A Jar of Dreams,* relates some of the important events of her childhood and young adulthood in the 1930s and 1940s. The younger daughter of Japanese-born parents, Uchida grew up in Berkeley, California, and always felt American, even though she was aware she looked different from her Caucasian friends. A trip to Japan with her family in the 1930s evoked the opposite response—there she fit in visually, but she found the Japanese language and many of the customs strange. Uchida writes movingly of her family's hardships during World War II. Her father, falsely accused of being a spy, was sent to a prison camp in Montana, and the entire family was forced into a relocation camp in Utah, even though Yoshiko and her sister were native-born Americans. In an epilogue, Uchida describes coming to terms with herself as an Asian American and expresses the hope that her books will help the sansei (third-generation Japanese Americans) develop pride in their heritage as well. Illustrated with black-and-white family photos, this will be fascinating reading for history students, Japanese Americans, and fans of Uchida's books.

Phyllis Graves

SOURCE: A review of *The Invisible Thread: An Autobiography,* in *School Library Journal,* Vol. 38, No. 4, April, 1992, p. 144.

In a clear, smoothly written style, with frequent dialogue and occasional figurative use of language or wry humor, Uchida describes her family history and happy childhood; her parents' traditional, arranged marriage; her father's business success; and their rich life, which blended Japanese and American cultures. She also recounts the Uchidas' experiences during World War II. For readers who don't know about the Japanese-American concentration camps, her book is an eye-opener. This autobiography is not a complete picture of the author; rather, it is the story of the stark contrast between her innocent early years and those she spent in internment, accompanied by black-and-white photographs. Another well-written book, Daniel S. Dave's *Behind Barbed Wire,* elaborates on these events, but Uchida's story is thought-provoking and important for giving young people a firsthand account of our inhumanity to others and for providing them with an individual's look at her personal development as a writer.

Liz deBeer

SOURCE: A review of *The Invisible Thread: An Autobiography,* in *Multicultural Review,* Vol. 1, No. 3, July, 1992, p. 68.

The Invisible Thread traces the author's life before and during internment with 12,000 other Japanese-Americans in United States concentration camps during World War II. The book begins by depicting the family's life before Japan bombed Pearl Harbor, revealing a typically American lifestyle with sibling spats and dating worries. Yoshiko also shares some of her anxieties about her dual Japanese/American identity as well as her beginnings as a writer.

By the middle of the book the Uchida family was imprisoned "not because we had done anything wrong, but simply because we *looked* like the enemy." They were forced to move from their comfortable Berkeley, California, home to an army barrack in Utah that measured about 18 by 20 feet. Black-and-white photographs of the family before and during their imprisonment reveal the strain of their confinement.

This well-written autobiography sensitively depicts the author's horror, allowing young readers to learn from her experience without frightening them. As she wrote in her Epilogue, Yoshiko hopes the book will allow readers "to see Japanese Americans not in the usual stereotypical way, but as fellow human beings. For although it is important for each of us to cherish our own special heritage. . . . we must all celebrate our common humanity."

This prolific, award-winning author has once again created a book to help readers learn and appreciate Japanese-American culture. The moving plot will make this book a favorite with pre-adolescents and adolescents. Because the narrator is female and the book cover is pastel with a photo of the author as a young girl, this book will have special appeal to females.

📖 *THE MAGIC PURSE* (adapted by Uchida, 1993)

Publishers Weekly

SOURCE: A review of *The Magic Purse,* in *Publishers Weekly,* Vol. 240, No. 27, July 5, 1993, p. 72.

On his way to the Iseh shrine, a young farmer meets a ghostly maiden who begs him to take a message to her parents in the Red Swamp. Though others attempt to dissuade him from the dangerous journey, he risks the snakes and crocodiles of the swamp because he has a "kind and gentle heart" and wants to help the young woman. Although he never sees her again, the red purse she has given him mysteriously fills with money overnight, and he becomes prosperous beyond measure. His friends rejoice at his good fortune, telling him, "Only a man with a kind heart would have delivered the letter. . . . And only a man of courage would have ventured alone into the Red Swamp. Surely you deserve all the riches that have come your way." For the most part, Uchida avoids the inherent preachiness of this old Japanese tale, and her elegant retelling is well paced and dotted with lyrical imagery. In a departure from the contemporary flavor of her other books for children (*Who Said Red?; Rain Talk*), [Keiko] Narahashi clearly evokes Japanese scroll paintings through her boldly outlined, seemingly spontaneous watercolors. Her luminous art sets the mood perfectly for Uchida's magical tale.

Elizabeth Bush

SOURCE: A review of *The Magic Purse,* in *Booklist,* Vol. 90, No. 3, October 1, 1993, p. 349.

A poor, young Japanese farmer interrupts his pilgrimage to the temple to carry a letter from a beautiful wraithlike maiden, held captive by the Black Swamp lord, to her parents in the treacherous Red Swamp. His courage and kindness are rewarded with an ever-filled purse and a tray of gold pieces. Forever after, the now-prosperous farmer brings an offering of rice cakes and wine to the Black Swamp; in return, he receives a flower and hears the maiden's haunting plea, "Don't forget me." Although the story has classic folktale trappings, Uchida's retelling lacks tension. The task is accomplished with facility and little dread, and the point of the farmer's journey, the temple visit, is thinly developed. However, the imagery of the tale provides a wonderful springboard for Narahashi's watercolors. Boldly brushed black strokes of swamp trees and mountains shimmer like wet ink. The diaphanous rendering of the maiden and the Swamps calls into question the reality of the farmer's visions, but then the solidity of the magic purse itself confirms his experience. This might be used as a supplement to units on Japan, but, unfortunately, notes on sources of the tale and its adaptation are not given.

John Philbrook

SOURCE: A review of *The Magic Purse,* in *School Library Journal,* Vol. 39, No. 11, November, 1993, p. 103.

A poor young man wishes to go on a pilgrimage with his friends, but lacks the money. Seeing them depart makes him so impetuous he sets out after them. Losing his way, he crosses a swamp, where a beautiful young woman asks him to take a letter to her parents in another swamp in Osaka. After he conquers his fear and accepts, she gives him a magic purse full of gold coins. He accomplishes his errand, and the woman's swamp-spirit parents also generously reward him. He now makes the pilgrimage in style, though missing his friends. He lives well to the end of his days, honoring the swamp maiden every year and, refreshingly for a folktale, following her instructions to always leave one coin in the purse. Though less elaborate than Uchida's retelling in Marianne Yamaguchi's *The Sea of Gold, and Other Tales from Japan,* this is nonetheless a satisfying retelling, replete with stylish prose, flowing dialogue, and convincing detail. Narahashi's watercolor-and-ink illustrations are evocative of the spooky swamp and Japanese countryside. Temple shade and farm somnolence are especially well captured in realistic yet dreamy pictures.

Hanna B. Zeiger

SOURCE: A review of *The Magic Purse,* in *The Horn Book Magazine,* Vol. LXX, No. 1, January-February, 1994, p. 80.

In this retelling of an old tale from Japan, a poor, young farmer hurries to catch up with friends who are making a spring pilgrimage to the shrine at Iseh. Taking a road which he thinks is a shortcut, he finds himself in the terrible and dismal Black Swamp, where he sees the apparition of a young girl floating across the water toward him. Explaining that she is imprisoned by the ruler of the swamp, she begs the young farmer to take a letter to her parents in the Red Swamp near Osaka. Troubled by her plight, he agrees and is rewarded by the gift of a magic purse that refills itself with coins. As he continues his journey, he is warned by people along the way that death awaits anyone who enters the Red Swamp, but the memory of the girl gives him the courage to go on. Despite his fears, he fulfills his task in a strange, mystical visit with the girls' parents and is given more gold as a reward. When he returns to his village, he builds a fine house and always helps those in need. And every spring, he returns to the Black Swamp in memory of the young girl he can never forget. Both the tale and the watercolor illustrations have the haunting quality of otherworldliness found in classic Japanese ghost films.

THE BRACELET (1993)

Roger Sutton

SOURCE: A review of *The Bracelet,* in *Bulletin of the Center for Children's Books,* Vol. 47, No. 1, September, 1993, p. 25.

"It was crazy, Emi thought. They loved America, but America didn't love them back." When Emi and her family are taken away during World War II to a Japanese-American internment camp, she brings a precious remembrance, a gold chain bracelet from Laurie, Emi's best friend in the second grade. While settling in to their barely converted horse stall at the Tanforan Racetracks, Emi loses the bracelet but is assured by her mother that Laurie, like Emi's father who has been previously taken away, like all the possessions they left behind, will be carried in their hearts to "take with us no matter where we are sent." While somewhat fragmentary in its structure and conclusion, the book (previously published as a short story) is a gentle, honest introduction to the treatment of the Japanese-Americans during the war, and [Joanna] Yardley's delicate pencil-and-watercolor paintings are cleanly drawn and richly colored, with scant pencil lines softly framing the sad scenes. A brief afterword gives a context for the story, allowing parents or librarians to give historical weight to a feeling all kids can share, the pain of missing a friend.

Hazel Rochman

SOURCE: A review of *The Bracelet,* in *Booklist,* Vol. 90, No. 2, September 15, 1993, p. 162.

Like many other books by Uchida, this picture book story is based on her own experience as a Japanese

American interned in a prison camp during World War II. A brief afterword summarizes the general facts and figures of the injustice and the recent restitution, but the story and pictures are about one child, Emi, and her bewilderment and sadness: leaving her empty house, saying goodbye to her best friend, traveling with her mother and older sister to the abandoned Tanforan Racetracks, and trying to make a home in a dark, dirty horse stall. Before Emi leaves Berkeley, her best friend gives her a bracelet. Emi's heartbroken when she loses the gift in the camp, but she comes to realize that she doesn't need a bracelet to remember what she loved and left behind. The bracelet becomes a metaphor for the gift of friendship, the loss, and the enduring bond. Yardley's watercolor paintings show the long lines of people and the barbed wire and also the heartfelt emotion, as when Emi hugs her friend goodbye. Rooted as this story is, it is about the wartime refugee experience everywhere, and kids will identify with the injustice that could suddenly invade an ordinary home right here on their street.

Kyoko Mori

SOURCE: "You're Never Too Old to Be Homesick," in *The New York Times Book Review,* November 14, 1993, p. 21.

Yoshiko Uchida's story **The Bracelet** features an American-born nisei girl, Emi, during World War II, when her family is ordered to a relocation camp.

Ms. Uchida, the author of many books for children, including **A Jar of Dreams,** does not hold back from painful truths. The book begins with the tears Emi sheds to see her empty house "like a gift box with no gift inside—filled with a lot of nothing." When her family arrives at their barracks at the detention camp; we are told, "No matter what anybody called it, it was just a dark, dirty horse stall that still smelled of horses."

Often, Ms. Uchida enriches her narrative by describing what is *not*. When the doorbell rings, Emi expects a government messenger coming to retract the relocation order. Instead, she finds her best friend, Laurie Madison, who has not come to walk to school, to go roller-skating or to show off a new dress. Though she brings a gift, it is not for a birthday, but a farewell gift of a golden bracelet.

The story continues using these narrative principles scrutinizing painful truths, defining things by what they are not. No miracle happens to spare Emi's painful uprooting. She loses the bracelet but realizes that she does not need it to remember Laurie, just as she does not need to see her home to remember it. The story ends with an anticipation of another move rather than a return home: "They would soon be sent to a camp in the Utah desert, but Laurie would still be in her heart even there."

We come to know Emi, through her thoughts, as a strong and likable girl. The minor characters in the story, too, are briefly but deftly portrayed, from Emi's older sister, who takes an angrier attitude toward relocation, to a family friend at the camp who politely rushes off to fetch mattresses because he does not want to linger and see Emi's mother cry.

The illustrations by Joanna Yardley underscore the dawning of hope implied by Emi's realization that no one can take away what is in her heart. The opening pictures of her home are full of pinks, light blues, greens. In the scenes of the journey and the camp at night the palette darkens to grays, browns, navy blue and eerie yellows. At the end, the light blue sky, white shirts on the line and Emi's red sweater and shoes again evoke cheerfulness as we realize that an empty gift box need not be a metaphor for despair. Though the box is "filled with a lot of nothing," people like Emi—people who are courageous—can sustain memory and hope on almost nothing.

Eva Mitnick

SOURCE: A review of *The Bracelet,* in *The Five Owls,* Vol. VIII, No. 3, January-February, 1994, pp. 61-2.

Many fine books about the internment of Japanese-Americans during World War II exist, but few are intended for younger readers. The late Yoshiko Uchida's new picture book is a perfect candidate to fill this gap.

Second-grader Emi and her family are all packed up and ready to leave their Berkeley, California, home for Tanforan Racetracks, which has been transformed into a prison camp; Emi's father has already been sent to a prisoner-of-war camp in Montana. The doorbell rings: it is Emi's best friend Laurie, who has come to say goodbye and to give her a gold bracelet, which Emi vows to wear forever. However, when Emi arrives at the camp, she discovers that the bracelet is missing; a thorough search of the dark and dirty horse stall that will be the family's "apartment" and of the muddy racetrack yields nothing.

Emi is devastated at this loss of the one physical thing that links her to Laurie. But as Emi thinks about her friend, she suddenly realizes that she doesn't really need the bracelet to remember Laurie, that she can remember Laurie and her father and her old life perfectly inside her head. This idea is reinforced by her mother, who comments, "Those are things we carry in our hearts and take with us no matter where we are sent."

Emi's story is told affectionately but without a scrap of sentimentality. Emi is terrified at being sent away from her home and community, and her understanding of the reasons for this event is that of a seven-year-old: "They were treated like the enemy because they *looked* like the enemy."

Realistic paintings in a muted but colorful palette face the text on every page. The reader gets a vivid sense of Emi's community with its small bungalows and of the stark camp surrounded by barbedwire. Well-written and handsome, this is a much-needed jewel of a book.

📖 THE WISE OLD WOMAN (adapted by Uchida, 1994)

Publishers Weekly

SOURCE: A review of *The Wise Old Woman,* in *Publishers Weekly,* Vol. 241, No. 43, October 24, 1994, p. 61.

Extolling the wisdom of elders may sound like a bland topic, but Uchida's brisk storytelling and [Martin] Springett's surprising, Japanese-woodblock-meets-superhero illustration style edge this Japanese folktale with suspense. "'Anyone over seventy is no longer useful,' the lord declared, 'and must be taken into the mountains and left to die.'" Defying this harsh proclamation, a farmer keeps his aged mother in hiding for two years. When a nearby ruler threatens to conquer the village unless the local lord can perform three seemingly impossible tasks, only the farmer's mother succeeds in solving the puzzles. From now on, the lord declares, elders "will be treated with respect and honor, and will share with us the wisdom of their years." What's not for a parent to love here? And the clever solutions to the three tasks, plus the familiar visual cues of good-versus-evil, should gratify the younger generation, too.

Kirkus Reviews

SOURCE: A review of *The Wise Old Woman,* in *Kirkus Reviews,* Vol. LXII, No. 22, November 15, 1994, p. 1545.

In medieval Japan a young farmer lives with his old mother in a village ruled by a cruel young lord who has decreed that all the villagers who reach the age of 70 must be taken into the mountains and left to die. On her 70th birthday, the farmer's mother tells her son to take her away, but he can't bear to leave her alone to die. He digs a secret room in his house, where his mother lives for two years without being discovered. But then the powerful Lord Higa sends men to invade the village, and they give the cruel young lord a test. If he can pass it, the village will be spared. Given three impossible tasks, he sets them before the wise men of the village. They can't solve them, but the farmer's mother can, and the cruel young lord, upon hearing who saved his village, reverses his decree. Uchida tells this folktale with simplicity and grace. Springett's bold illustrations lend a modern feel to the traditional setting, perfectly matching the tone of the tale.

A wonderful way to explain respect for the elderly.

Kenneth Oppel

SOURCE: A review of *The Wise Old Woman,* in *Quill and Quire,* Vol. 60, No. 12, December, 1994, p. 32.

In Yoshiko Uchida's retelling of a Japanese folktale, a cruel young lord decrees that all people over 70 should be left to die in the mountains. But a young farmer, unable to part with his beloved mother, hides her under his house. Two years later, three warriors arrive and announce that the village will be destroyed unless the people can solve three impossible tasks. The wise men of the village prove useless, invocations to the gods go unanswered, and even the wise badger of the forest finds the tasks too daunting. It is the old woman who knows all the answers—and so not only is the village saved from destruction, but the cruel young lord repents and announces that henceforth old people "will be treated with respect and honour, and will share with us the wisdom of their years."

Martin Springett's illustrations are bound to appeal to kids—bold and stylized, they recall traditional Japanese woodcuts and paintings. And Uchida crafts her language with similar precision. The omniscient narration, common in folk and fairy tales, distances us from the characters, but at the same time generates remarkable pathos. Most impressive is the narrative's restraint, as in the early scene in which the farmer carries his mother up the mountain on his back, but is unable to abandon her.

A clinical (and cynical) reader might find the story a little too politically calculated—anti-ageist, anti-sexist—but the themes here are undeniably important for all of us, and will have particular relevance to young readers, who may often find their grandparents tedious, their stories and memories boring. *The Wise Old Woman* seems additionally topical as our own nation's aging population is increasingly seen more as a tax burden than as a societal asset.

John Philbrook

SOURCE: A review of *The Wise Old Woman,* in *School Library Journal,* Vol. 41, No. 7, July, 1995, p. 75.

In medieval Japan, a cruel lord declares old people useless and decrees that they be abandoned in the mountains when they reach the age of 70. A young farmer, who is a devoted son, digs a room under his house to hide his mother. Then, when a more powerful lord threatens to conquer the village unless three seemingly impossible tasks be accomplished, the farmer is the only one who comes up with ingenious solutions. Finally, he confesses to the suspicious lord that it was his mother who came up with the answers. The man reverses his decree, as he realizes that wisdom can come with age. This is a fuller and richer retelling than that which appears in Uchida's *The Sea of Gold and Other Tales from Japan.* Springett's exquisite airbrush-and-ink illustrations accurately anchor the tale in the mid-Edo period, simulating woodblock prints with particularly rich blues. Verbally and visually elegant, emotionally touching, with a timeless moral, this *Wise Old Woman* is one no library can afford to be without.

Additional coverage of Uchida's life and career is contained in the following sources published by The Gale Group: *Authors and Artists for Young Adults,* Vol. 16; *Contemporary Authors New Revision Series,* Vol. 61; *Junior DISCovering Authors; Major Authors and Illustrators for Children and Young Adults; Something about the Author Autobiography Series,* Vol. 1; and *Something about the Author,* Vols. 1, 53.

CUMULATIVE INDEXES

How to Use This Index

CUMULATIVE INDEX TO AUTHORS

Author Index

CUMULATIVE INDEX TO NATIONALITIES

Nationality Index

CUMULATIVE INDEX TO TITLES

Title Index

Title Index

Title Index

Title Index

Title Index

Title Index

Title Index

Title Index

Title Index

Title Index

Title Index

Title Index

Title Index

Title Index

Title Index

Title Index

Title Index

ISBN 0-7876-2905-7

90000